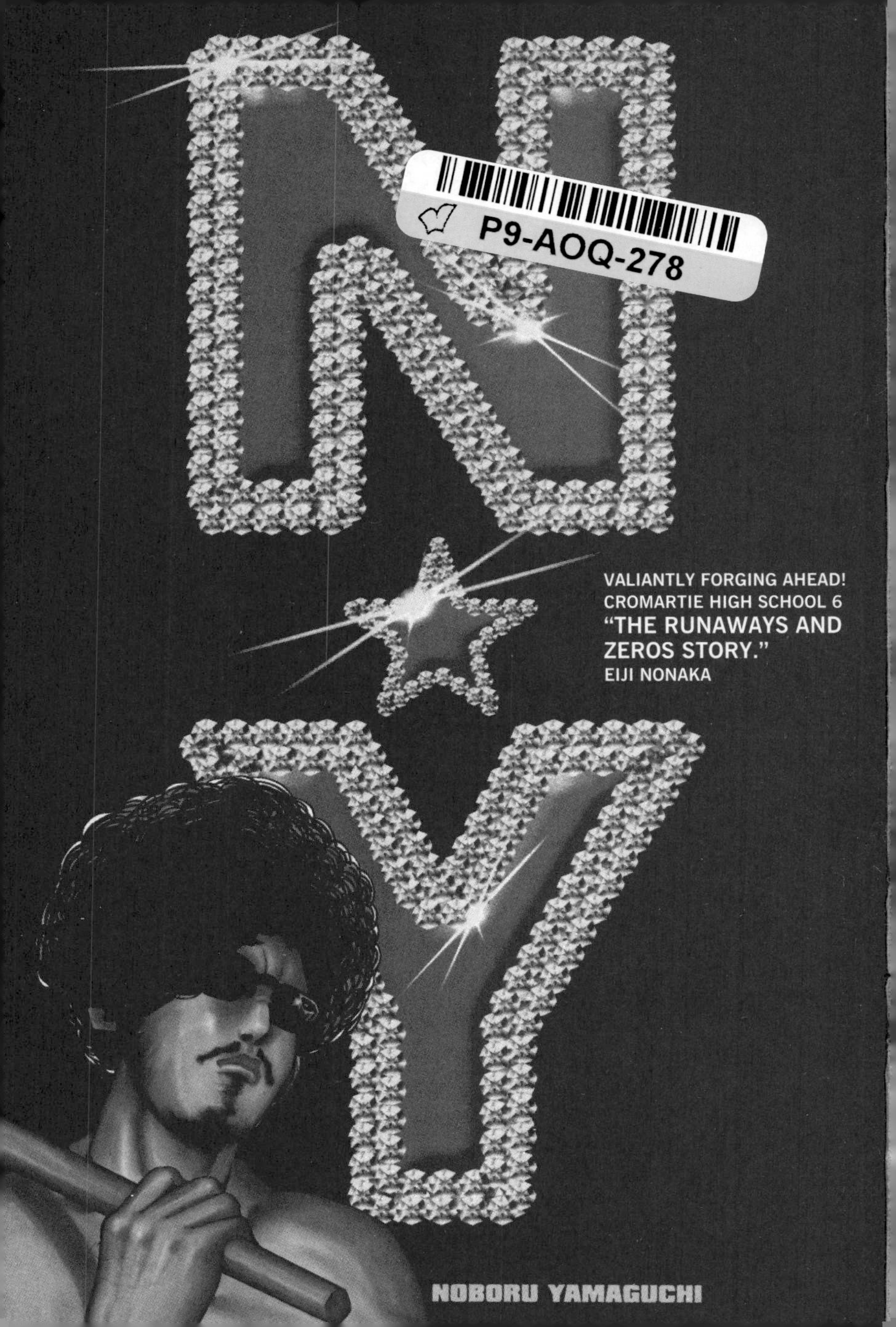
N
Y
VALIANTLY FORGING AHEAD!
CROMARTIE HIGH SCHOOL 6
"THE RUNAWAYS AND ZEROS STORY."
EIJI NONAKA
NOBORU YAMAGUCHI

TABLE OF CONTENTS

CHAPTER 121: **STARMAN**

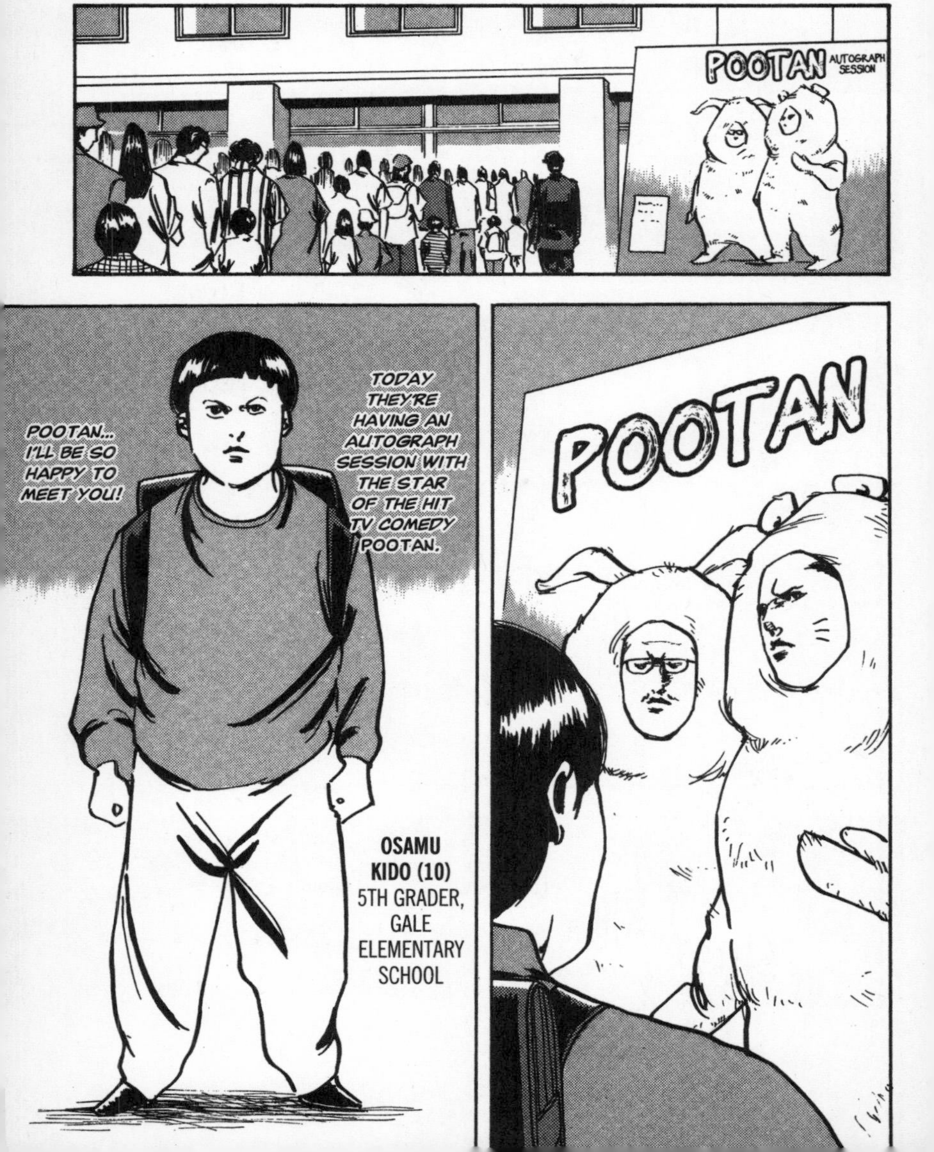
POOTAN AUTOGRAPH SESSION
POOTAN
TODAY THEY'RE HAVING AN AUTOGRAPH SESSION WITH THE STAR OF THE HIT TV COMEDY POOTAN.
POOTAN... I'LL BE SO HAPPY TO MEET YOU!
OSAMU KIDO (10) 5TH GRADER, GALE ELEMENTARY SCHOOL

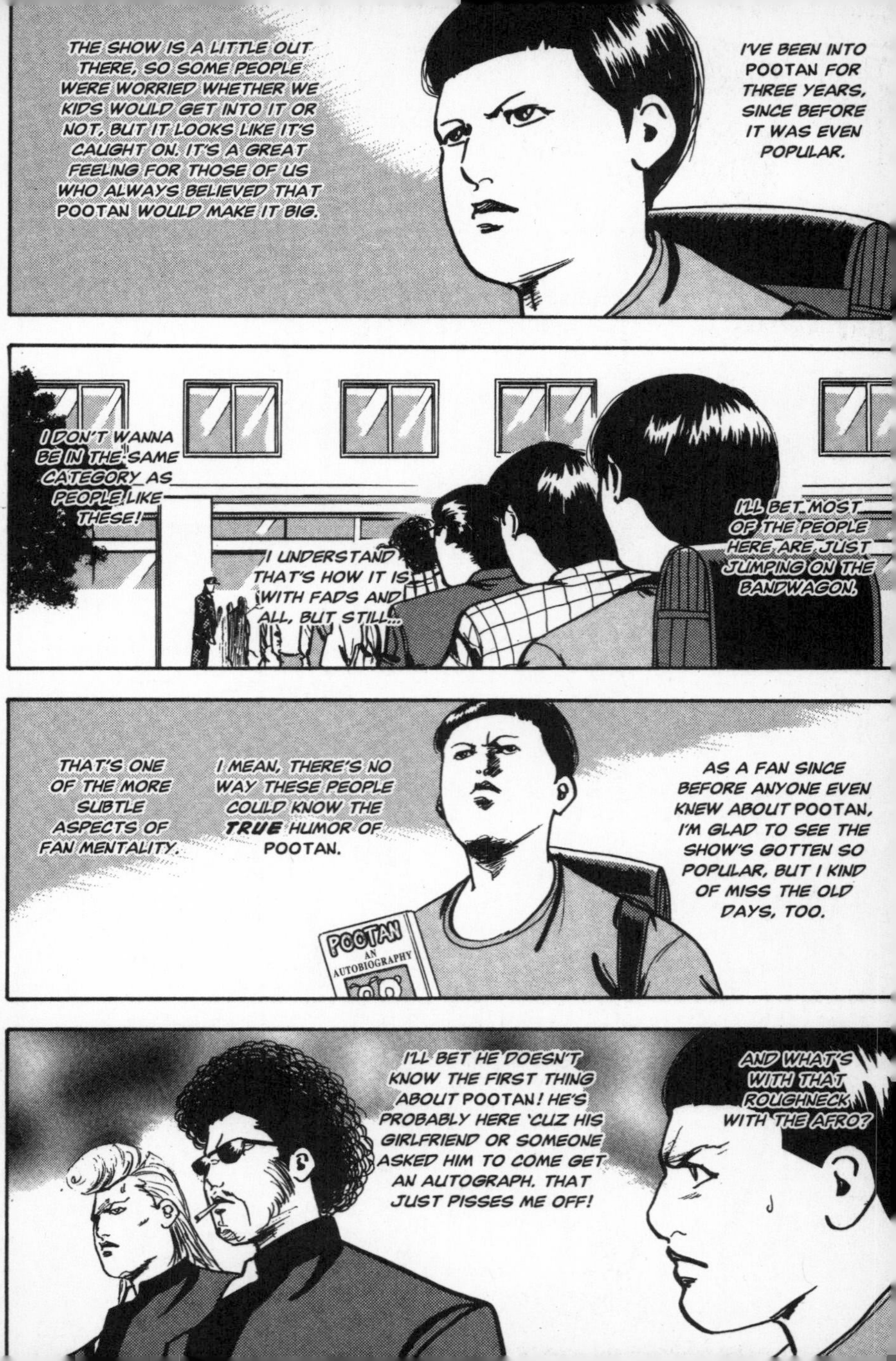
I'VE BEEN INTO POOTAN FOR THREE YEARS, SINCE BEFORE IT WAS EVEN POPULAR.
THE SHOW IS A LITTLE OUT THERE, SO SOME PEOPLE WERE WORRIED WHETHER WE KIDS WOULD GET INTO IT OR NOT, BUT IT LOOKS LIKE IT'S CAUGHT ON. IT'S A GREAT FEELING FOR THOSE OF US WHO ALWAYS BELIEVED THAT POOTAN WOULD MAKE IT BIG.
I'LL BET MOST OF THE PEOPLE HERE ARE JUST JUMPING ON THE BANDWAGON.
I UNDERSTAND THAT'S HOW IT IS WITH FADS AND ALL, BUT STILL...
I DON'T WANNA BE IN THE SAME CATEGORY AS PEOPLE LIKE THESE!
AS A FAN SINCE BEFORE ANYONE EVEN KNEW ABOUT POOTAN, I'M GLAD TO SEE THE SHOW'S GOTTEN SO POPULAR, BUT I KIND OF MISS THE OLD DAYS, TOO.
I MEAN, THERE'S NO WAY THESE PEOPLE COULD KNOW THE TRUE HUMOR OF POOTAN.
THAT'S ONE OF THE MORE SUBTLE ASPECTS OF FAN MENTALITY.
POOTAN AN AUTOBIOGRAPHY
AND WHAT'S WITH THAT ROUGHNECK WITH THE AFRO?
I'LL BET HE DOESN'T KNOW THE FIRST THING ABOUT POOTAN! HE'S PROBABLY HERE 'CUZ HIS GIRLFRIEND OR SOMEONE ASKED HIM TO COME GET AN AUTOGRAPH. THAT JUST PISSES ME OFF!

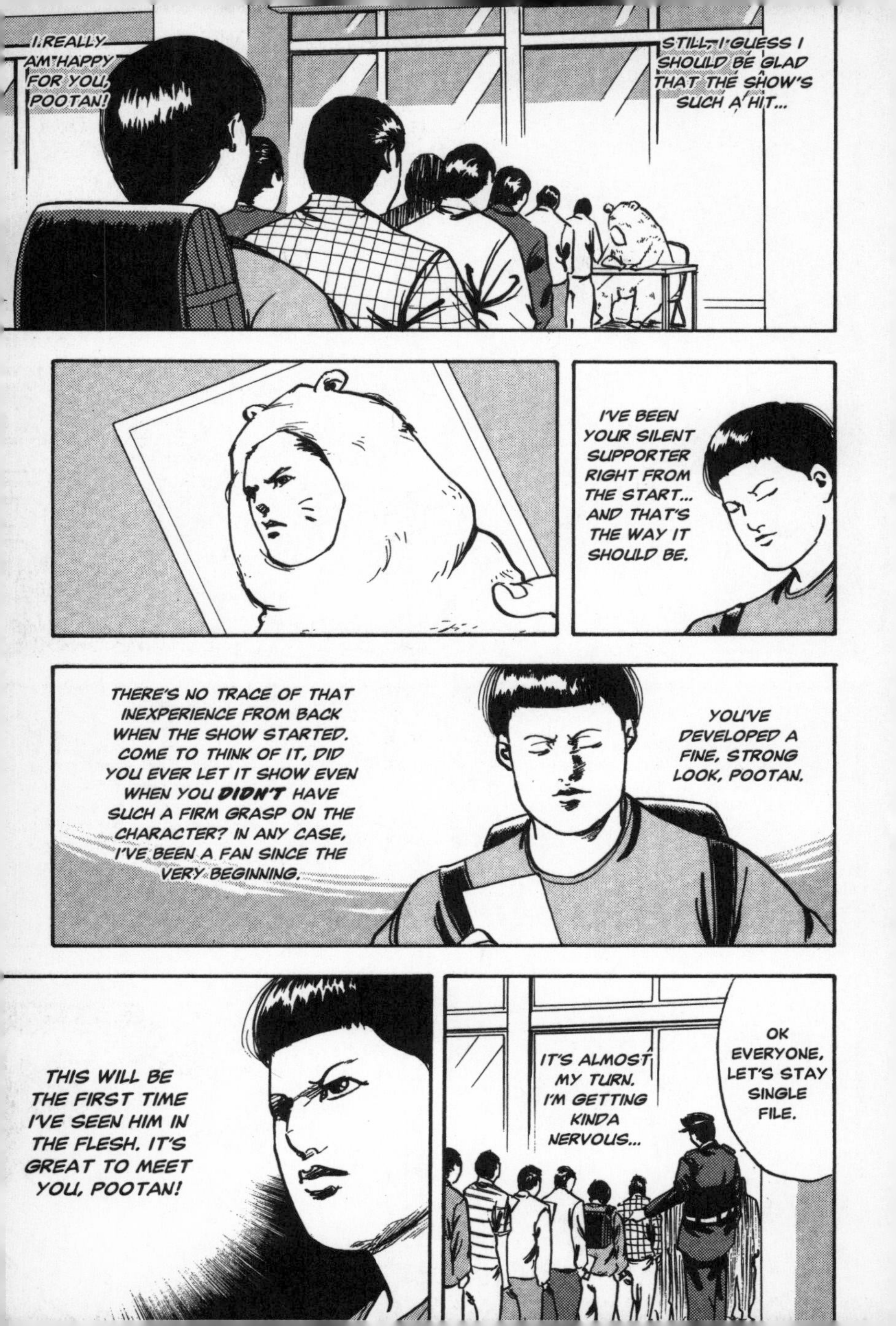
I REALLY AM HAPPY FOR YOU, POOTAN!
STILL, I GUESS I SHOULD BE GLAD THAT THE SHOW'S SUCH A HIT...
I'VE BEEN YOUR SILENT SUPPORTER RIGHT FROM THE START... AND THAT'S THE WAY IT SHOULD BE.
THERE'S NO TRACE OF THAT INEXPERIENCE FROM BACK WHEN THE SHOW STARTED. COME TO THINK OF IT, DID YOU EVER LET IT SHOW EVEN WHEN YOU DIDN'T HAVE SUCH A FIRM GRASP ON THE CHARACTER? IN ANY CASE, I'VE BEEN A FAN SINCE THE VERY BEGINNING.
YOU'VE DEVELOPED A FINE, STRONG LOOK, POOTAN.
THIS WILL BE THE FIRST TIME I'VE SEEN HIM IN THE FLESH. IT'S GREAT TO MEET YOU, POOTAN!
IT'S ALMOST MY TURN. I'M GETTING KINDA NERVOUS...
OK EVERYONE, LET'S STAY SINGLE FILE.

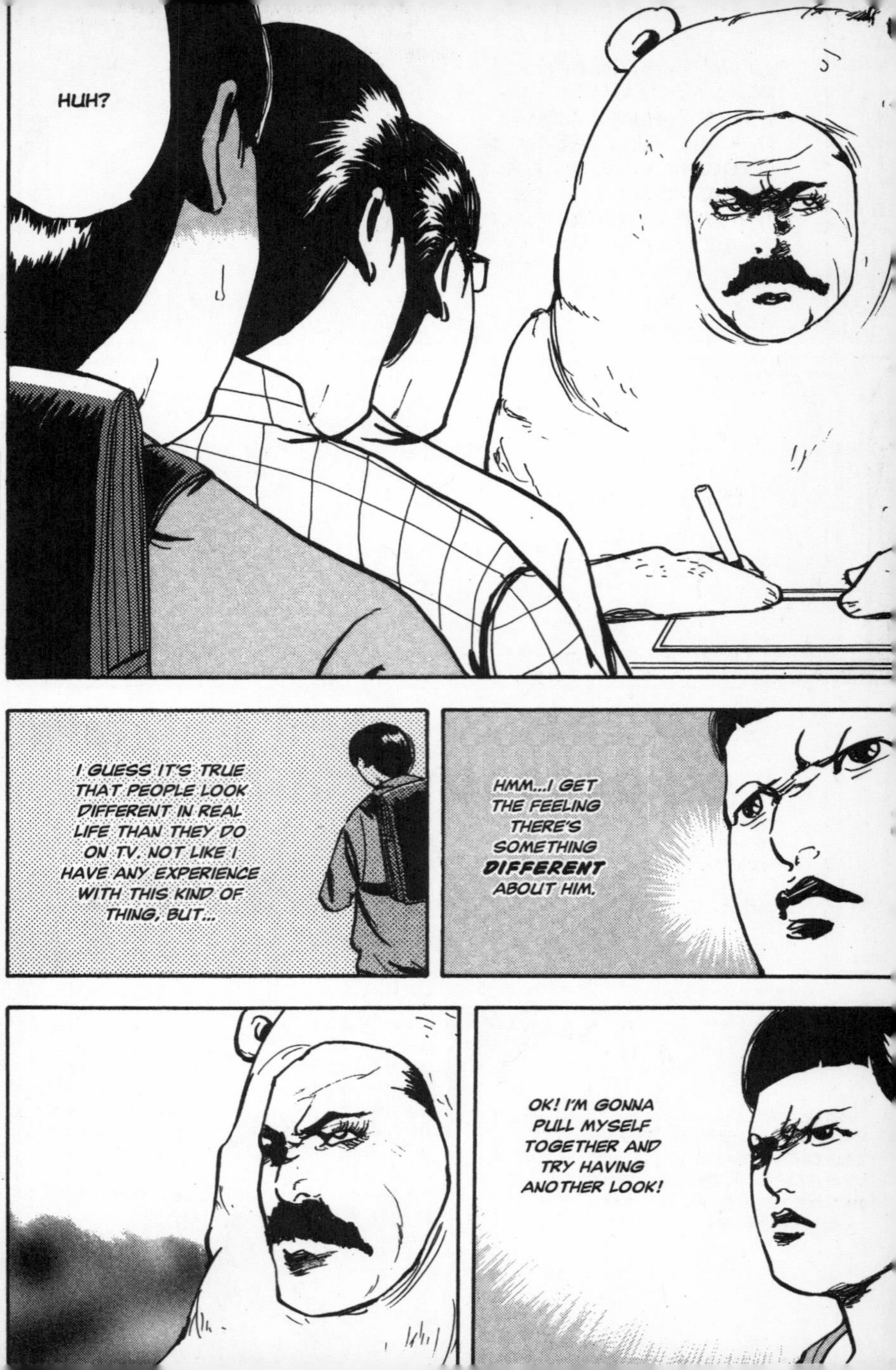
HUH?
I GUESS IT'S TRUE THAT PEOPLE LOOK DIFFERENT IN REAL LIFE THAN THEY DO ON TV. NOT LIKE I HAVE ANY EXPERIENCE WITH THIS KIND OF THING, BUT...
HMM...I GET THE FEELING THERE'S SOMETHING DIFFERENT ABOUT HIM.
OK! I'M GONNA PULL MYSELF TOGETHER AND TRY HAVING ANOTHER LOOK!

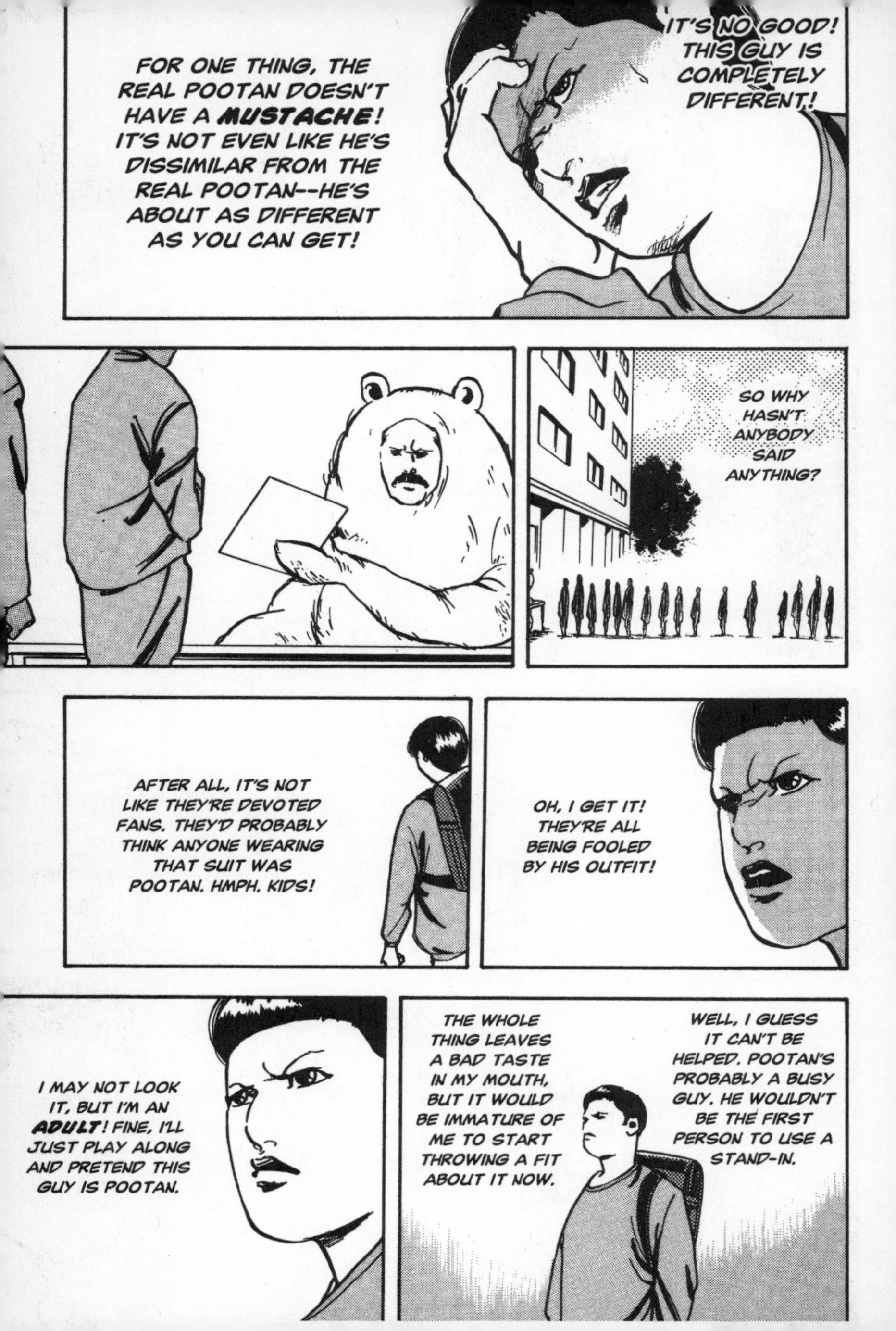
FOR ONE THING, THE REAL POOTAN DOESN'T HAVE A MUSTACHE! IT'S NOT EVEN LIKE HE'S DISSIMILAR FROM THE REAL POOTAN--HE'S ABOUT AS DIFFERENT AS YOU CAN GET!
IT'S NO GOOD! THIS GUY IS COMPLETELY DIFFERENT!
SO WHY HASN'T ANYBODY SAID ANYTHING?
AFTER ALL, IT'S NOT LIKE THEY'RE DEVOTED FANS. THEY'D PROBABLY THINK ANYONE WEARING THAT SUIT WAS POOTAN. HMPH. KIDS!
OH, I GET IT! THEY'RE ALL BEING FOOLED BY HIS OUTFIT!
I MAY NOT LOOK IT, BUT I'M AN ADULT! FINE, I'LL JUST PLAY ALONG AND PRETEND THIS GUY IS POOTAN.
THE WHOLE THING LEAVES A BAD TASTE IN MY MOUTH, BUT IT WOULD BE IMMATURE OF ME TO START THROWING A FIT ABOUT IT NOW.
WELL, I GUESS IT CAN'T BE HELPED. POOTAN'S PROBABLY A BUSY GUY. HE WOULDN'T BE THE FIRST PERSON TO USE A STAND-IN.

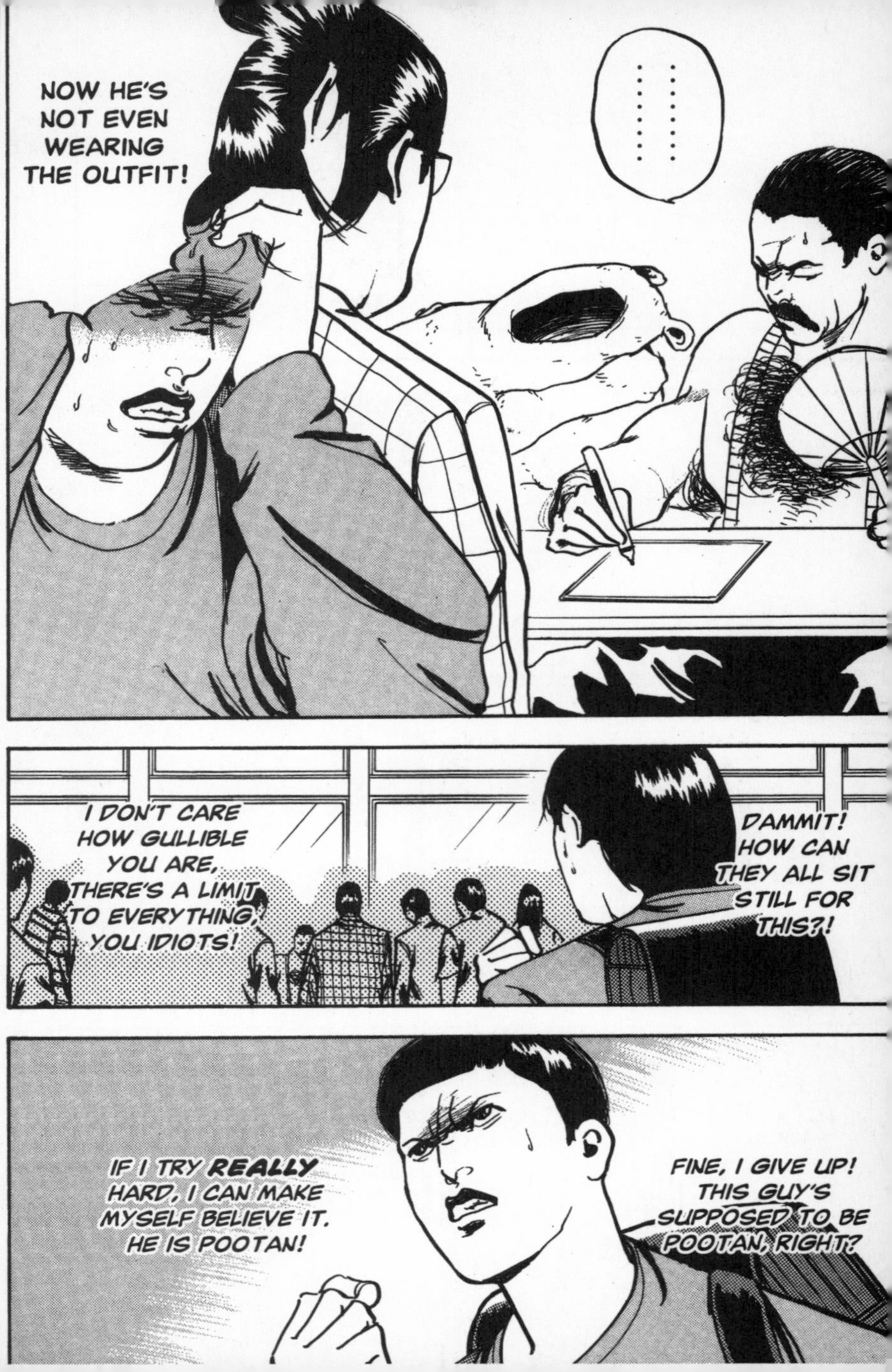
NOW HE'S NOT EVEN WEARING THE OUTFIT!
......
DAMMIT! HOW CAN THEY ALL SIT STILL FOR THIS?!
I DON'T CARE HOW GULLIBLE YOU ARE, THERE'S A LIMIT TO EVERYTHING, YOU IDIOTS!
FINE, I GIVE UP! THIS GUY'S SUPPOSED TO BE POOTAN, RIGHT?
IF I TRY **REALLY** HARD, I CAN MAKE MYSELF BELIEVE IT. HE IS POOTAN!

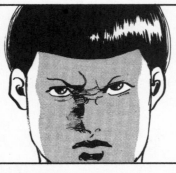

POOTAN!

YES, INDEED. WITHOUT A DOUBT, THIS IS...

HE'S POOTAN!

THERE'S NO TWO WAYS ABOUT IT...

IT'S POOTAN WHO'S SHAKING MY HAND.

IT'S POOTAN WHO'S GIVING ME HIS AUTOGRAPH.

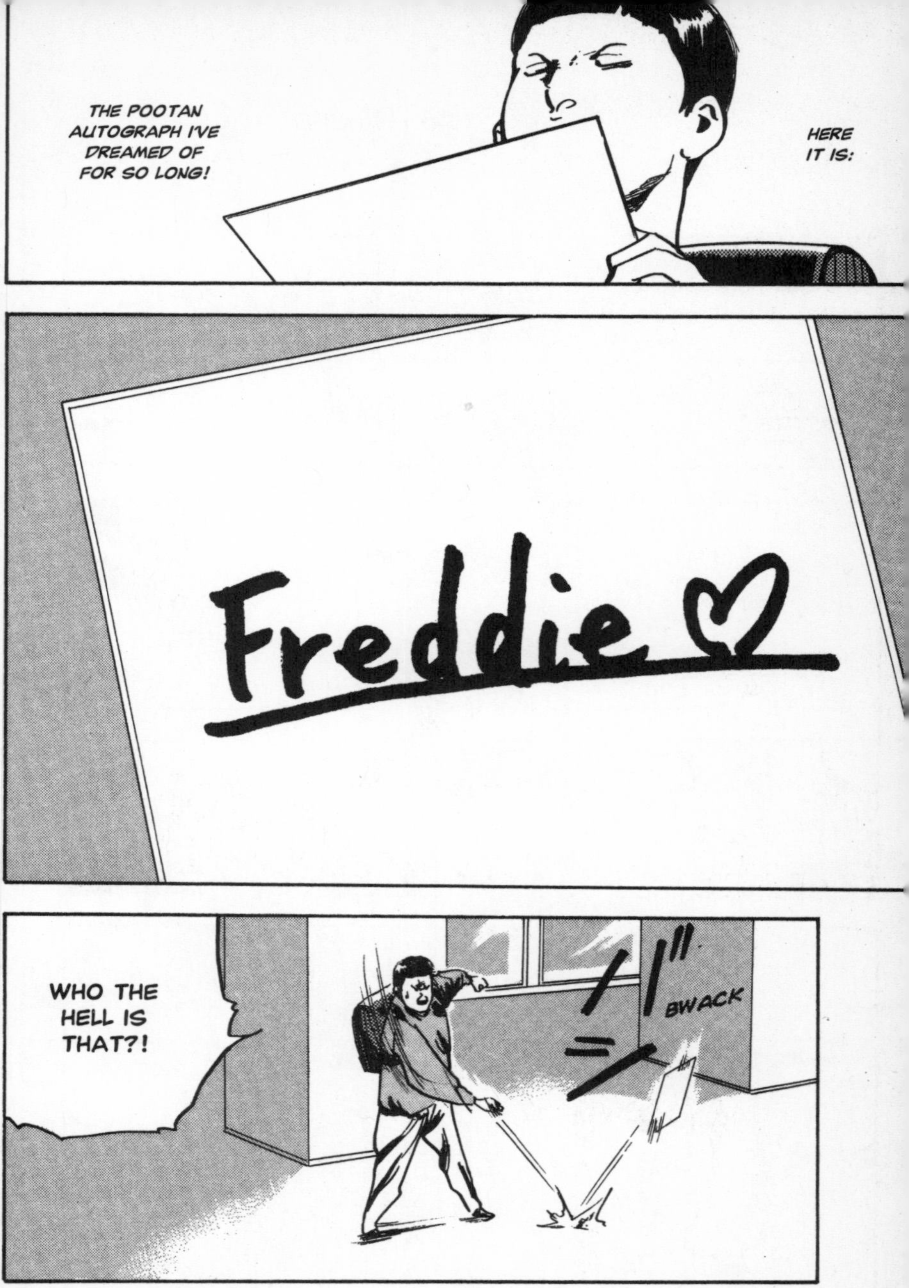
THE POOTAN AUTOGRAPH I'VE DREAMED OF FOR SO LONG!
HERE IT IS:
Freddie
WHO THE HELL IS THAT?!
BWACK

THIS IS FREDDIE'S NEW PART TIME JOB.

CHAPTER 122: NOW I'M HERE

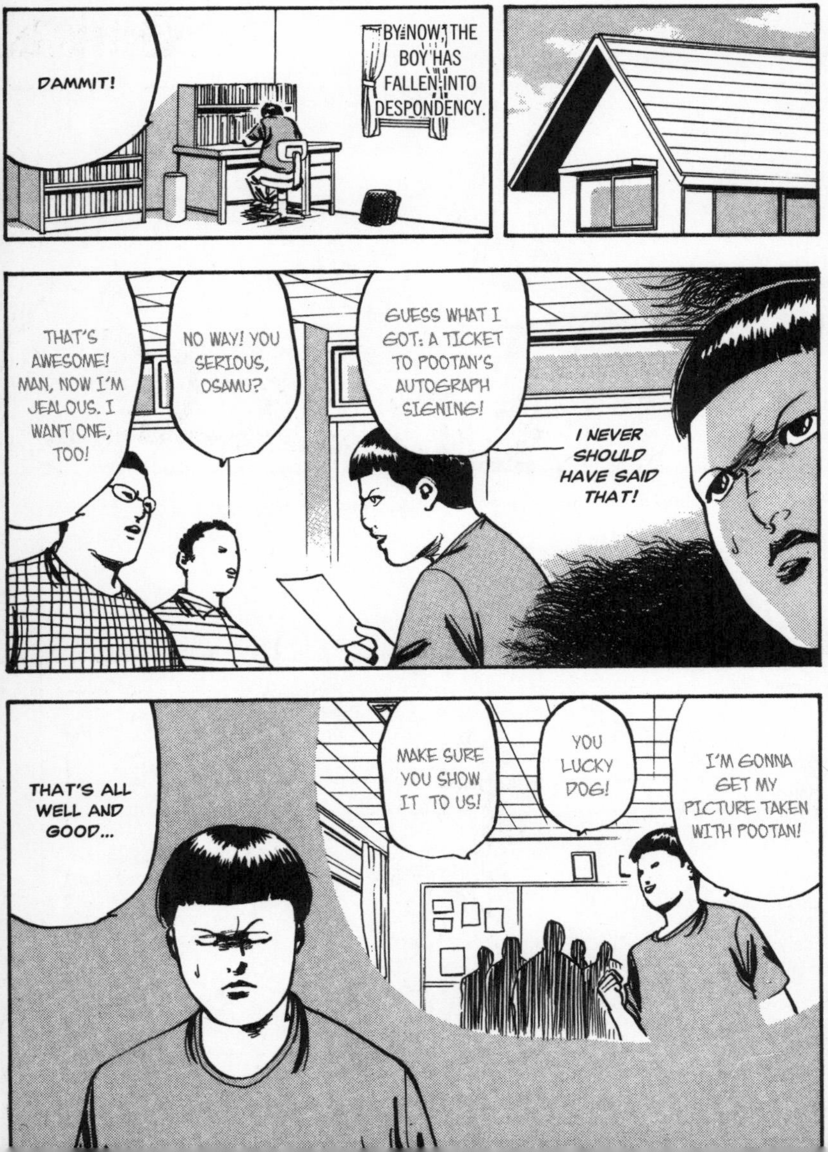

BY NOW, THE BOY HAS FALLEN INTO DESPONDENCY.
DAMMIT!
I NEVER SHOULD HAVE SAID THAT!
GUESS WHAT I GOT: A TICKET TO POOTAN'S AUTOGRAPH SIGNING!
NO WAY! YOU SERIOUS, OSAMU?
THAT'S AWESOME! MAN, NOW I'M JEALOUS. I WANT ONE, TOO!
I'M GONNA GET MY PICTURE TAKEN WITH POOTAN!
YOU LUCKY DOG!
MAKE SURE YOU SHOW IT TO US!
THAT'S ALL WELL AND GOOD...

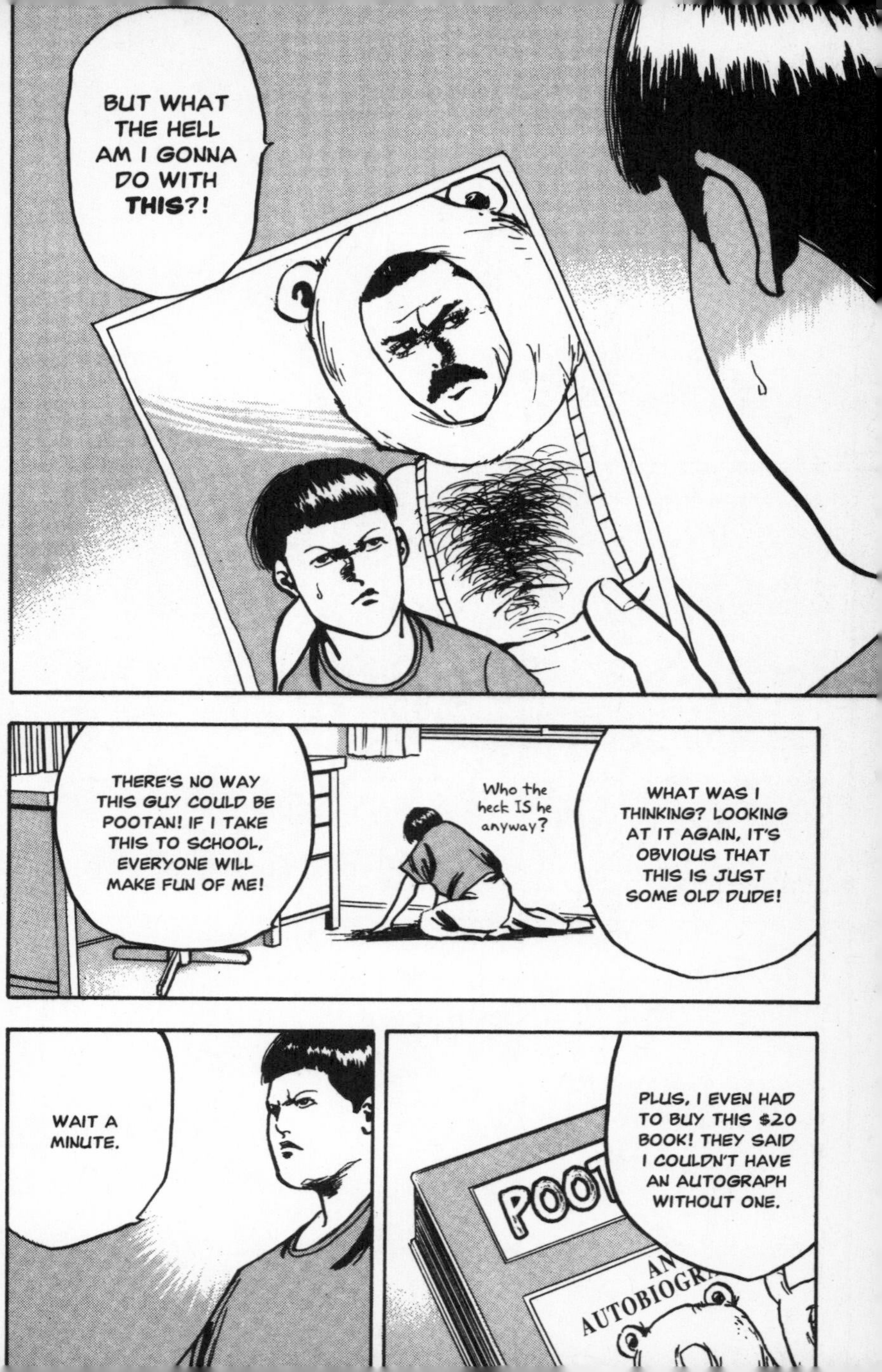
BUT WHAT THE HELL AM I GONNA DO WITH **THIS**?!
WHAT WAS I THINKING? LOOKING AT IT AGAIN, IT'S OBVIOUS THAT THIS IS JUST SOME OLD DUDE!
Who the heck IS he anyway?
THERE'S NO WAY THIS GUY COULD BE POOTAN! IF I TAKE THIS TO SCHOOL, EVERYONE WILL MAKE FUN OF ME!
PLUS, I EVEN HAD TO BUY THIS $20 BOOK! THEY SAID I COULDN'T HAVE AN AUTOGRAPH WITHOUT ONE.
WAIT A MINUTE.

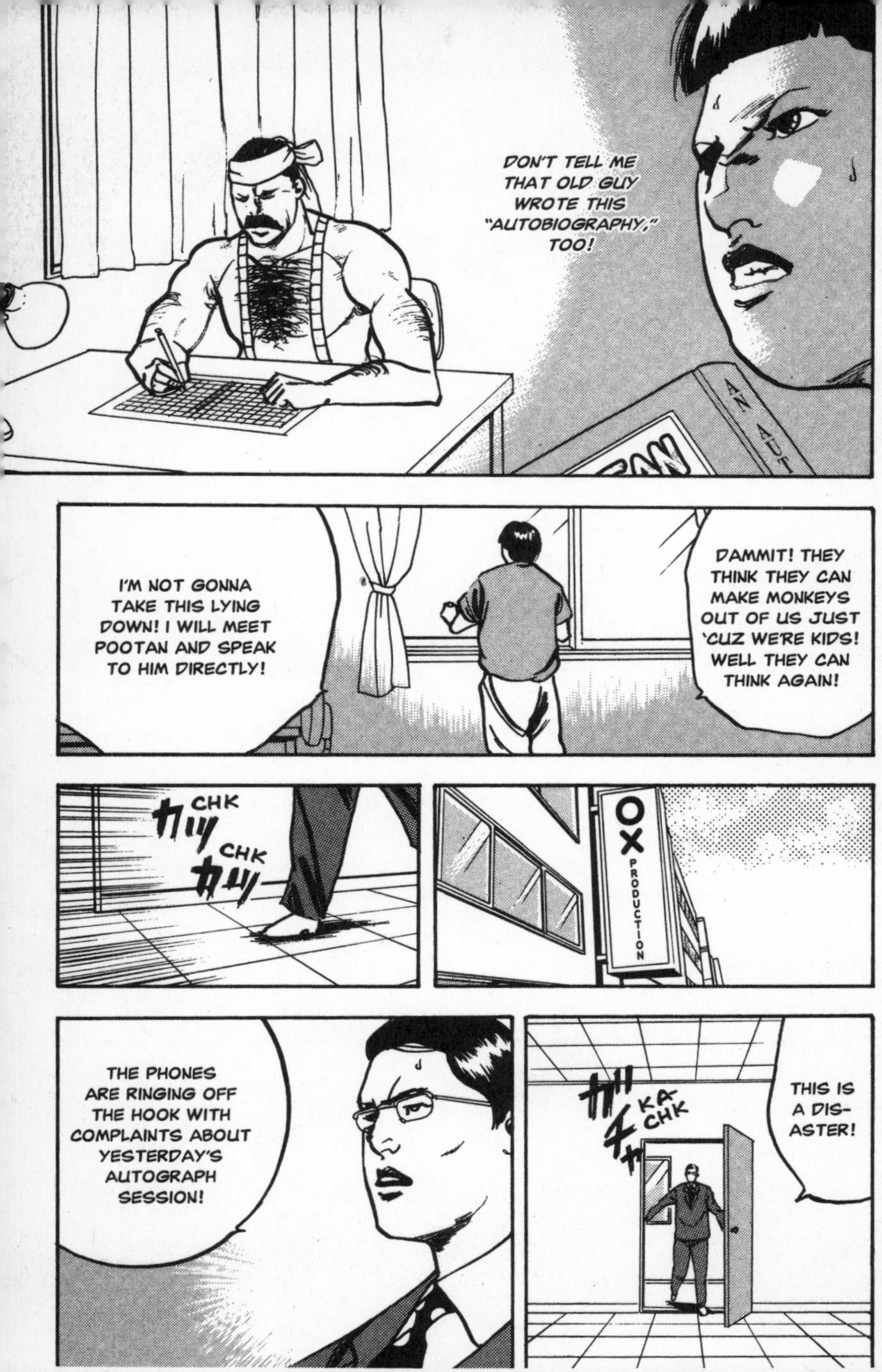
DON'T TELL ME THAT OLD GUY WROTE THIS "AUTOBIOGRAPHY," TOO!
AN AUT
DAMMIT! THEY THINK THEY CAN MAKE MONKEYS OUT OF US JUST 'CUZ WE'RE KIDS! WELL THEY CAN THINK AGAIN!
I'M NOT GONNA TAKE THIS LYING DOWN! I WILL MEET POOTAN AND SPEAK TO HIM DIRECTLY!
OX PRODUCTION
カッ CHK
カッ CHK
ガチャ KA CHK
THIS IS A DIS-ASTER!
THE PHONES ARE RINGING OFF THE HOOK WITH COMPLAINTS ABOUT YESTERDAY'S AUTOGRAPH SESSION!

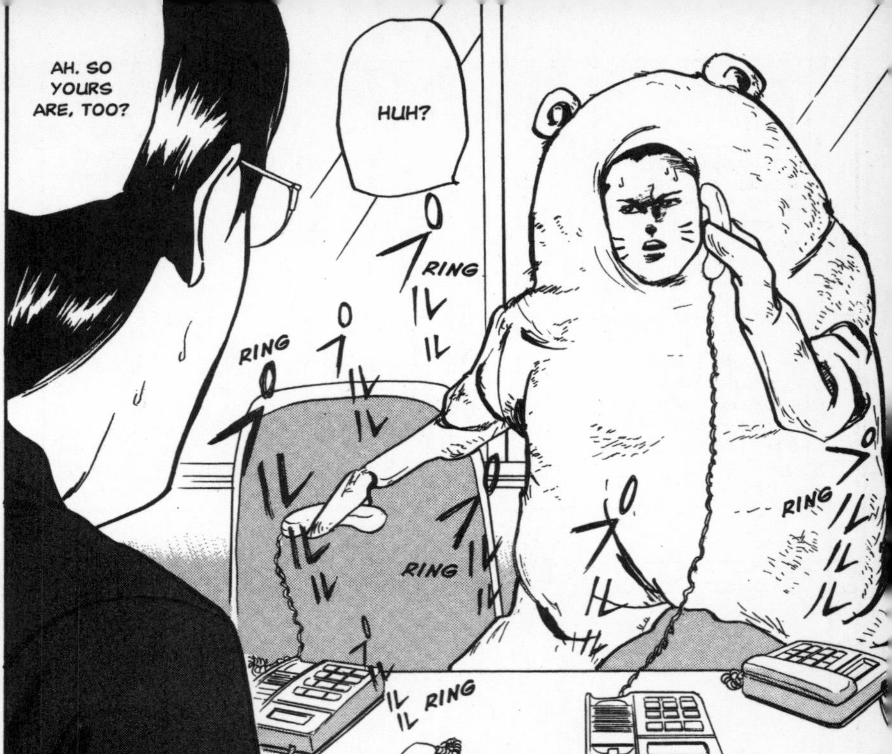
AH. SO YOURS ARE, TOO?
HUH?
RING
RING
RING
RING
RING

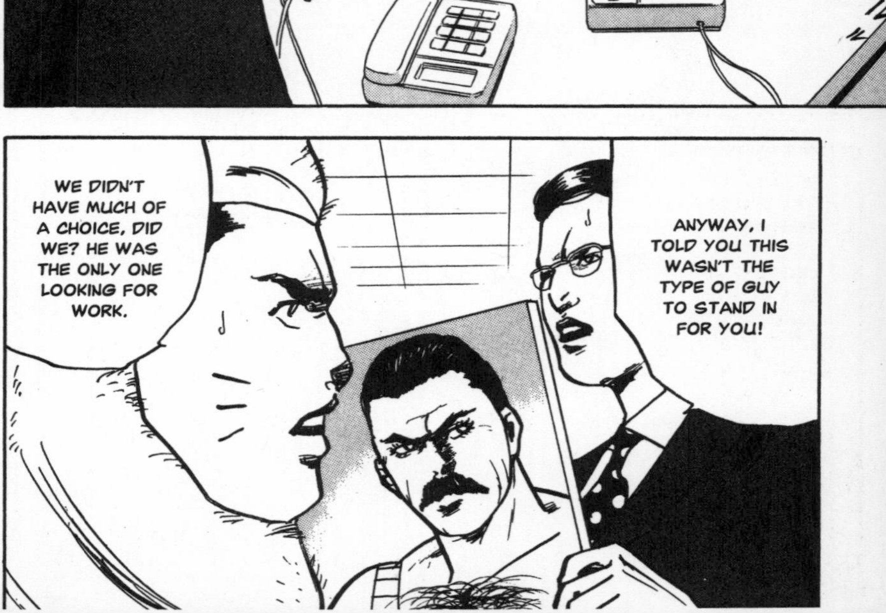
ANYWAY, I TOLD YOU THIS WASN'T THE TYPE OF GUY TO STAND IN FOR YOU!
WE DIDN'T HAVE MUCH OF A CHOICE, DID WE? HE WAS THE ONLY ONE LOOKING FOR WORK.

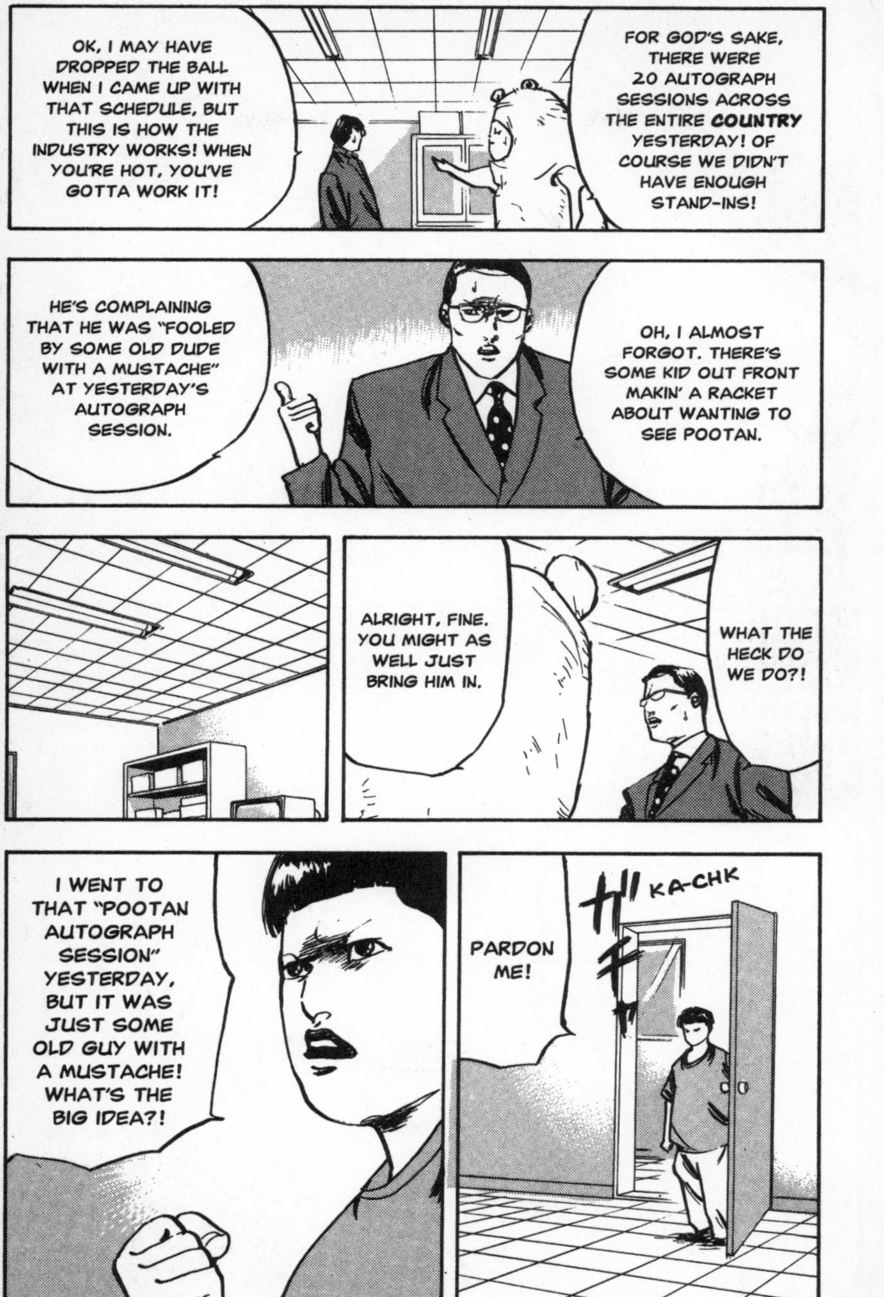
OK, I MAY HAVE DROPPED THE BALL WHEN I CAME UP WITH THAT SCHEDULE, BUT THIS IS HOW THE INDUSTRY WORKS! WHEN YOU'RE HOT, YOU'VE GOTTA WORK IT!
FOR GOD'S SAKE, THERE WERE 20 AUTOGRAPH SESSIONS ACROSS THE ENTIRE **COUNTRY** YESTERDAY! OF COURSE WE DIDN'T HAVE ENOUGH STAND-INS!
HE'S COMPLAINING THAT HE WAS "FOOLED BY SOME OLD DUDE WITH A MUSTACHE" AT YESTERDAY'S AUTOGRAPH SESSION.
OH, I ALMOST FORGOT. THERE'S SOME KID OUT FRONT MAKIN' A RACKET ABOUT WANTING TO SEE POOTAN.
ALRIGHT, FINE. YOU MIGHT AS WELL JUST BRING HIM IN.
WHAT THE HECK DO WE DO?!
I WENT TO THAT "POOTAN AUTOGRAPH SESSION" YESTERDAY, BUT IT WAS JUST SOME OLD GUY WITH A MUSTACHE! WHAT'S THE BIG IDEA?!
KA-CHK
PARDON ME!

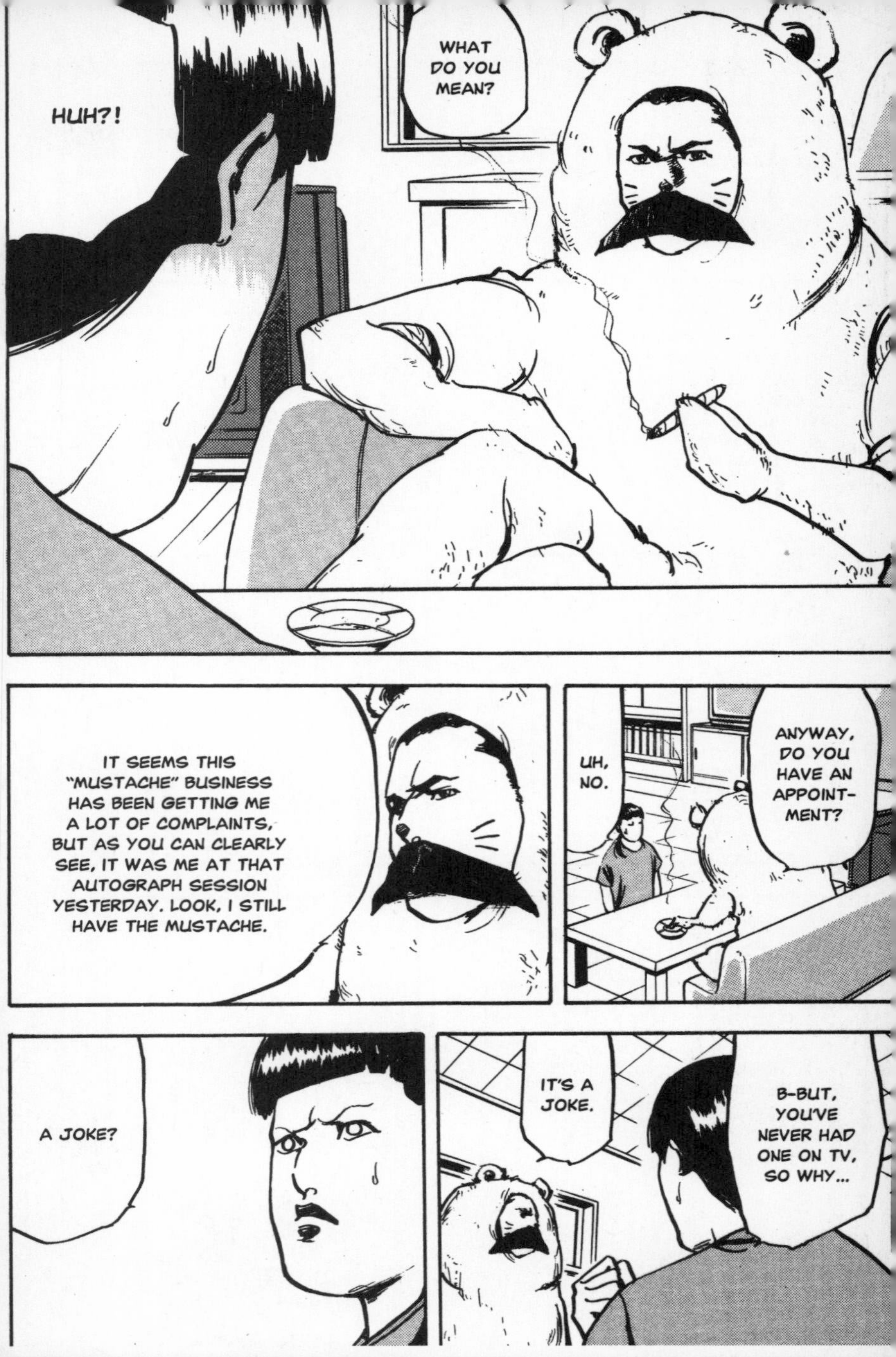
WHAT DO YOU MEAN?
HUH?!
ANYWAY, DO YOU HAVE AN APPOINT-MENT?
UH, NO.
IT SEEMS THIS "MUSTACHE" BUSINESS HAS BEEN GETTING ME A LOT OF COMPLAINTS, BUT AS YOU CAN CLEARLY SEE, IT WAS ME AT THAT AUTOGRAPH SESSION YESTERDAY. LOOK, I STILL HAVE THE MUSTACHE.
B-BUT, YOU'VE NEVER HAD ONE ON TV, SO WHY...
IT'S A JOKE.
A JOKE?

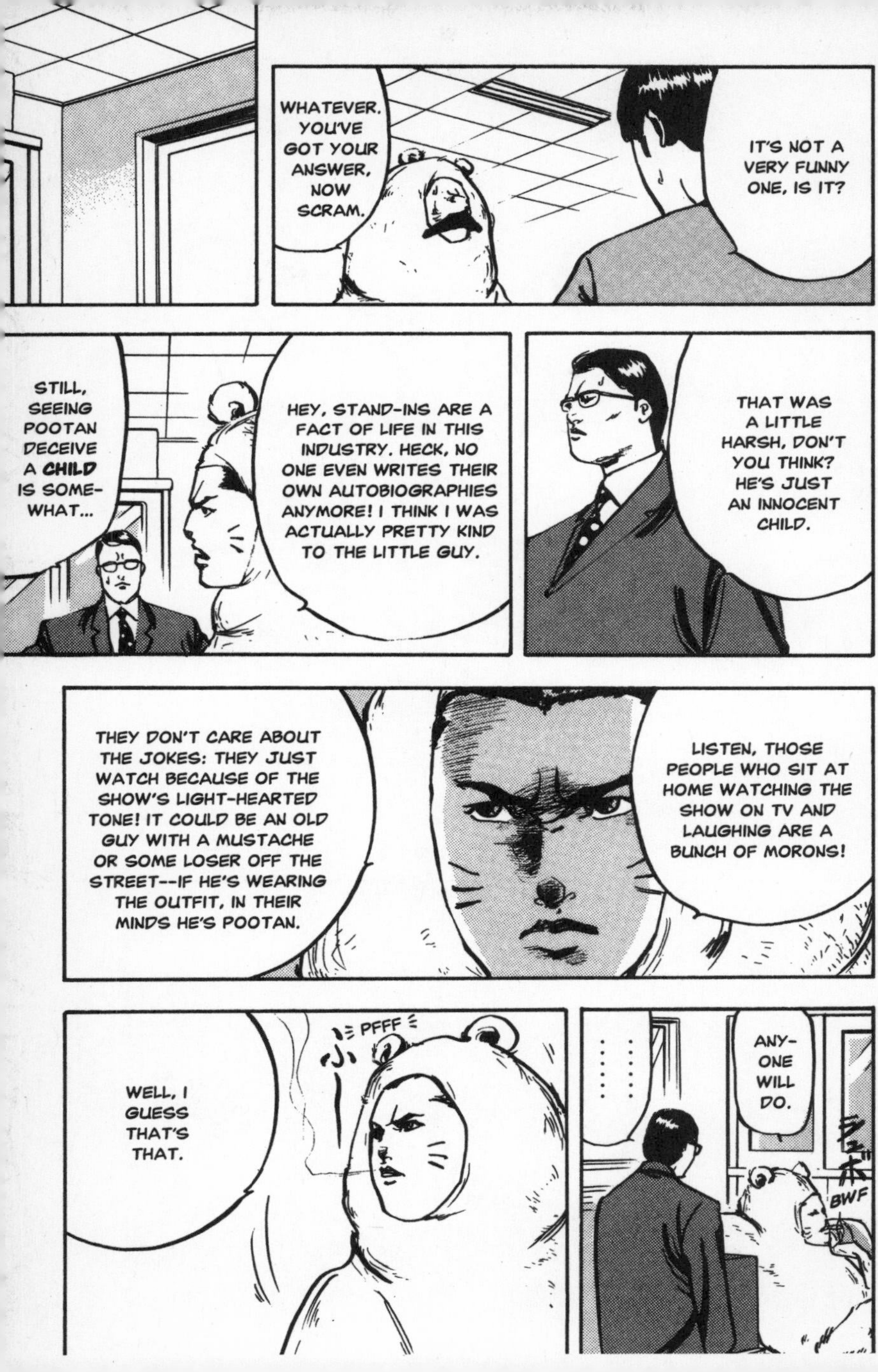

IT'S NOT A VERY FUNNY ONE, IS IT?
WHATEVER. YOU'VE GOT YOUR ANSWER, NOW SCRAM.
THAT WAS A LITTLE HARSH, DON'T YOU THINK? HE'S JUST AN INNOCENT CHILD.
HEY, STAND-INS ARE A FACT OF LIFE IN THIS INDUSTRY. HECK, NO ONE EVEN WRITES THEIR OWN AUTOBIOGRAPHIES ANYMORE! I THINK I WAS ACTUALLY PRETTY KIND TO THE LITTLE GUY.
STILL, SEEING POOTAN DECEIVE A **CHILD** IS SOME-WHAT...
LISTEN, THOSE PEOPLE WHO SIT AT HOME WATCHING THE SHOW ON TV AND LAUGHING ARE A BUNCH OF MORONS!
THEY DON'T CARE ABOUT THE JOKES: THEY JUST WATCH BECAUSE OF THE SHOW'S LIGHT-HEARTED TONE! IT COULD BE AN OLD GUY WITH A MUSTACHE OR SOME LOSER OFF THE STREET--IF HE'S WEARING THE OUTFIT, IN THEIR MINDS HE'S POOTAN.
ANY-ONE WILL DO.
BWF
......
PFFF
WELL, I GUESS THAT'S THAT.

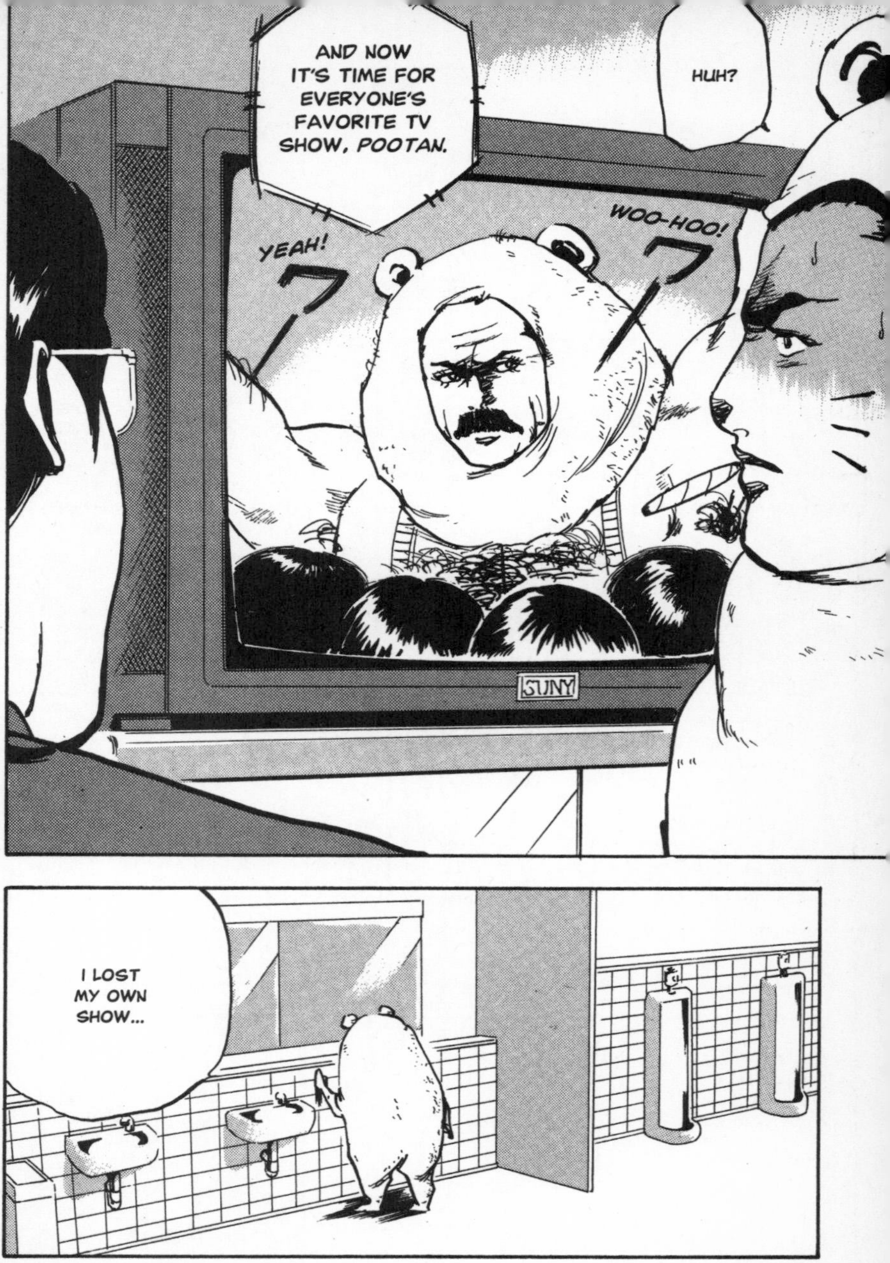
AND NOW IT'S TIME FOR EVERYONE'S FAVORITE TV SHOW, *POOTAN.*
YEAH!
WOO-HOO!
HUH?
SUNY
I LOST MY OWN SHOW...

HE LOOKS GOOD FROM BEHIND.

CHAPTER 123: **NO ONE BUT YOU**

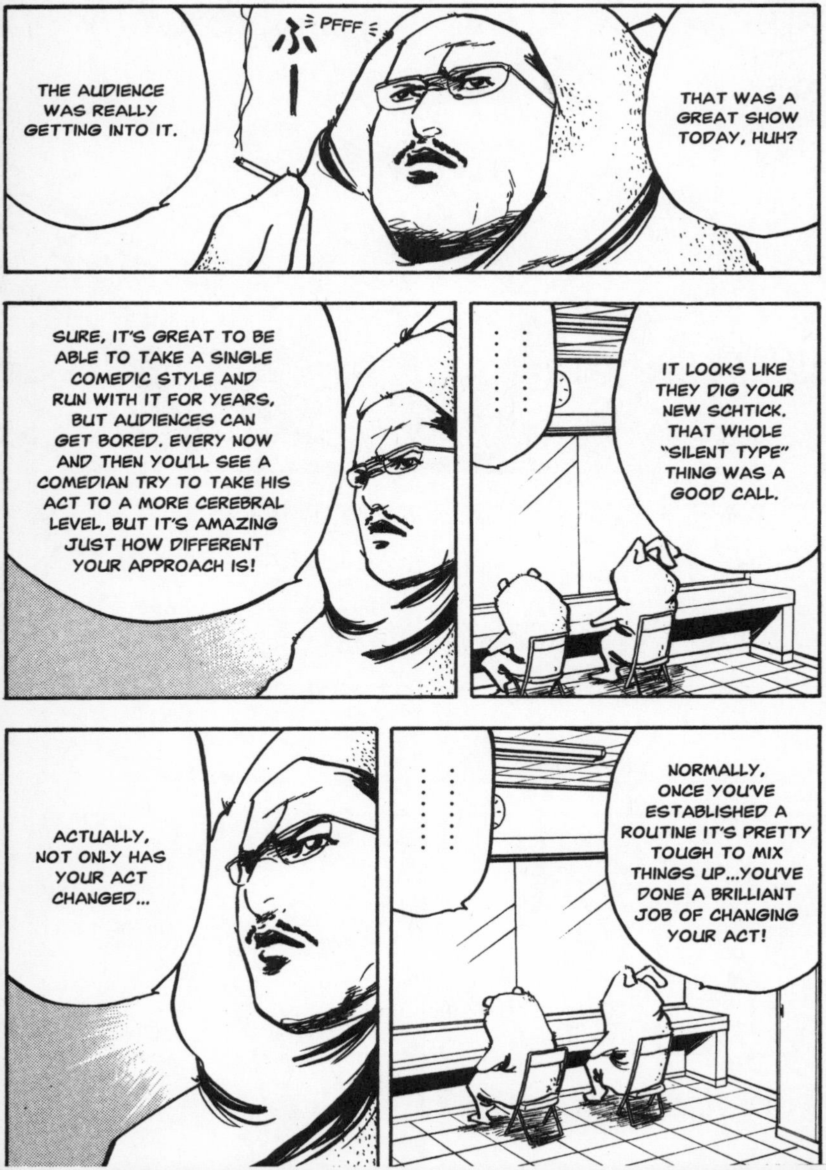

ふー PFFF
THAT WAS A GREAT SHOW TODAY, HUH?
THE AUDIENCE WAS REALLY GETTING INTO IT.
IT LOOKS LIKE THEY DIG YOUR NEW SCHTICK. THAT WHOLE "SILENT TYPE" THING WAS A GOOD CALL.
SURE, IT'S GREAT TO BE ABLE TO TAKE A SINGLE COMEDIC STYLE AND RUN WITH IT FOR YEARS, BUT AUDIENCES CAN GET BORED. EVERY NOW AND THEN YOU'LL SEE A COMEDIAN TRY TO TAKE HIS ACT TO A MORE CEREBRAL LEVEL, BUT IT'S AMAZING JUST HOW DIFFERENT YOUR APPROACH IS!
NORMALLY, ONCE YOU'VE ESTABLISHED A ROUTINE IT'S PRETTY TOUGH TO MIX THINGS UP...YOU'VE DONE A BRILLIANT JOB OF CHANGING YOUR ACT!
ACTUALLY, NOT ONLY HAS YOUR ACT CHANGED...

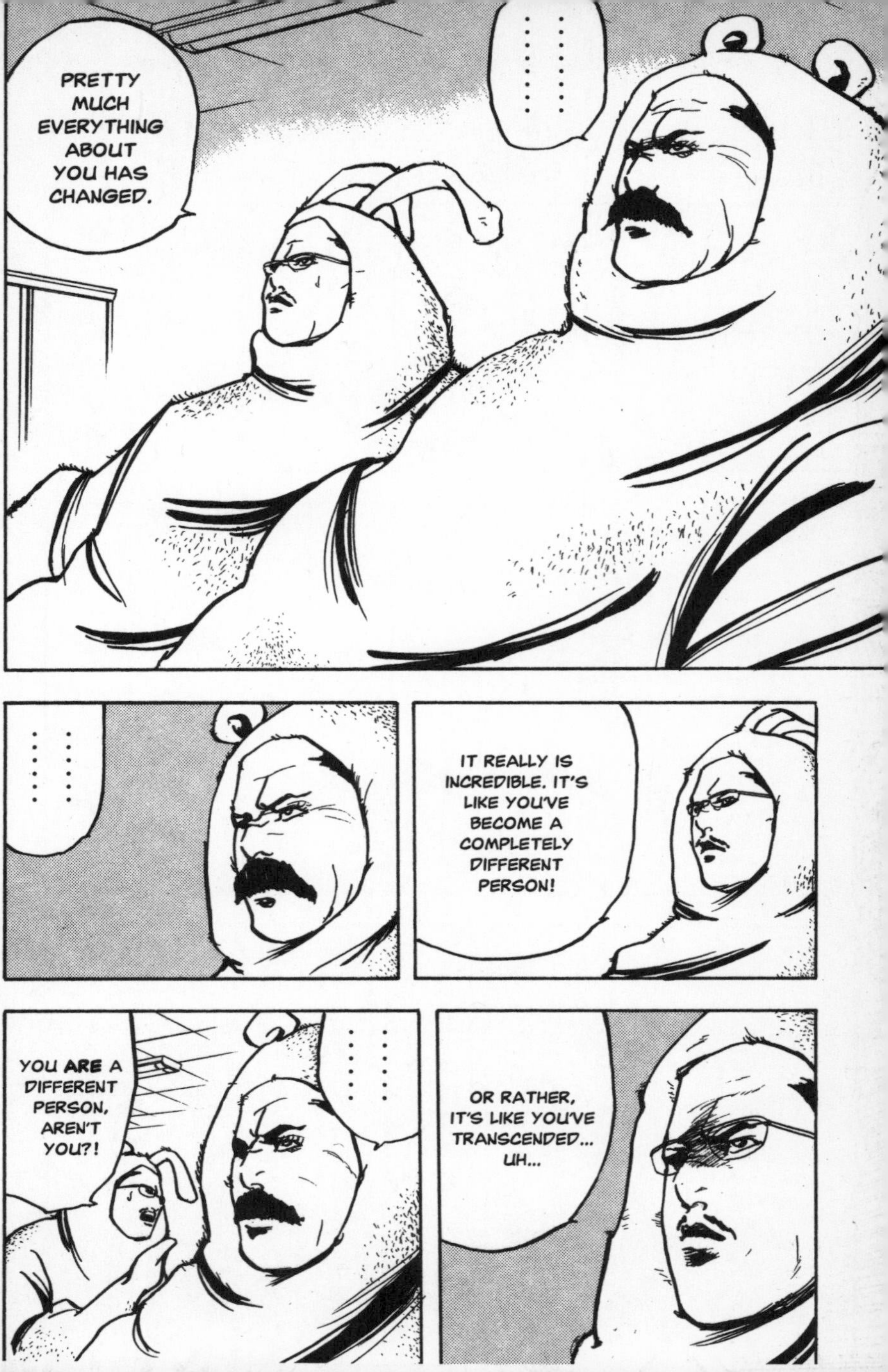
PRETTY MUCH EVERYTHING ABOUT YOU HAS CHANGED.
......
......
IT REALLY IS INCREDIBLE. IT'S LIKE YOU'VE BECOME A COMPLETELY DIFFERENT PERSON!
YOU **ARE** A DIFFERENT PERSON, AREN'T YOU?!
......
OR RATHER, IT'S LIKE YOU'VE TRANSCENDED... UH...

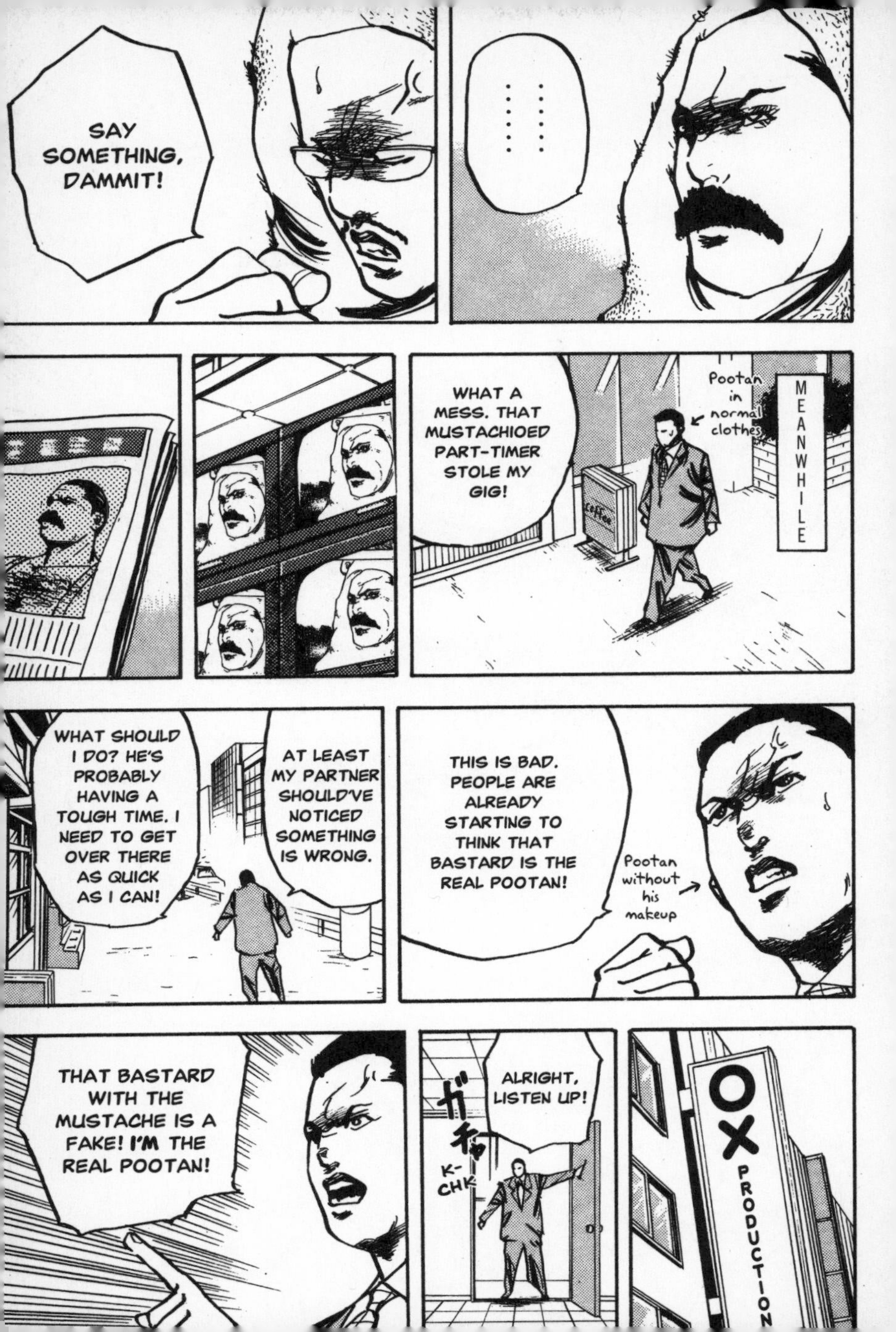
......
SAY SOMETHING, DAMMIT!
MEANWHILE
Pootan in normal clothes
WHAT A MESS. THAT MUSTACHIOED PART-TIMER STOLE MY GIG!
Coffee
THIS IS BAD. PEOPLE ARE ALREADY STARTING TO THINK THAT BASTARD IS THE REAL POOTAN!
Pootan without his makeup
AT LEAST MY PARTNER SHOULD'VE NOTICED SOMETHING IS WRONG.
WHAT SHOULD I DO? HE'S PROBABLY HAVING A TOUGH TIME. I NEED TO GET OVER THERE AS QUICK AS I CAN!
OX PRODUCTION
ガチャ
K-CHK
ALRIGHT, LISTEN UP!
THAT BASTARD WITH THE MUSTACHE IS A FAKE! I'M THE REAL POOTAN!

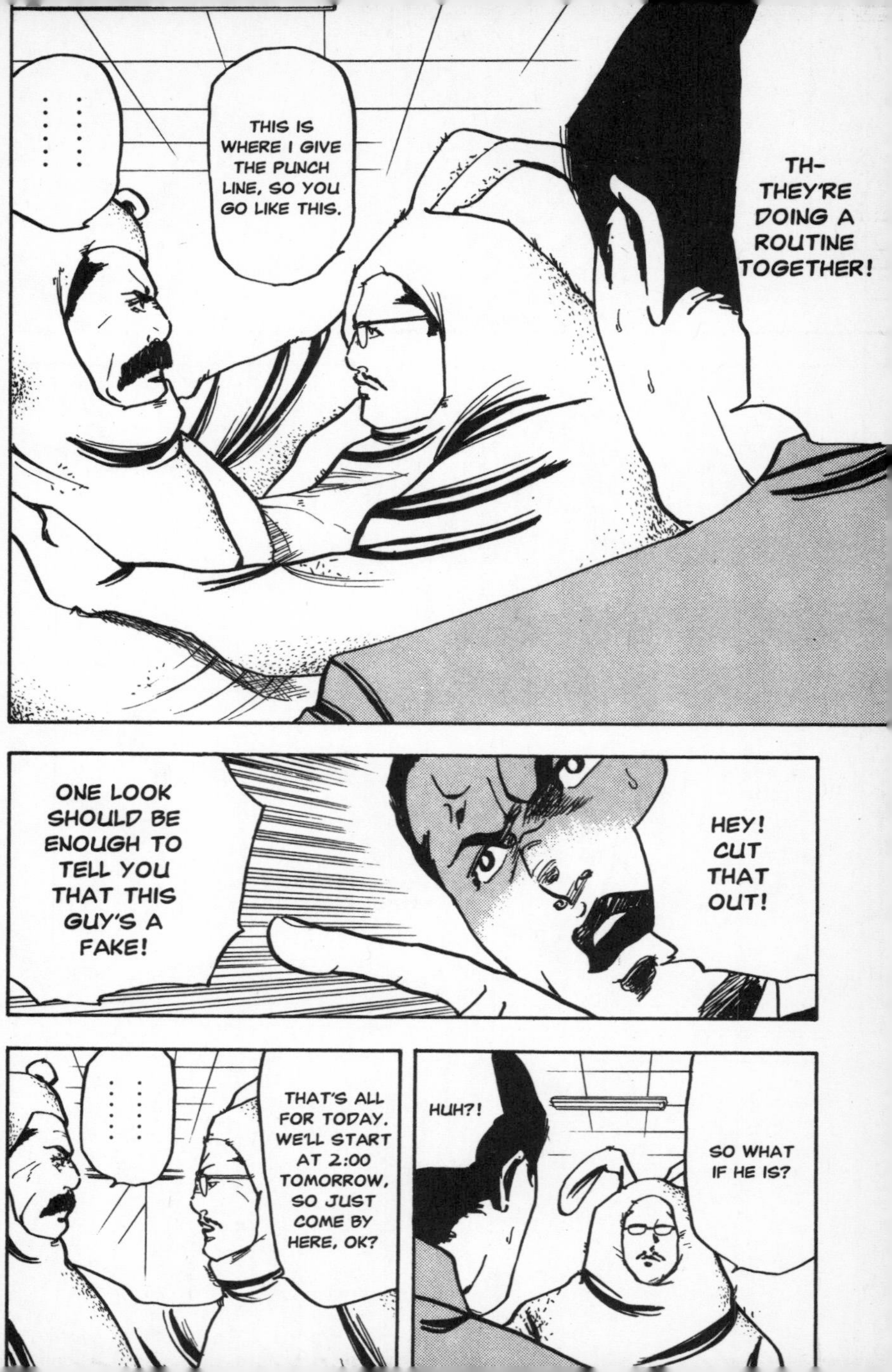

TH- THEY'RE DOING A ROUTINE TOGETHER!
THIS IS WHERE I GIVE THE PUNCH LINE, SO YOU GO LIKE THIS.
......
HEY! CUT THAT OUT!
ONE LOOK SHOULD BE ENOUGH TO TELL YOU THAT THIS GUY'S A FAKE!
THAT'S ALL FOR TODAY. WE'LL START AT 2:00 TOMORROW, SO JUST COME BY HERE, OK?
......
SO WHAT IF HE IS?
HUH?!

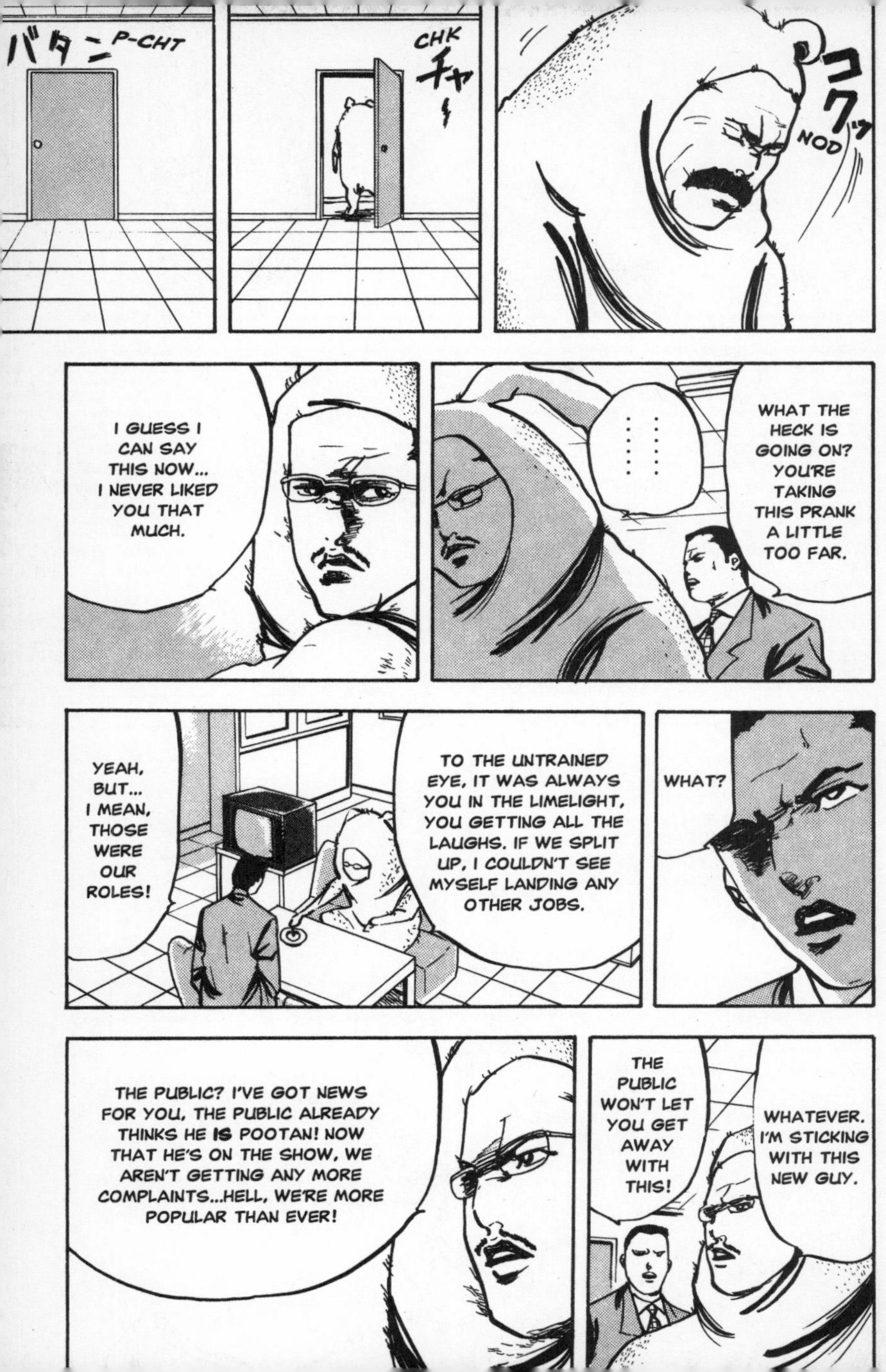
コクッ
NOD
チャ
CHK
バタン
P-CHT
WHAT THE HECK IS GOING ON? YOU'RE TAKING THIS PRANK A LITTLE TOO FAR.
......
I GUESS I CAN SAY THIS NOW... I NEVER LIKED YOU THAT MUCH.
WHAT?
TO THE UNTRAINED EYE, IT WAS ALWAYS YOU IN THE LIMELIGHT, YOU GETTING ALL THE LAUGHS. IF WE SPLIT UP, I COULDN'T SEE MYSELF LANDING ANY OTHER JOBS.
YEAH, BUT... I MEAN, THOSE WERE OUR ROLES!
WHATEVER. I'M STICKING WITH THIS NEW GUY.
THE PUBLIC WON'T LET YOU GET AWAY WITH THIS!
THE PUBLIC? I'VE GOT NEWS FOR YOU, THE PUBLIC ALREADY THINKS HE **IS** POOTAN! NOW THAT HE'S ON THE SHOW, WE AREN'T GETTING ANY MORE COMPLAINTS...HELL, WE'RE MORE POPULAR THAN EVER!

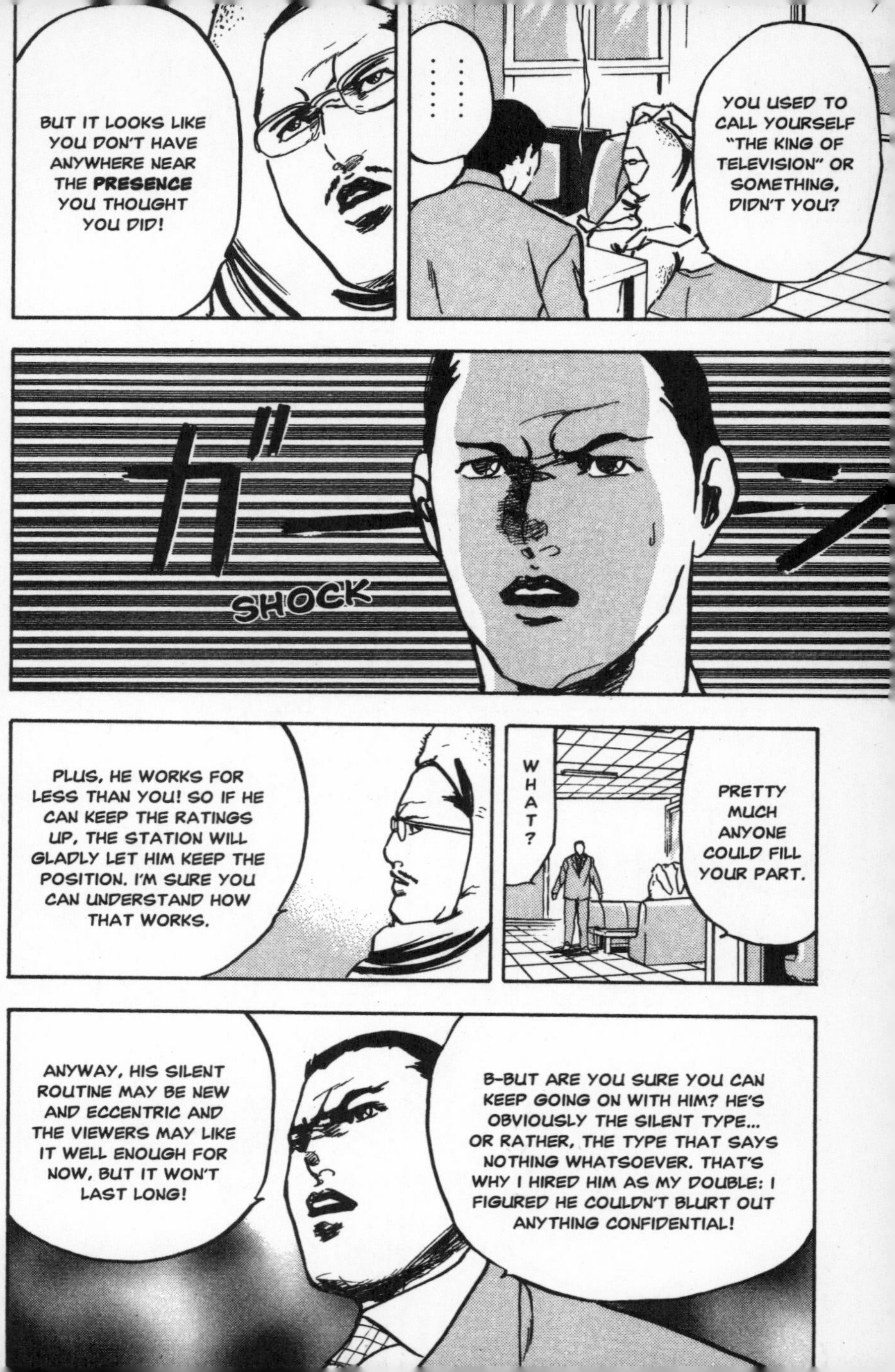
BUT IT LOOKS LIKE YOU DON'T HAVE ANYWHERE NEAR THE **PRESENCE** YOU THOUGHT YOU DID!
......
YOU USED TO CALL YOURSELF "THE KING OF TELEVISION" OR SOMETHING, DIDN'T YOU?
ガーン
SHOCK
PLUS, HE WORKS FOR LESS THAN YOU! SO IF HE CAN KEEP THE RATINGS UP, THE STATION WILL GLADLY LET HIM KEEP THE POSITION. I'M SURE YOU CAN UNDERSTAND HOW THAT WORKS.
WHAT?
PRETTY MUCH ANYONE COULD FILL YOUR PART.
ANYWAY, HIS SILENT ROUTINE MAY BE NEW AND ECCENTRIC AND THE VIEWERS MAY LIKE IT WELL ENOUGH FOR NOW, BUT IT WON'T LAST LONG!
B-BUT ARE YOU SURE YOU CAN KEEP GOING ON WITH HIM? HE'S OBVIOUSLY THE SILENT TYPE... OR RATHER, THE TYPE THAT SAYS NOTHING WHATSOEVER. THAT'S WHY I HIRED HIM AS MY DOUBLE: I FIGURED HE COULDN'T BLURT OUT ANYTHING CONFIDENTIAL!

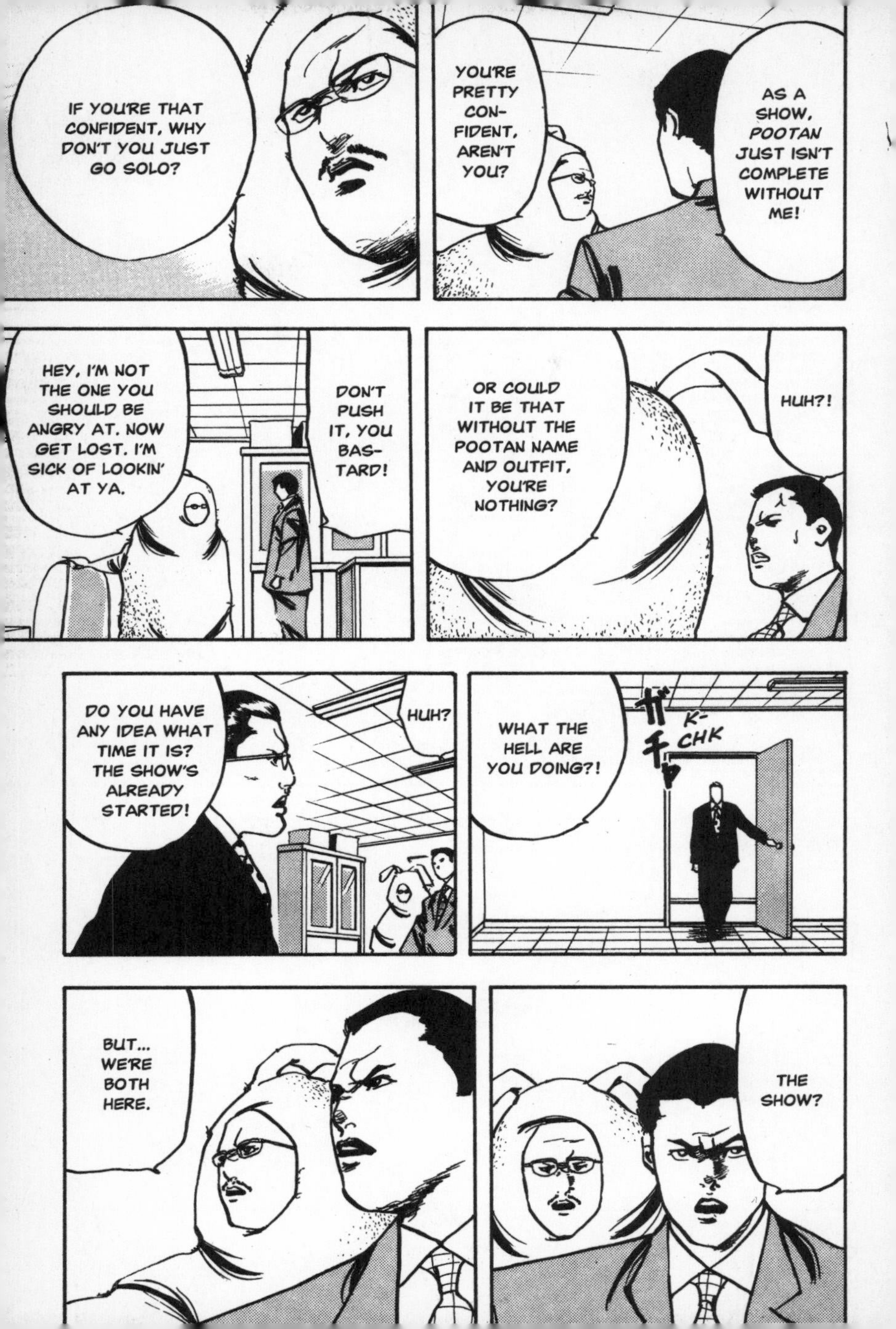
AS A SHOW, POOTAN JUST ISN'T COMPLETE WITHOUT ME!
YOU'RE PRETTY CON-FIDENT, AREN'T YOU?
IF YOU'RE THAT CONFIDENT, WHY DON'T YOU JUST GO SOLO?
OR COULD IT BE THAT WITHOUT THE POOTAN NAME AND OUTFIT, YOU'RE NOTHING?
HUH?!
DON'T PUSH IT, YOU BAS-TARD!
HEY, I'M NOT THE ONE YOU SHOULD BE ANGRY AT. NOW GET LOST. I'M SICK OF LOOKIN' AT YA.
ガチャ
K-CHK
WHAT THE HELL ARE YOU DOING?!
HUH?
DO YOU HAVE ANY IDEA WHAT TIME IT IS? THE SHOW'S ALREADY STARTED!
THE SHOW?
BUT... WE'RE BOTH HERE.

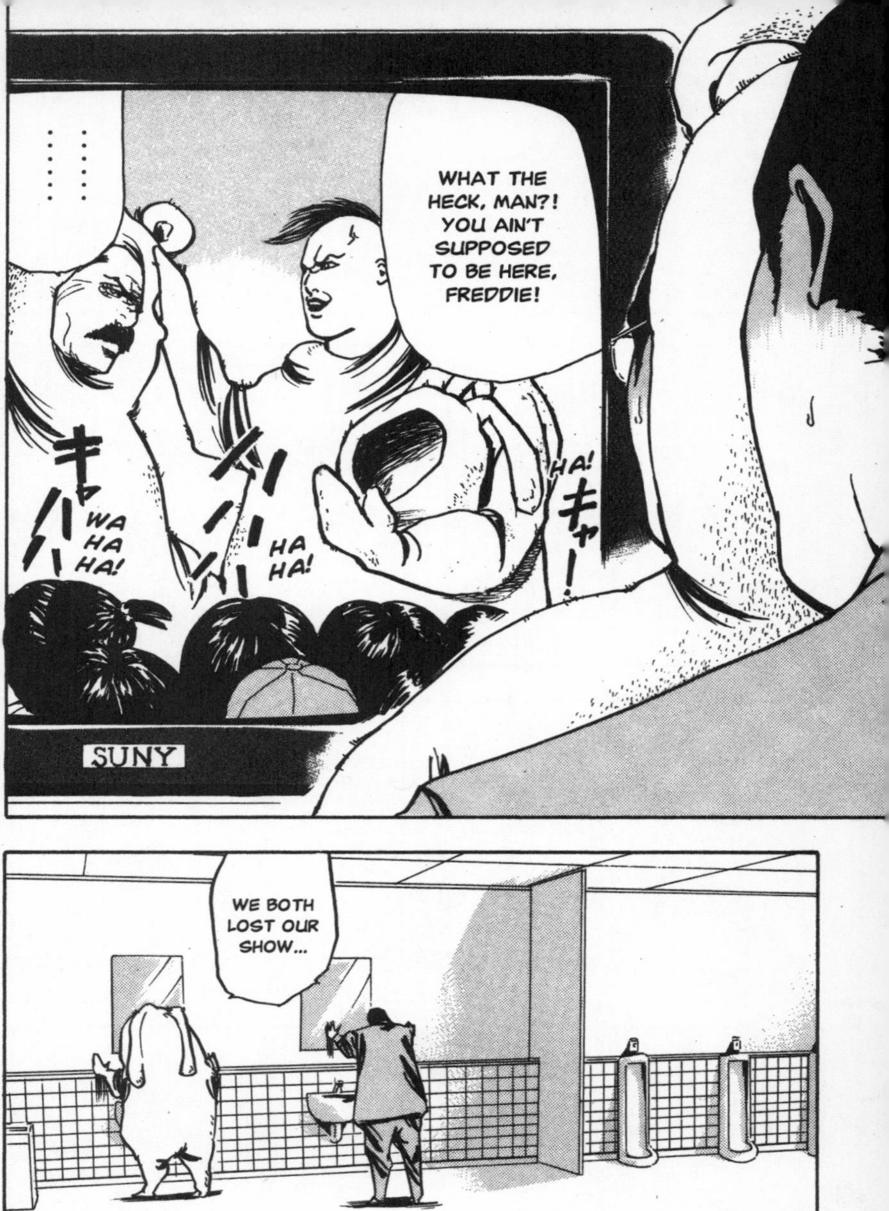
......
WHAT THE HECK, MAN?! YOU AIN'T SUPPOSED TO BE HERE, FREDDIE!
WA HA HA!
HA HA!
HA!
SUNY
WE BOTH LOST OUR SHOW...

IN THE BATHROOM AGAIN!

CHAPTER 124: A KIND OF MAGIC

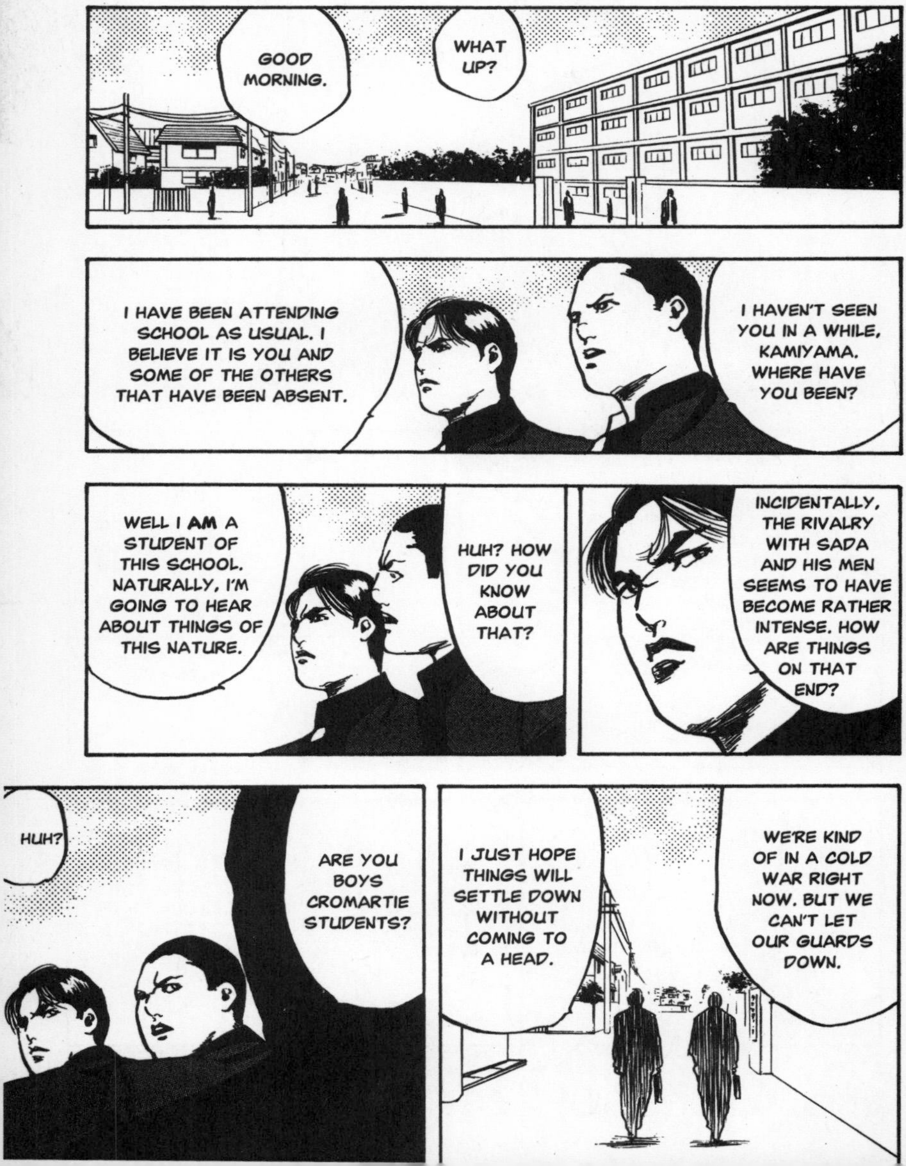
WHAT UP?
GOOD MORNING.
I HAVEN'T SEEN YOU IN A WHILE, KAMIYAMA. WHERE HAVE YOU BEEN?
I HAVE BEEN ATTENDING SCHOOL AS USUAL. I BELIEVE IT IS YOU AND SOME OF THE OTHERS THAT HAVE BEEN ABSENT.
INCIDENTALLY, THE RIVALRY WITH SADA AND HIS MEN SEEMS TO HAVE BECOME RATHER INTENSE. HOW ARE THINGS ON THAT END?
HUH? HOW DID YOU KNOW ABOUT THAT?
WELL I AM A STUDENT OF THIS SCHOOL. NATURALLY, I'M GOING TO HEAR ABOUT THINGS OF THIS NATURE.
WE'RE KIND OF IN A COLD WAR RIGHT NOW. BUT WE CAN'T LET OUR GUARDS DOWN.
I JUST HOPE THINGS WILL SETTLE DOWN WITHOUT COMING TO A HEAD.
ARE YOU BOYS CROMARTIE STUDENTS?
HUH?

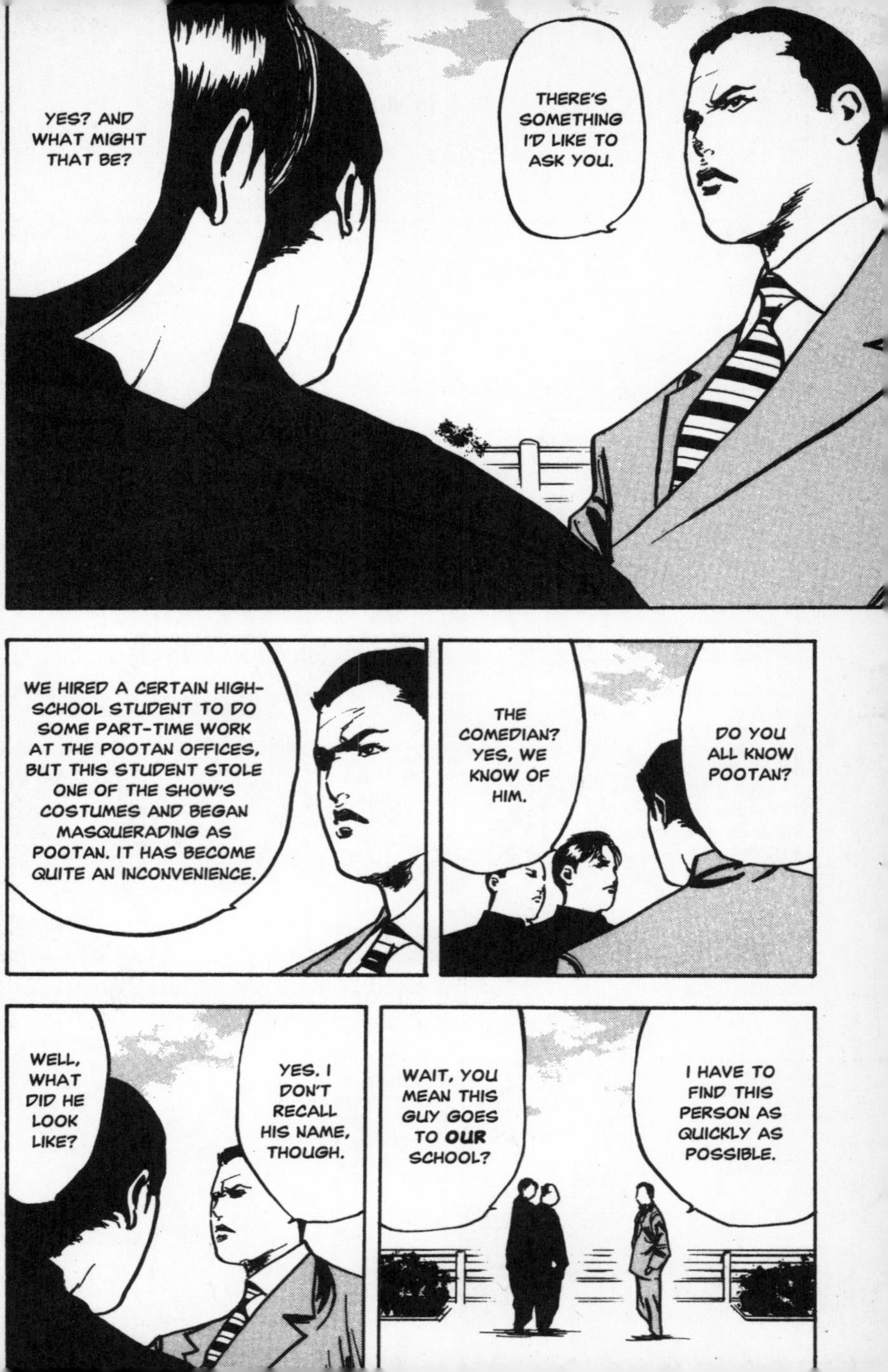
THERE'S SOMETHING I'D LIKE TO ASK YOU.
YES? AND WHAT MIGHT THAT BE?
DO YOU ALL KNOW POOTAN?
THE COMEDIAN? YES, WE KNOW OF HIM.
WE HIRED A CERTAIN HIGH-SCHOOL STUDENT TO DO SOME PART-TIME WORK AT THE POOTAN OFFICES, BUT THIS STUDENT STOLE ONE OF THE SHOW'S COSTUMES AND BEGAN MASQUERADING AS POOTAN. IT HAS BECOME QUITE AN INCONVENIENCE.
I HAVE TO FIND THIS PERSON AS QUICKLY AS POSSIBLE.
WAIT, YOU MEAN THIS GUY GOES TO **OUR** SCHOOL?
YES. I DON'T RECALL HIS NAME, THOUGH.
WELL, WHAT DID HE LOOK LIKE?

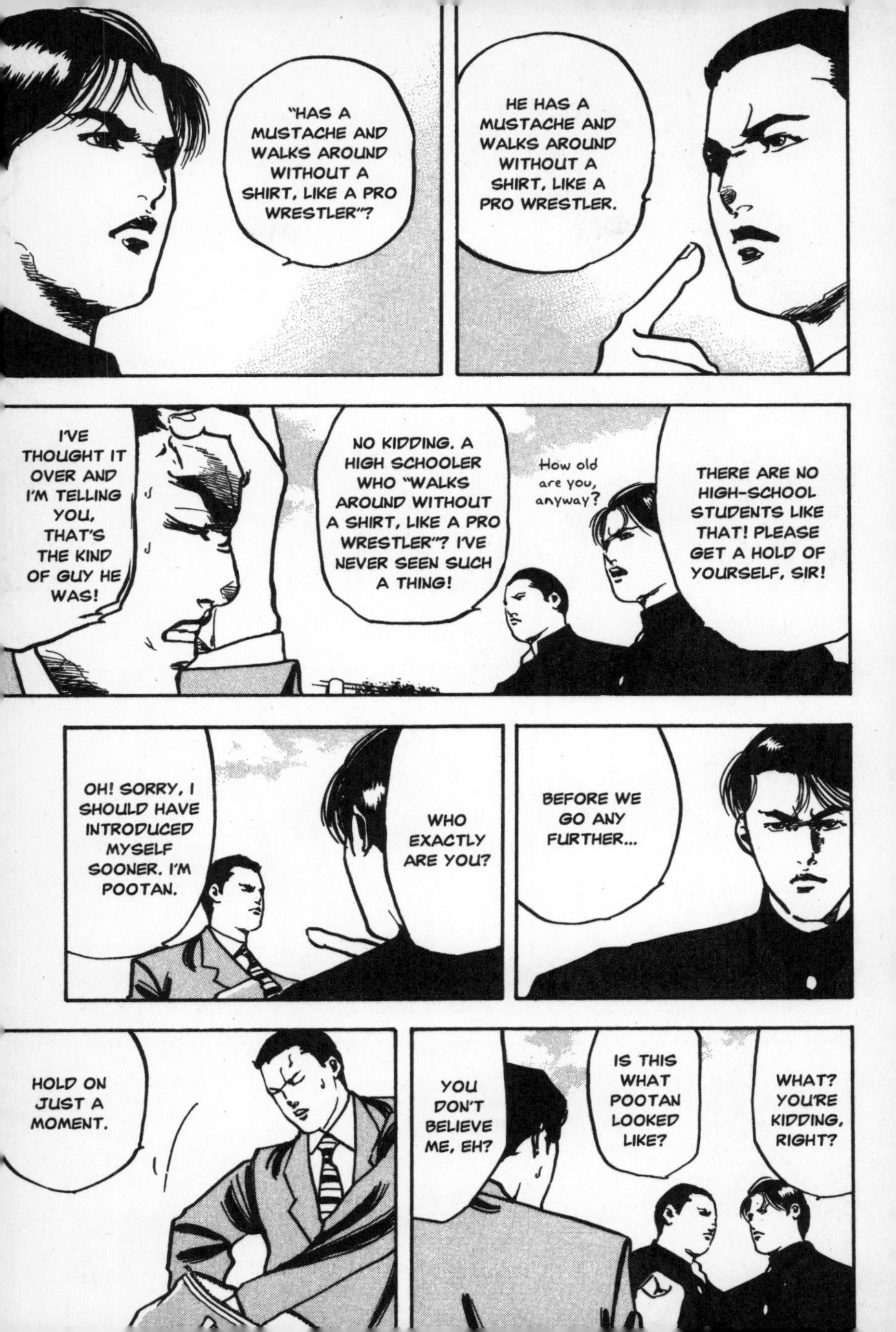
HE HAS A MUSTACHE AND WALKS AROUND WITHOUT A SHIRT, LIKE A PRO WRESTLER.
"HAS A MUSTACHE AND WALKS AROUND WITHOUT A SHIRT, LIKE A PRO WRESTLER"?
THERE ARE NO HIGH-SCHOOL STUDENTS LIKE THAT! PLEASE GET A HOLD OF YOURSELF, SIR!
How old are you, anyway?
NO KIDDING. A HIGH SCHOOLER WHO "WALKS AROUND WITHOUT A SHIRT, LIKE A PRO WRESTLER"? I'VE NEVER SEEN SUCH A THING!
I'VE THOUGHT IT OVER AND I'M TELLING YOU, THAT'S THE KIND OF GUY HE WAS!
BEFORE WE GO ANY FURTHER...
WHO EXACTLY ARE YOU?
OH! SORRY, I SHOULD HAVE INTRODUCED MYSELF SOONER. I'M POOTAN.
WHAT? YOU'RE KIDDING, RIGHT?
IS THIS WHAT POOTAN LOOKED LIKE?
YOU DON'T BELIEVE ME, EH?
HOLD ON JUST A MOMENT.

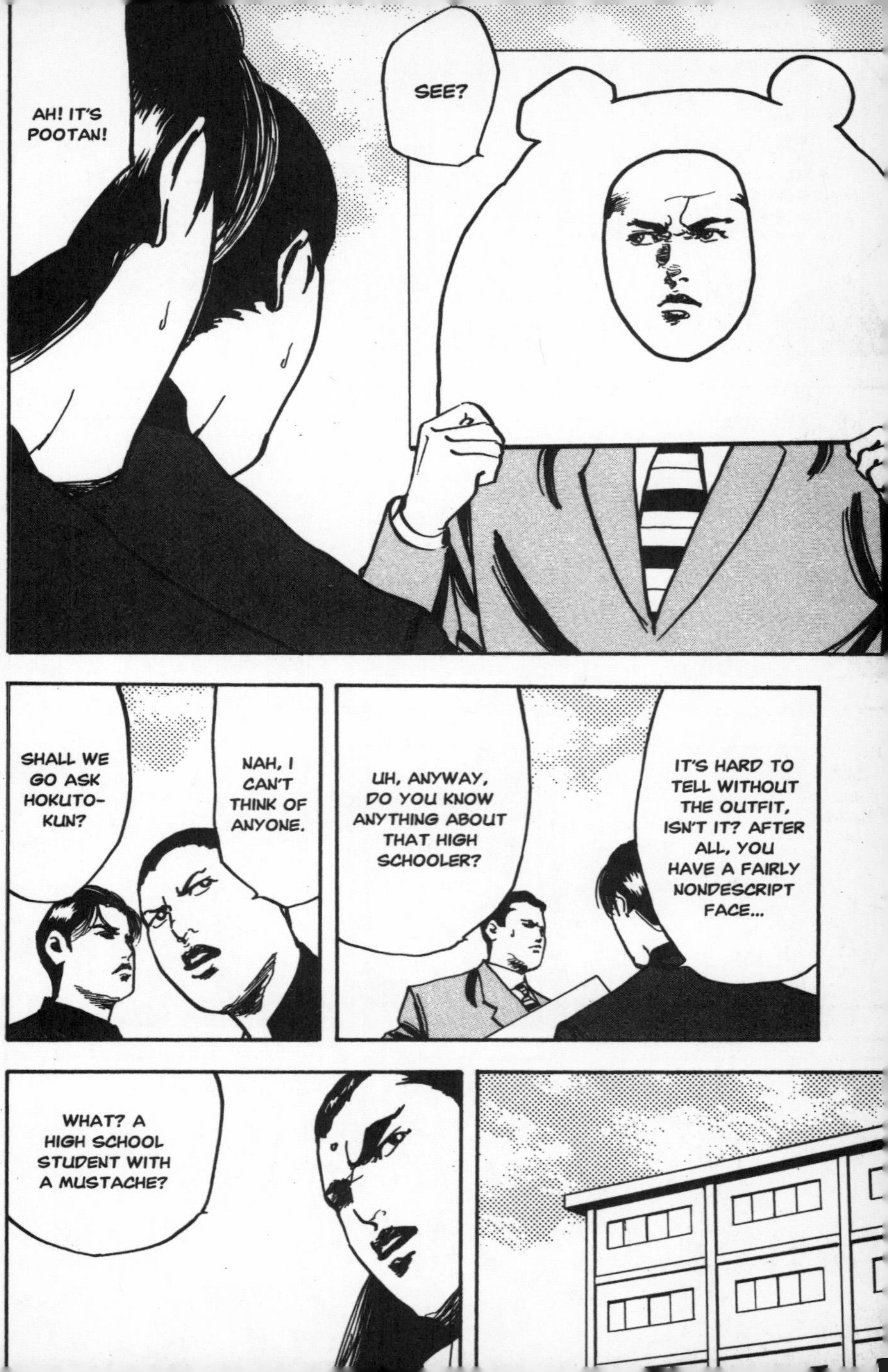
SEE?
AH! IT'S POOTAN!
IT'S HARD TO TELL WITHOUT THE OUTFIT, ISN'T IT? AFTER ALL, YOU HAVE A FAIRLY NONDESCRIPT FACE...
UH, ANYWAY, DO YOU KNOW ANYTHING ABOUT THAT HIGH SCHOOLER?
NAH, I CAN'T THINK OF ANYONE.
SHALL WE GO ASK HOKUTO-KUN?
WHAT? A HIGH SCHOOL STUDENT WITH A MUSTACHE?

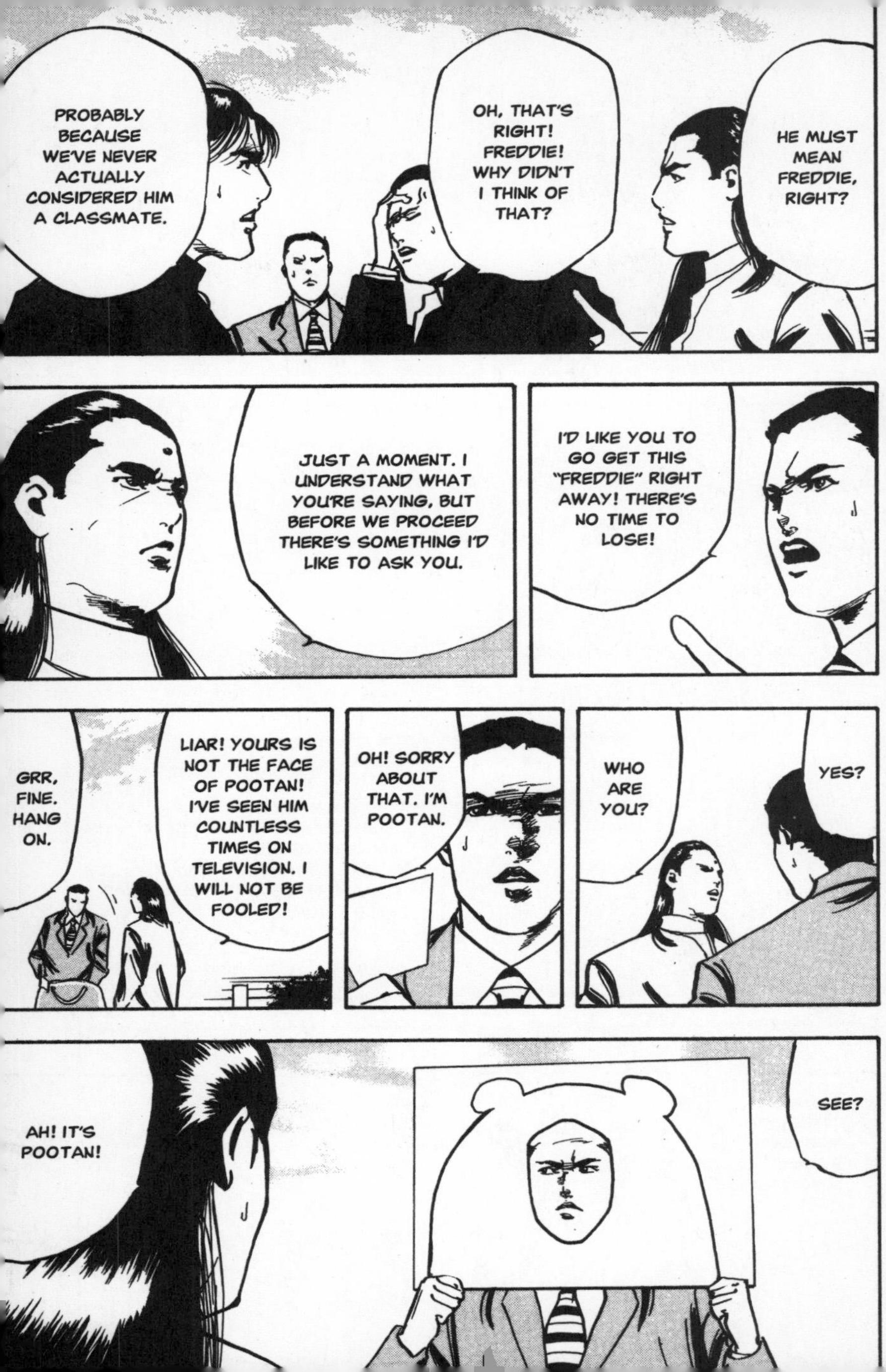
HE MUST MEAN FREDDIE, RIGHT?
OH, THAT'S RIGHT! FREDDIE! WHY DIDN'T I THINK OF THAT?
PROBABLY BECAUSE WE'VE NEVER ACTUALLY CONSIDERED HIM A CLASSMATE.
I'D LIKE YOU TO GO GET THIS "FREDDIE" RIGHT AWAY! THERE'S NO TIME TO LOSE!
JUST A MOMENT. I UNDERSTAND WHAT YOU'RE SAYING, BUT BEFORE WE PROCEED THERE'S SOMETHING I'D LIKE TO ASK YOU.
YES?
WHO ARE YOU?
OH! SORRY ABOUT THAT. I'M POOTAN.
LIAR! YOURS IS NOT THE FACE OF POOTAN! I'VE SEEN HIM COUNTLESS TIMES ON TELEVISION. I WILL NOT BE FOOLED!
GRR, FINE. HANG ON.
SEE?
AH! IT'S POOTAN!

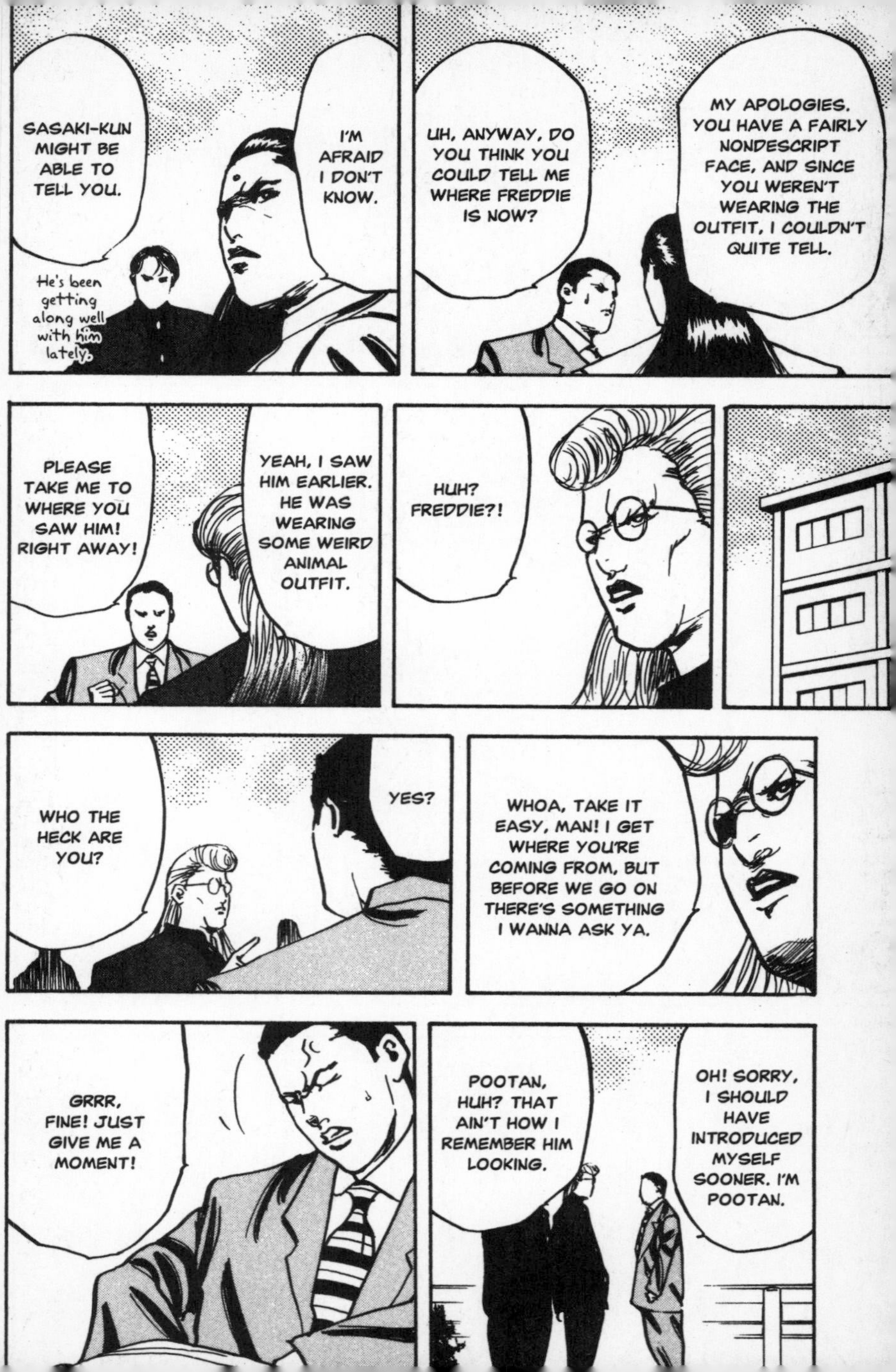
MY APOLOGIES. YOU HAVE A FAIRLY NONDESCRIPT FACE, AND SINCE YOU WEREN'T WEARING THE OUTFIT, I COULDN'T QUITE TELL.
UH, ANYWAY, DO YOU THINK YOU COULD TELL ME WHERE FREDDIE IS NOW?
I'M AFRAID I DON'T KNOW.
SASAKI-KUN MIGHT BE ABLE TO TELL YOU.
He's been getting along well with him lately.
HUH? FREDDIE?!
YEAH, I SAW HIM EARLIER. HE WAS WEARING SOME WEIRD ANIMAL OUTFIT.
PLEASE TAKE ME TO WHERE YOU SAW HIM! RIGHT AWAY!
WHOA, TAKE IT EASY, MAN! I GET WHERE YOU'RE COMING FROM, BUT BEFORE WE GO ON THERE'S SOMETHING I WANNA ASK YA.
YES?
WHO THE HECK ARE YOU?
OH! SORRY, I SHOULD HAVE INTRODUCED MYSELF SOONER. I'M POOTAN.
POOTAN, HUH? THAT AIN'T HOW I REMEMBER HIM LOOKING.
GRRR, FINE! JUST GIVE ME A MOMENT!

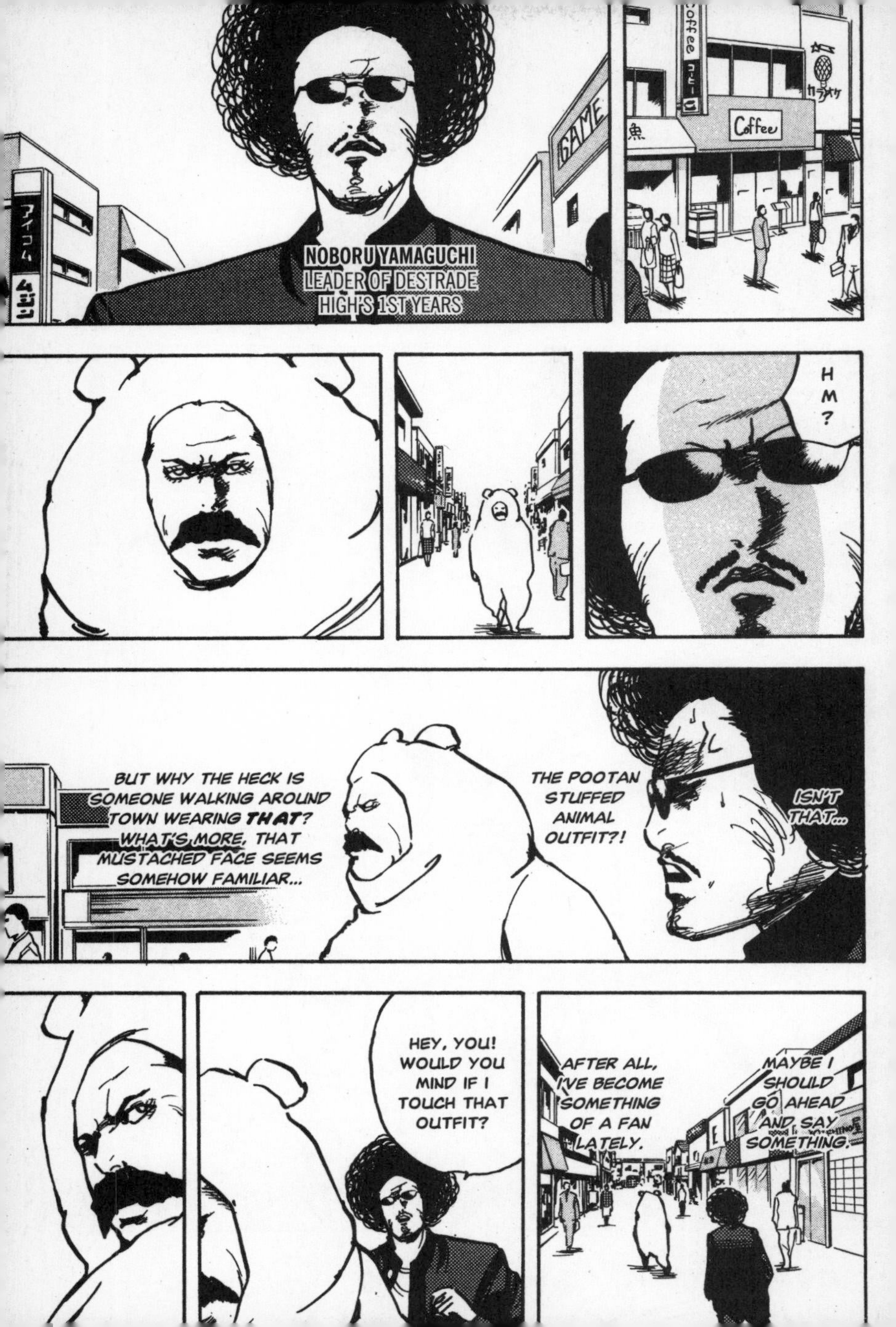
NOBORU YAMAGUCHI
LEADER OF DESTRADE HIGH'S 1ST YEARS
Coffee
GAME
Coffee
HM?
ISN'T THAT...
THE POOTAN STUFFED ANIMAL OUTFIT?!
BUT WHY THE HECK IS SOMEONE WALKING AROUND TOWN WEARING THAT? WHAT'S MORE, THAT MUSTACHED FACE SEEMS SOMEHOW FAMILIAR...
MAYBE I SHOULD GO AHEAD AND SAY SOMETHING.
AFTER ALL, I'VE BECOME SOMETHING OF A FAN LATELY.
HEY, YOU! WOULD YOU MIND IF I TOUCH THAT OUTFIT?

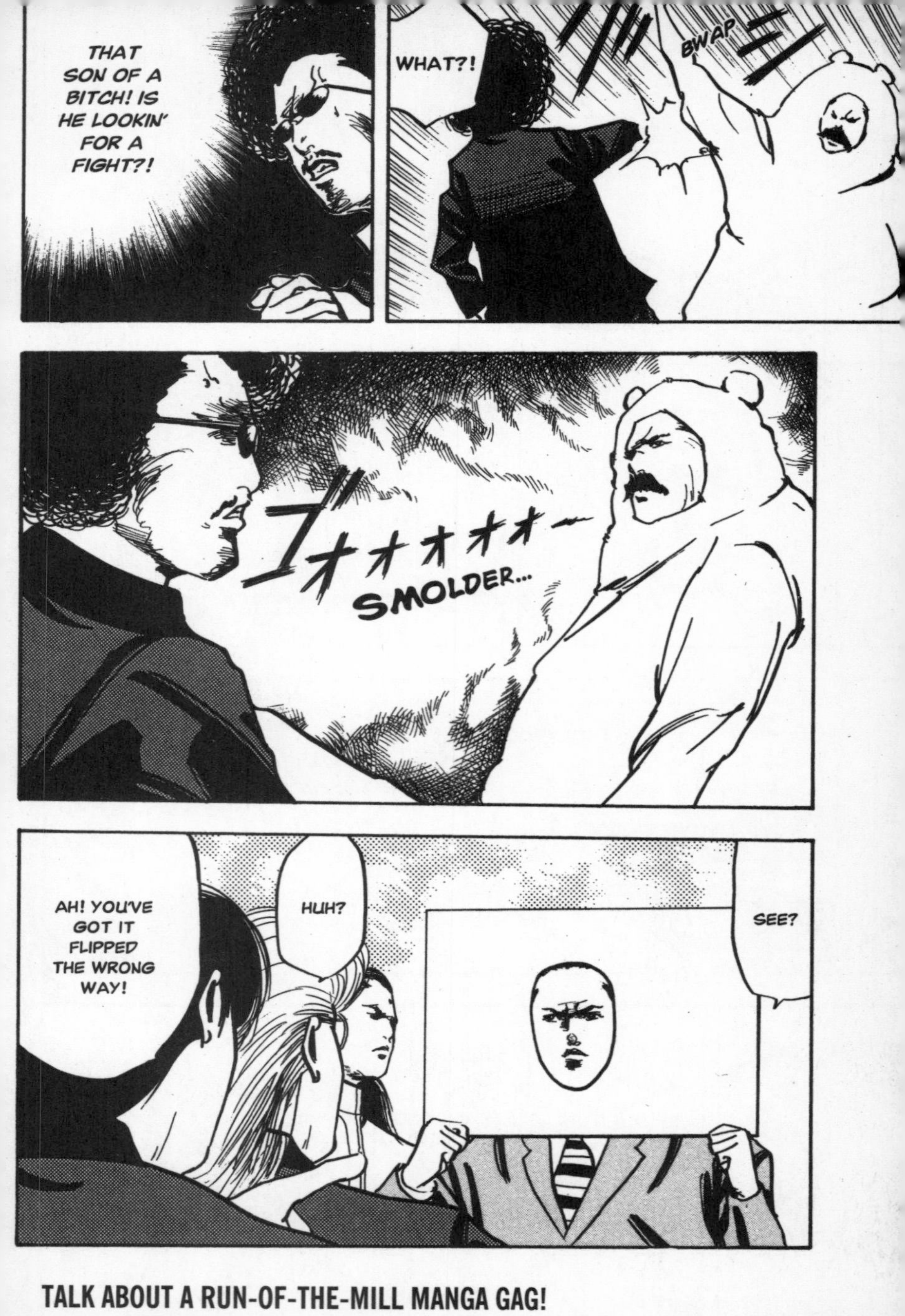
BWAP
WHAT?!
THAT SON OF A BITCH! IS HE LOOKIN' FOR A FIGHT?!
ゴオオオオオー
SMOLDER...
SEE?
HUH?
AH! YOU'VE GOT IT FLIPPED THE WRONG WAY!

TALK ABOUT A RUN-OF-THE-MILL MANGA GAG!

CHAPTER 125: **UNDER PRESSURE**

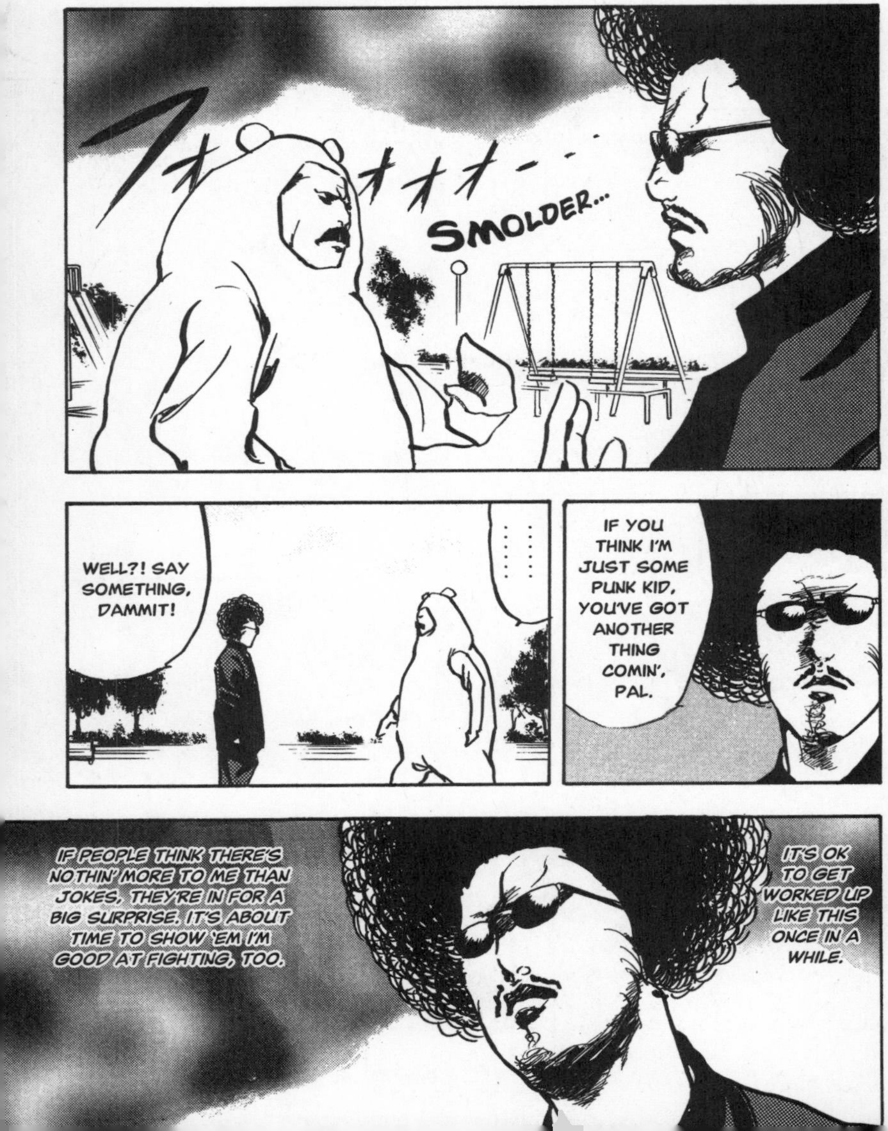
SMOLDER...
WELL?! SAY SOMETHING, DAMMIT!
......
IF YOU THINK I'M JUST SOME PUNK KID, YOU'VE GOT ANOTHER THING COMIN', PAL.
IF PEOPLE THINK THERE'S NOTHIN' MORE TO ME THAN JOKES, THEY'RE IN FOR A BIG SURPRISE. IT'S ABOUT TIME TO SHOW 'EM I'M GOOD AT FIGHTING, TOO.
IT'S OK TO GET WORKED UP LIKE THIS ONCE IN A WHILE.

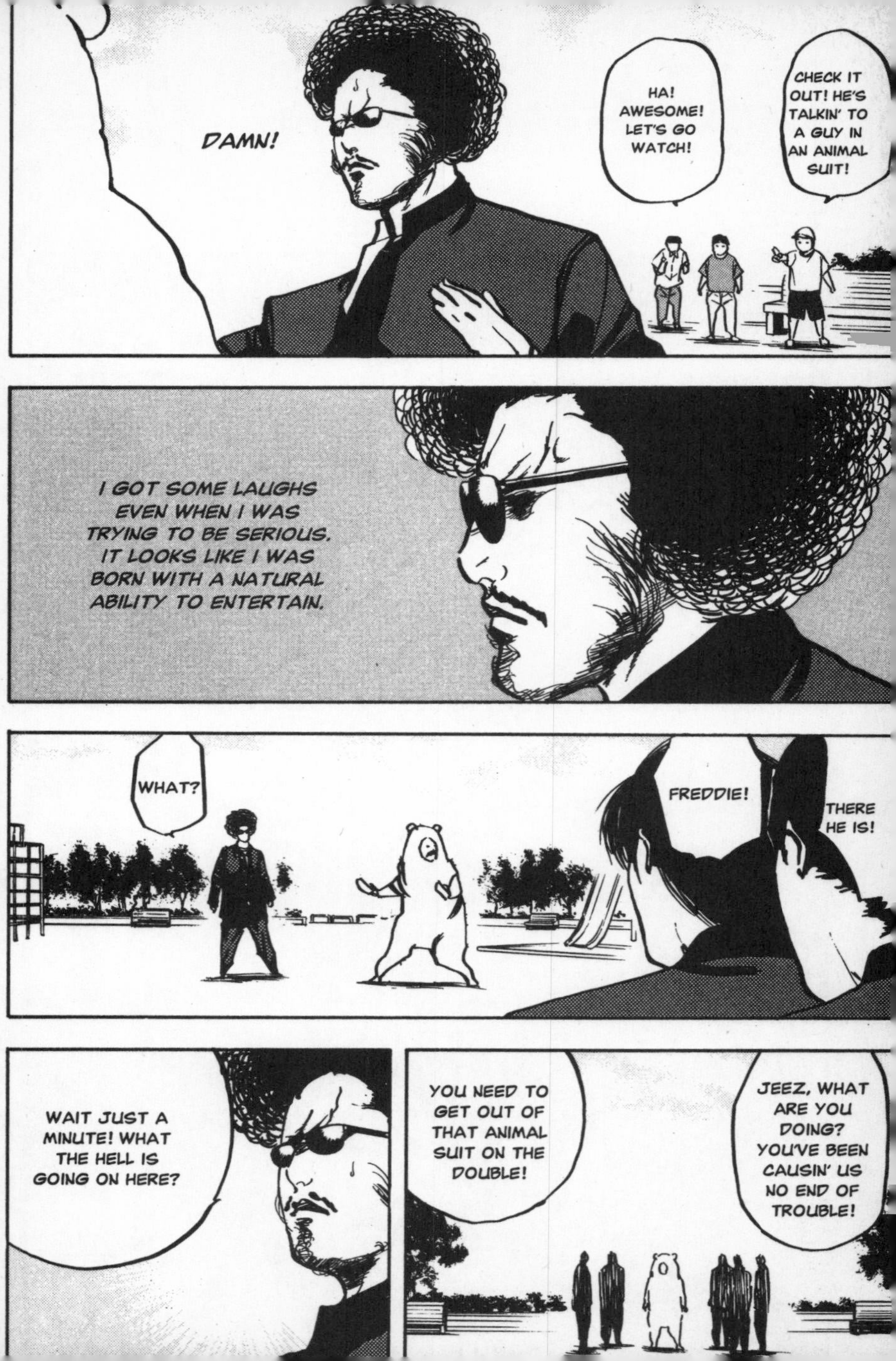
DAMN!
HA! AWESOME! LET'S GO WATCH!
CHECK IT OUT! HE'S TALKIN' TO A GUY IN AN ANIMAL SUIT!
I GOT SOME LAUGHS EVEN WHEN I WAS TRYING TO BE SERIOUS. IT LOOKS LIKE I WAS BORN WITH A NATURAL ABILITY TO ENTERTAIN.
WHAT?
FREDDIE!
THERE HE IS!
WAIT JUST A MINUTE! WHAT THE HELL IS GOING ON HERE?
YOU NEED TO GET OUT OF THAT ANIMAL SUIT ON THE DOUBLE!
JEEZ, WHAT ARE YOU DOING? YOU'VE BEEN CAUSIN' US NO END OF TROUBLE!

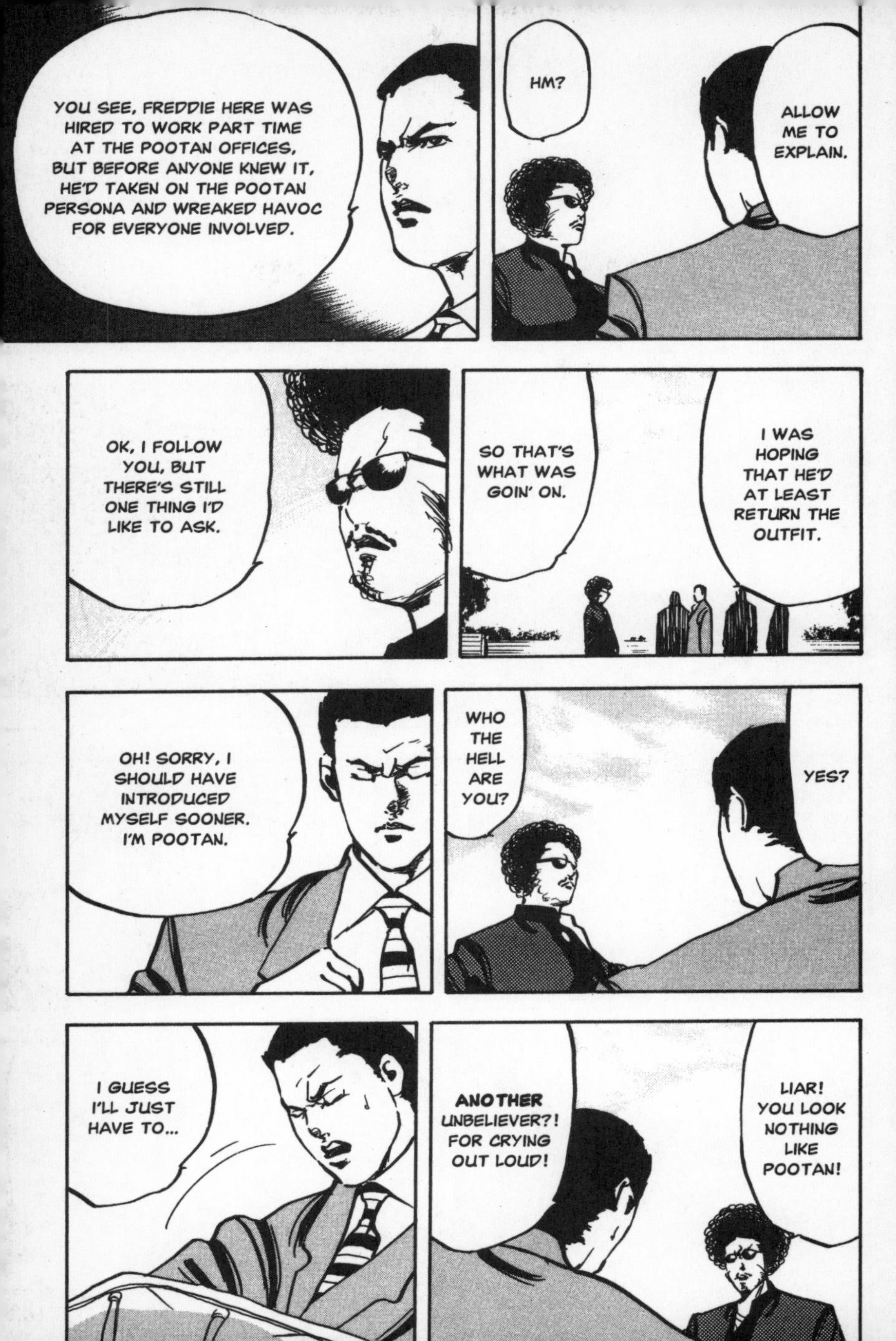
ALLOW ME TO EXPLAIN.
HM?
YOU SEE, FREDDIE HERE WAS HIRED TO WORK PART TIME AT THE POOTAN OFFICES, BUT BEFORE ANYONE KNEW IT, HE'D TAKEN ON THE POOTAN PERSONA AND WREAKED HAVOC FOR EVERYONE INVOLVED.
I WAS HOPING THAT HE'D AT LEAST RETURN THE OUTFIT.
SO THAT'S WHAT WAS GOIN' ON.
OK, I FOLLOW YOU, BUT THERE'S STILL ONE THING I'D LIKE TO ASK.
YES?
WHO THE HELL ARE YOU?
OH! SORRY, I SHOULD HAVE INTRODUCED MYSELF SOONER. I'M POOTAN.
LIAR! YOU LOOK NOTHING LIKE POOTAN!
ANOTHER UNBELIEVER?! FOR CRYING OUT LOUD!
I GUESS I'LL JUST HAVE TO...

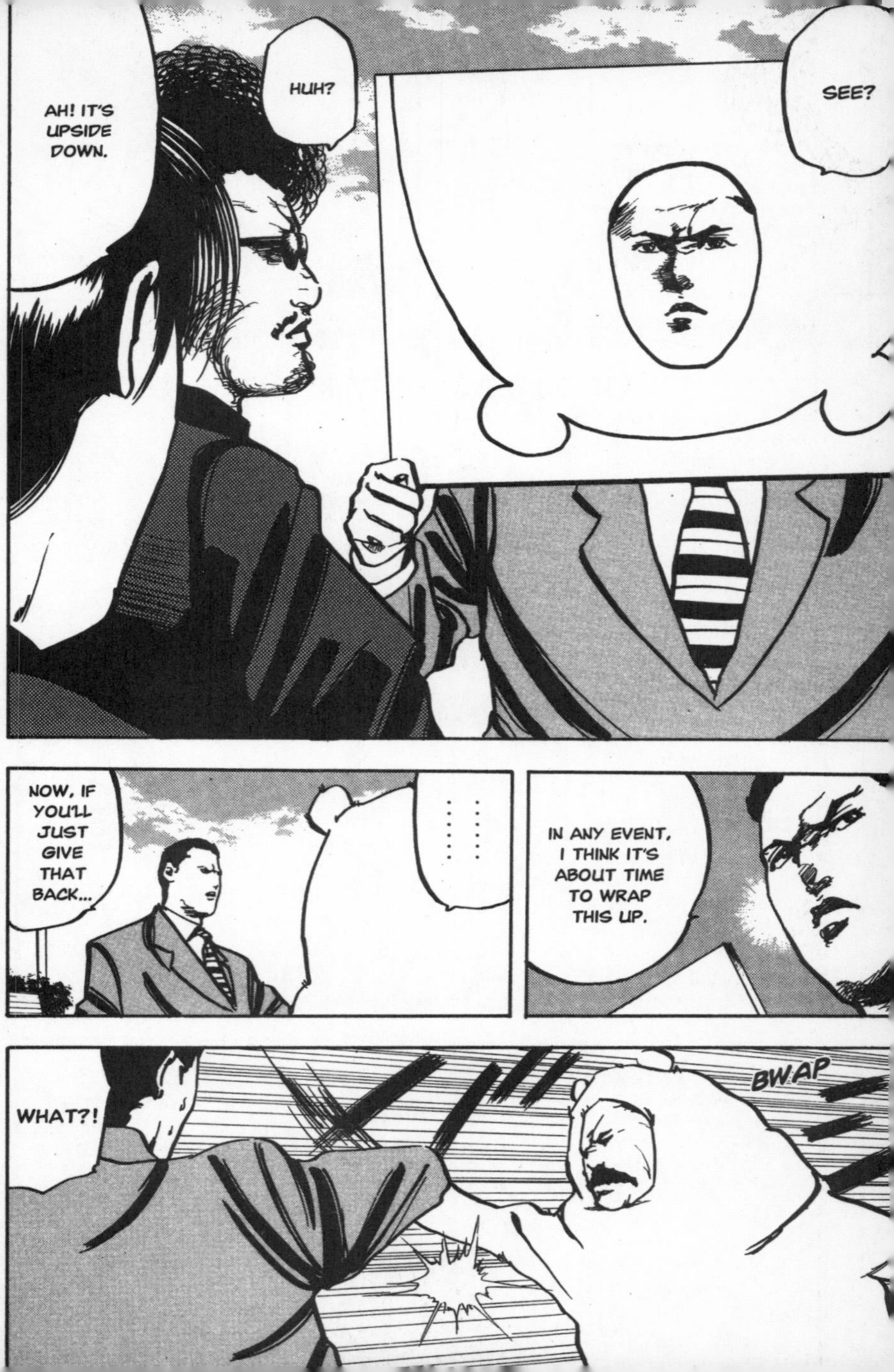
SEE?
HUH?
AH! IT'S UPSIDE DOWN.
IN ANY EVENT, I THINK IT'S ABOUT TIME TO WRAP THIS UP.
......
NOW, IF YOU'LL JUST GIVE THAT BACK...
BWAP
WHAT?!

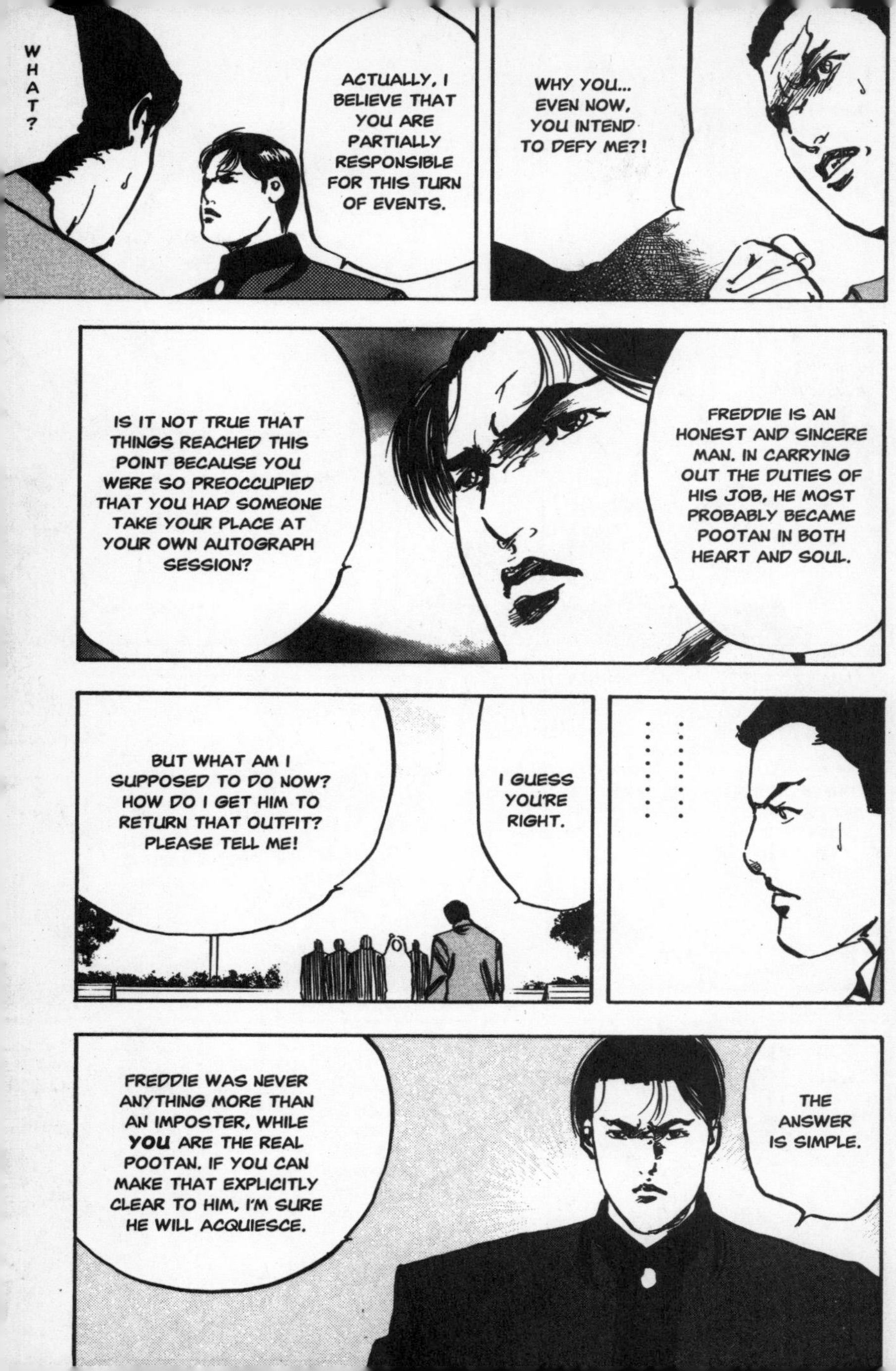

WHY YOU... EVEN NOW, YOU INTEND TO DEFY ME?!
ACTUALLY, I BELIEVE THAT YOU ARE PARTIALLY RESPONSIBLE FOR THIS TURN OF EVENTS.
WHAT?
FREDDIE IS AN HONEST AND SINCERE MAN. IN CARRYING OUT THE DUTIES OF HIS JOB, HE MOST PROBABLY BECAME POOTAN IN BOTH HEART AND SOUL.
IS IT NOT TRUE THAT THINGS REACHED THIS POINT BECAUSE YOU WERE SO PREOCCUPIED THAT YOU HAD SOMEONE TAKE YOUR PLACE AT YOUR OWN AUTOGRAPH SESSION?
......
I GUESS YOU'RE RIGHT.
BUT WHAT AM I SUPPOSED TO DO NOW? HOW DO I GET HIM TO RETURN THAT OUTFIT? PLEASE TELL ME!
THE ANSWER IS SIMPLE.
FREDDIE WAS NEVER ANYTHING MORE THAN AN IMPOSTER, WHILE **YOU** ARE THE REAL POOTAN. IF YOU CAN MAKE THAT EXPLICITLY CLEAR TO HIM, I'M SURE HE WILL ACQUIESCE.

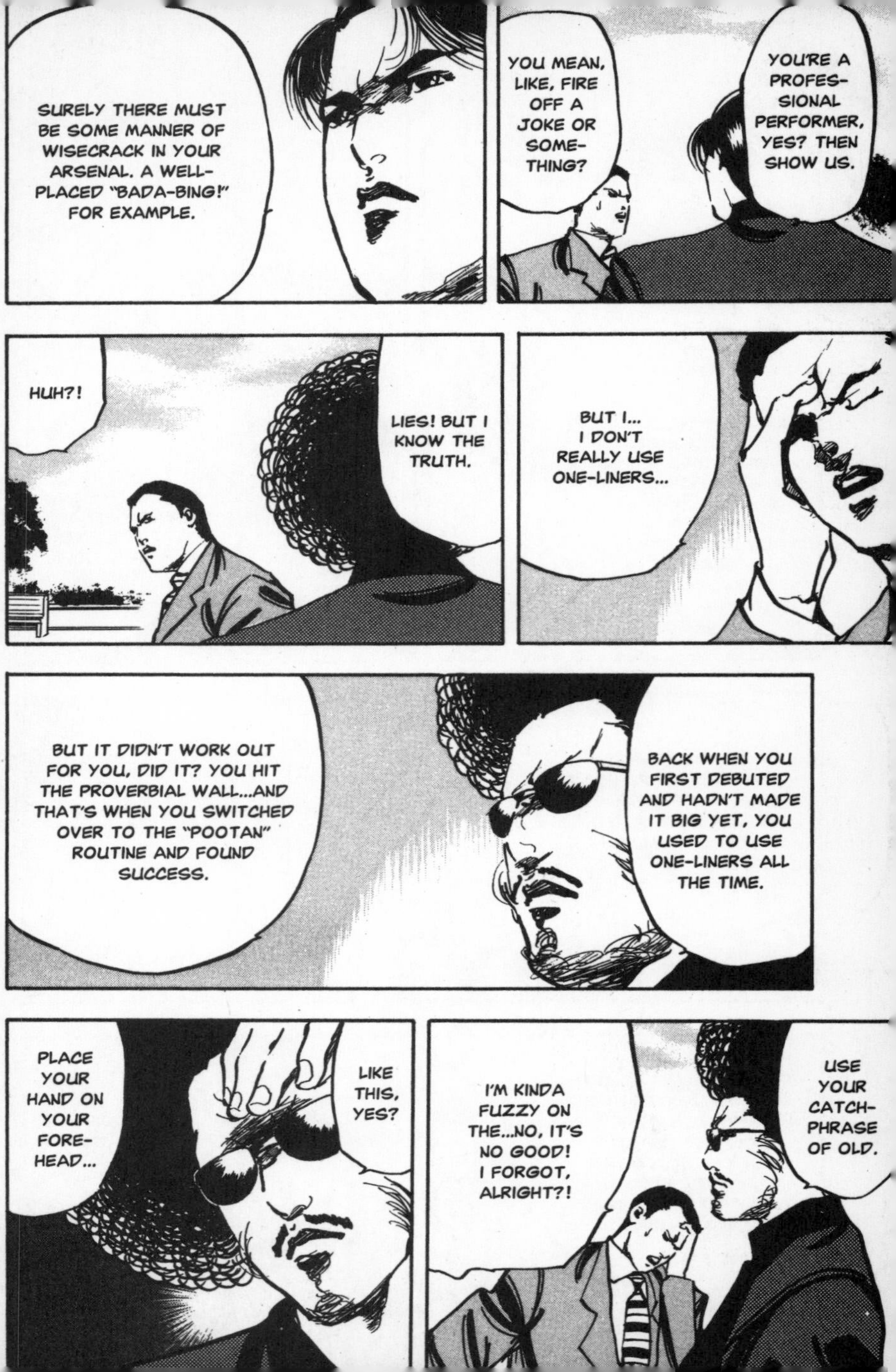
YOU'RE A PROFES-SIONAL PERFORMER, YES? THEN SHOW US.
YOU MEAN, LIKE, FIRE OFF A JOKE OR SOME-THING?
SURELY THERE MUST BE SOME MANNER OF WISECRACK IN YOUR ARSENAL. A WELL-PLACED "BADA-BING!" FOR EXAMPLE.
BUT I... I DON'T REALLY USE ONE-LINERS...
LIES! BUT I KNOW THE TRUTH.
HUH?!
BACK WHEN YOU FIRST DEBUTED AND HADN'T MADE IT BIG YET, YOU USED TO USE ONE-LINERS ALL THE TIME.
BUT IT DIDN'T WORK OUT FOR YOU, DID IT? YOU HIT THE PROVERBIAL WALL...AND THAT'S WHEN YOU SWITCHED OVER TO THE "POOTAN" ROUTINE AND FOUND SUCCESS.
USE YOUR CATCH-PHRASE OF OLD.
I'M KINDA FUZZY ON THE...NO, IT'S NO GOOD! I FORGOT, ALRIGHT?!
LIKE THIS, YES?
PLACE YOUR HAND ON YOUR FORE-HEAD...

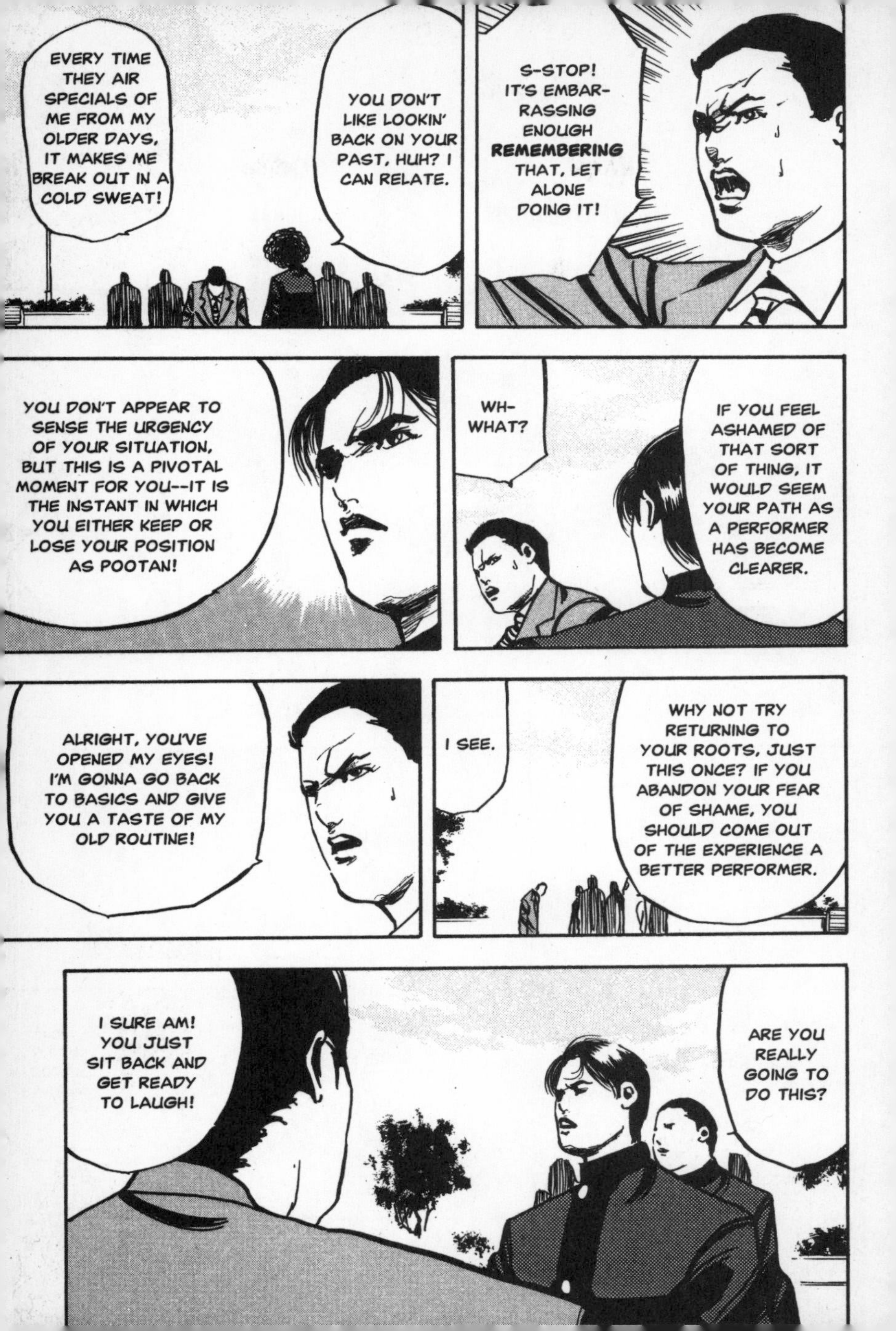
EVERY TIME THEY AIR SPECIALS OF ME FROM MY OLDER DAYS, IT MAKES ME BREAK OUT IN A COLD SWEAT!
YOU DON'T LIKE LOOKIN' BACK ON YOUR PAST, HUH? I CAN RELATE.
S-STOP! IT'S EMBARRASSING ENOUGH REMEMBERING THAT, LET ALONE DOING IT!
YOU DON'T APPEAR TO SENSE THE URGENCY OF YOUR SITUATION, BUT THIS IS A PIVOTAL MOMENT FOR YOU--IT IS THE INSTANT IN WHICH YOU EITHER KEEP OR LOSE YOUR POSITION AS POOTAN!
WH- WHAT?
IF YOU FEEL ASHAMED OF THAT SORT OF THING, IT WOULD SEEM YOUR PATH AS A PERFORMER HAS BECOME CLEARER.
ALRIGHT, YOU'VE OPENED MY EYES! I'M GONNA GO BACK TO BASICS AND GIVE YOU A TASTE OF MY OLD ROUTINE!
I SEE.
WHY NOT TRY RETURNING TO YOUR ROOTS, JUST THIS ONCE? IF YOU ABANDON YOUR FEAR OF SHAME, YOU SHOULD COME OUT OF THE EXPERIENCE A BETTER PERFORMER.
I SURE AM! YOU JUST SIT BACK AND GET READY TO LAUGH!
ARE YOU REALLY GOING TO DO THIS?

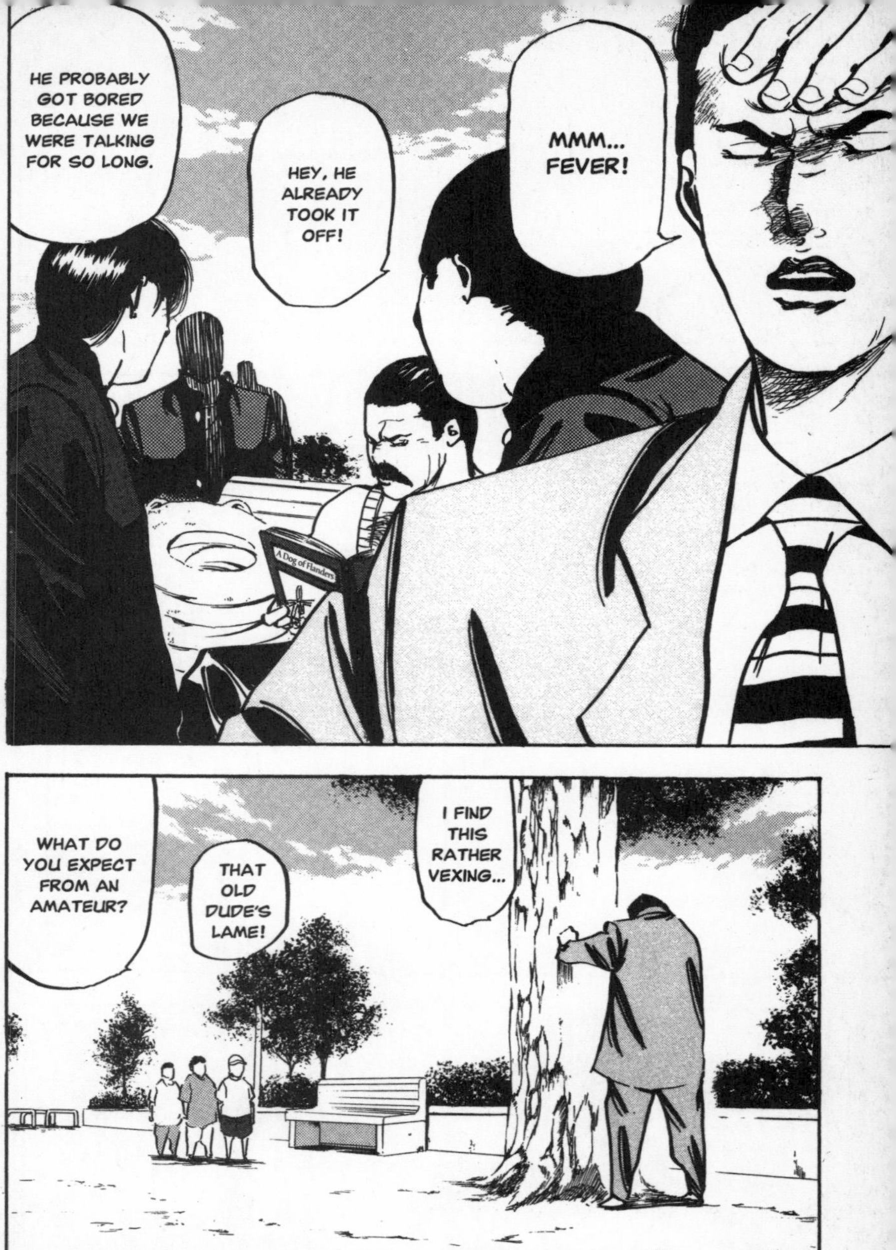
HE PROBABLY GOT BORED BECAUSE WE WERE TALKING FOR SO LONG.
HEY, HE ALREADY TOOK IT OFF!
MMM... FEVER!
A Dog of Flanders
WHAT DO YOU EXPECT FROM AN AMATEUR?
THAT OLD DUDE'S LAME!
I FIND THIS RATHER VEXING...

YEAH, THAT'S NOT SO FUNNY.

A HAPHAZARD INTRODUCTION TO THE CHARACTERS

TAKASHI KAMIYAMA

Known as "the honors student," Kamiyama is the protagonist of our story. Or rather, he should be. The fact that he will be absent for long stretches and yet the narrative can continue without a hitch has been a cause of recent consternation. He was once absent for two full months...and yet he is the protagonist. In truth, the more that Kamiyama is pushed into the background, the more power and influence he amasses. The 1st years that rally around him may well end up becoming a sort of "Kamiyama Corps"! I kind of miss the old Kamiyama, the one who, back when our story first began, used to freak all these hoods out.

SHINJIRO HAYASHIDA

Known as "Mr. Perfect Idiot," Hayashida is in his own way among the elite of Cromartie High. His dizzying absurdity is so masterfully refined that no one could possibly keep up with him. Whenever you hear that "Wait a second" and Hayashida puts in his two cents, you can rest assured that the conversation is going to get kicked up (or would that be down?) a couple notches. Of course, all our wonderfully enlightened readers are already aware of this.

AKIRA MAEDA

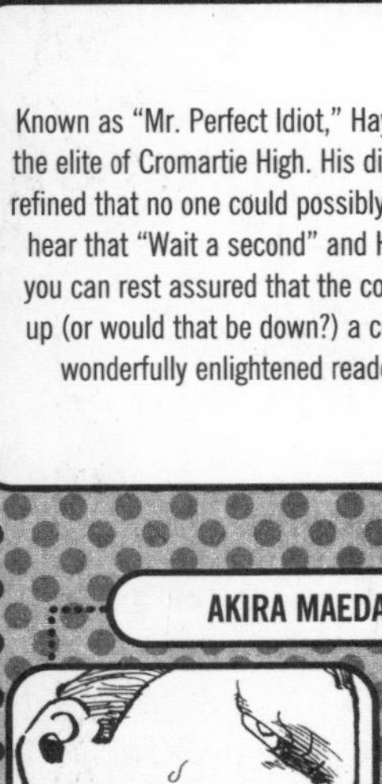

Known as "the Dragon of Razors." Not that anyone actually calls him that. As Cromartie's most straightforward character, Maeda rises farther above the others with each passing day. He has the important task of teaching the younger readers that doing the right thing isn't always the right way to go, a dilemma we tend to face as adults. When all you youngsters out there settle down and become company employees, you'll finally understand the depths of Maeda's sorrow! (LOL)

A HAPHAZARD INTRODUCTION TO THE CHARACTERS

FREDDIE

Known as...actually, I still can't figure out who this guy is! (LOL) He's really warmed up to everyone now, as opposed to how he was when he first appeared. Where once he was feared, Freddie is now loved and adored by all. The only things we know for sure are that he's apparently a good singer and his blood type is B. Whether or not he's even a high-school student remains unclear. I wonder if that's OK...

TAKESHI HOKUTO

Hokuto was born into a wealthy family and is the leader of the Hokuto Corps, which (to the shock of our readers) was revealed in the last volume to actually exist. His goal of controlling all the high schools in Japan--something so absurd that it could only appear in a manga--is now a thing of the past. He has settled down quite a bit, but I actually get the feeling he's becoming more and more irresponsible. Hokuto is known as "the strongest fighter of impossible battles." And no wisecracks as to why he's the only one wearing a white uniform!

HOKUTO'S HENCHMAN

Known as "Hokuto's Henchman." (LOL) I mean, there's nothing else to call him! In the last volume, he put himself on the line to try to prevent a split in the Hokuto Corps. At least, that's how it looked. Though he has yet to reveal his name, this particular henchman occupies an unexpectedly choice position in the manga. What's more, he is (narratively speaking) rather convenient, so he tends to show up in the story a lot. How long can this poor fellow continue to remain nameless? (LOL)

CHAPTER 126: **WATCH THAT MAN**

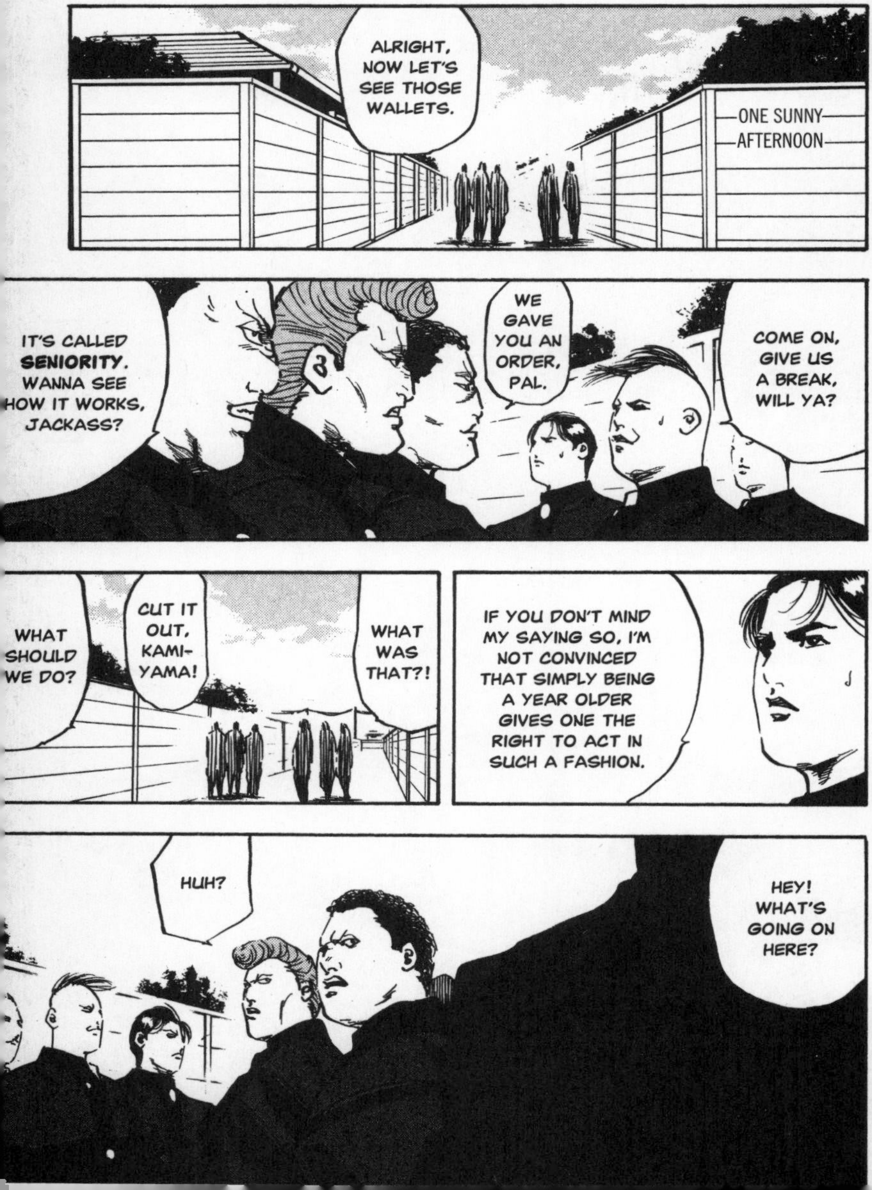
—ONE SUNNY—
—AFTERNOON—
ALRIGHT, NOW LET'S SEE THOSE WALLETS.
COME ON, GIVE US A BREAK, WILL YA?
WE GAVE YOU AN ORDER, PAL.
IT'S CALLED **SENIORITY**. WANNA SEE HOW IT WORKS, JACKASS?
IF YOU DON'T MIND MY SAYING SO, I'M NOT CONVINCED THAT SIMPLY BEING A YEAR OLDER GIVES ONE THE RIGHT TO ACT IN SUCH A FASHION.
WHAT WAS THAT?!
CUT IT OUT, KAMI-YAMA!
WHAT SHOULD WE DO?
HEY! WHAT'S GOING ON HERE?
HUH?

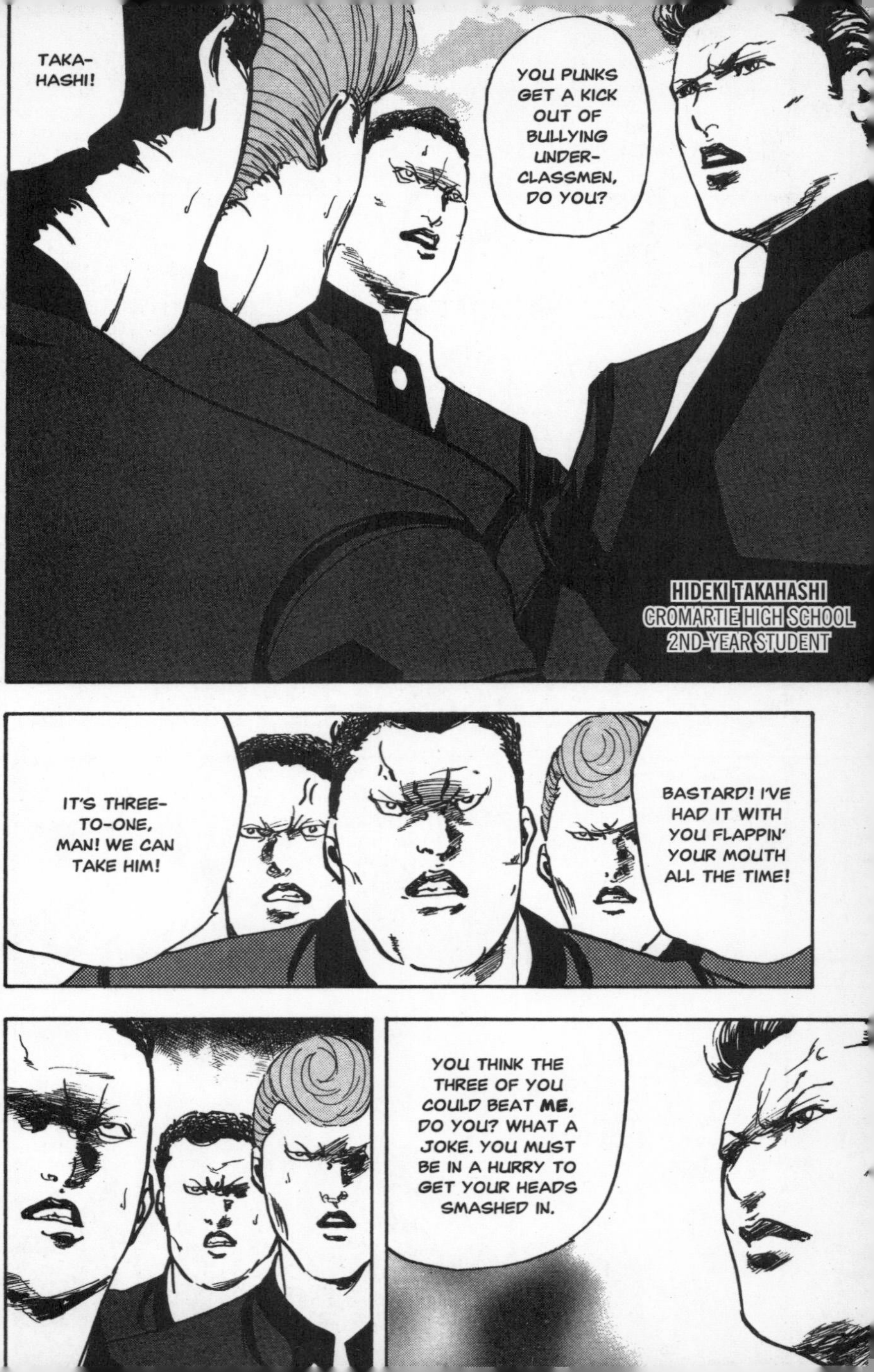

YOU PUNKS GET A KICK OUT OF BULLYING UNDER-CLASSMEN, DO YOU?
HIDEKI TAKAHASHI
CROMARTIE HIGH SCHOOL
2ND-YEAR STUDENT
TAKA-HASHI!
BASTARD! I'VE HAD IT WITH YOU FLAPPIN' YOUR MOUTH ALL THE TIME!
IT'S THREE-TO-ONE, MAN! WE CAN TAKE HIM!
YOU THINK THE THREE OF YOU COULD BEAT **ME**, DO YOU? WHAT A JOKE. YOU MUST BE IN A HURRY TO GET YOUR HEADS SMASHED IN.

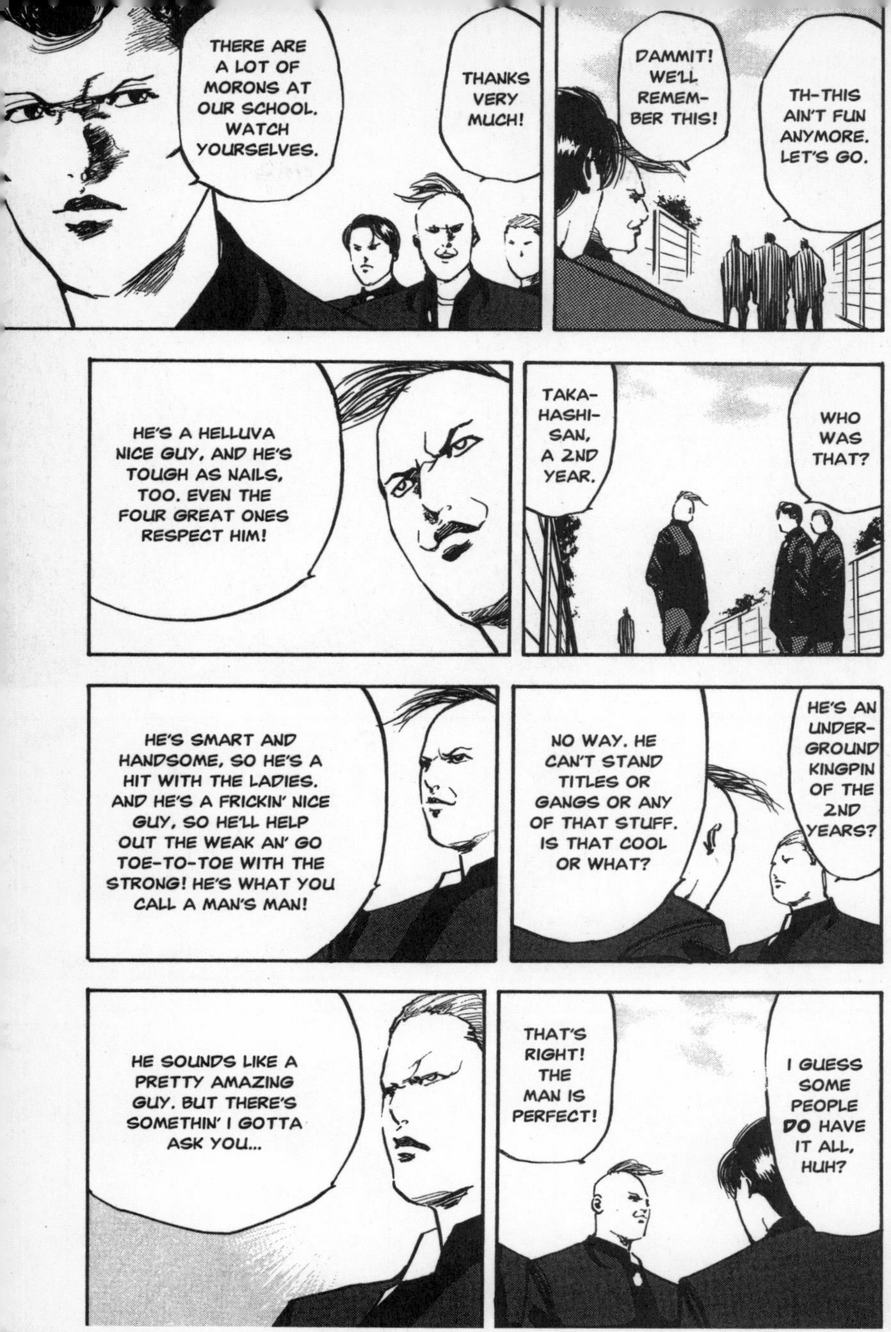

TH-THIS AIN'T FUN ANYMORE. LET'S GO.
DAMMIT! WE'LL REMEMBER THIS!
THERE ARE A LOT OF MORONS AT OUR SCHOOL. WATCH YOURSELVES.
THANKS VERY MUCH!
WHO WAS THAT?
TAKA-HASHI-SAN, A 2ND YEAR.
HE'S A HELLUVA NICE GUY, AND HE'S TOUGH AS NAILS, TOO. EVEN THE FOUR GREAT ONES RESPECT HIM!
HE'S AN UNDER-GROUND KINGPIN OF THE 2ND YEARS?
NO WAY. HE CAN'T STAND TITLES OR GANGS OR ANY OF THAT STUFF. IS THAT COOL OR WHAT?
HE'S SMART AND HANDSOME, SO HE'S A HIT WITH THE LADIES. AND HE'S A FRICKIN' NICE GUY, SO HE'LL HELP OUT THE WEAK AN' GO TOE-TO-TOE WITH THE STRONG! HE'S WHAT YOU CALL A MAN'S MAN!
I GUESS SOME PEOPLE **DO** HAVE IT ALL, HUH?
THAT'S RIGHT! THE MAN IS PERFECT!
HE SOUNDS LIKE A PRETTY AMAZING GUY. BUT THERE'S SOMETHIN' I GOTTA ASK YOU...

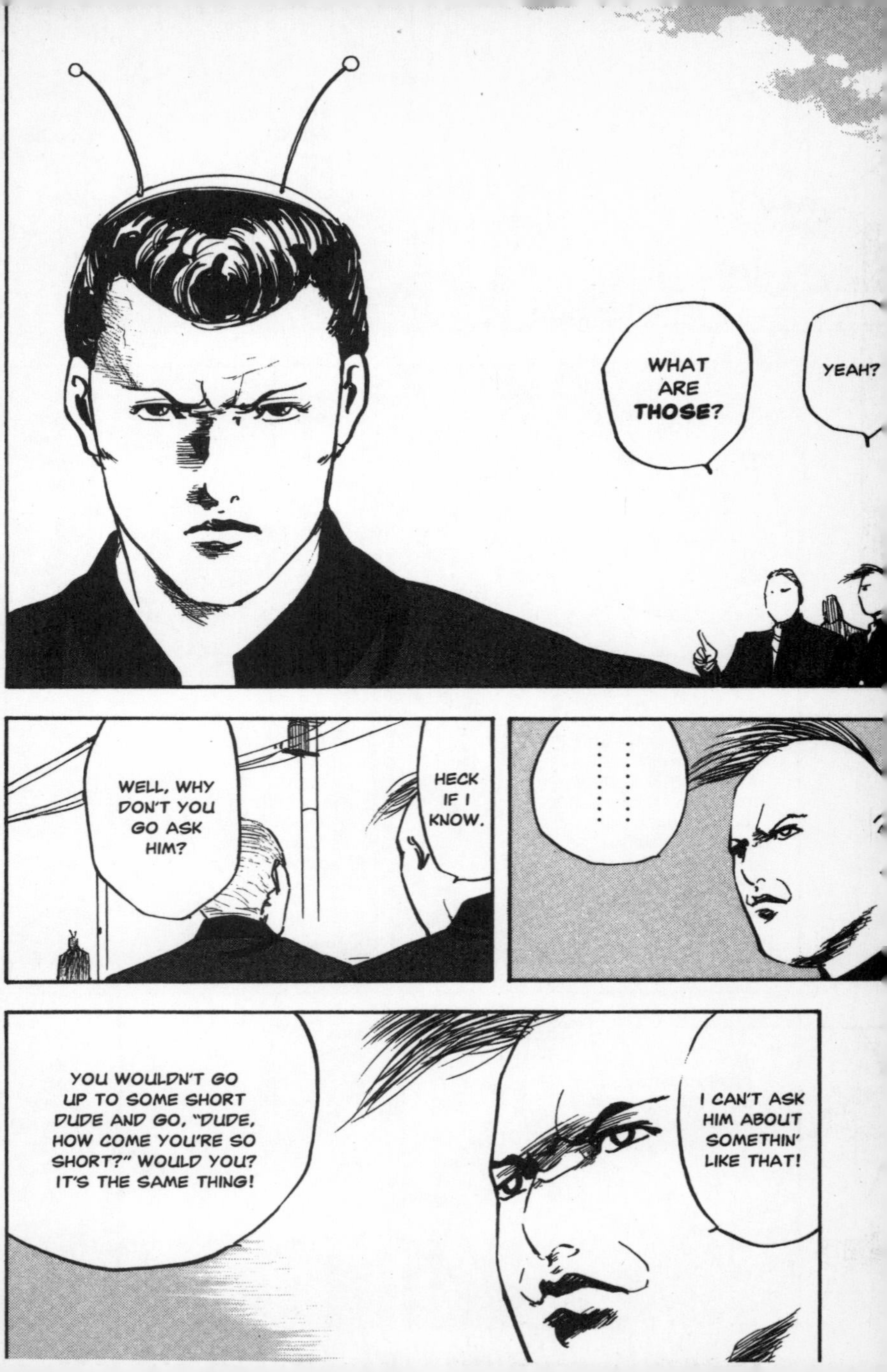
YEAH?
WHAT ARE THOSE?
HECK IF I KNOW.
WELL, WHY DON'T YOU GO ASK HIM?
......
......
I CAN'T ASK HIM ABOUT SOMETHIN' LIKE THAT!
YOU WOULDN'T GO UP TO SOME SHORT DUDE AND GO, "DUDE, HOW COME YOU'RE SO SHORT?" WOULD YOU? IT'S THE SAME THING!

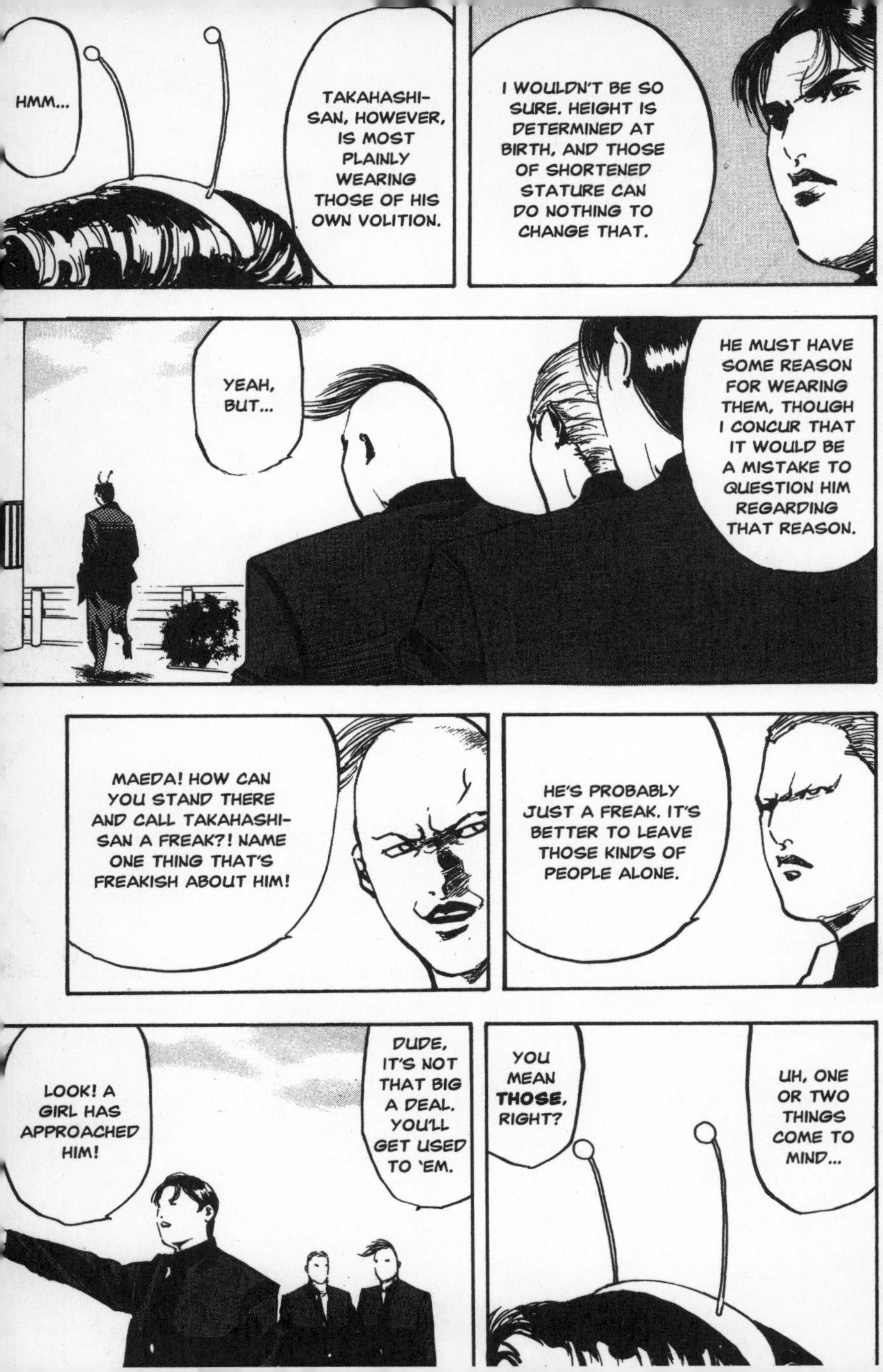
I WOULDN'T BE SO SURE. HEIGHT IS DETERMINED AT BIRTH, AND THOSE OF SHORTENED STATURE CAN DO NOTHING TO CHANGE THAT.
TAKAHASHI-SAN, HOWEVER, IS MOST PLAINLY WEARING THOSE OF HIS OWN VOLITION.
HMM...
HE MUST HAVE SOME REASON FOR WEARING THEM, THOUGH I CONCUR THAT IT WOULD BE A MISTAKE TO QUESTION HIM REGARDING THAT REASON.
YEAH, BUT...
HE'S PROBABLY JUST A FREAK. IT'S BETTER TO LEAVE THOSE KINDS OF PEOPLE ALONE.
MAEDA! HOW CAN YOU STAND THERE AND CALL TAKAHASHI-SAN A FREAK?! NAME ONE THING THAT'S FREAKISH ABOUT HIM!
UH, ONE OR TWO THINGS COME TO MIND...
YOU MEAN **THOSE**, RIGHT?
DUDE, IT'S NOT THAT BIG A DEAL. YOU'LL GET USED TO 'EM.
LOOK! A GIRL HAS APPROACHED HIM!

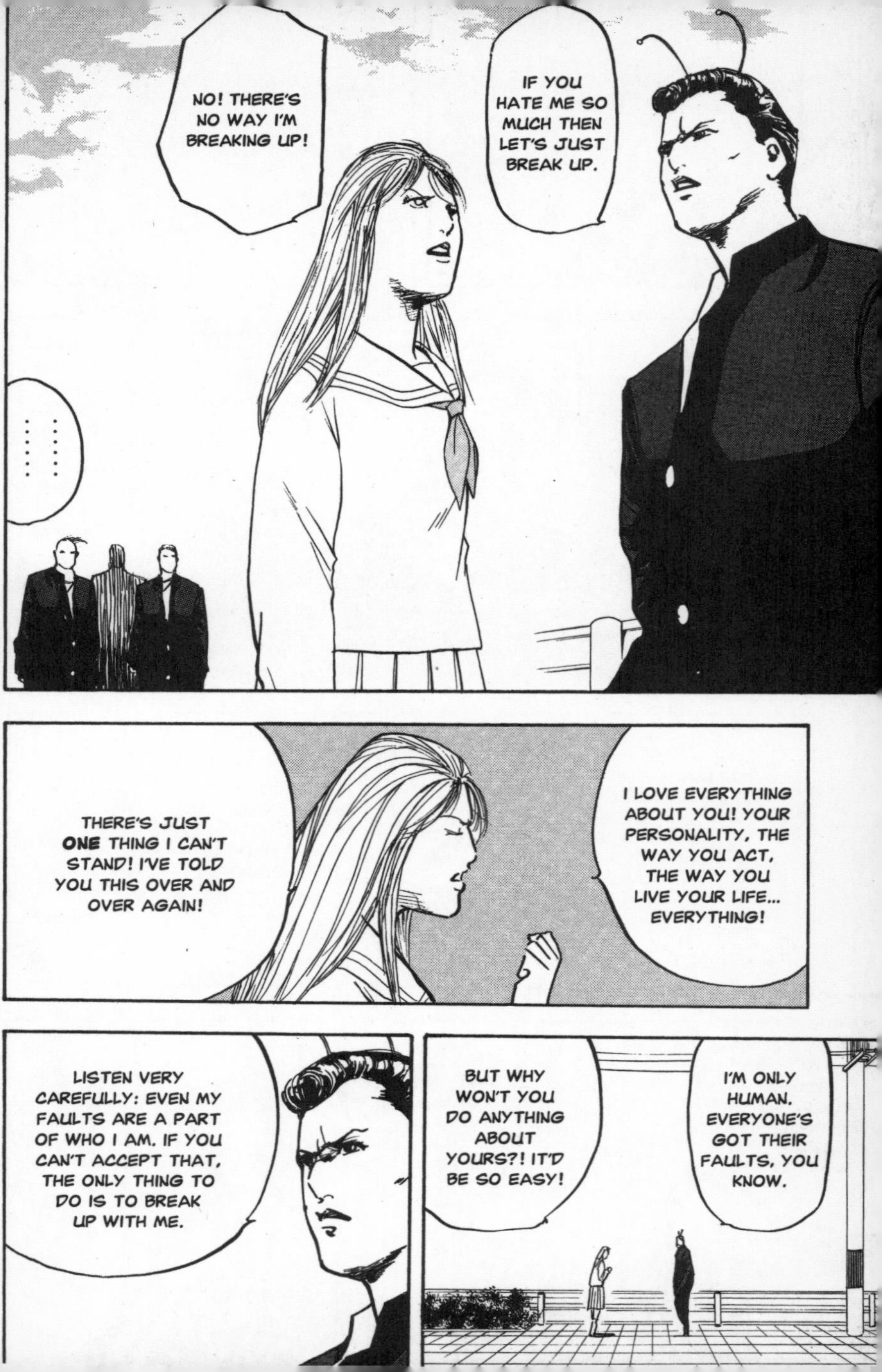
IF YOU HATE ME SO MUCH THEN LET'S JUST BREAK UP.
NO! THERE'S NO WAY I'M BREAKING UP!
......
I LOVE EVERYTHING ABOUT YOU! YOUR PERSONALITY, THE WAY YOU ACT, THE WAY YOU LIVE YOUR LIFE... EVERYTHING!
THERE'S JUST **ONE** THING I CAN'T STAND! I'VE TOLD YOU THIS OVER AND OVER AGAIN!
I'M ONLY HUMAN. EVERYONE'S GOT THEIR FAULTS, YOU KNOW.
BUT WHY WON'T YOU DO ANYTHING ABOUT YOURS?! IT'D BE SO EASY!
LISTEN VERY CAREFULLY: EVEN MY FAULTS ARE A PART OF WHO I AM. IF YOU CAN'T ACCEPT THAT, THE ONLY THING TO DO IS TO BREAK UP WITH ME.

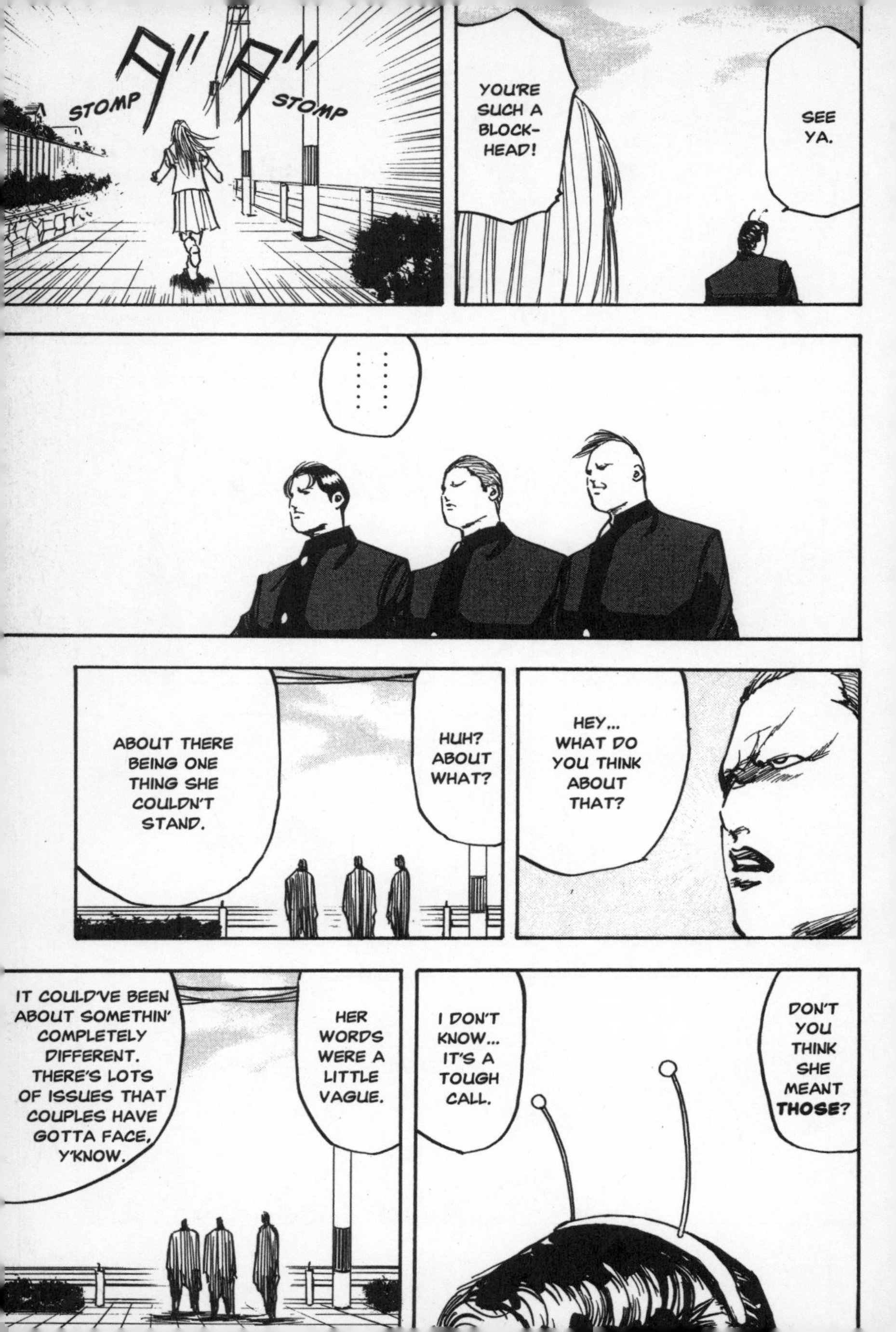

SEE YA.
YOU'RE SUCH A BLOCK-HEAD!
STOMP
STOMP
......
HEY... WHAT DO YOU THINK ABOUT THAT?
HUH? ABOUT WHAT?
ABOUT THERE BEING ONE THING SHE COULDN'T STAND.
DON'T YOU THINK SHE MEANT **THOSE**?
I DON'T KNOW... IT'S A TOUGH CALL.
HER WORDS WERE A LITTLE VAGUE.
IT COULD'VE BEEN ABOUT SOMETHIN' COMPLETELY DIFFERENT. THERE'S LOTS OF ISSUES THAT COUPLES HAVE GOTTA FACE, Y'KNOW.

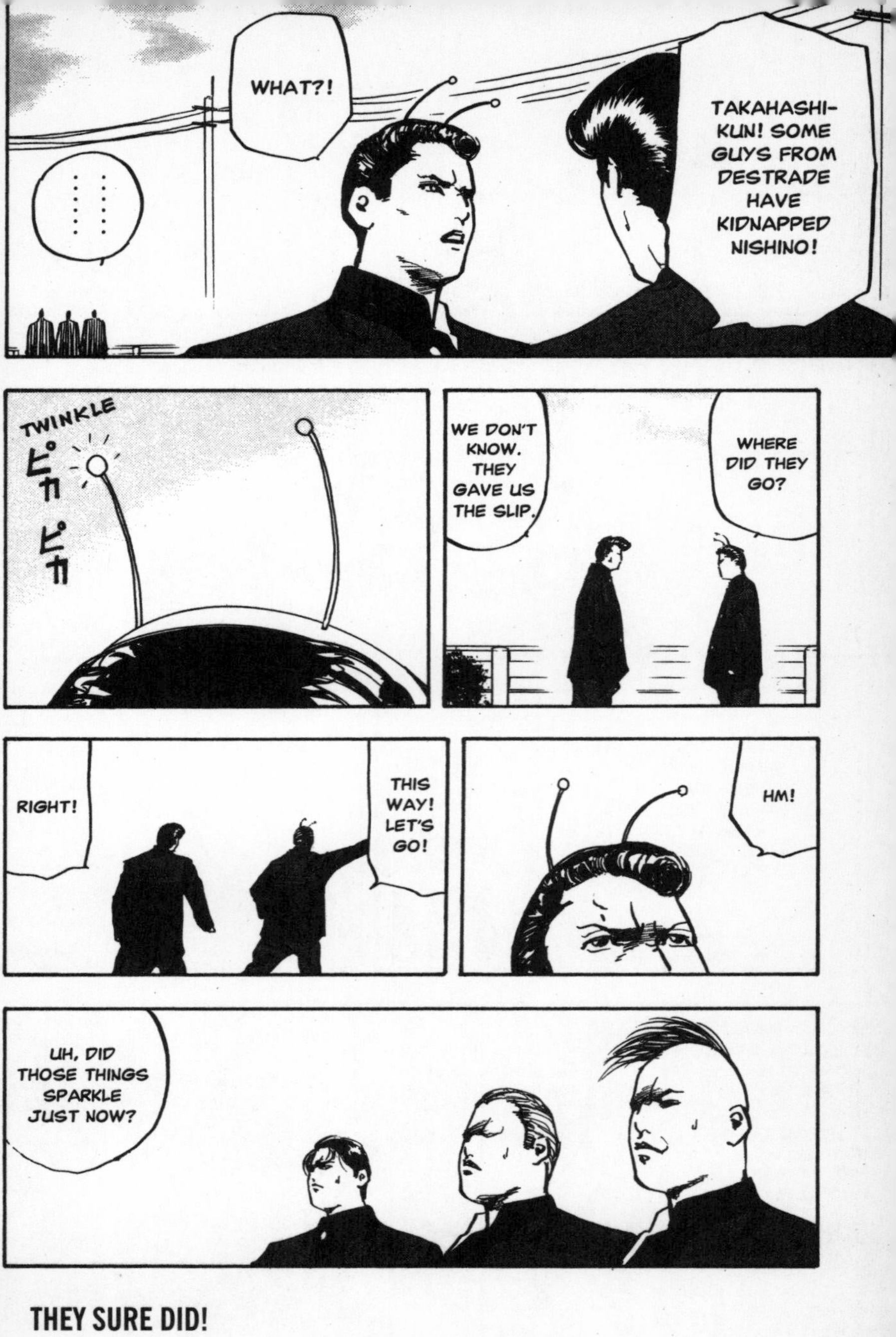
TAKAHASHI-KUN! SOME GUYS FROM DESTRADE HAVE KIDNAPPED NISHINO!
WHAT?!
......
WHERE DID THEY GO?
WE DON'T KNOW. THEY GAVE US THE SLIP.
TWINKLE
ピカ ピカ
HM!
THIS WAY! LET'S GO!
RIGHT!
UH, DID THOSE THINGS SPARKLE JUST NOW?

THEY SURE DID!

CHAPTER 127: **SENSE OF DOUBT**

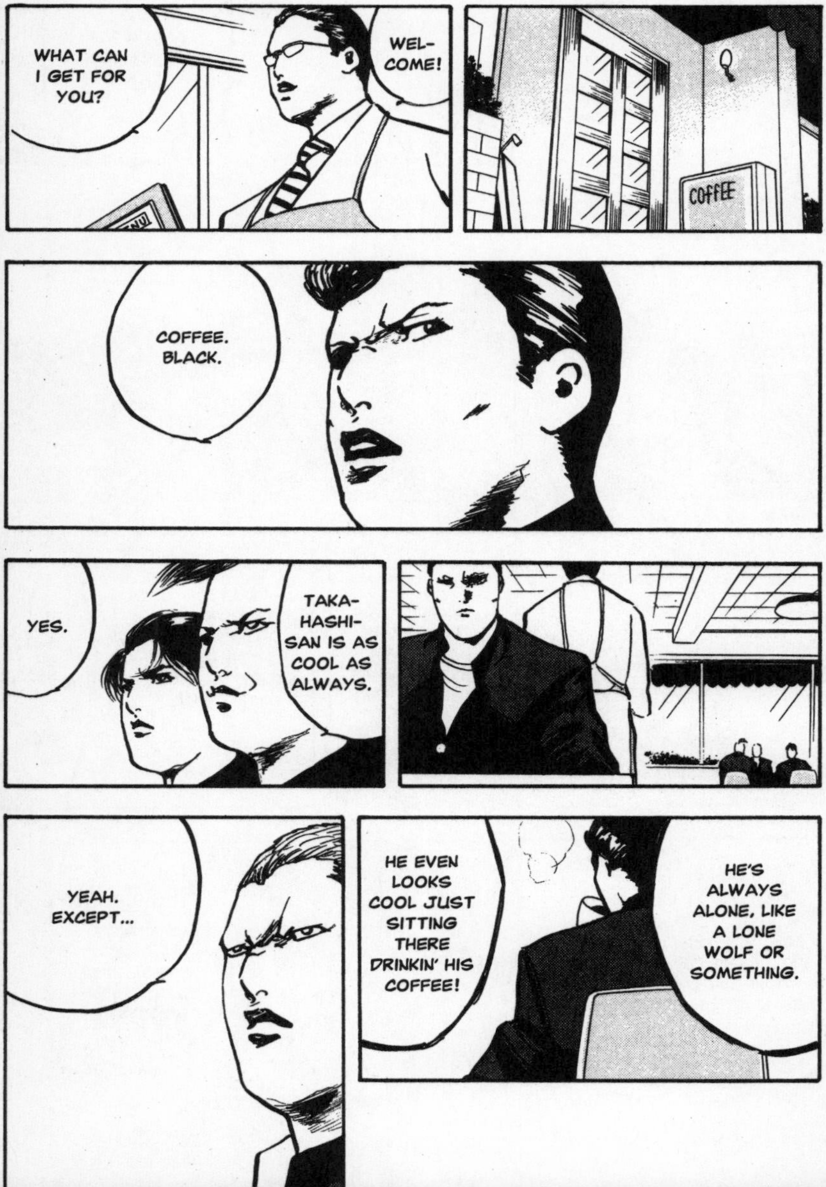

COFFEE
WEL-COME!
WHAT CAN I GET FOR YOU?
COFFEE. BLACK.
TAKA-HASHI-SAN IS AS COOL AS ALWAYS.
YES.
HE'S ALWAYS ALONE, LIKE A LONE WOLF OR SOMETHING.
HE EVEN LOOKS COOL JUST SITTING THERE DRINKIN' HIS COFFEE!
YEAH. EXCEPT...

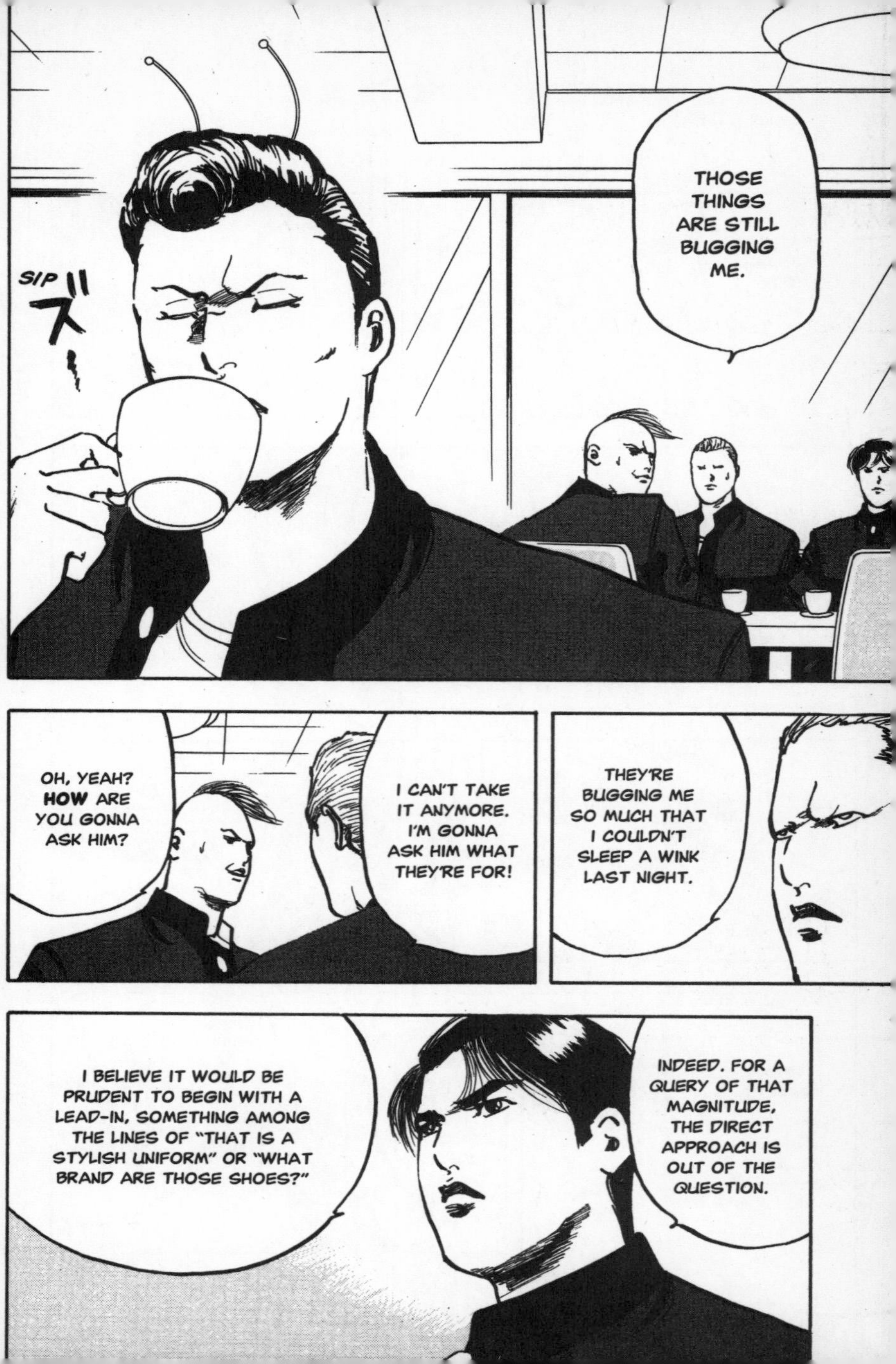
THOSE THINGS ARE STILL BUGGING ME.
SIP ズ
THEY'RE BUGGING ME SO MUCH THAT I COULDN'T SLEEP A WINK LAST NIGHT.
I CAN'T TAKE IT ANYMORE. I'M GONNA ASK HIM WHAT THEY'RE FOR!
OH, YEAH? **HOW** ARE YOU GONNA ASK HIM?
INDEED. FOR A QUERY OF THAT MAGNITUDE, THE DIRECT APPROACH IS OUT OF THE QUESTION.
I BELIEVE IT WOULD BE PRUDENT TO BEGIN WITH A LEAD-IN, SOMETHING AMONG THE LINES OF "THAT IS A STYLISH UNIFORM" OR "WHAT BRAND ARE THOSE SHOES?"

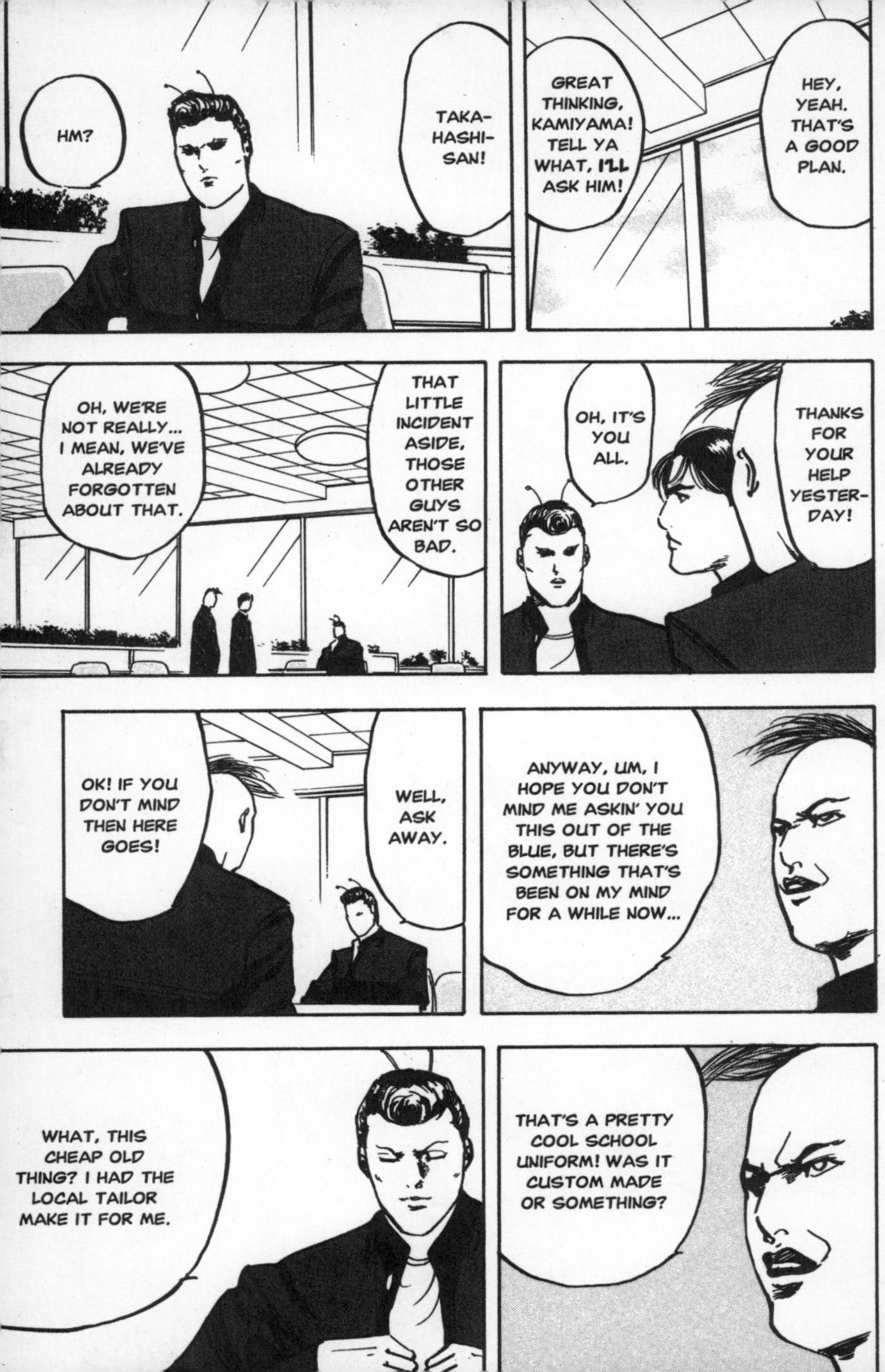
HEY, YEAH. THAT'S A GOOD PLAN.
GREAT THINKING, KAMIYAMA! TELL YA WHAT, I'LL ASK HIM!
TAKA-HASHI-SAN!
HM?
THANKS FOR YOUR HELP YESTER-DAY!
OH, IT'S YOU ALL.
THAT LITTLE INCIDENT ASIDE, THOSE OTHER GUYS AREN'T SO BAD.
OH, WE'RE NOT REALLY... I MEAN, WE'VE ALREADY FORGOTTEN ABOUT THAT.
ANYWAY, UM, I HOPE YOU DON'T MIND ME ASKIN' YOU THIS OUT OF THE BLUE, BUT THERE'S SOMETHING THAT'S BEEN ON MY MIND FOR A WHILE NOW...
WELL, ASK AWAY.
OK! IF YOU DON'T MIND THEN HERE GOES!
THAT'S A PRETTY COOL SCHOOL UNIFORM! WAS IT CUSTOM MADE OR SOMETHING?
WHAT, THIS CHEAP OLD THING? I HAD THE LOCAL TAILOR MAKE IT FOR ME.

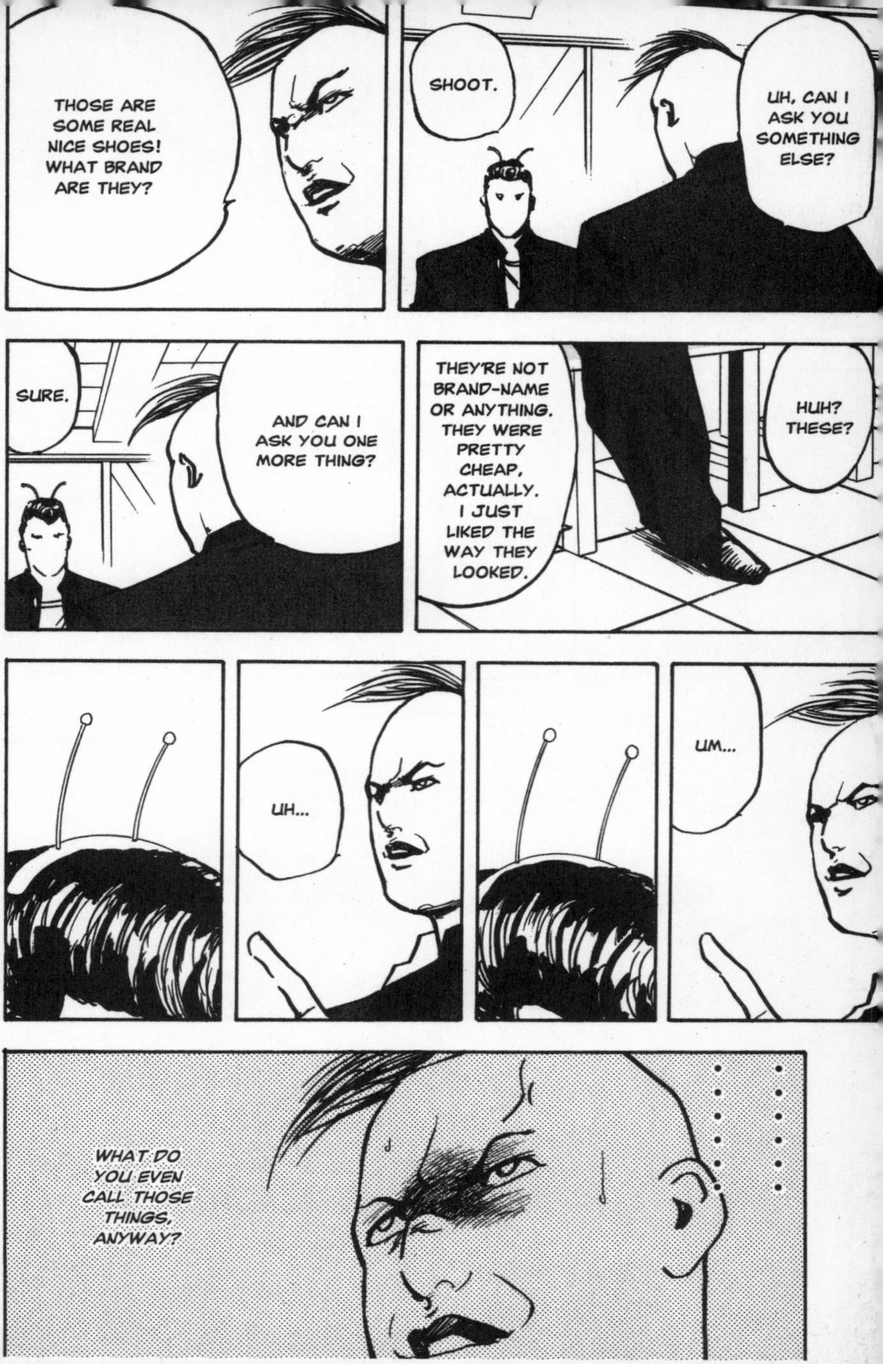
UH, CAN I ASK YOU SOMETHING ELSE?
SHOOT.
THOSE ARE SOME REAL NICE SHOES! WHAT BRAND ARE THEY?
HUH? THESE?
THEY'RE NOT BRAND-NAME OR ANYTHING. THEY WERE PRETTY CHEAP, ACTUALLY. I JUST LIKED THE WAY THEY LOOKED.
AND CAN I ASK YOU ONE MORE THING?
SURE.
UM...
UH...
WHAT DO YOU EVEN CALL THOSE THINGS, ANYWAY?

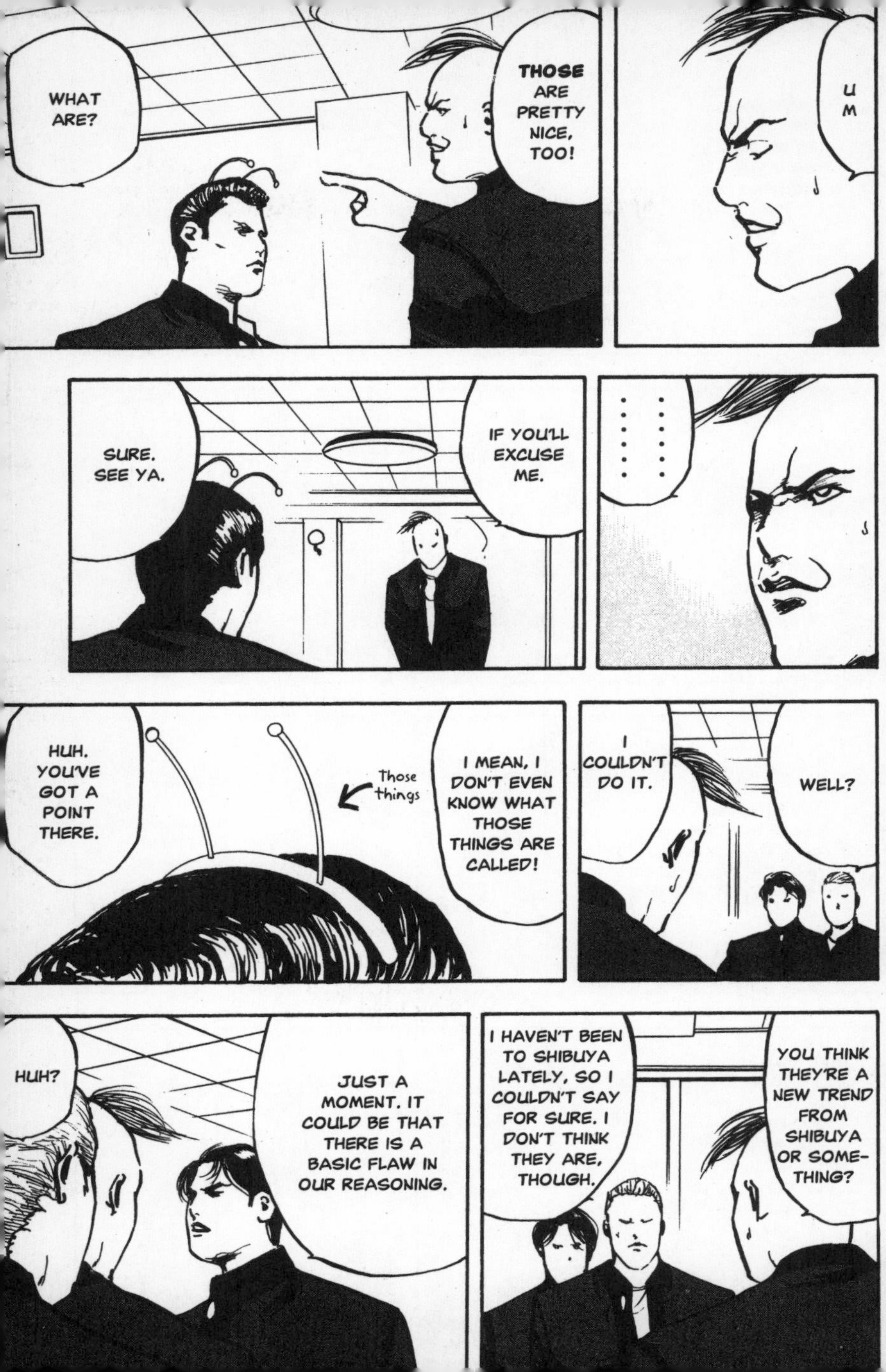

UM
THOSE ARE PRETTY NICE, TOO!
WHAT ARE?
......
IF YOU'LL EXCUSE ME.
SURE. SEE YA.
WELL?
I COULDN'T DO IT.
I MEAN, I DON'T EVEN KNOW WHAT THOSE THINGS ARE CALLED!
Those things
HUH. YOU'VE GOT A POINT THERE.
YOU THINK THEY'RE A NEW TREND FROM SHIBUYA OR SOME-THING?
I HAVEN'T BEEN TO SHIBUYA LATELY, SO I COULDN'T SAY FOR SURE. I DON'T THINK THEY ARE, THOUGH.
JUST A MOMENT. IT COULD BE THAT THERE IS A BASIC FLAW IN OUR REASONING.
HUH?

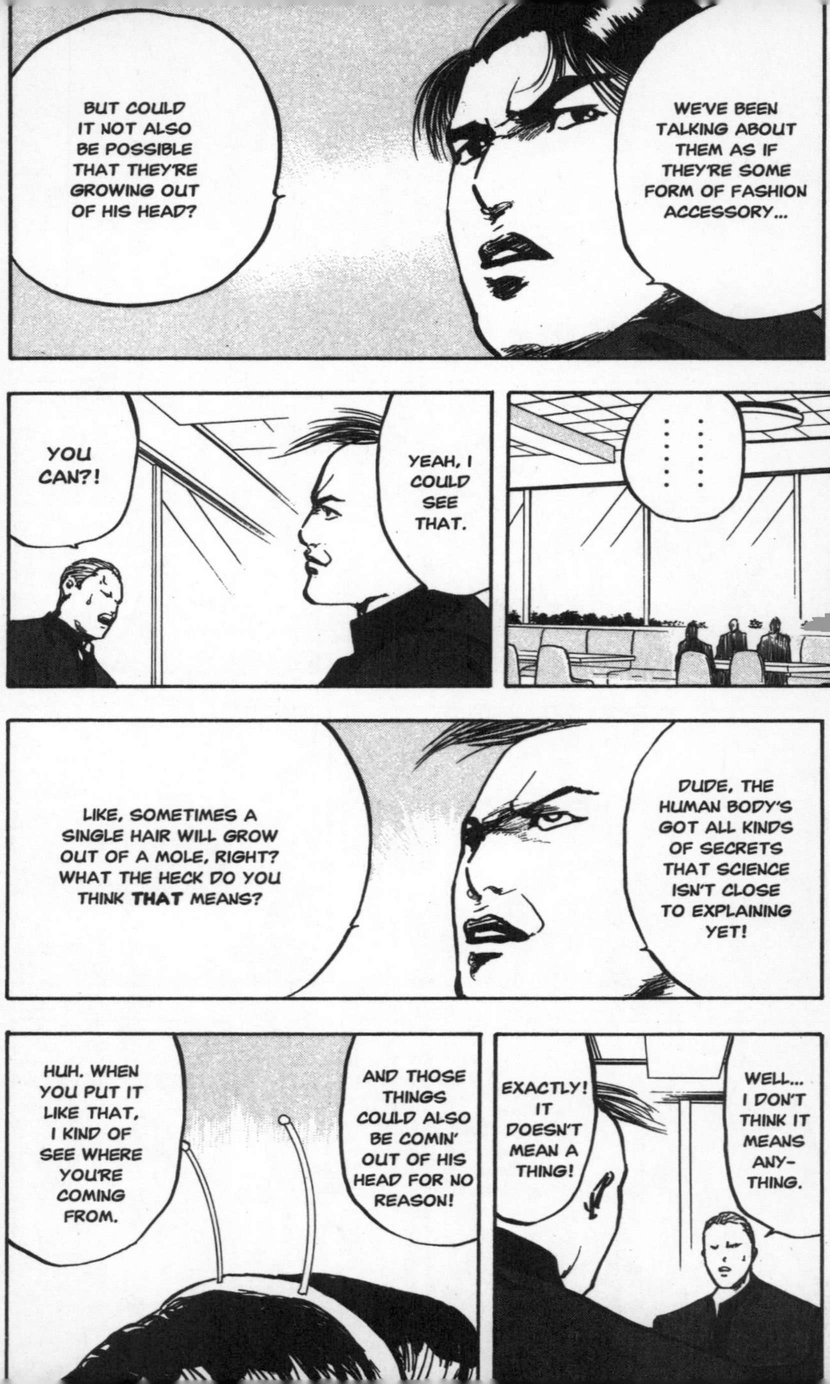

WE'VE BEEN TALKING ABOUT THEM AS IF THEY'RE SOME FORM OF FASHION ACCESSORY...
BUT COULD IT NOT ALSO BE POSSIBLE THAT THEY'RE GROWING OUT OF HIS HEAD?
......
YEAH, I COULD SEE THAT.
YOU CAN?!
DUDE, THE HUMAN BODY'S GOT ALL KINDS OF SECRETS THAT SCIENCE ISN'T CLOSE TO EXPLAINING YET!
LIKE, SOMETIMES A SINGLE HAIR WILL GROW OUT OF A MOLE, RIGHT? WHAT THE HECK DO YOU THINK **THAT** MEANS?
WELL... I DON'T THINK IT MEANS ANY-THING.
EXACTLY! IT DOESN'T MEAN A THING!
AND THOSE THINGS COULD ALSO BE COMIN' OUT OF HIS HEAD FOR NO REASON!
HUH. WHEN YOU PUT IT LIKE THAT, I KIND OF SEE WHERE YOU'RE COMING FROM.

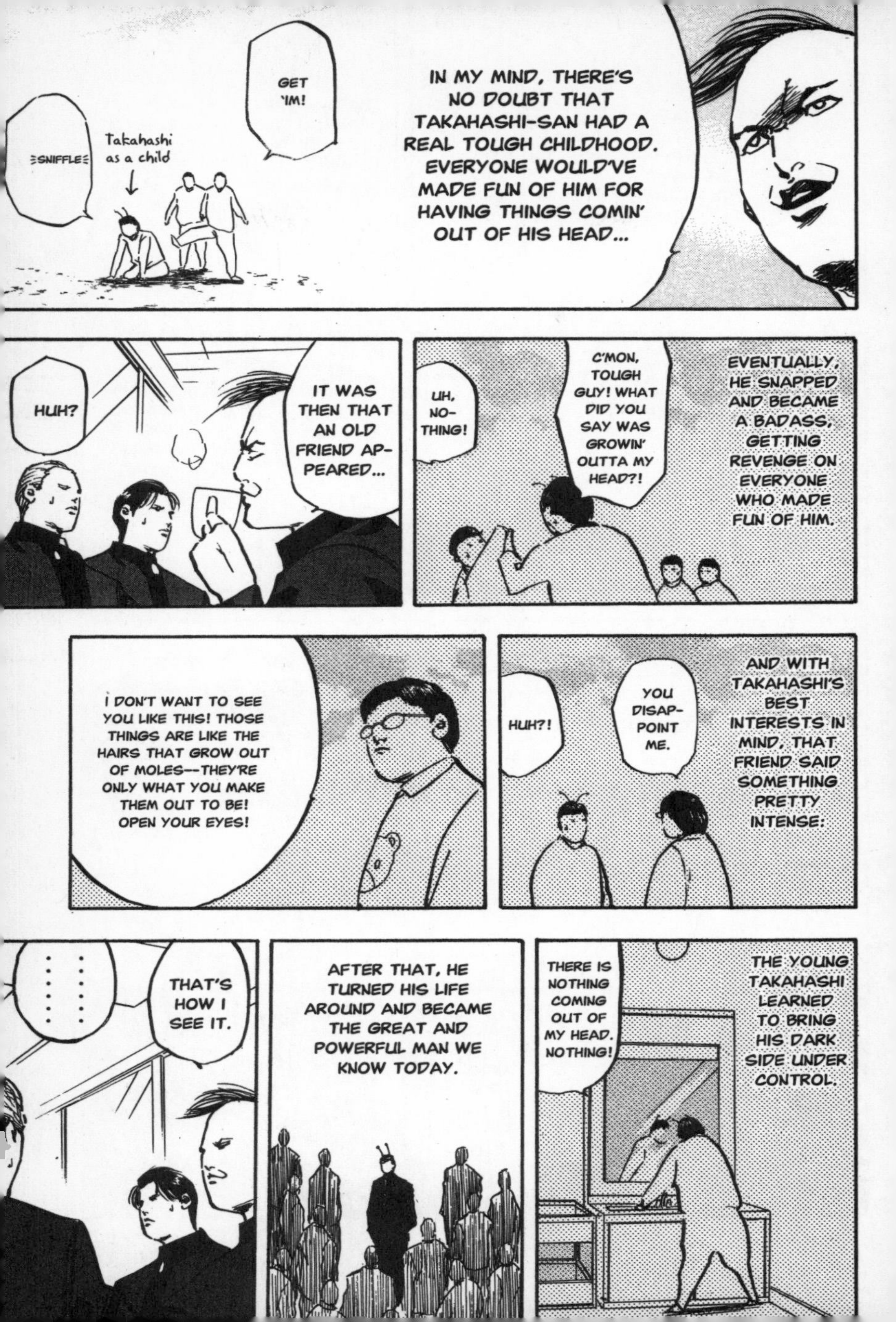

IN MY MIND, THERE'S NO DOUBT THAT TAKAHASHI-SAN HAD A REAL TOUGH CHILDHOOD. EVERYONE WOULD'VE MADE FUN OF HIM FOR HAVING THINGS COMIN' OUT OF HIS HEAD...
GET 'IM!
Takahashi as a child
SNIFFLE
EVENTUALLY, HE SNAPPED AND BECAME A BADASS, GETTING REVENGE ON EVERYONE WHO MADE FUN OF HIM.
C'MON, TOUGH GUY! WHAT DID YOU SAY WAS GROWIN' OUTTA MY HEAD?!
UH, NO-THING!
IT WAS THEN THAT AN OLD FRIEND AP-PEARED...
HUH?
AND WITH TAKAHASHI'S BEST INTERESTS IN MIND, THAT FRIEND SAID SOMETHING PRETTY INTENSE:
YOU DISAP-POINT ME.
HUH?!
I DON'T WANT TO SEE YOU LIKE THIS! THOSE THINGS ARE LIKE THE HAIRS THAT GROW OUT OF MOLES--THEY'RE ONLY WHAT YOU MAKE THEM OUT TO BE! OPEN YOUR EYES!
THE YOUNG TAKAHASHI LEARNED TO BRING HIS DARK SIDE UNDER CONTROL.
THERE IS NOTHING COMING OUT OF MY HEAD. NOTHING!
AFTER THAT, HE TURNED HIS LIFE AROUND AND BECAME THE GREAT AND POWERFUL MAN WE KNOW TODAY.
THAT'S HOW I SEE IT.
......

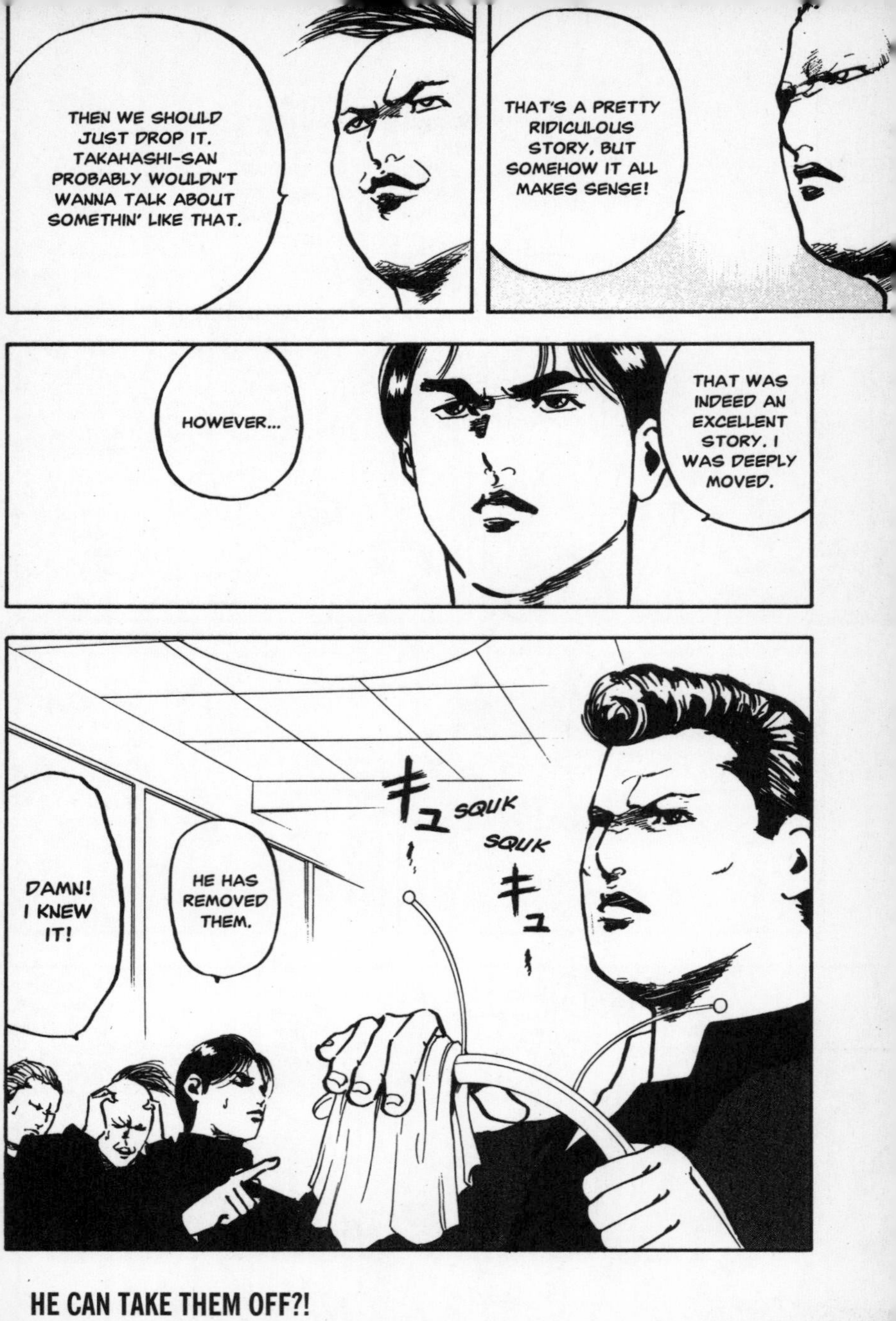
THAT'S A PRETTY RIDICULOUS STORY, BUT SOMEHOW IT ALL MAKES SENSE!
THEN WE SHOULD JUST DROP IT. TAKAHASHI-SAN PROBABLY WOULDN'T WANNA TALK ABOUT SOMETHIN' LIKE THAT.
THAT WAS INDEED AN EXCELLENT STORY. I WAS DEEPLY MOVED.
HOWEVER...
キュ
SQUK
SQUK
キュ
HE HAS REMOVED THEM.
DAMN! I KNEW IT!

HE CAN TAKE THEM OFF?!

CHAPTER 128: **I DO IT FOR YOU**

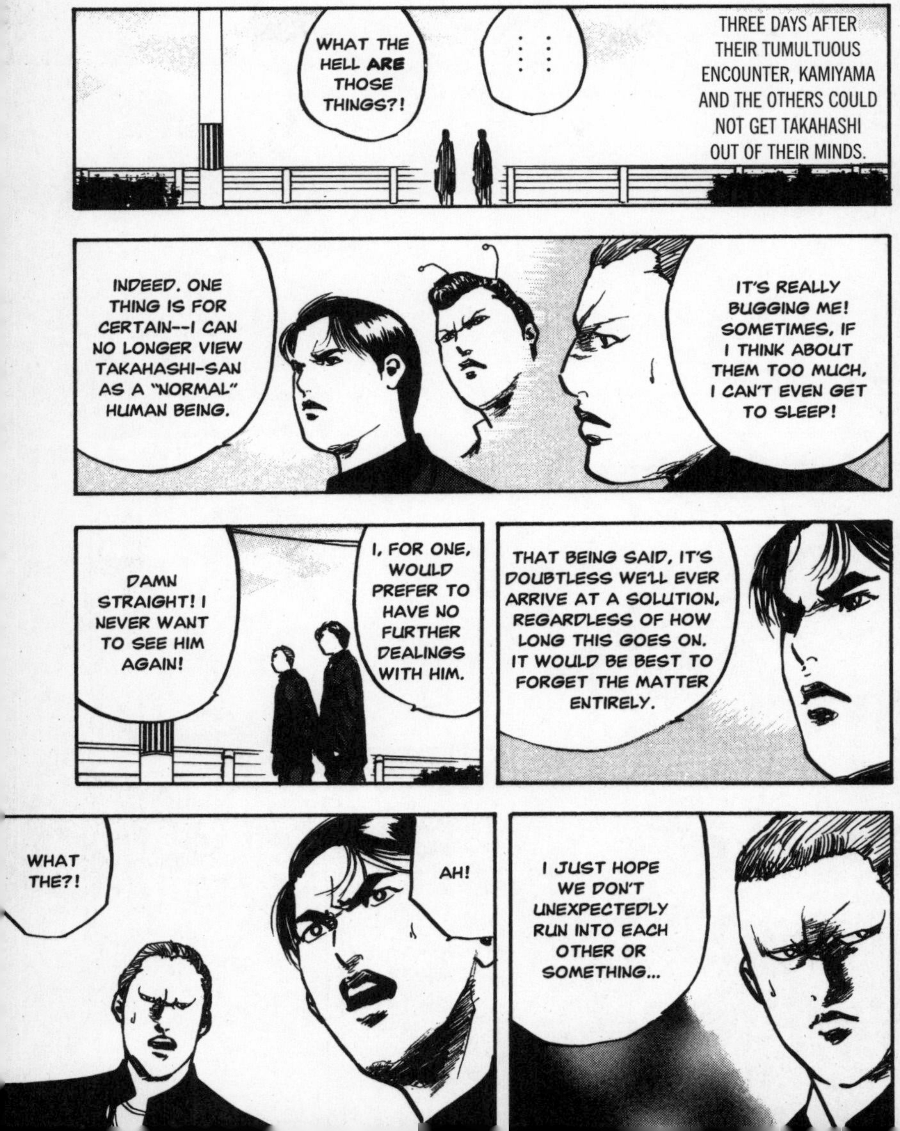
THREE DAYS AFTER THEIR TUMULTUOUS ENCOUNTER, KAMIYAMA AND THE OTHERS COULD NOT GET TAKAHASHI OUT OF THEIR MINDS.
......
WHAT THE HELL **ARE** THOSE THINGS?!
IT'S REALLY BUGGING ME! SOMETIMES, IF I THINK ABOUT THEM TOO MUCH, I CAN'T EVEN GET TO SLEEP!
INDEED. ONE THING IS FOR CERTAIN--I CAN NO LONGER VIEW TAKAHASHI-SAN AS A "NORMAL" HUMAN BEING.
THAT BEING SAID, IT'S DOUBTLESS WE'LL EVER ARRIVE AT A SOLUTION, REGARDLESS OF HOW LONG THIS GOES ON. IT WOULD BE BEST TO FORGET THE MATTER ENTIRELY.
I, FOR ONE, WOULD PREFER TO HAVE NO FURTHER DEALINGS WITH HIM.
DAMN STRAIGHT! I NEVER WANT TO SEE HIM AGAIN!
I JUST HOPE WE DON'T UNEXPECTEDLY RUN INTO EACH OTHER OR SOMETHING...
AH!
WHAT THE?!

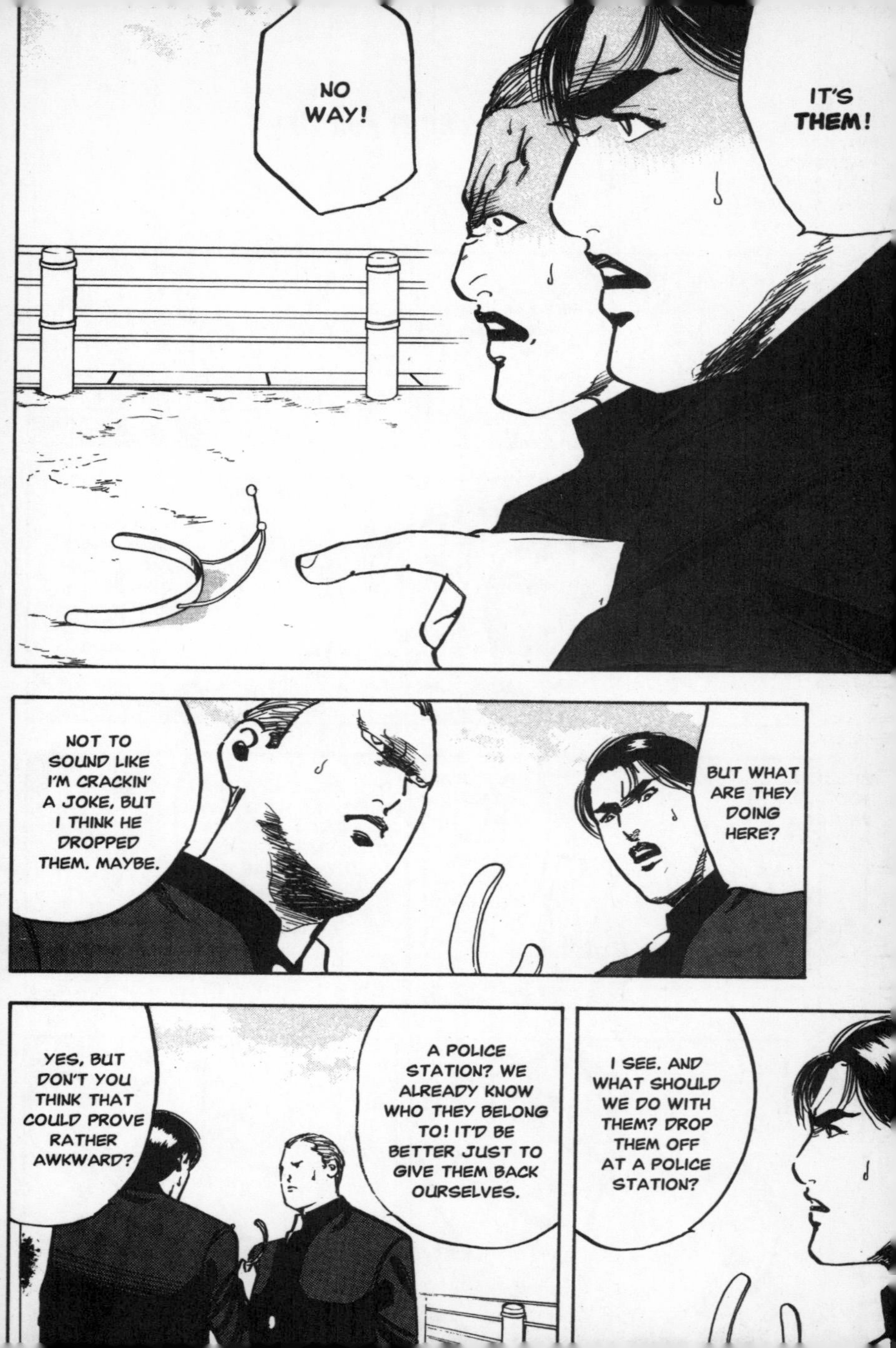
IT'S THEM!
NO WAY!
BUT WHAT ARE THEY DOING HERE?
NOT TO SOUND LIKE I'M CRACKIN' A JOKE, BUT I THINK HE DROPPED THEM. MAYBE.
I SEE. AND WHAT SHOULD WE DO WITH THEM? DROP THEM OFF AT A POLICE STATION?
A POLICE STATION? WE ALREADY KNOW WHO THEY BELONG TO! IT'D BE BETTER JUST TO GIVE THEM BACK OURSELVES.
YES, BUT DON'T YOU THINK THAT COULD PROVE RATHER AWKWARD?

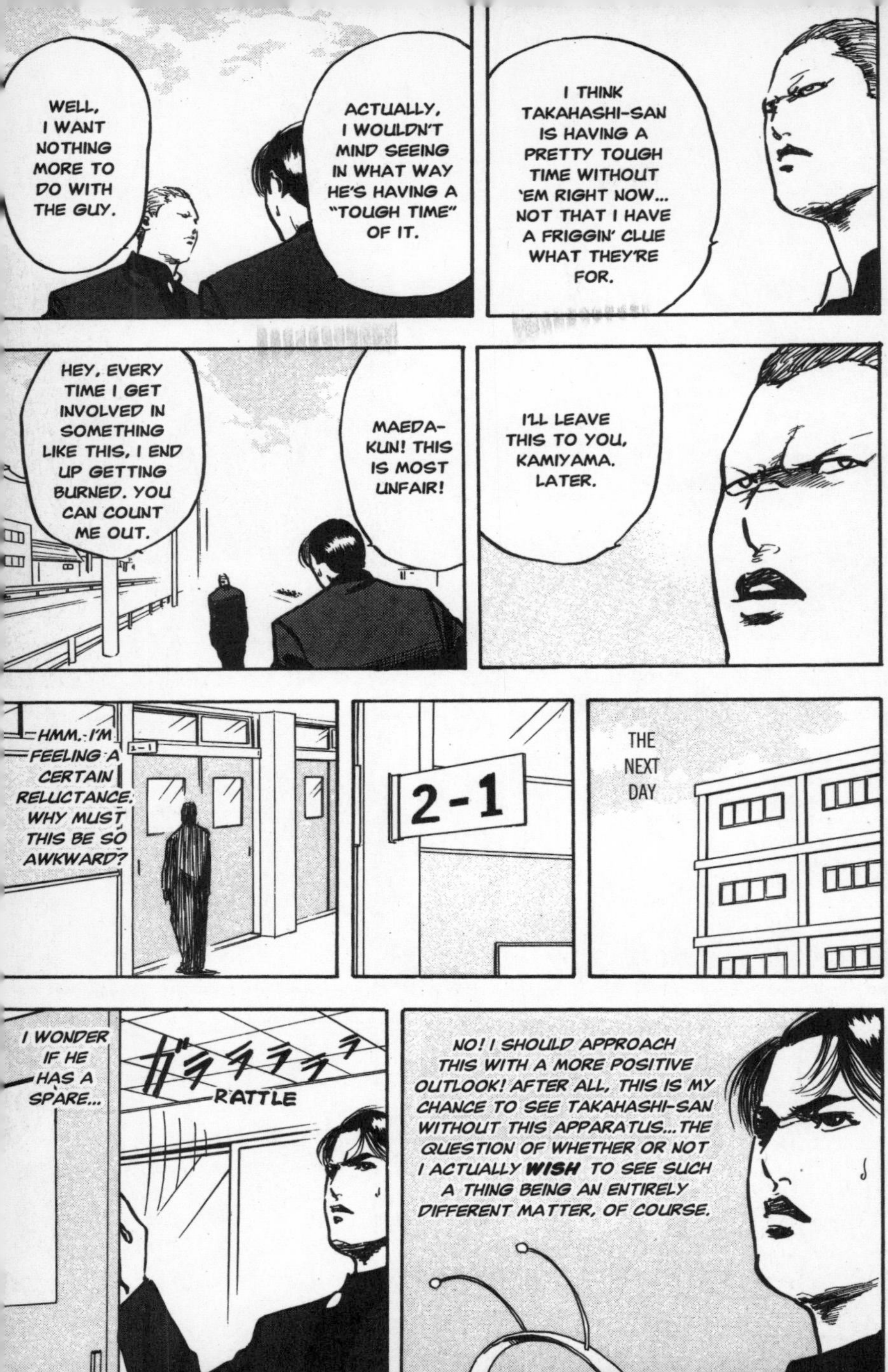
WELL, I WANT NOTHING MORE TO DO WITH THE GUY.
ACTUALLY, I WOULDN'T MIND SEEING IN WHAT WAY HE'S HAVING A "TOUGH TIME" OF IT.
I THINK TAKAHASHI-SAN IS HAVING A PRETTY TOUGH TIME WITHOUT 'EM RIGHT NOW... NOT THAT I HAVE A FRIGGIN' CLUE WHAT THEY'RE FOR.
HEY, EVERY TIME I GET INVOLVED IN SOMETHING LIKE THIS, I END UP GETTING BURNED. YOU CAN COUNT ME OUT.
MAEDA-KUN! THIS IS MOST UNFAIR!
I'LL LEAVE THIS TO YOU, KAMIYAMA. LATER.
HMM. I'M FEELING A CERTAIN RELUCTANCE. WHY MUST THIS BE SO AWKWARD?
2-1
THE NEXT DAY
I WONDER IF HE HAS A SPARE...
ガラララララ
RATTLE
NO! I SHOULD APPROACH THIS WITH A MORE POSITIVE OUTLOOK! AFTER ALL, THIS IS MY CHANCE TO SEE TAKAHASHI-SAN WITHOUT THIS APPARATUS... THE QUESTION OF WHETHER OR NOT I ACTUALLY WISH TO SEE SUCH A THING BEING AN ENTIRELY DIFFERENT MATTER, OF COURSE.

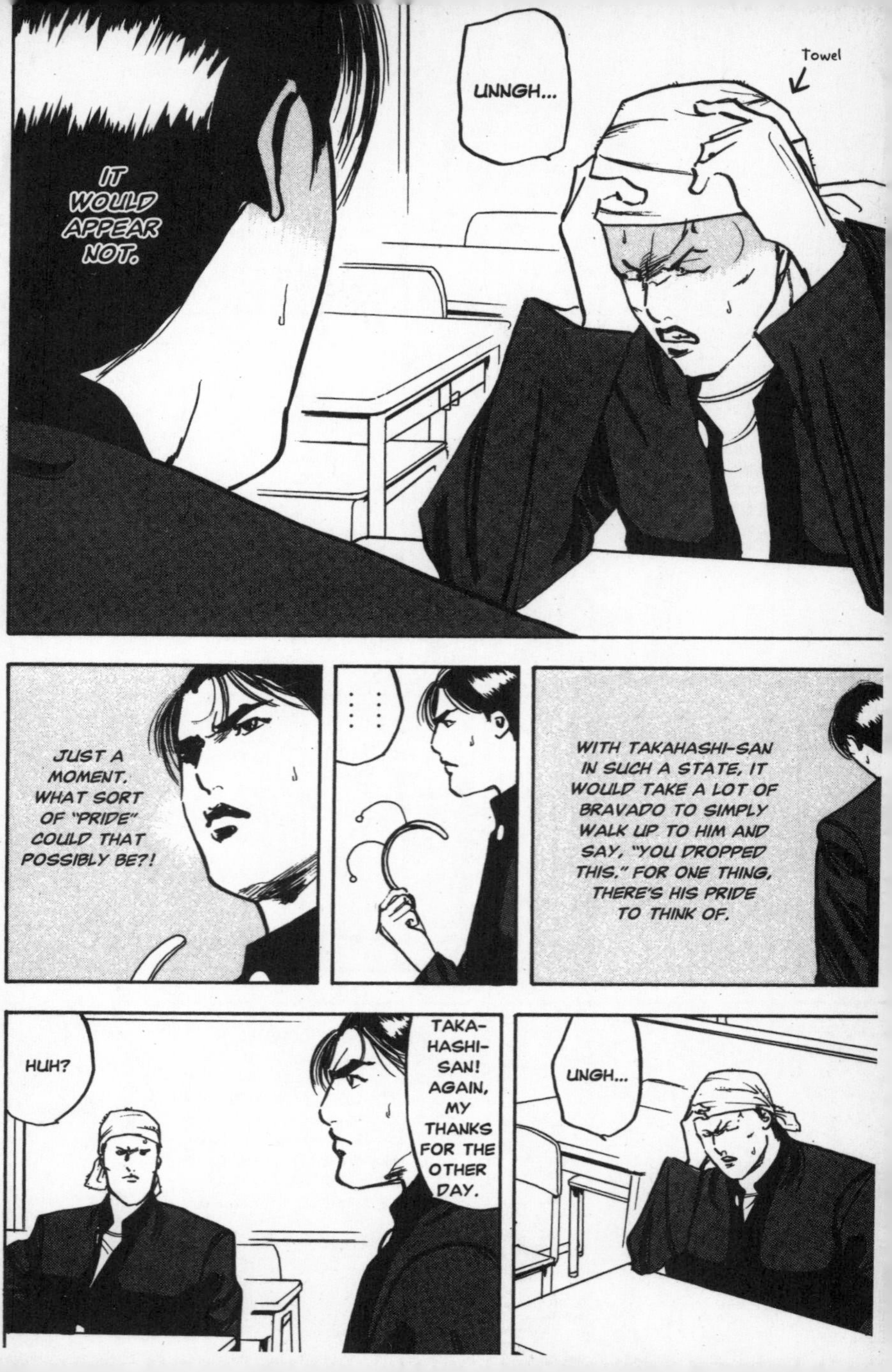
Towel
UNNGH...
IT WOULD APPEAR NOT.
WITH TAKAHASHI-SAN IN SUCH A STATE, IT WOULD TAKE A LOT OF BRAVADO TO SIMPLY WALK UP TO HIM AND SAY, "YOU DROPPED THIS." FOR ONE THING, THERE'S HIS PRIDE TO THINK OF.
......
JUST A MOMENT. WHAT SORT OF "PRIDE" COULD THAT POSSIBLY BE?!
UNGH...
TAKAHASHI-SAN! AGAIN, MY THANKS FOR THE OTHER DAY.
HUH?

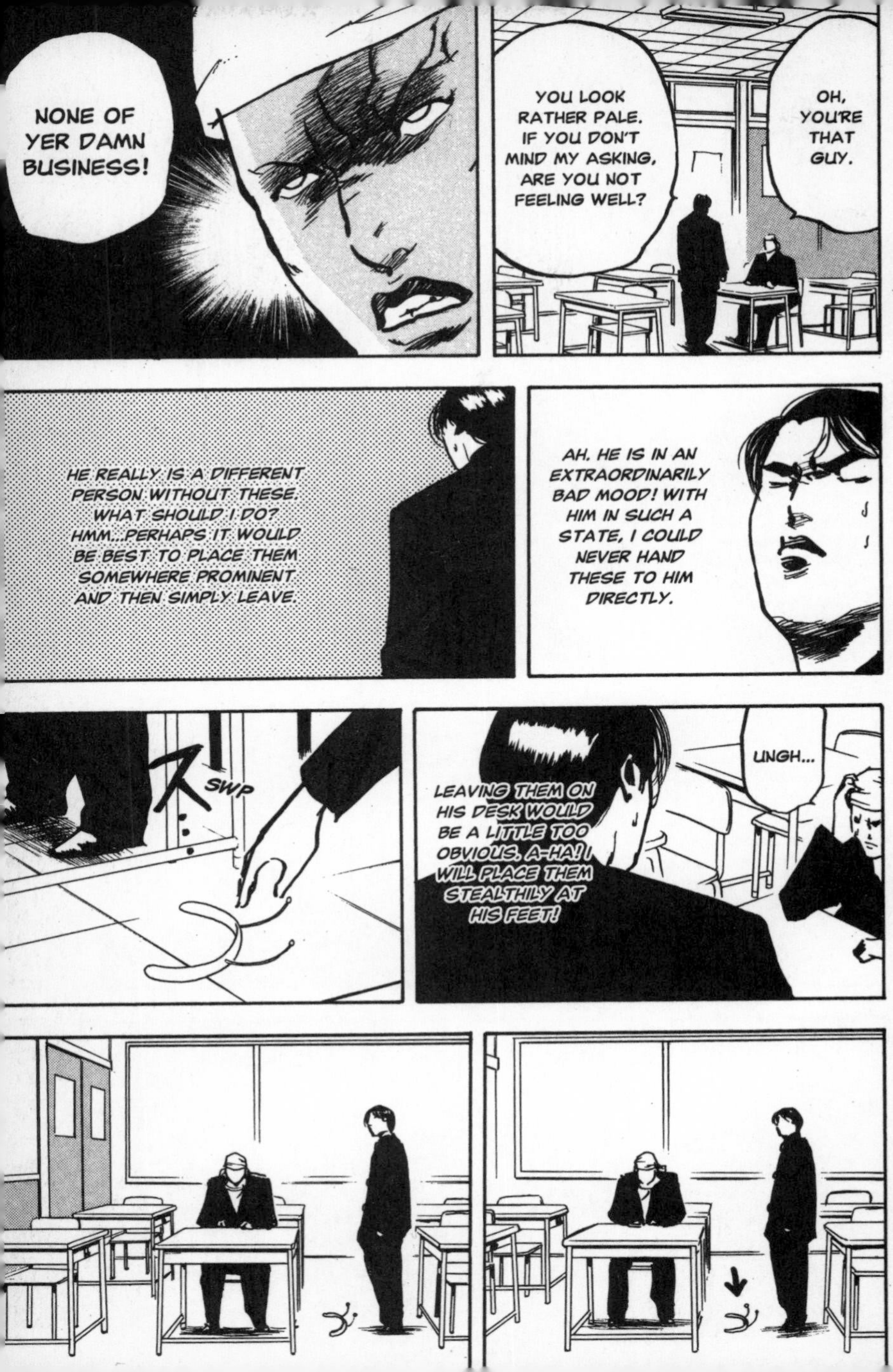
OH, YOU'RE THAT GUY.
YOU LOOK RATHER PALE. IF YOU DON'T MIND MY ASKING, ARE YOU NOT FEELING WELL?
NONE OF YER DAMN BUSINESS!
AH. HE IS IN AN EXTRAORDINARILY BAD MOOD! WITH HIM IN SUCH A STATE, I COULD NEVER HAND THESE TO HIM DIRECTLY.
HE REALLY IS A DIFFERENT PERSON WITHOUT THESE. WHAT SHOULD I DO? HMM...PERHAPS IT WOULD BE BEST TO PLACE THEM SOMEWHERE PROMINENT AND THEN SIMPLY LEAVE.
UNGH...
LEAVING THEM ON HIS DESK WOULD BE A LITTLE TOO OBVIOUS. A-HA! I WILL PLACE THEM STEALTHILY AT HIS FEET!
SWP

OH, NO! HE DIDN'T NOTICE THEM AT ALL!

コロ K-TNK
K-TNK コロ

BWACK

DAMMIT!

I DON'T THINK IT'S ENOUGH TO AFFECT THEIR FUNCTIONALITY. STILL, IT'S NOT MAKING THINGS ANY EASIER THAT I HAVE NO IDEA WHAT THAT FUNCTIONALITY IS SUPPOSED TO BE!

WHAT'S MORE, THEY'VE SUSTAINED MINOR DAMAGE.

THERE'S NOTHING FOR IT--I'M JUST GOING TO HAVE TO DROP THEM IN PLAIN SIGHT. IT'S A BOLD MOVE, BUT I'M OUT OF OPTIONS!

THIS ISN'T GOOD?! I HAVE TO DO SOMETHING QUICK!

AH. VERY WELL.

LOOK, IF YOU DON'T HAVE ANYTHING TO SAY THEN BEAT IT!

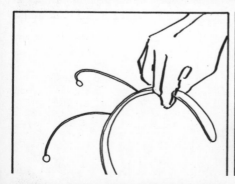

YEAH, SURE.

IF YOU'LL EXCUSE ME.

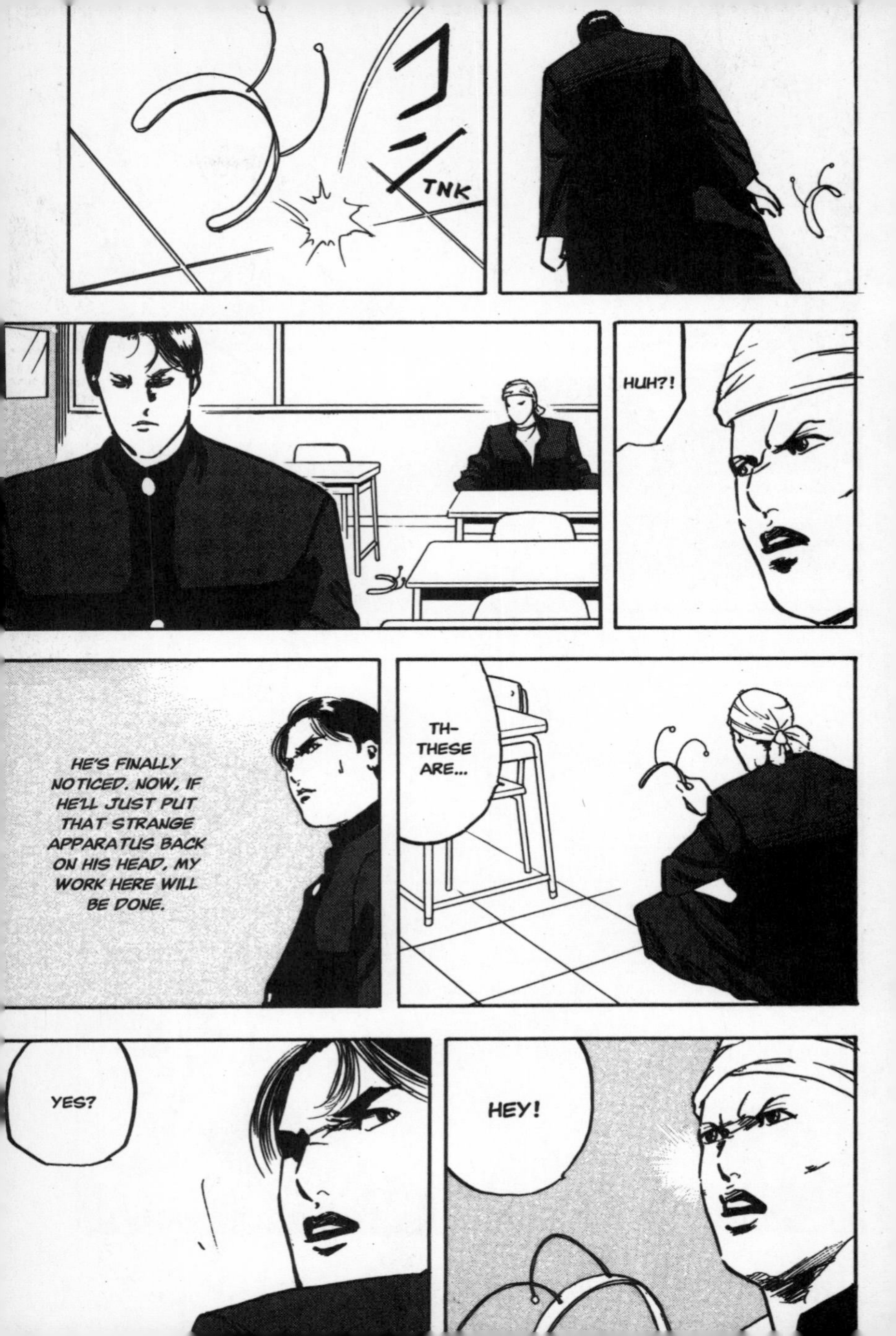
TNK
HUH?!
TH- THESE ARE...
HE'S FINALLY NOTICED. NOW, IF HE'LL JUST PUT THAT STRANGE APPARATUS BACK ON HIS HEAD, MY WORK HERE WILL BE DONE.
HEY!
YES?

HUH?
YOU DROPPED THIS.
TRY TO BE MORE CAREFUL, HUH?
TH-THANK YOU VERY MUCH.

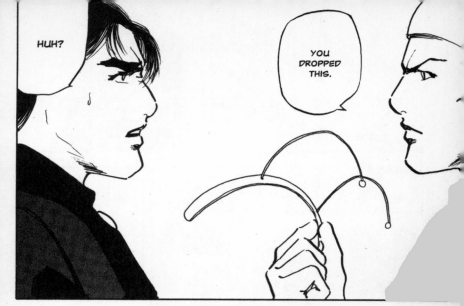

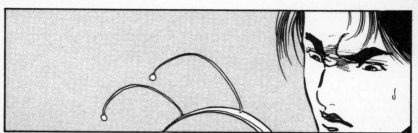

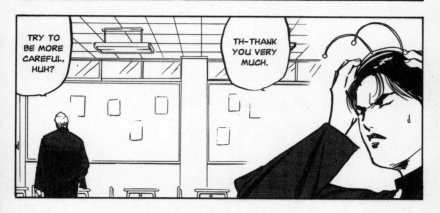

WHAT THE HELL *ARE* THOSE THINGS?

CHAPTER 129: **BOYS KEEP SWINGING**

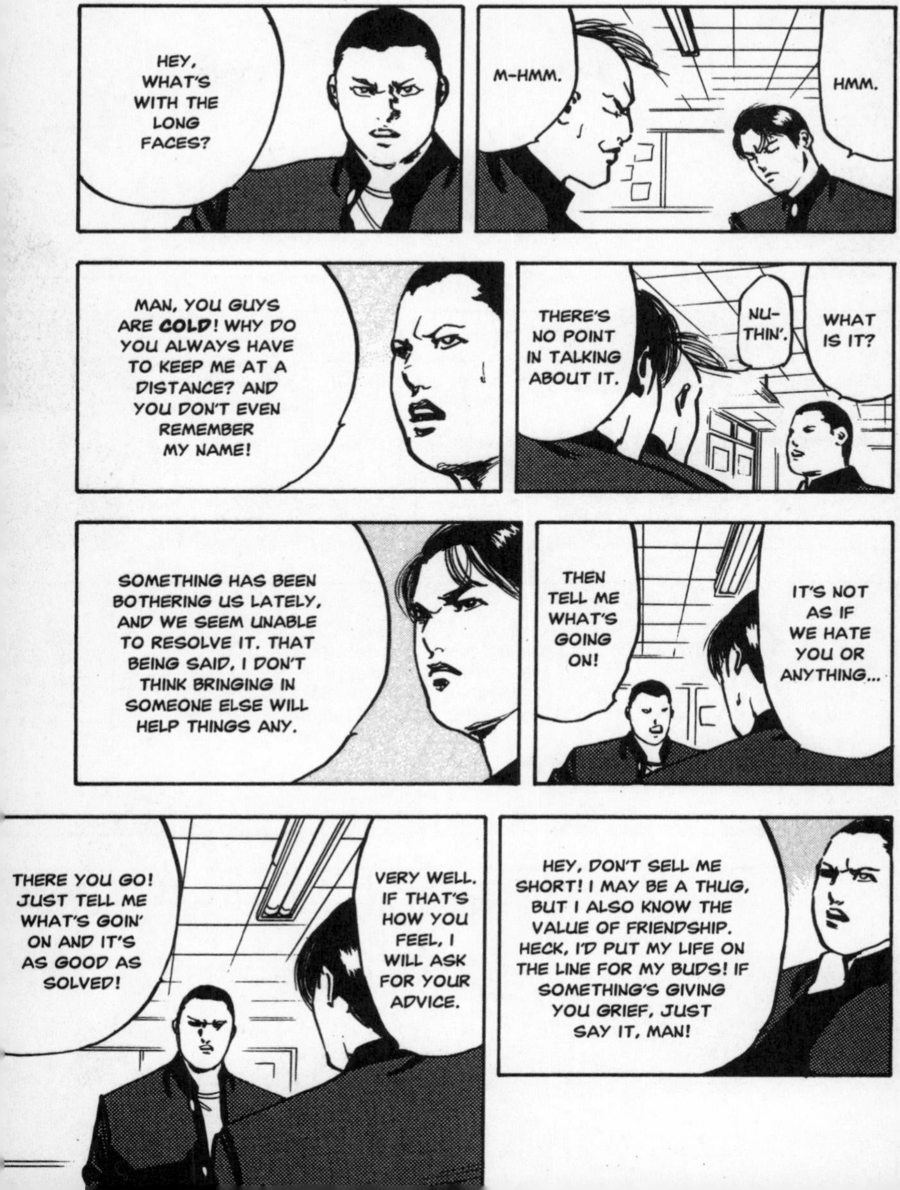
HMM.
M-HMM.
HEY, WHAT'S WITH THE LONG FACES?
WHAT IS IT?
NU-THIN'.
THERE'S NO POINT IN TALKING ABOUT IT.
MAN, YOU GUYS ARE COLD! WHY DO YOU ALWAYS HAVE TO KEEP ME AT A DISTANCE? AND YOU DON'T EVEN REMEMBER MY NAME!
IT'S NOT AS IF WE HATE YOU OR ANYTHING...
THEN TELL ME WHAT'S GOING ON!
SOMETHING HAS BEEN BOTHERING US LATELY, AND WE SEEM UNABLE TO RESOLVE IT. THAT BEING SAID, I DON'T THINK BRINGING IN SOMEONE ELSE WILL HELP THINGS ANY.
HEY, DON'T SELL ME SHORT! I MAY BE A THUG, BUT I ALSO KNOW THE VALUE OF FRIENDSHIP. HECK, I'D PUT MY LIFE ON THE LINE FOR MY BUDS! IF SOMETHING'S GIVING YOU GRIEF, JUST SAY IT, MAN!
VERY WELL. IF THAT'S HOW YOU FEEL, I WILL ASK FOR YOUR ADVICE.
THERE YOU GO! JUST TELL ME WHAT'S GOIN' ON AND IT'S AS GOOD AS SOLVED!

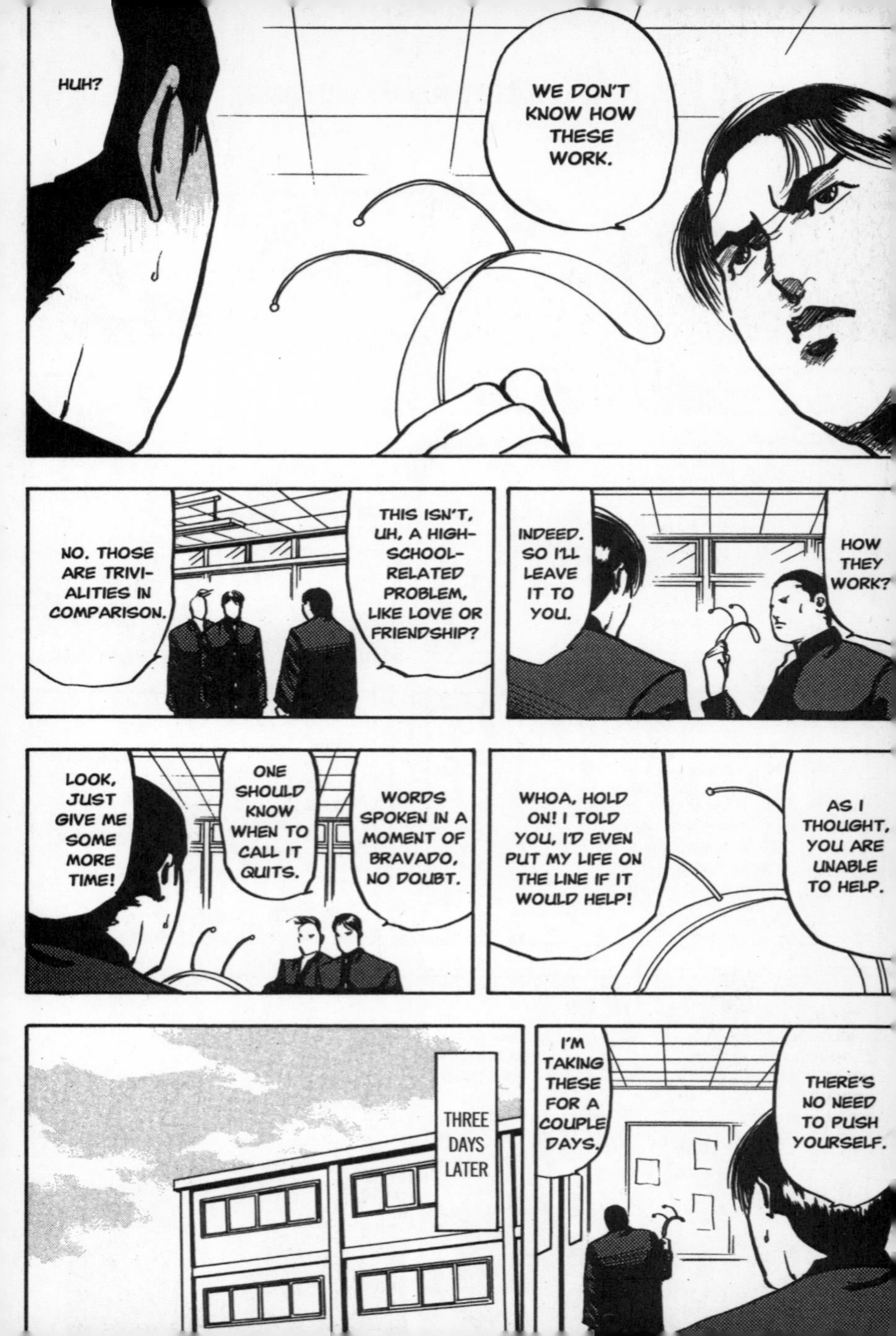
WE DON'T KNOW HOW THESE WORK.
HUH?
HOW THEY WORK?
INDEED. SO I'LL LEAVE IT TO YOU.
THIS ISN'T, UH, A HIGH-SCHOOL-RELATED PROBLEM, LIKE LOVE OR FRIENDSHIP?
NO. THOSE ARE TRIVI-ALITIES IN COMPARISON.
AS I THOUGHT, YOU ARE UNABLE TO HELP.
WHOA, HOLD ON! I TOLD YOU, I'D EVEN PUT MY LIFE ON THE LINE IF IT WOULD HELP!
WORDS SPOKEN IN A MOMENT OF BRAVADO, NO DOUBT.
ONE SHOULD KNOW WHEN TO CALL IT QUITS.
LOOK, JUST GIVE ME SOME MORE TIME!
THERE'S NO NEED TO PUSH YOURSELF.
I'M TAKING THESE FOR A COUPLE DAYS.
THREE DAYS LATER

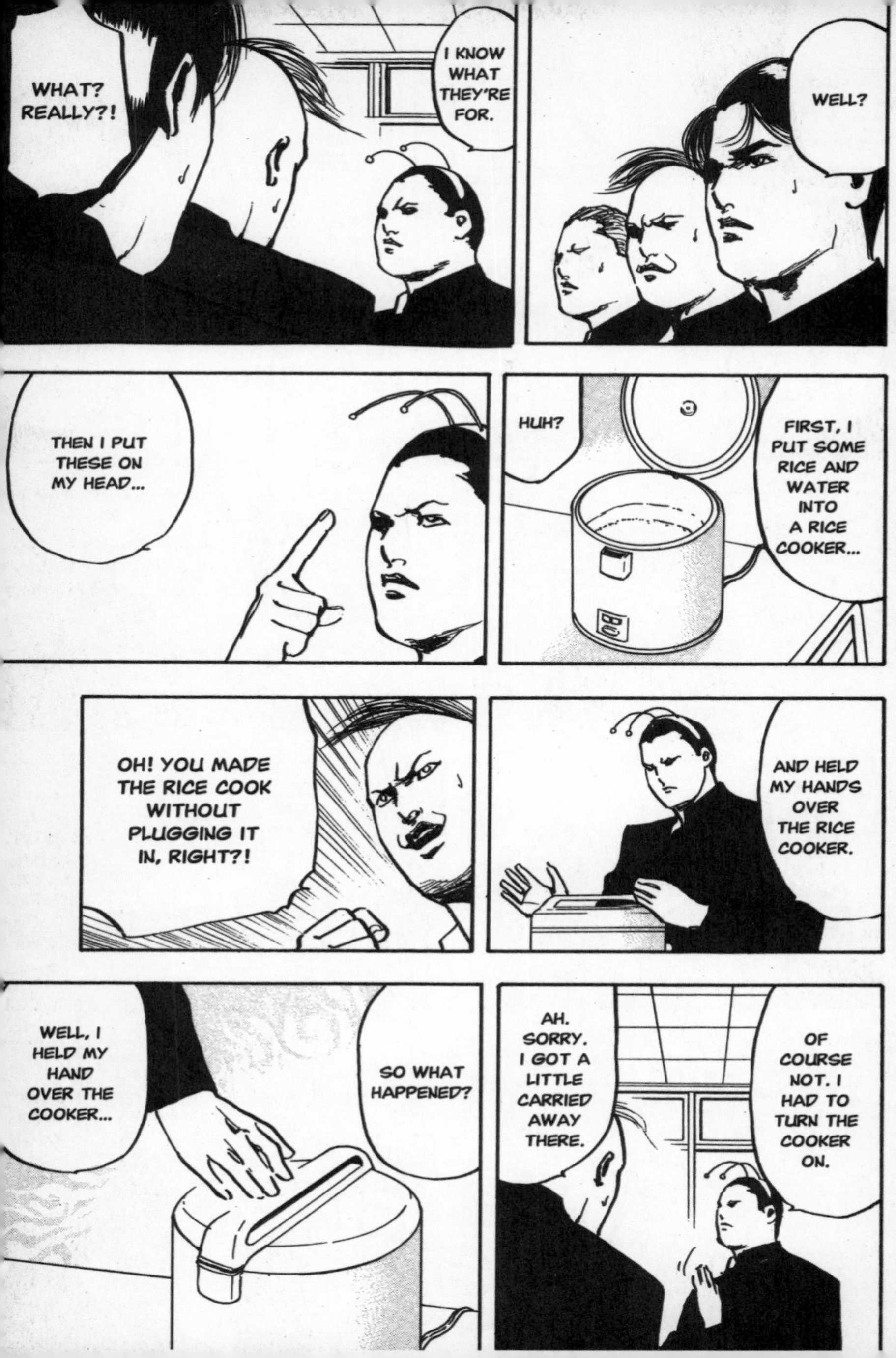
WELL?
I KNOW WHAT THEY'RE FOR.
WHAT? REALLY?!
FIRST, I PUT SOME RICE AND WATER INTO A RICE COOKER...
HUH?
THEN I PUT THESE ON MY HEAD...
AND HELD MY HANDS OVER THE RICE COOKER.
OH! YOU MADE THE RICE COOK WITHOUT PLUGGING IT IN, RIGHT?!
OF COURSE NOT. I HAD TO TURN THE COOKER ON.
AH. SORRY. I GOT A LITTLE CARRIED AWAY THERE.
SO WHAT HAPPENED?
WELL, I HELD MY HAND OVER THE COOKER...

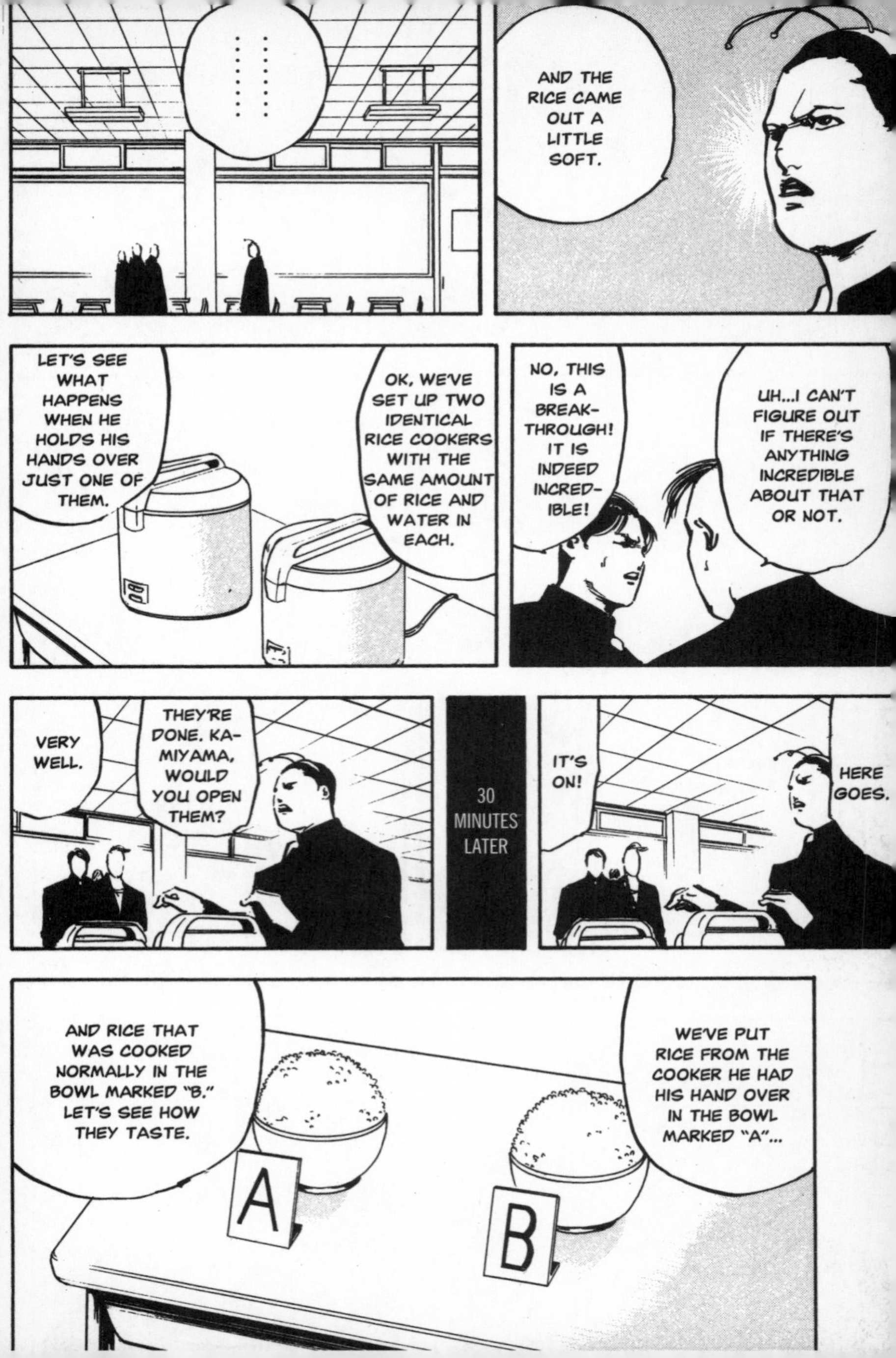
AND THE RICE CAME OUT A LITTLE SOFT.
......
UH...I CAN'T FIGURE OUT IF THERE'S ANYTHING INCREDIBLE ABOUT THAT OR NOT.
NO, THIS IS A BREAK-THROUGH! IT IS INDEED INCRED-IBLE!
OK, WE'VE SET UP TWO IDENTICAL RICE COOKERS WITH THE SAME AMOUNT OF RICE AND WATER IN EACH.
LET'S SEE WHAT HAPPENS WHEN HE HOLDS HIS HANDS OVER JUST ONE OF THEM.
HERE GOES.
IT'S ON!
30 MINUTES LATER
THEY'RE DONE. KA-MIYAMA, WOULD YOU OPEN THEM?
VERY WELL.
WE'VE PUT RICE FROM THE COOKER HE HAD HIS HAND OVER IN THE BOWL MARKED "A"...
AND RICE THAT WAS COOKED NORMALLY IN THE BOWL MARKED "B." LET'S SEE HOW THEY TASTE.
A
B

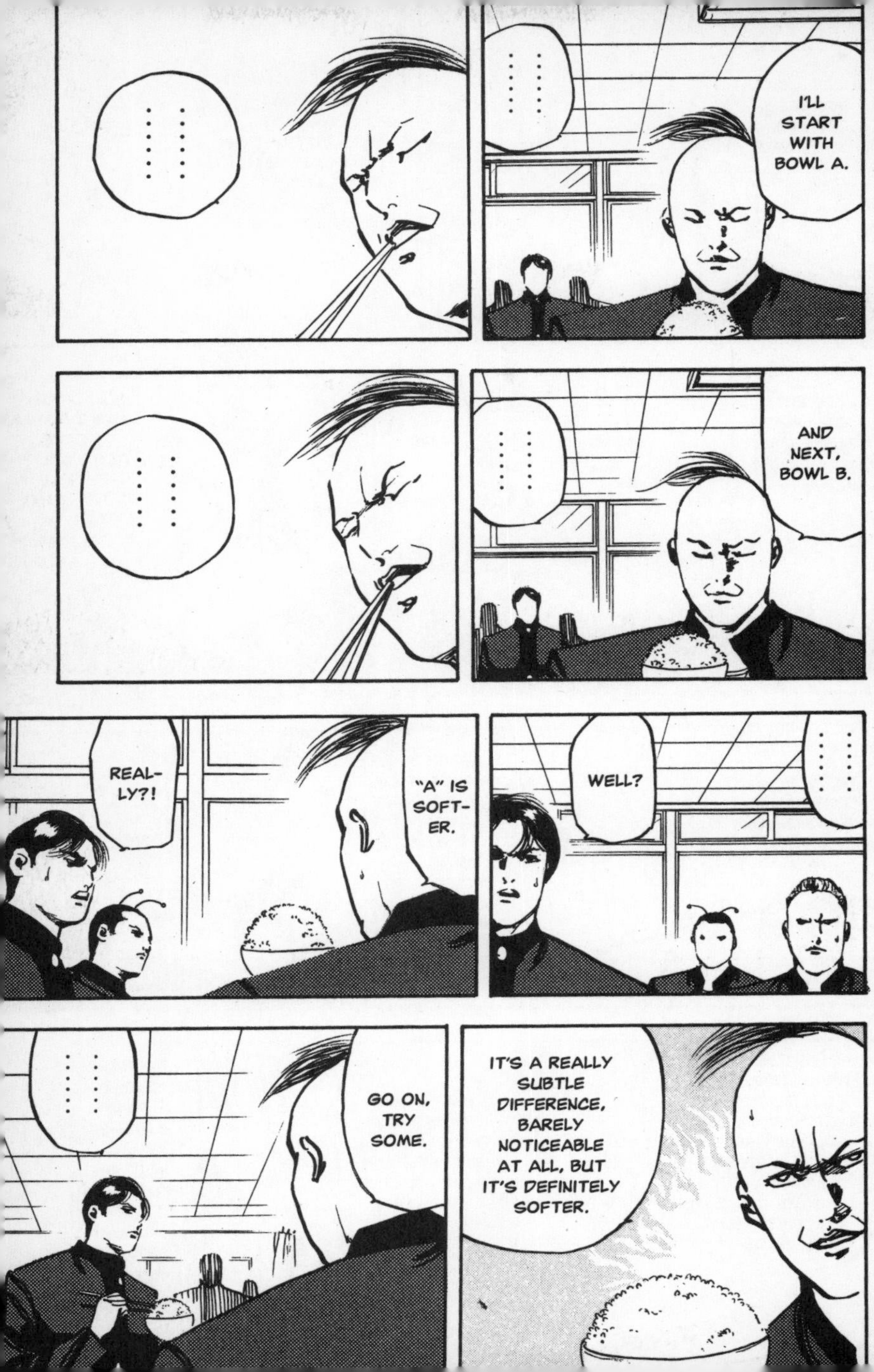
I'LL START WITH BOWL A.
......
......
AND NEXT, BOWL B.
......
......
......
WELL?
"A" IS SOFT-ER.
REAL-LY?!
IT'S A REALLY SUBTLE DIFFERENCE, BARELY NOTICEABLE AT ALL, BUT IT'S DEFINITELY SOFTER.
GO ON, TRY SOME.
......

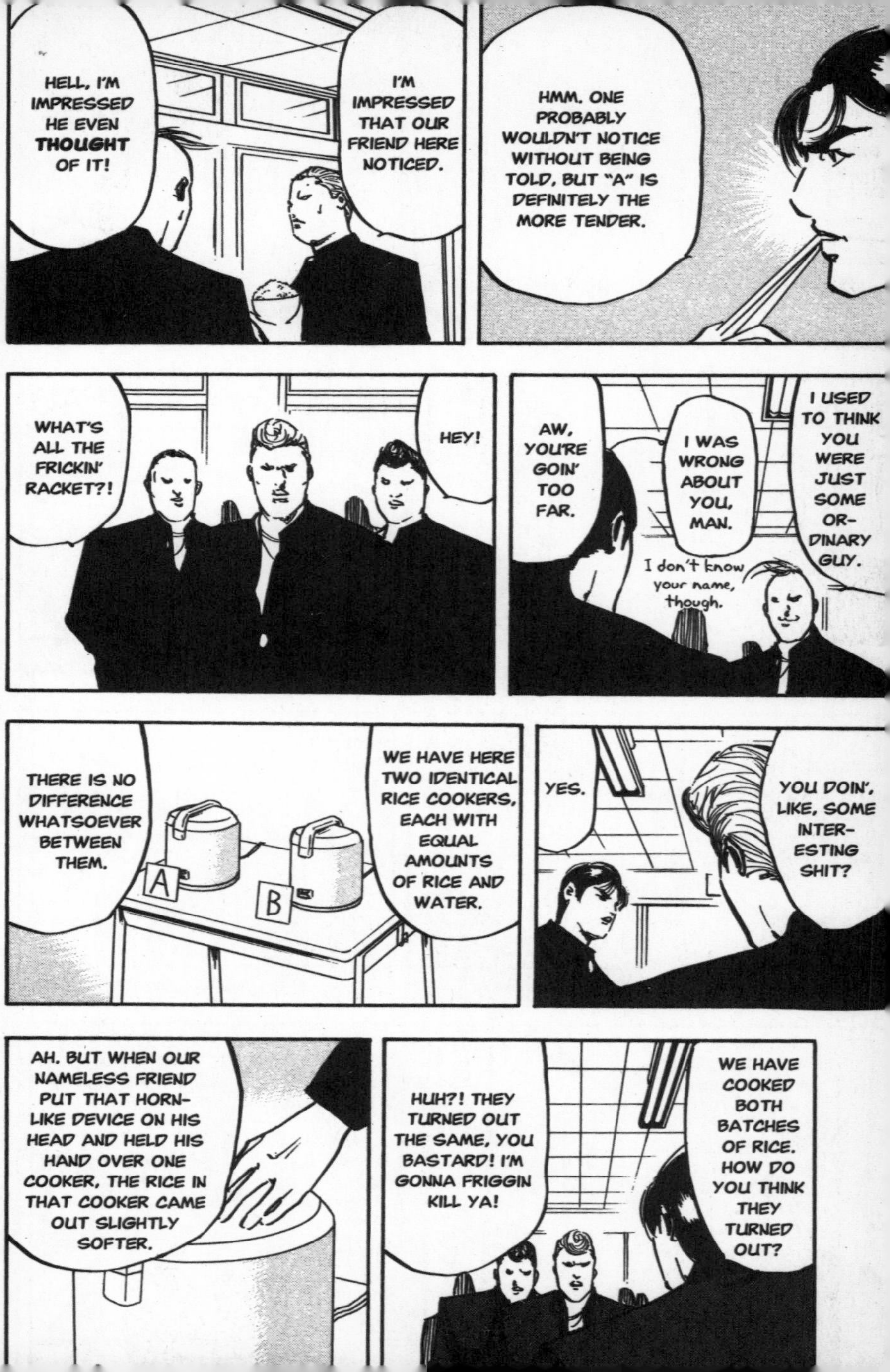
HMM. ONE PROBABLY WOULDN'T NOTICE WITHOUT BEING TOLD, BUT "A" IS DEFINITELY THE MORE TENDER.
I'M IMPRESSED THAT OUR FRIEND HERE NOTICED.
HELL, I'M IMPRESSED HE EVEN **THOUGHT** OF IT!
I USED TO THINK YOU WERE JUST SOME OR-DINARY GUY.
I WAS WRONG ABOUT YOU, MAN.
I don't know your name, though.
AW, YOU'RE GOIN' TOO FAR.
HEY!
WHAT'S ALL THE FRICKIN' RACKET?!
YOU DOIN', LIKE, SOME INTER-ESTING SHIT?
YES.
WE HAVE HERE TWO IDENTICAL RICE COOKERS, EACH WITH EQUAL AMOUNTS OF RICE AND WATER.
THERE IS NO DIFFERENCE WHATSOEVER BETWEEN THEM.
A
B
WE HAVE COOKED BOTH BATCHES OF RICE. HOW DO YOU THINK THEY TURNED OUT?
HUH?! THEY TURNED OUT THE SAME, YOU BASTARD! I'M GONNA FRIGGIN KILL YA!
AH. BUT WHEN OUR NAMELESS FRIEND PUT THAT HORN-LIKE DEVICE ON HIS HEAD AND HELD HIS HAND OVER ONE COOKER, THE RICE IN THAT COOKER CAME OUT SLIGHTLY SOFTER.

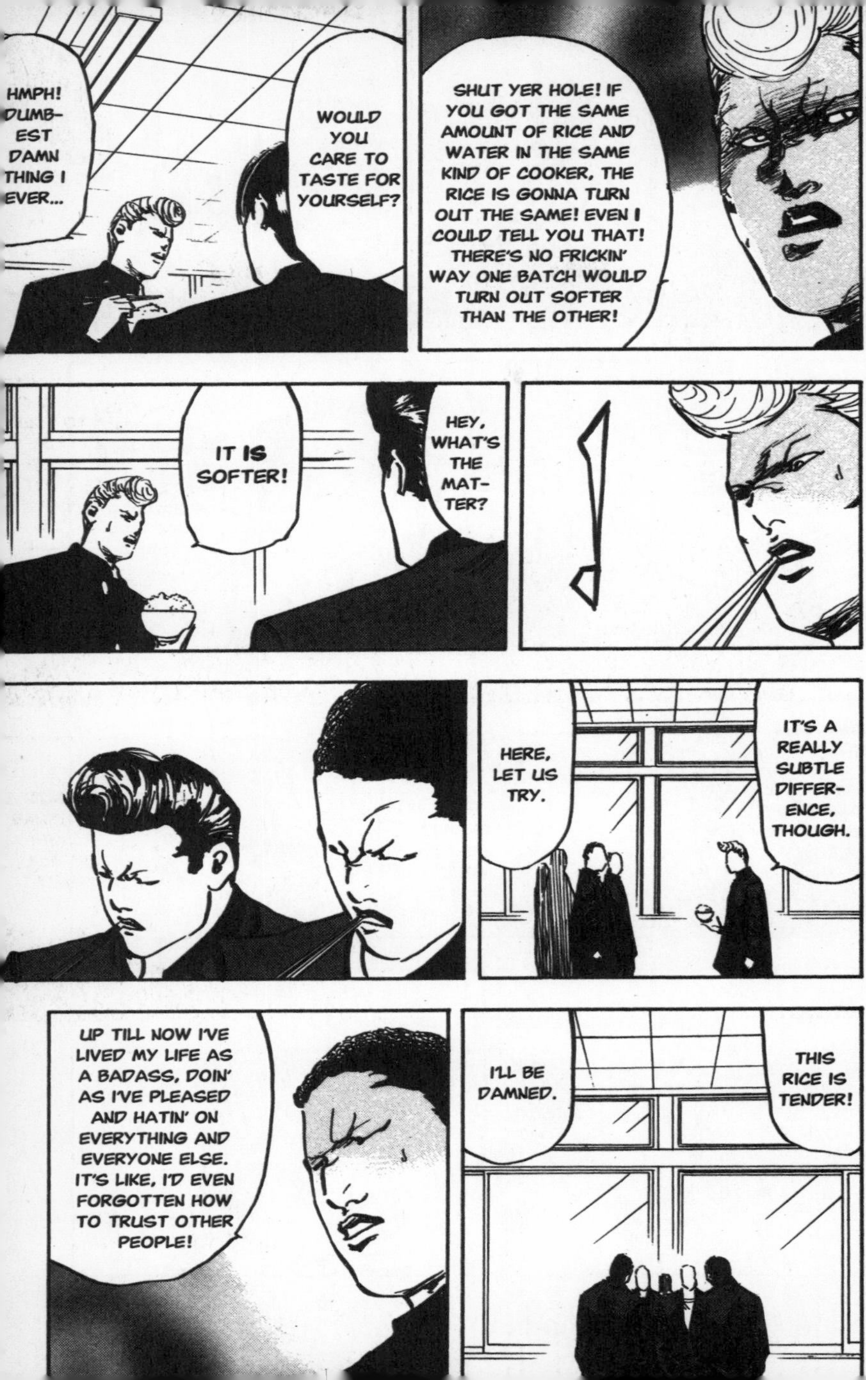
HMPH! DUMB-EST DAMN THING I EVER...
WOULD YOU CARE TO TASTE FOR YOURSELF?
SHUT YER HOLE! IF YOU GOT THE SAME AMOUNT OF RICE AND WATER IN THE SAME KIND OF COOKER, THE RICE IS GONNA TURN OUT THE SAME! EVEN I COULD TELL YOU THAT! THERE'S NO FRICKIN' WAY ONE BATCH WOULD TURN OUT SOFTER THAN THE OTHER!
IT IS SOFTER!
HEY, WHAT'S THE MAT-TER?
!
HERE, LET US TRY.
IT'S A REALLY SUBTLE DIFFER-ENCE, THOUGH.
UP TILL NOW I'VE LIVED MY LIFE AS A BADASS, DOIN' AS I'VE PLEASED AND HATIN' ON EVERYTHING AND EVERYONE ELSE. IT'S LIKE, I'D EVEN FORGOTTEN HOW TO TRUST OTHER PEOPLE!
I'LL BE DAMNED.
THIS RICE IS TENDER!

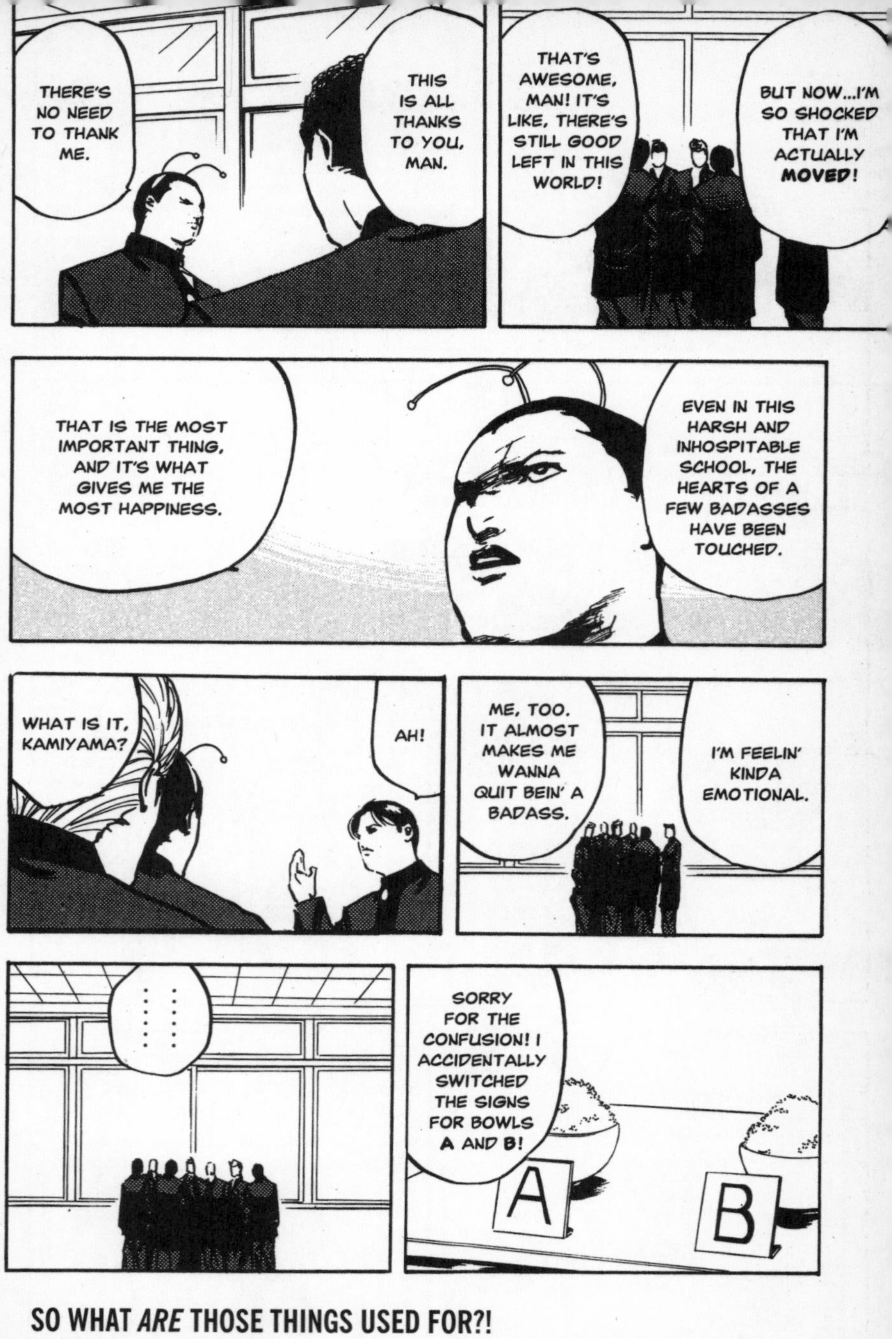
THERE'S NO NEED TO THANK ME.
THIS IS ALL THANKS TO YOU, MAN.
THAT'S AWESOME, MAN! IT'S LIKE, THERE'S STILL GOOD LEFT IN THIS WORLD!
BUT NOW...I'M SO SHOCKED THAT I'M ACTUALLY **MOVED**!
EVEN IN THIS HARSH AND INHOSPITABLE SCHOOL, THE HEARTS OF A FEW BADASSES HAVE BEEN TOUCHED.
THAT IS THE MOST IMPORTANT THING, AND IT'S WHAT GIVES ME THE MOST HAPPINESS.
I'M FEELIN' KINDA EMOTIONAL.
ME, TOO. IT ALMOST MAKES ME WANNA QUIT BEIN' A BADASS.
AH!
WHAT IS IT, KAMIYAMA?
SORRY FOR THE CONFUSION! I ACCIDENTALLY SWITCHED THE SIGNS FOR BOWLS A AND B!
A
B

SO WHAT *ARE* THOSE THINGS USED FOR?!

CHAPTER 130: **A DAY IN THE LIFE**

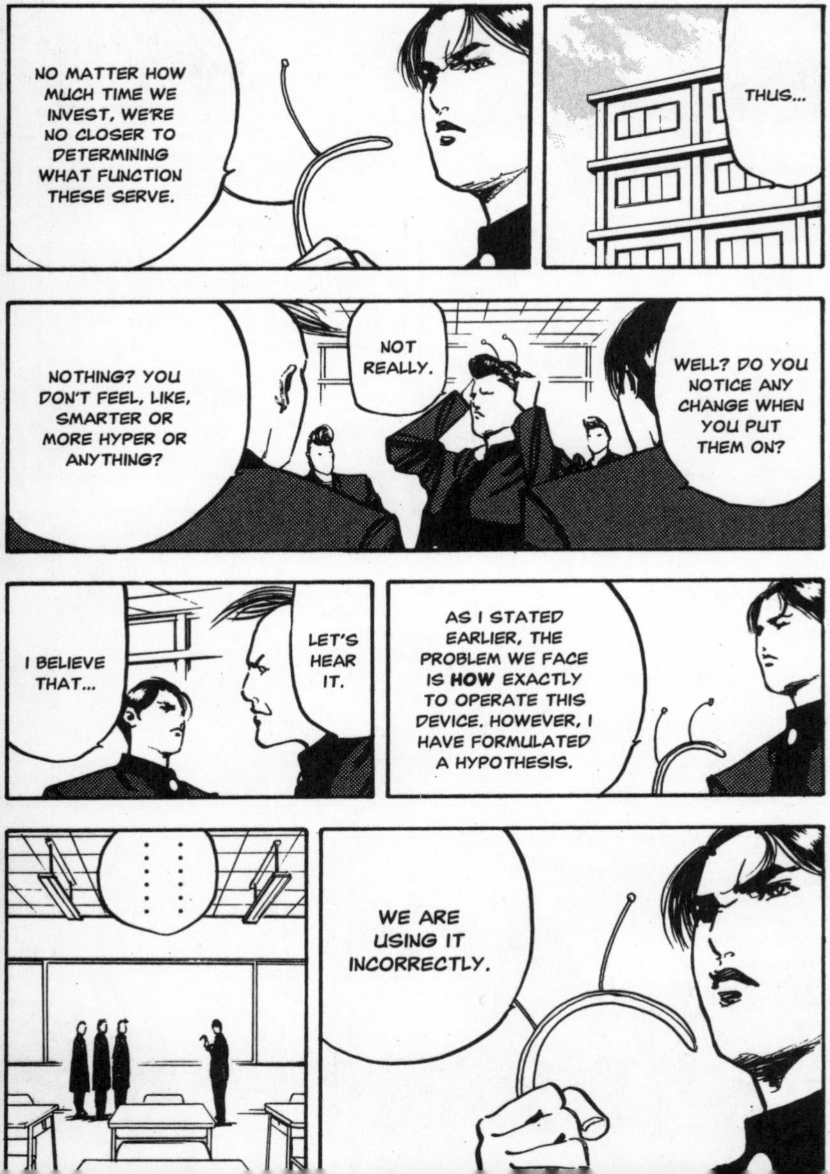

THUS...
NO MATTER HOW MUCH TIME WE INVEST, WE'RE NO CLOSER TO DETERMINING WHAT FUNCTION THESE SERVE.
WELL? DO YOU NOTICE ANY CHANGE WHEN YOU PUT THEM ON?
NOT REALLY.
NOTHING? YOU DON'T FEEL, LIKE, SMARTER OR MORE HYPER OR ANYTHING?
AS I STATED EARLIER, THE PROBLEM WE FACE IS HOW EXACTLY TO OPERATE THIS DEVICE. HOWEVER, I HAVE FORMULATED A HYPOTHESIS.
LET'S HEAR IT.
I BELIEVE THAT...
WE ARE USING IT INCORRECTLY.
......

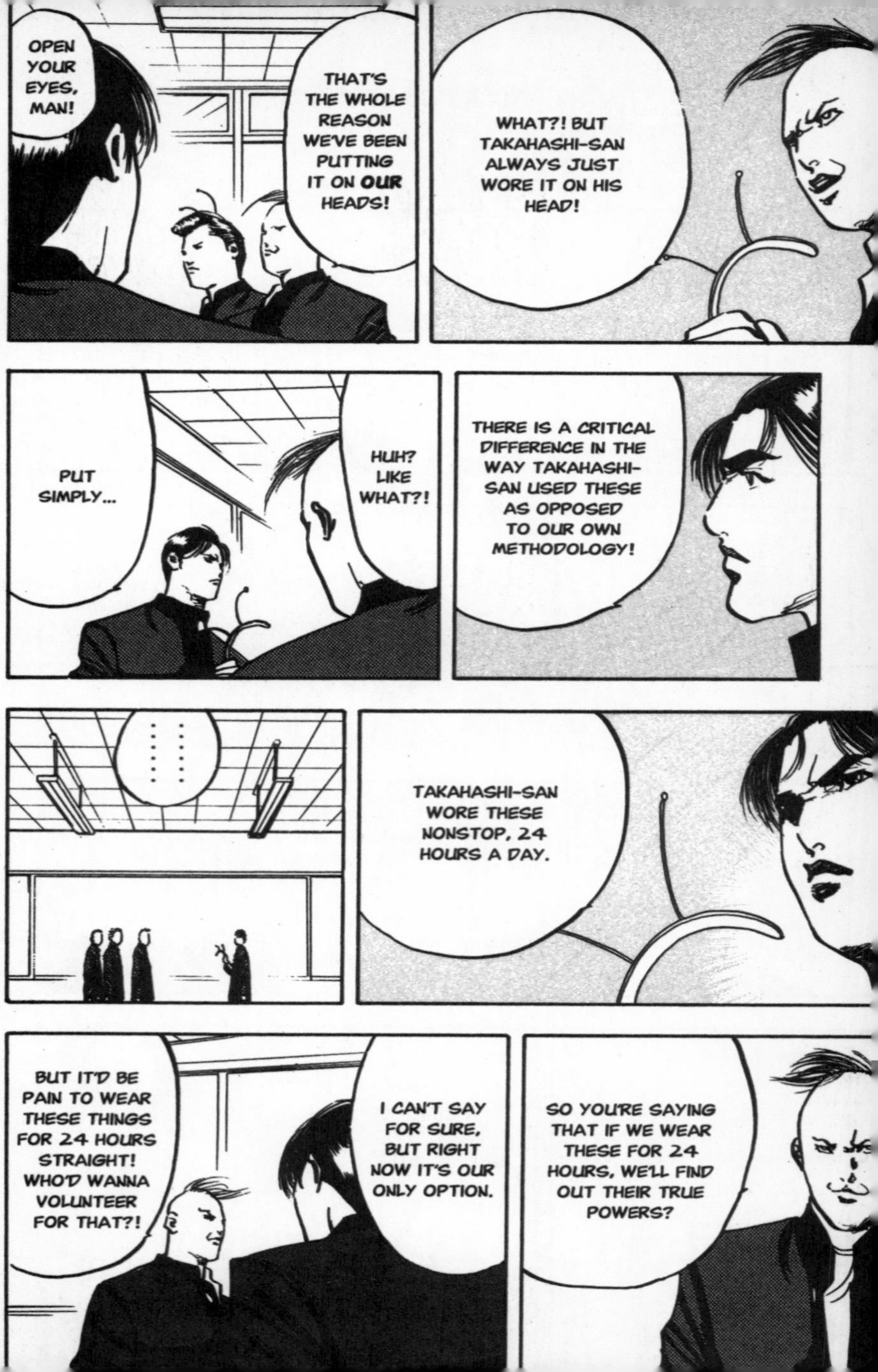

WHAT?! BUT TAKAHASHI-SAN ALWAYS JUST WORE IT ON HIS HEAD!
THAT'S THE WHOLE REASON WE'VE BEEN PUTTING IT ON **OUR** HEADS!
OPEN YOUR EYES, MAN!
THERE IS A CRITICAL DIFFERENCE IN THE WAY TAKAHASHI-SAN USED THESE AS OPPOSED TO OUR OWN METHODOLOGY!
HUH? LIKE WHAT?!
PUT SIMPLY...
TAKAHASHI-SAN WORE THESE NONSTOP, 24 HOURS A DAY.
......
SO YOU'RE SAYING THAT IF WE WEAR THESE FOR 24 HOURS, WE'LL FIND OUT THEIR TRUE POWERS?
I CAN'T SAY FOR SURE, BUT RIGHT NOW IT'S OUR ONLY OPTION.
BUT IT'D BE PAIN TO WEAR THESE THINGS FOR 24 HOURS STRAIGHT! WHO'D WANNA VOLUNTEER FOR THAT?!

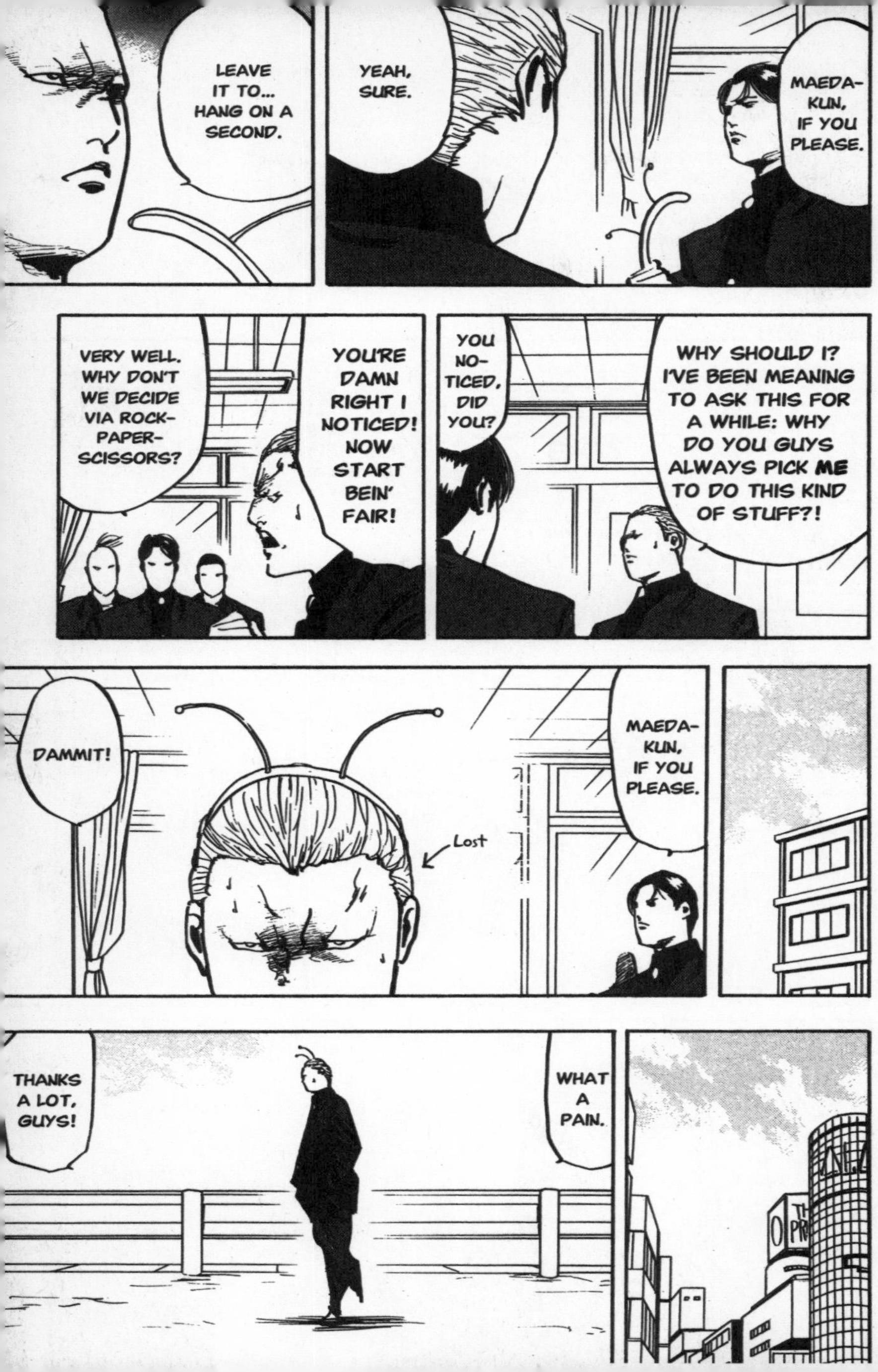

MAEDA-KUN, IF YOU PLEASE.
YEAH, SURE.
LEAVE IT TO... HANG ON A SECOND.
WHY SHOULD I? I'VE BEEN MEANING TO ASK THIS FOR A WHILE: WHY DO YOU GUYS ALWAYS PICK **ME** TO DO THIS KIND OF STUFF?!
YOU NOTICED, DID YOU?
YOU'RE DAMN RIGHT I NOTICED! NOW START BEIN' FAIR!
VERY WELL. WHY DON'T WE DECIDE VIA ROCK-PAPER-SCISSORS?
MAEDA-KUN, IF YOU PLEASE.
DAMMIT!
Lost
WHAT A PAIN.
THANKS A LOT, GUYS!

IT MIGHT JUST BE MY IMAGINATION, BUT EVER SINCE I PUT THESE ON, I FEEL LIKE SOMETHING HAS CHANGED INSIDE ME, OR MY LUCK HAS IMPROVED OR SOMETHING.

STILL, NOTHING HAS GONE RIGHT FOR ME LATELY...

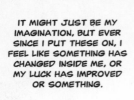

IT'S NOT LIKE IT'S A MAGIC PENDANT OR SOMETHING! HA!

YEAH, RIGHT. TALK ABOUT STUPID.

SPLSSH

TOK TOK TOK

I'M HOME.

K-CHK

CURRY AGAIN?

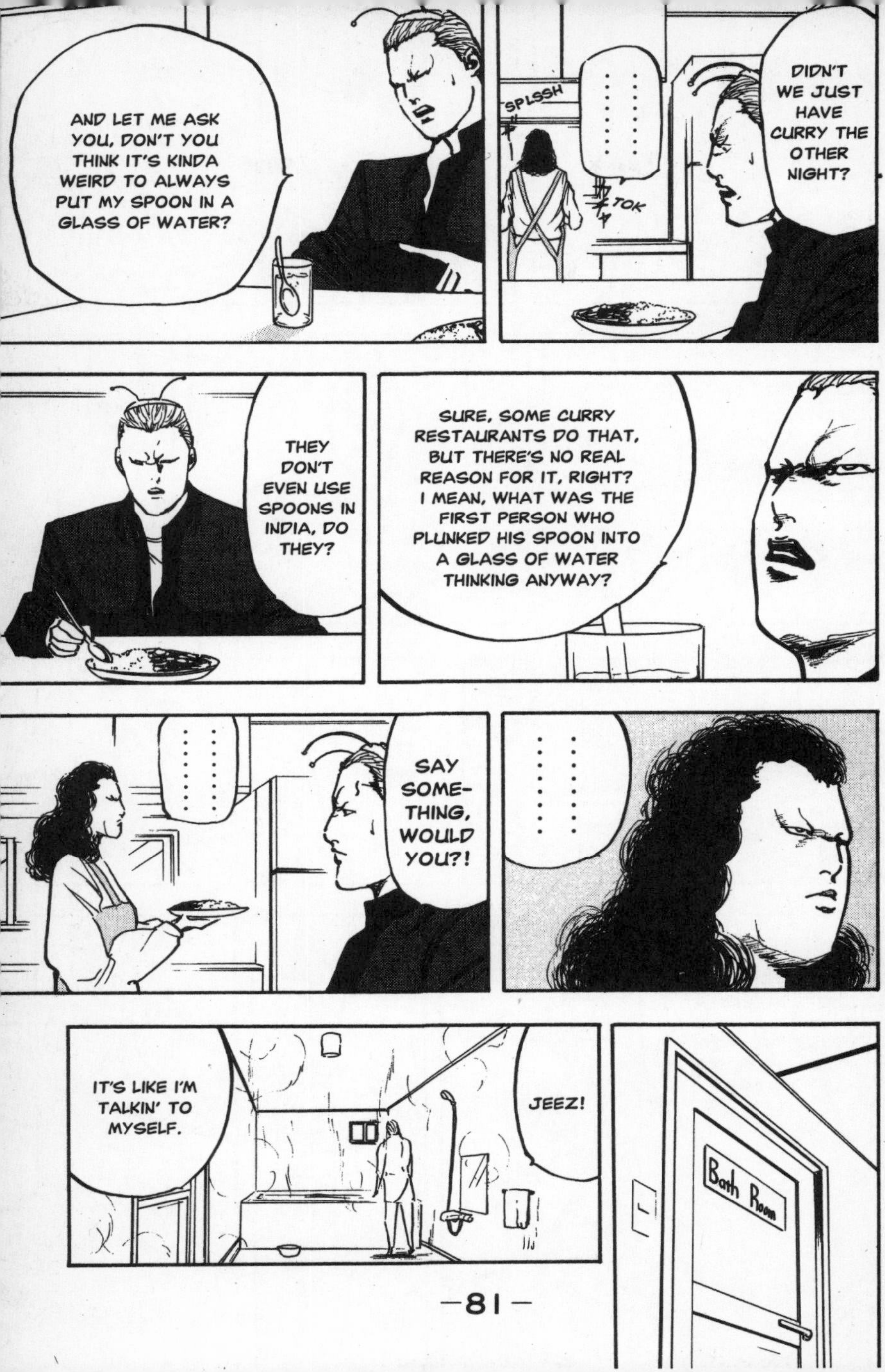
AND LET ME ASK YOU, DON'T YOU THINK IT'S KINDA WEIRD TO ALWAYS PUT MY SPOON IN A GLASS OF WATER?
DIDN'T WE JUST HAVE CURRY THE OTHER NIGHT?
SPLSSH
TOK
THEY DON'T EVEN USE SPOONS IN INDIA, DO THEY?
SURE, SOME CURRY RESTAURANTS DO THAT, BUT THERE'S NO REAL REASON FOR IT, RIGHT? I MEAN, WHAT WAS THE FIRST PERSON WHO PLUNKED HIS SPOON INTO A GLASS OF WATER THINKING ANYWAY?
SAY SOME-THING, WOULD YOU?!
IT'S LIKE I'M TALKIN' TO MYSELF.
JEEZ!
Bath Room

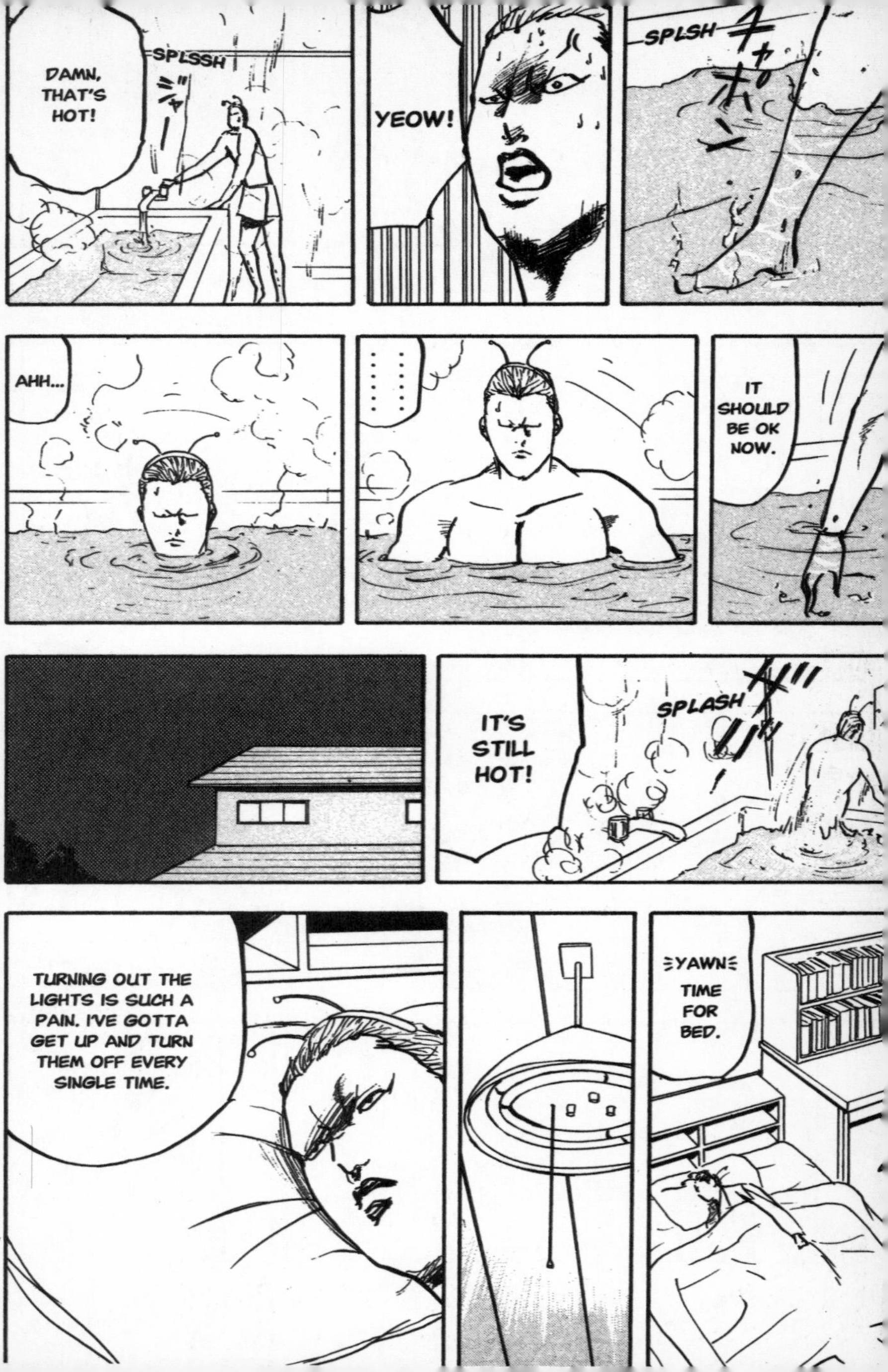
DAMN, THAT'S HOT!
SPLSSH
YEOW!
SPLSH
AHH...
......
IT SHOULD BE OK NOW.
IT'S STILL HOT!
SPLASH
TURNING OUT THE LIGHTS IS SUCH A PAIN. I'VE GOTTA GET UP AND TURN THEM OFF EVERY SINGLE TIME.
YAWN
TIME FOR BED.

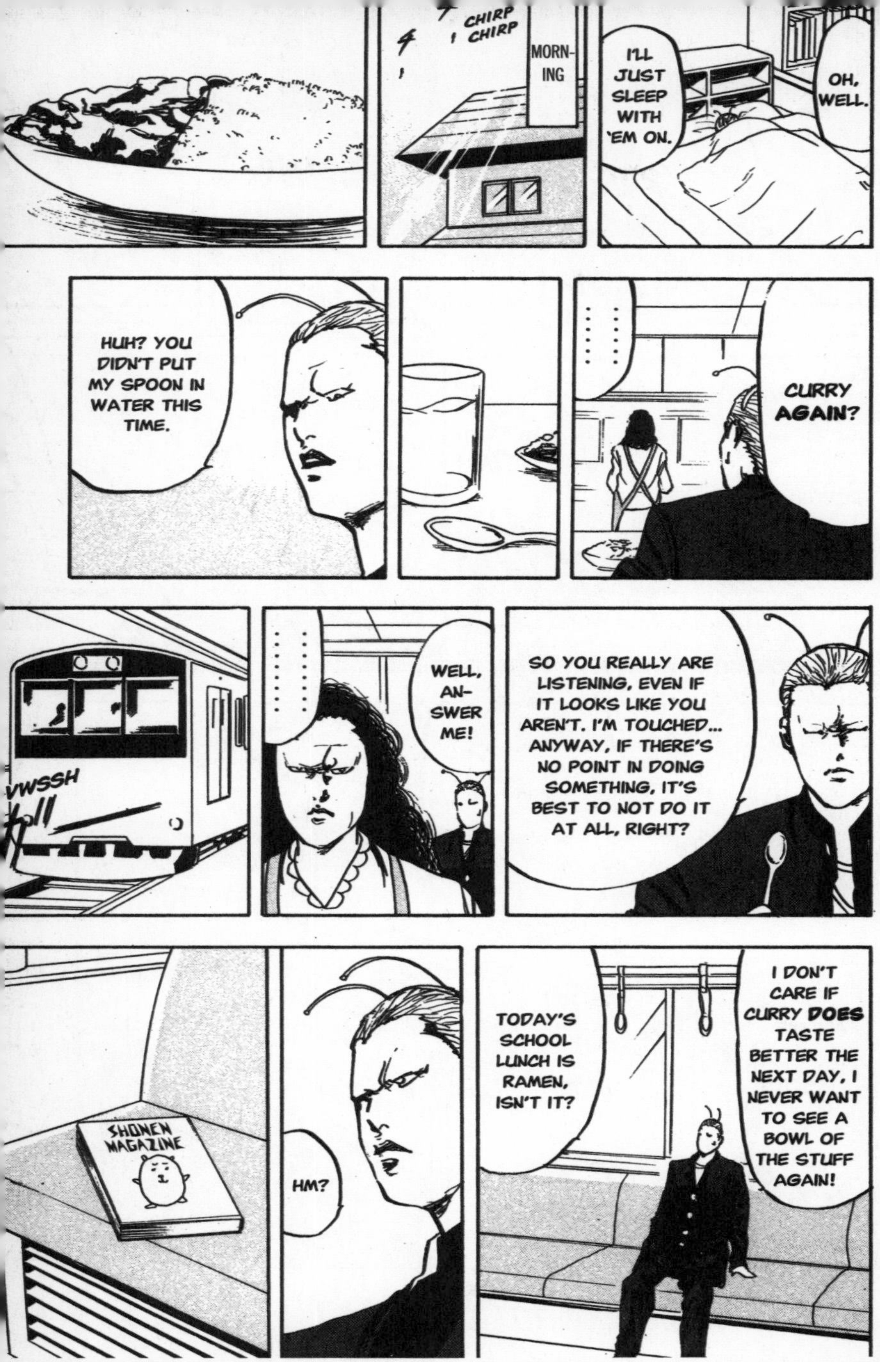

OH, WELL.
I'LL JUST SLEEP WITH 'EM ON.
MORNING
CHIRP CHIRP
CURRY AGAIN?
......
HUH? YOU DIDN'T PUT MY SPOON IN WATER THIS TIME.
SO YOU REALLY ARE LISTENING, EVEN IF IT LOOKS LIKE YOU AREN'T. I'M TOUCHED... ANYWAY, IF THERE'S NO POINT IN DOING SOMETHING, IT'S BEST TO NOT DO IT AT ALL, RIGHT?
WELL, ANSWER ME!
......
VWSSH
I DON'T CARE IF CURRY DOES TASTE BETTER THE NEXT DAY, I NEVER WANT TO SEE A BOWL OF THE STUFF AGAIN!
TODAY'S SCHOOL LUNCH IS RAMEN, ISN'T IT?
HM?
SHONEN MAGAZINE

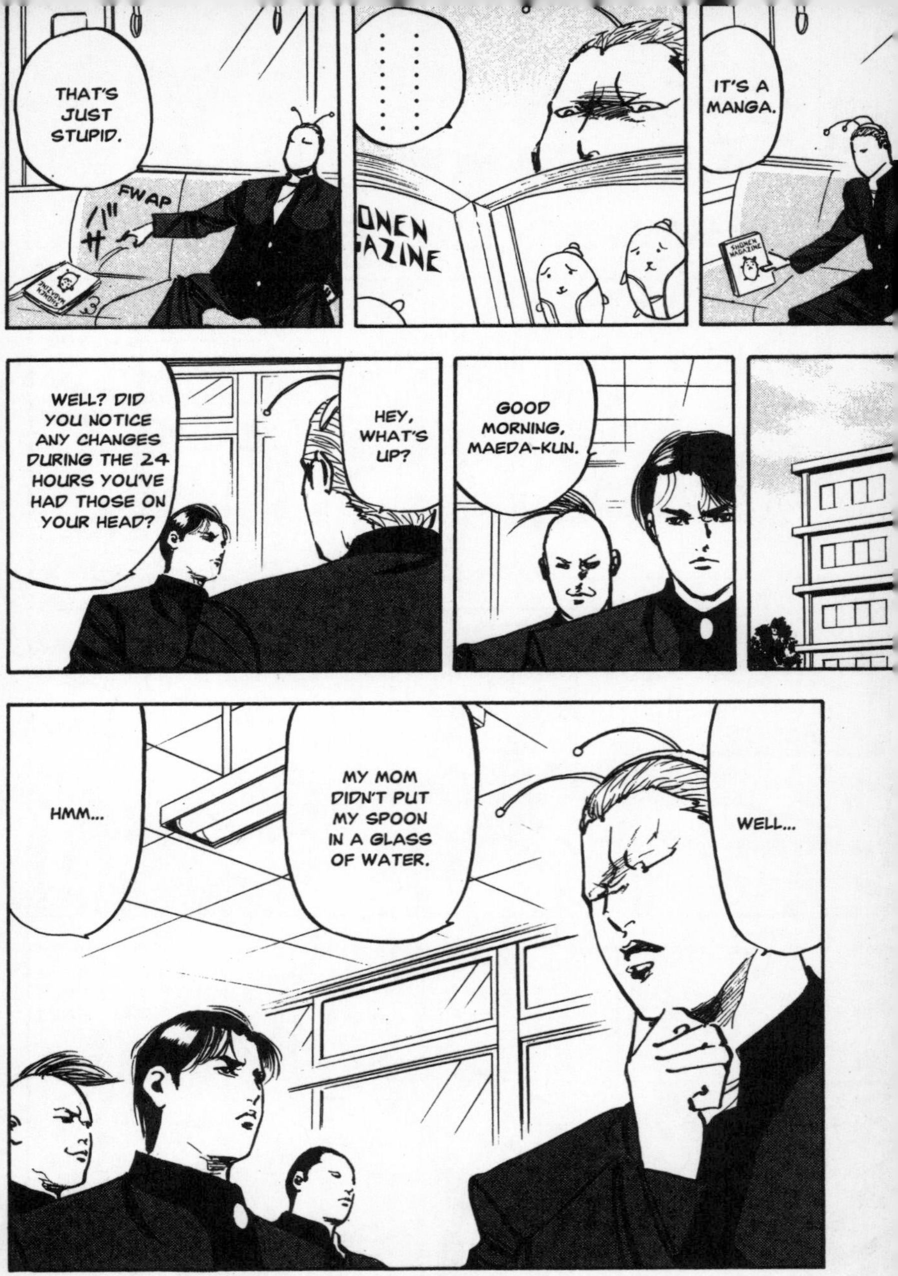
IT'S A MANGA.
......
THAT'S JUST STUPID.
FWAP
GOOD MORNING, MAEDA-KUN.
HEY, WHAT'S UP?
WELL? DID YOU NOTICE ANY CHANGES DURING THE 24 HOURS YOU'VE HAD THOSE ON YOUR HEAD?
WELL...
MY MOM DIDN'T PUT MY SPOON IN A GLASS OF WATER.
HMM...

YEAH, THAT'S PROBABLY UNRELATED.

CHAPTER 131: **START ME UP**

HUH.

MECHA-ZAWA-KUN HAS SEEMED RATHER DOWN LATELY.

YOU KNOW...

EVERY **PERSON,** HUH?

EVERY PERSON HAS PROBLEMS, YOU KNOW.

WELL, WE PROBLY SHOULDN'T GO STICKIN' OUR NECKS INTO HIS BUSINESS. LET'S JUST LEAVE HIM BE.

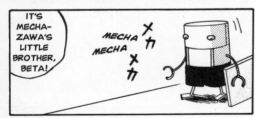

IT'S MECHA-ZAWA'S LITTLE BROTHER, BETA!

MECHA MECHA

HM?

WHAT?

THIS IS...

FWP

HUH?

WHAT IS HE HOLD-ING?

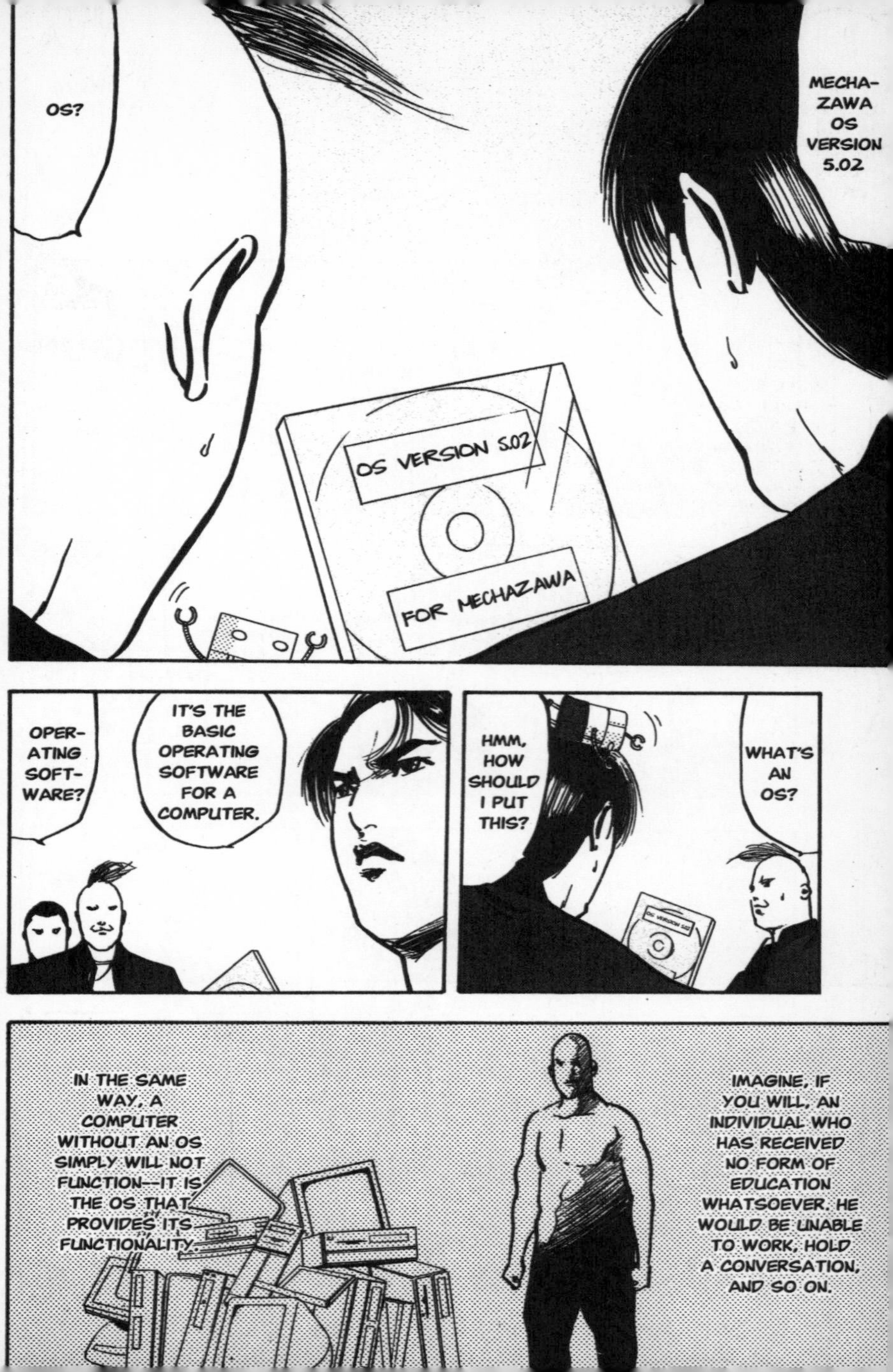
MECHA-ZAWA OS VERSION 5.02
OS?
OS VERSION 5.02
FOR MECHAZAWA
WHAT'S AN OS?
HMM, HOW SHOULD I PUT THIS?
IT'S THE BASIC OPERATING SOFTWARE FOR A COMPUTER.
OPER-ATING SOFT-WARE?
IMAGINE, IF YOU WILL, AN INDIVIDUAL WHO HAS RECEIVED NO FORM OF EDUCATION WHATSOEVER. HE WOULD BE UNABLE TO WORK, HOLD A CONVERSATION, AND SO ON.
IN THE SAME WAY, A COMPUTER WITHOUT AN OS SIMPLY WILL NOT FUNCTION--IT IS THE OS THAT PROVIDES ITS FUNCTIONALITY.

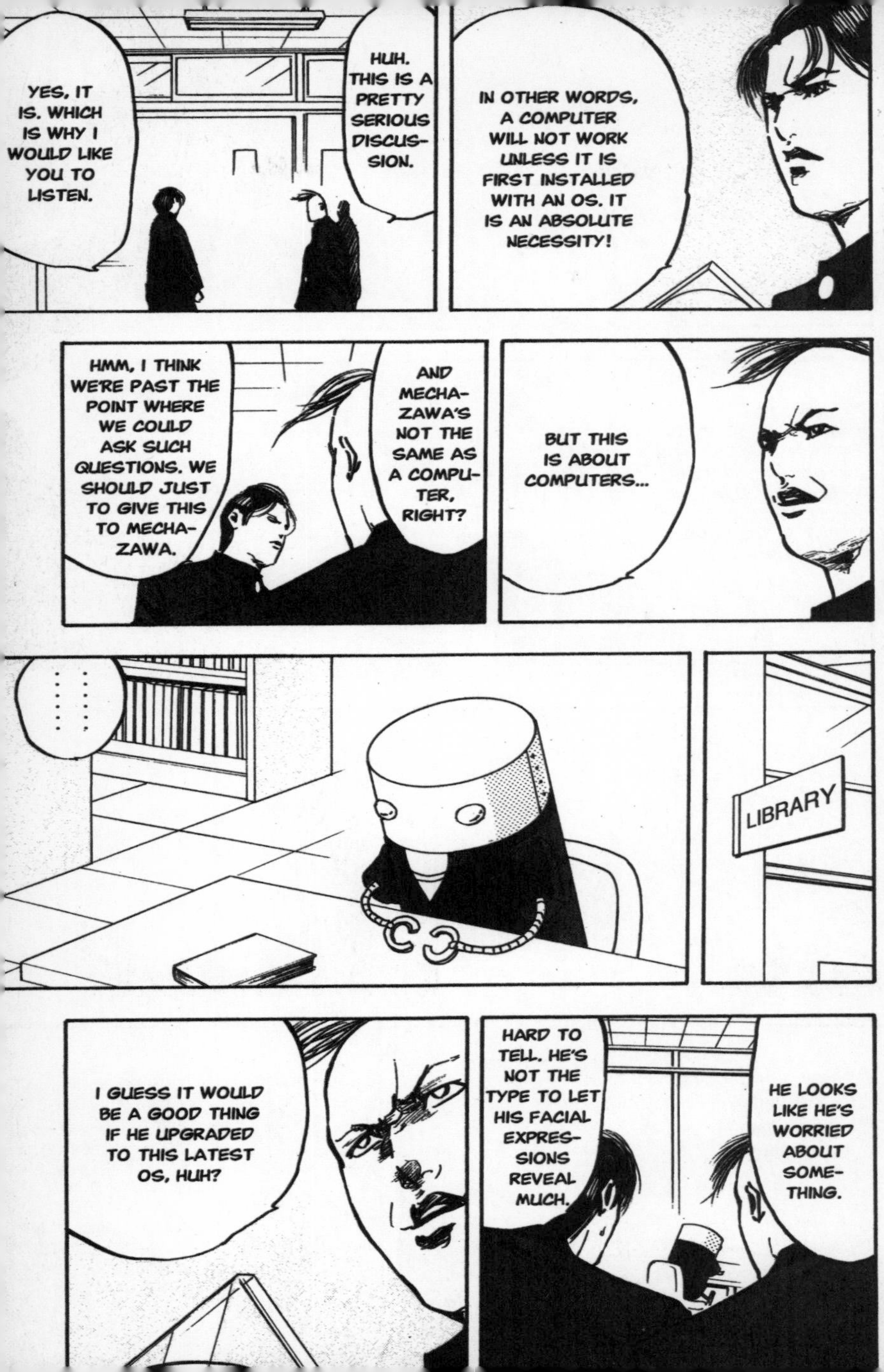
IN OTHER WORDS, A COMPUTER WILL NOT WORK UNLESS IT IS FIRST INSTALLED WITH AN OS. IT IS AN ABSOLUTE NECESSITY!
HUH. THIS IS A PRETTY SERIOUS DISCUSSION.
YES, IT IS. WHICH IS WHY I WOULD LIKE YOU TO LISTEN.
BUT THIS IS ABOUT COMPUTERS...
AND MECHAZAWA'S NOT THE SAME AS A COMPUTER, RIGHT?
HMM, I THINK WE'RE PAST THE POINT WHERE WE COULD ASK SUCH QUESTIONS. WE SHOULD JUST TO GIVE THIS TO MECHAZAWA.
LIBRARY
......
HE LOOKS LIKE HE'S WORRIED ABOUT SOMETHING.
HARD TO TELL. HE'S NOT THE TYPE TO LET HIS FACIAL EXPRESSIONS REVEAL MUCH.
I GUESS IT WOULD BE A GOOD THING IF HE UPGRADED TO THIS LATEST OS, HUH?

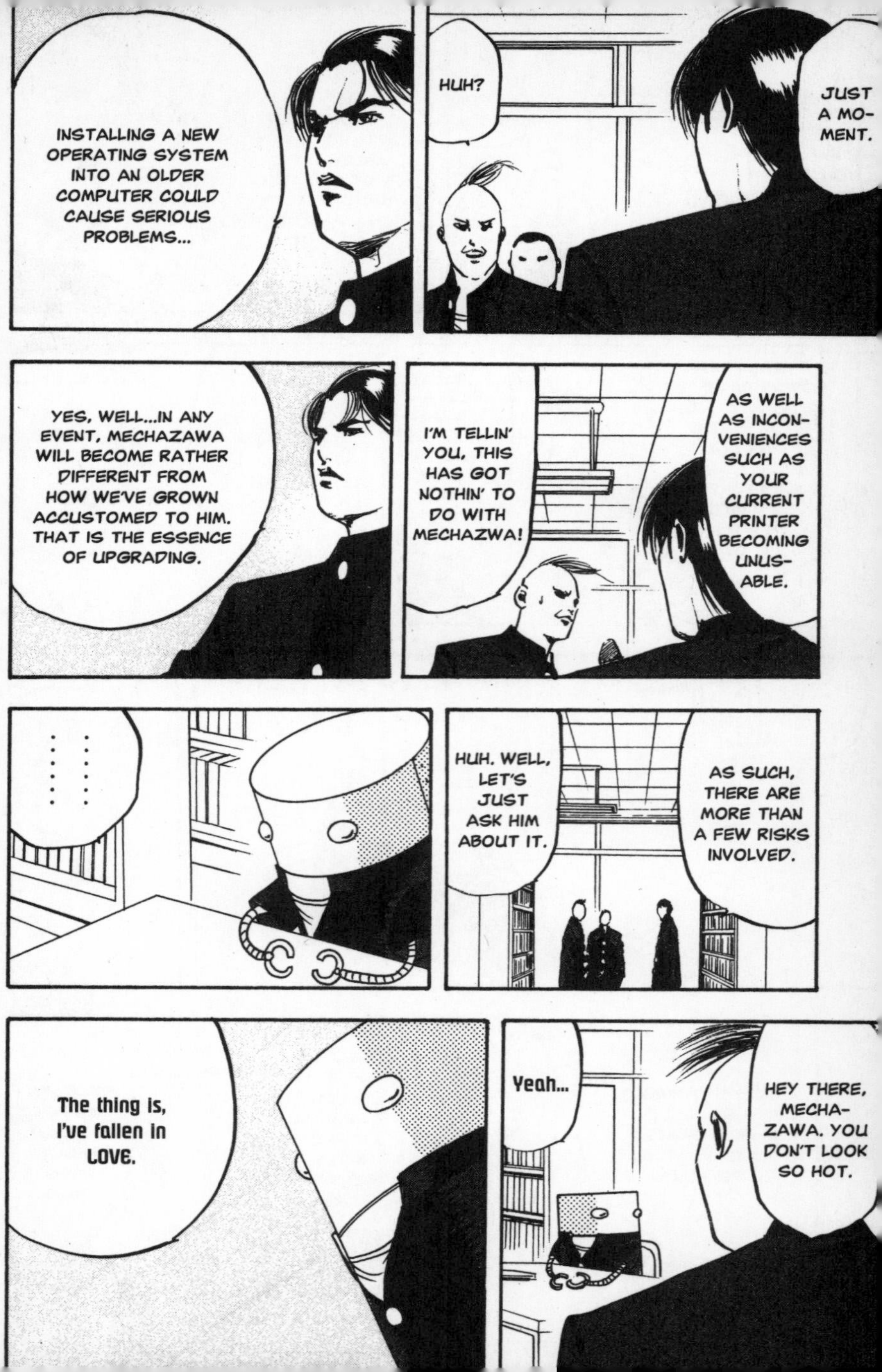
JUST A MO-MENT.
HUH?
INSTALLING A NEW OPERATING SYSTEM INTO AN OLDER COMPUTER COULD CAUSE SERIOUS PROBLEMS...
AS WELL AS INCON-VENIENCES SUCH AS YOUR CURRENT PRINTER BECOMING UNUS-ABLE.
I'M TELLIN' YOU, THIS HAS GOT NOTHIN' TO DO WITH MECHAZWA!
YES, WELL...IN ANY EVENT, MECHAZAWA WILL BECOME RATHER DIFFERENT FROM HOW WE'VE GROWN ACCUSTOMED TO HIM. THAT IS THE ESSENCE OF UPGRADING.
AS SUCH, THERE ARE MORE THAN A FEW RISKS INVOLVED.
HUH. WELL, LET'S JUST ASK HIM ABOUT IT.
......
HEY THERE, MECHA-ZAWA. YOU DON'T LOOK SO HOT.
Yeah...
The thing is, I've fallen in LOVE.

But how could a badass like me, the lowest of the low, end up falling for someone?!

HE'S FALLEN IN LOVE!

If I could, I'd start from scratch and have another go at life. Sheesh! Listen to me talkin' this kind of crap!

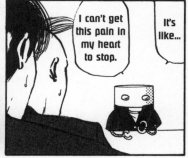

I can't get this pain in my heart to stop.

It's like...

Huh?

MECHA-ZAWA-KUN, WE'RE HERE TO HELP.

I GUESS THAT MAKES THIS PRETTY EASY.

HE WANTS ANOTHER GO AT LIFE!

KA-CHAK

Uh, OK.

JUST STAND WITH YOUR BACK FACING ME. THIS WILL BE OVER BEFORE YOU KNOW IT.

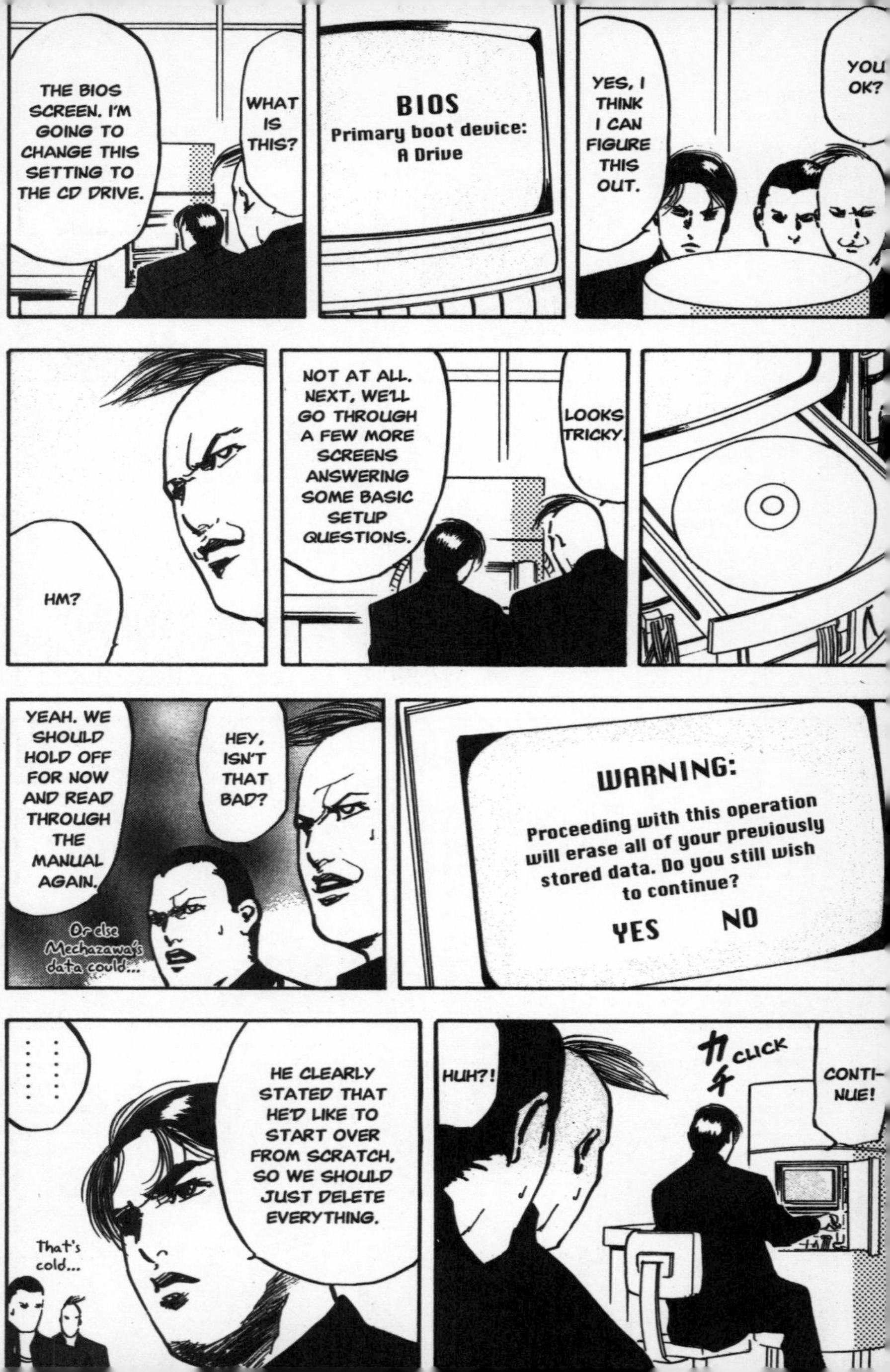
YOU OK?
YES, I THINK I CAN FIGURE THIS OUT.
BIOS
Primary boot device:
A Drive
WHAT IS THIS?
THE BIOS SCREEN. I'M GOING TO CHANGE THIS SETTING TO THE CD DRIVE.
LOOKS TRICKY.
NOT AT ALL. NEXT, WE'LL GO THROUGH A FEW MORE SCREENS ANSWERING SOME BASIC SETUP QUESTIONS.
HM?
WARNING:
Proceeding with this operation will erase all of your previously stored data. Do you still wish to continue?
YES NO
HEY, ISN'T THAT BAD?
YEAH. WE SHOULD HOLD OFF FOR NOW AND READ THROUGH THE MANUAL AGAIN.
Or else Mechazawa's data could...
CONTI-NUE!
カチ CLICK
HUH?!
......
HE CLEARLY STATED THAT HE'D LIKE TO START OVER FROM SCRATCH, SO WE SHOULD JUST DELETE EVERYTHING.
That's cold...

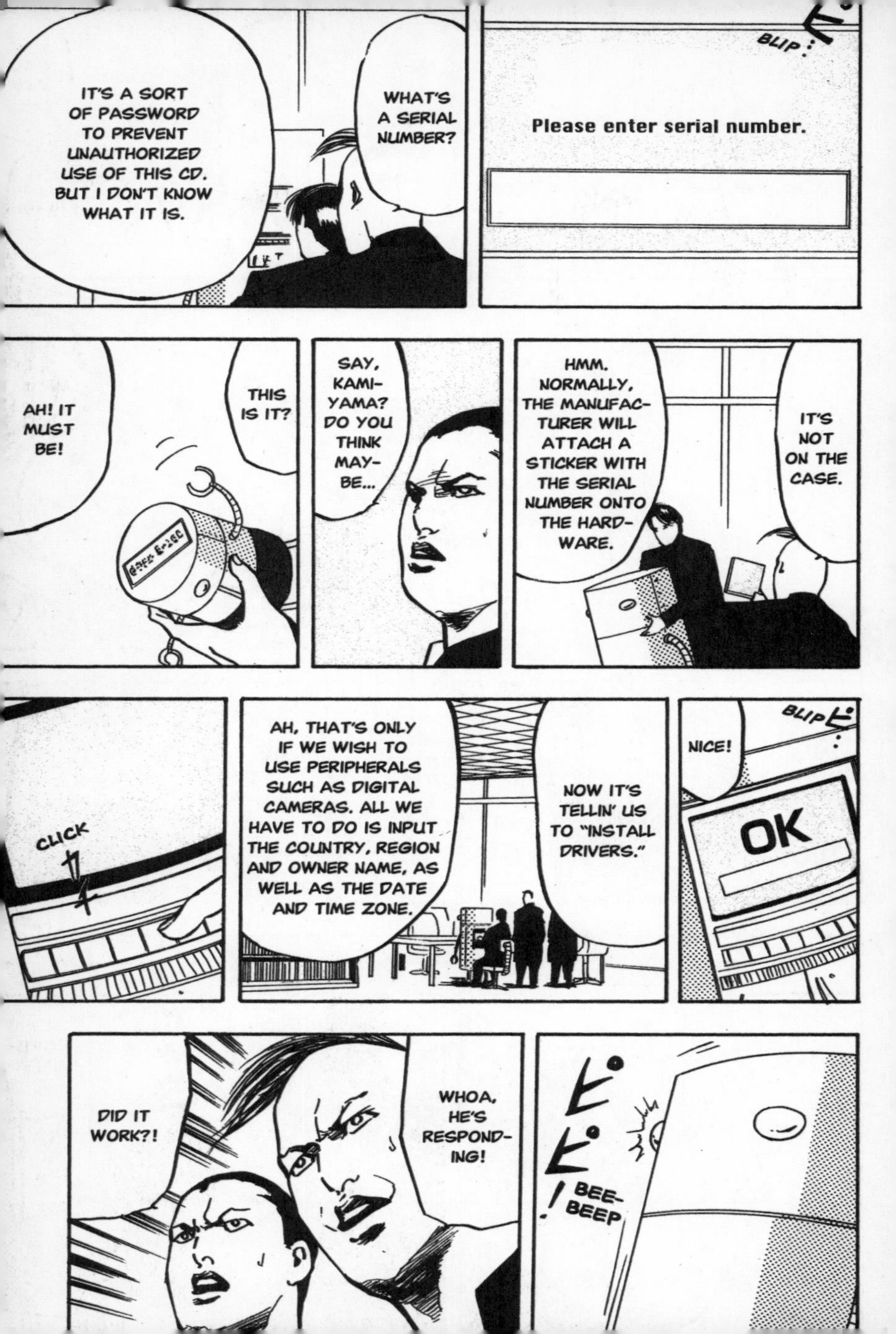
BLIP
Please enter serial number.
WHAT'S A SERIAL NUMBER?
IT'S A SORT OF PASSWORD TO PREVENT UNAUTHORIZED USE OF THIS CD. BUT I DON'T KNOW WHAT IT IS.
IT'S NOT ON THE CASE.
HMM. NORMALLY, THE MANUFACTURER WILL ATTACH A STICKER WITH THE SERIAL NUMBER ONTO THE HARDWARE.
SAY, KAMIYAMA? DO YOU THINK MAYBE...
THIS IS IT?
AH! IT MUST BE!
BLIP
NICE!
OK
NOW IT'S TELLIN' US TO "INSTALL DRIVERS."
AH, THAT'S ONLY IF WE WISH TO USE PERIPHERALS SUCH AS DIGITAL CAMERAS. ALL WE HAVE TO DO IS INPUT THE COUNTRY, REGION AND OWNER NAME, AS WELL AS THE DATE AND TIME ZONE.
CLICK
BEE-BEEP
WHOA, HE'S RESPONDING!
DID IT WORK?!

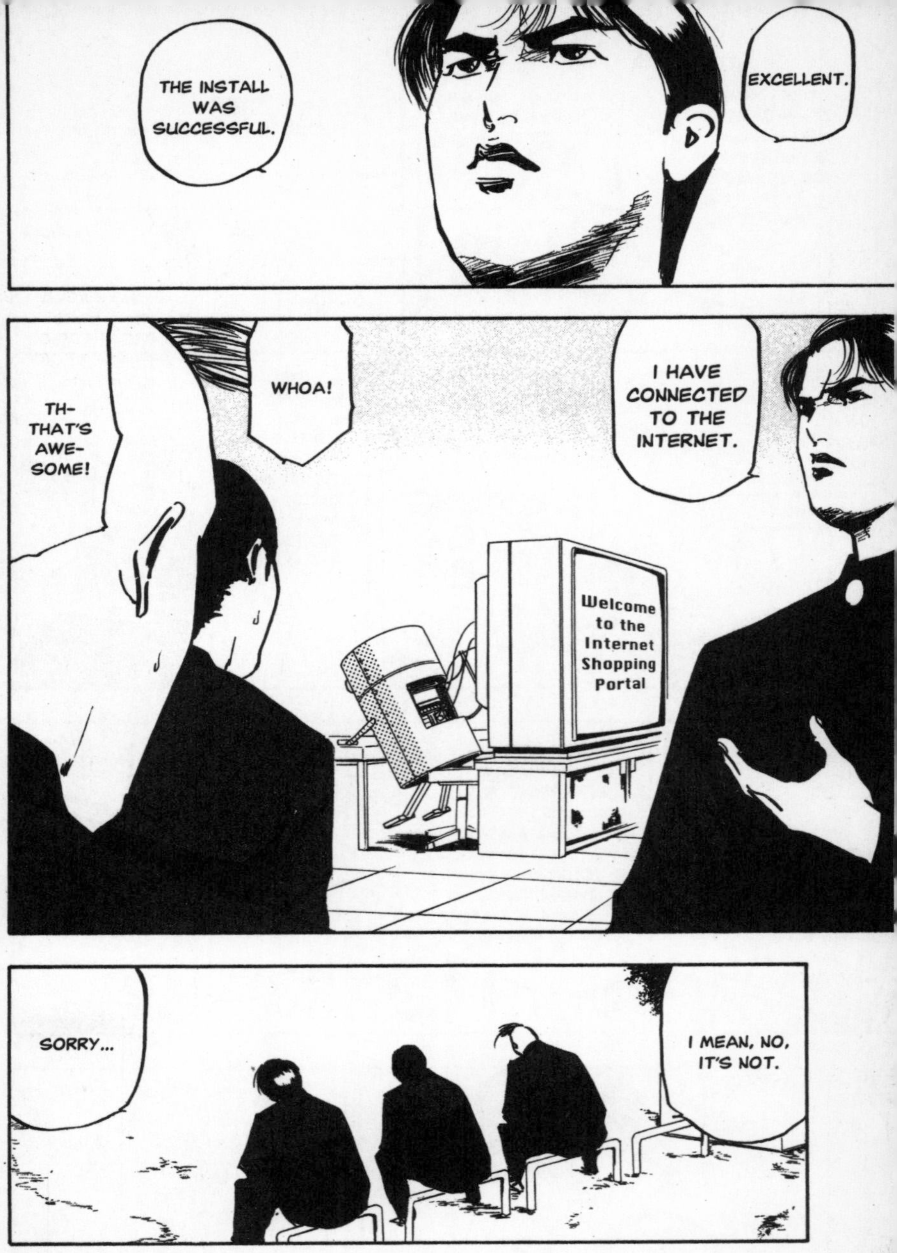
EXCELLENT.
THE INSTALL WAS SUCCESSFUL.
I HAVE CONNECTED TO THE INTERNET.
Welcome to the Internet Shopping Portal
WHOA!
TH- THAT'S AWE- SOME!
I MEAN, NO, IT'S NOT.
SORRY...

MECHAZAWA'S LOVE: TERMINATED.

CHAPTER 132: **I WANT TO BREAK FREE**

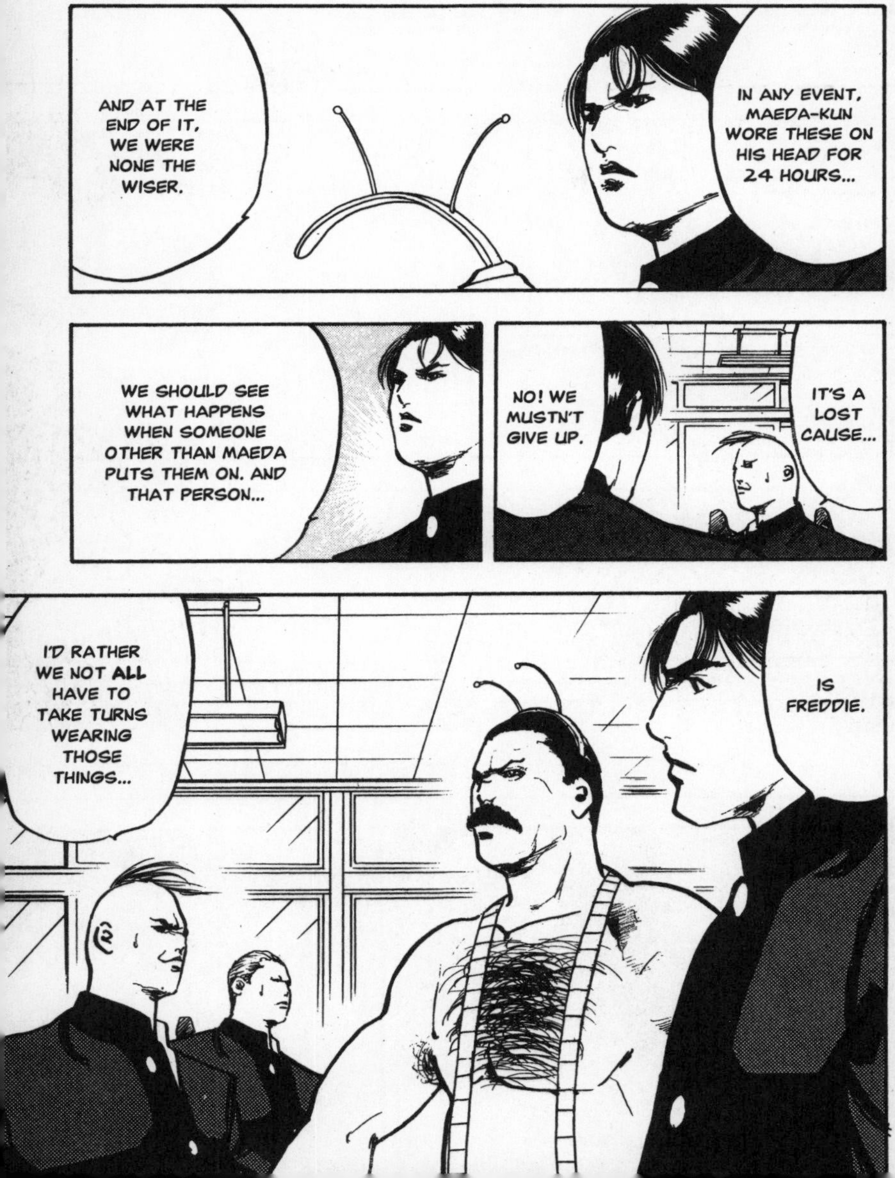
IN ANY EVENT, MAEDA-KUN WORE THESE ON HIS HEAD FOR 24 HOURS...
AND AT THE END OF IT, WE WERE NONE THE WISER.
IT'S A LOST CAUSE...
NO! WE MUSTN'T GIVE UP.
WE SHOULD SEE WHAT HAPPENS WHEN SOMEONE OTHER THAN MAEDA PUTS THEM ON. AND THAT PERSON...
IS FREDDIE.
I'D RATHER WE NOT ALL HAVE TO TAKE TURNS WEARING THOSE THINGS...

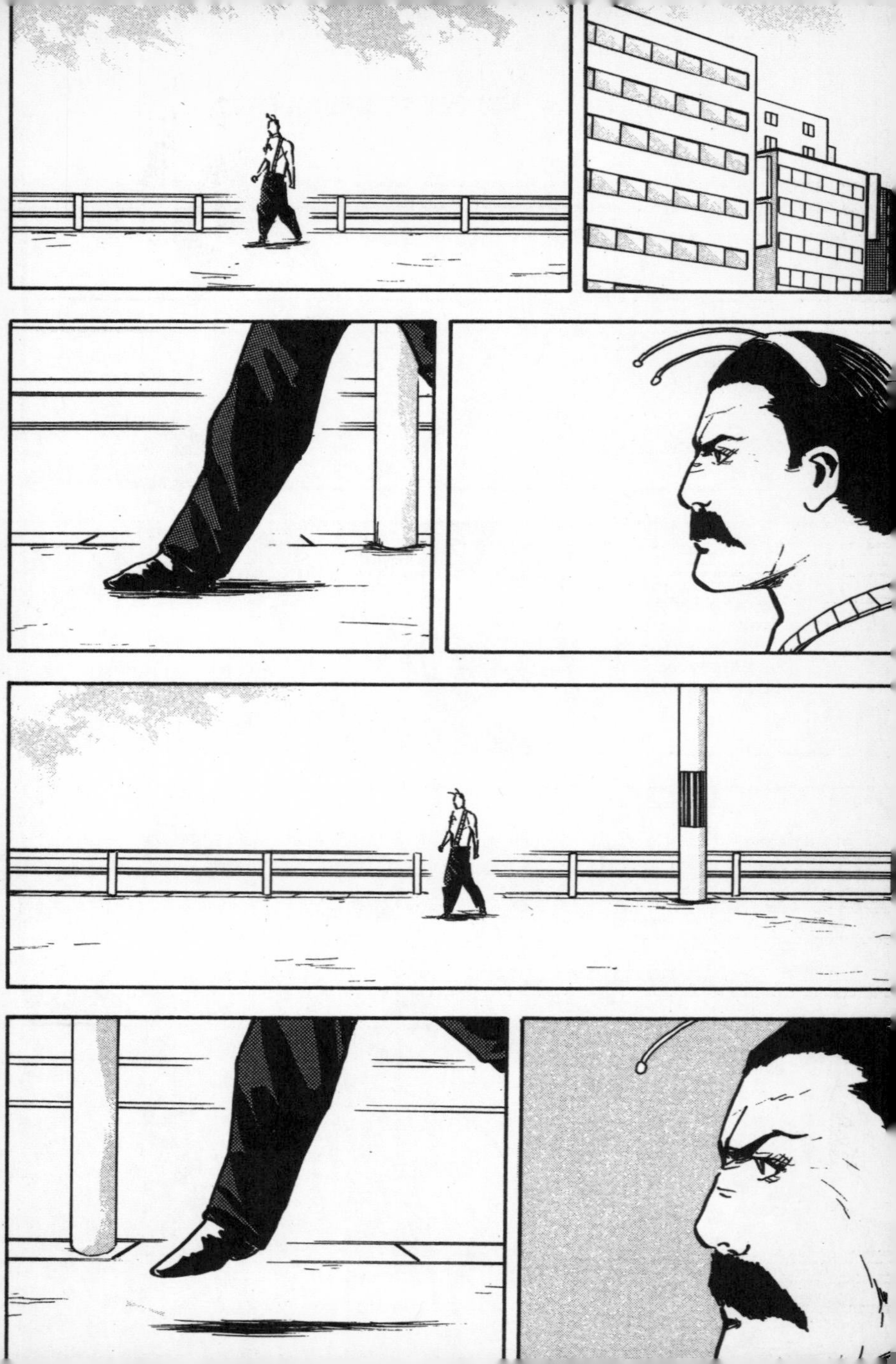

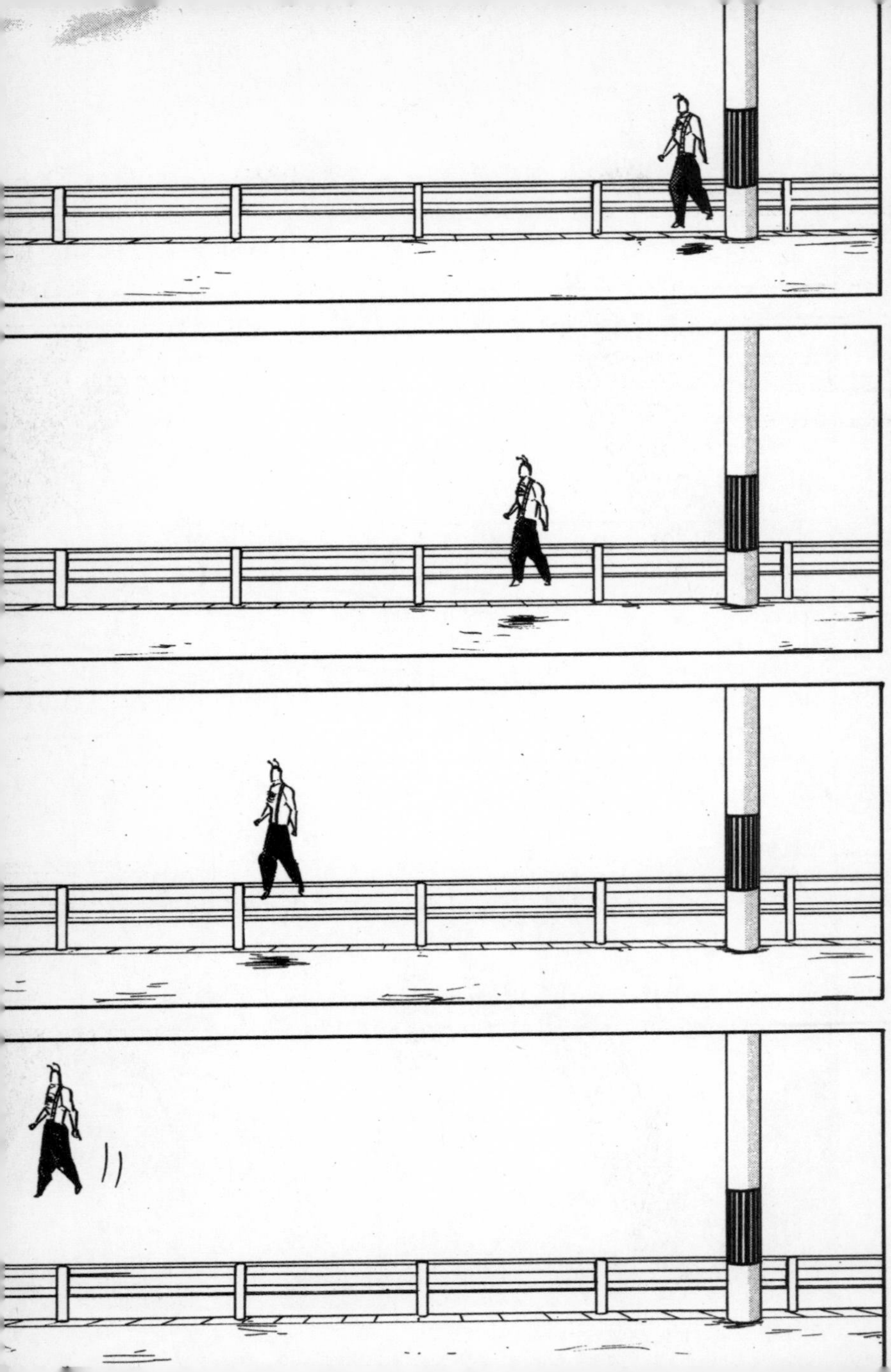

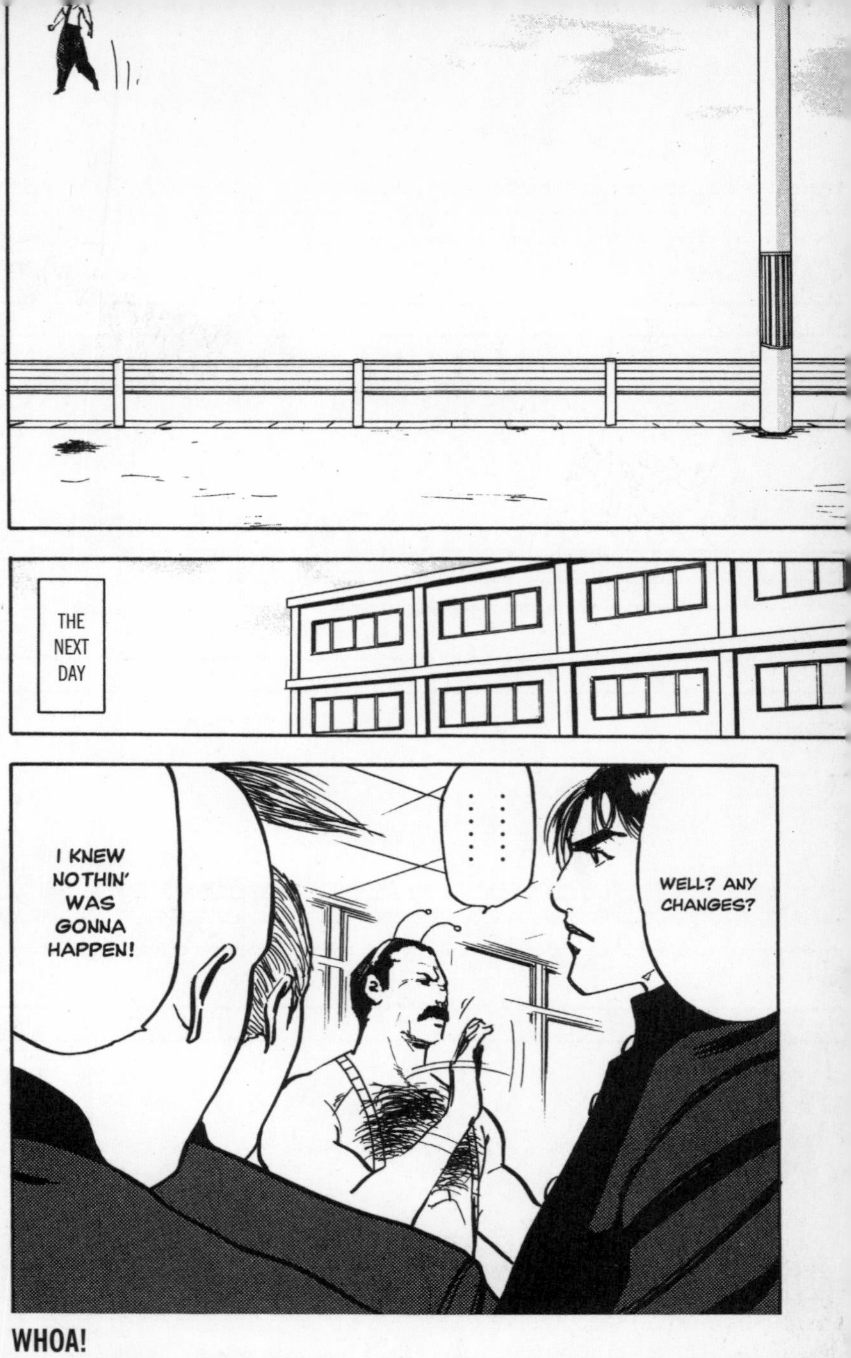
THE NEXT DAY
WELL? ANY CHANGES?
......
I KNEW NOTHIN' WAS GONNA HAPPEN!
WHOA!

CHAPTER 133: **THE LAST TIME**

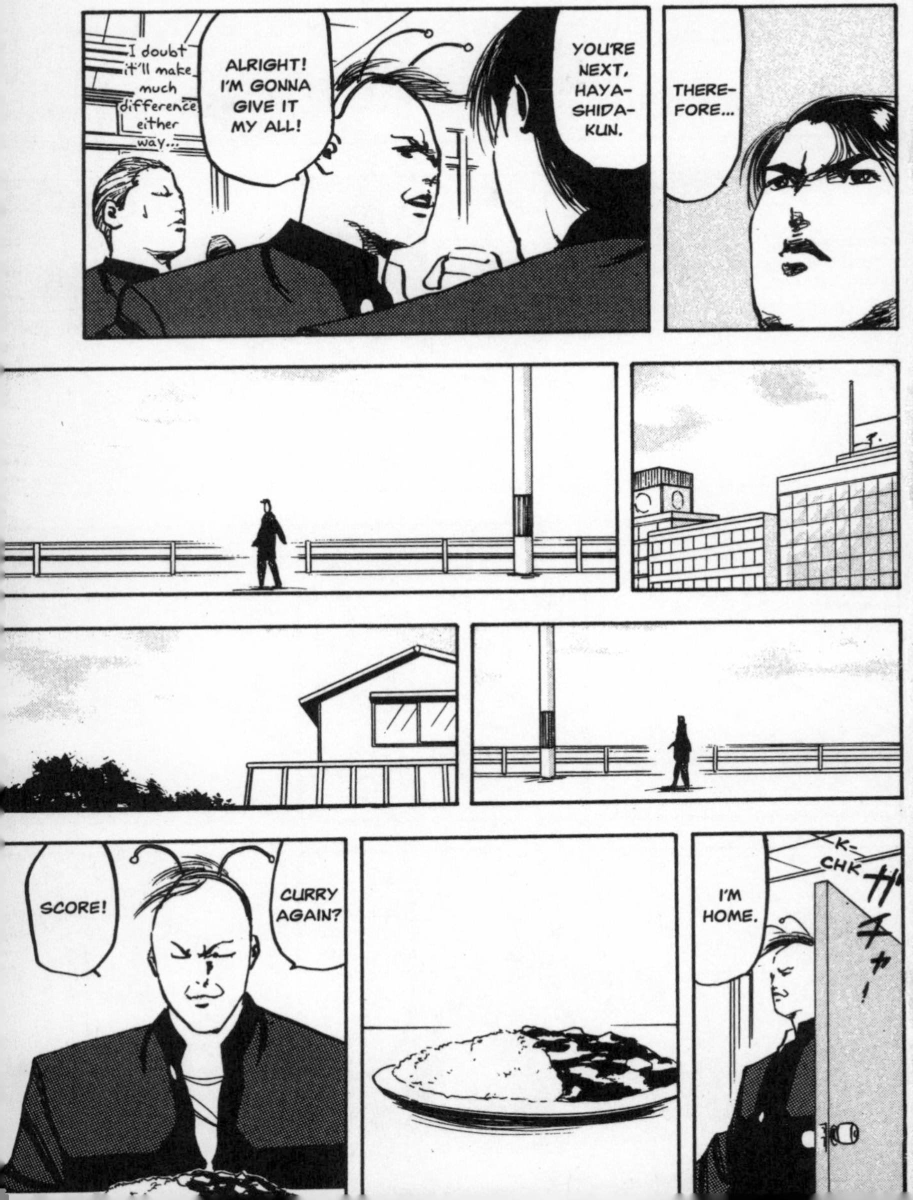
THERE-FORE...
YOU'RE NEXT, HAYA-SHIDA-KUN.
ALRIGHT! I'M GONNA GIVE IT MY ALL!
I doubt it'll make much difference either way...
K-CHK
ガチャ!
I'M HOME.
CURRY AGAIN?
SCORE!

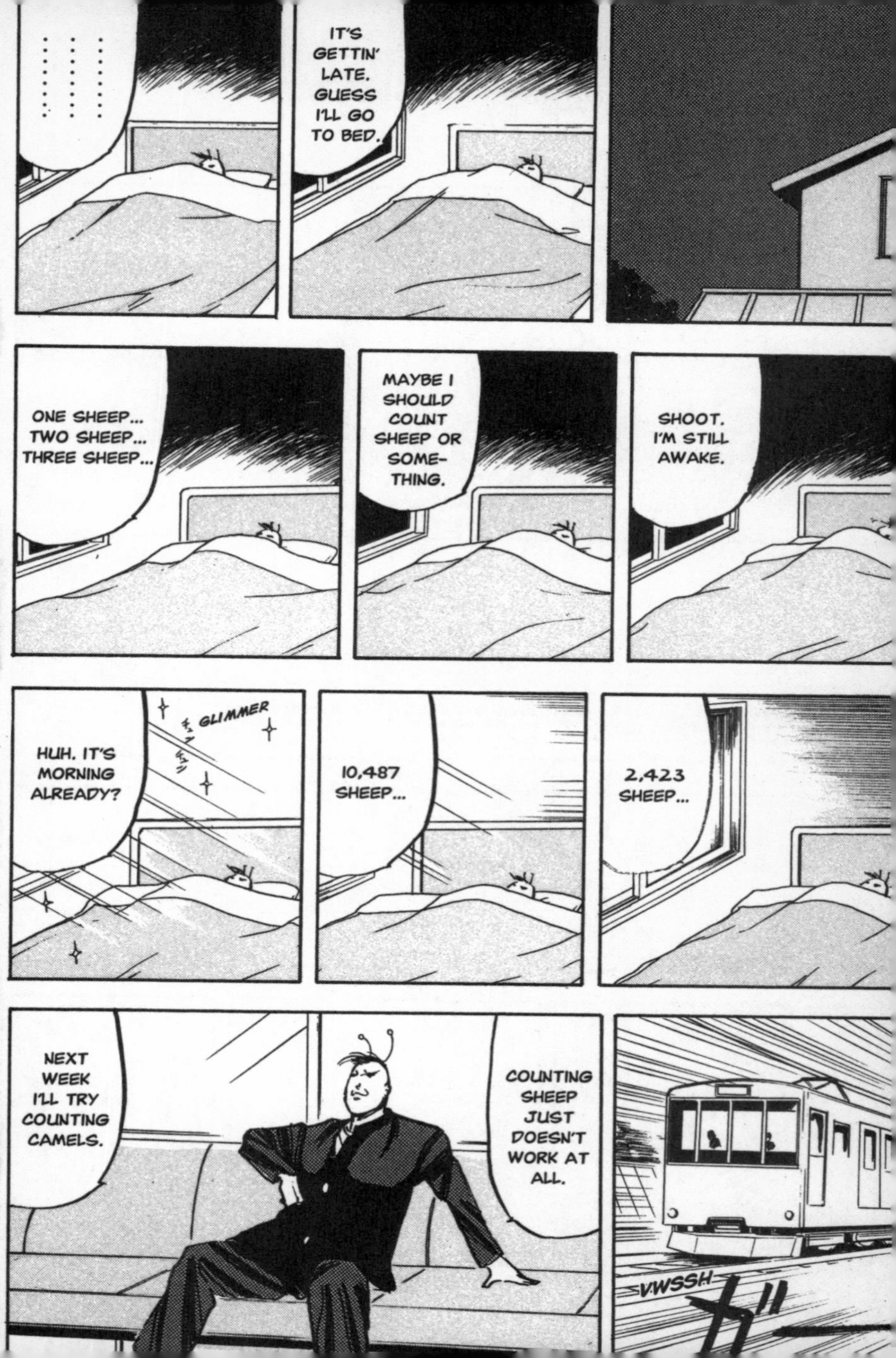
IT'S GETTIN' LATE. GUESS I'LL GO TO BED.
......
SHOOT. I'M STILL AWAKE.
MAYBE I SHOULD COUNT SHEEP OR SOMETHING.
ONE SHEEP... TWO SHEEP... THREE SHEEP...
2,423 SHEEP...
10,487 SHEEP...
GLIMMER
HUH. IT'S MORNING ALREADY?
VWSSH
COUNTING SHEEP JUST DOESN'T WORK AT ALL.
NEXT WEEK I'LL TRY COUNTING CAMELS.

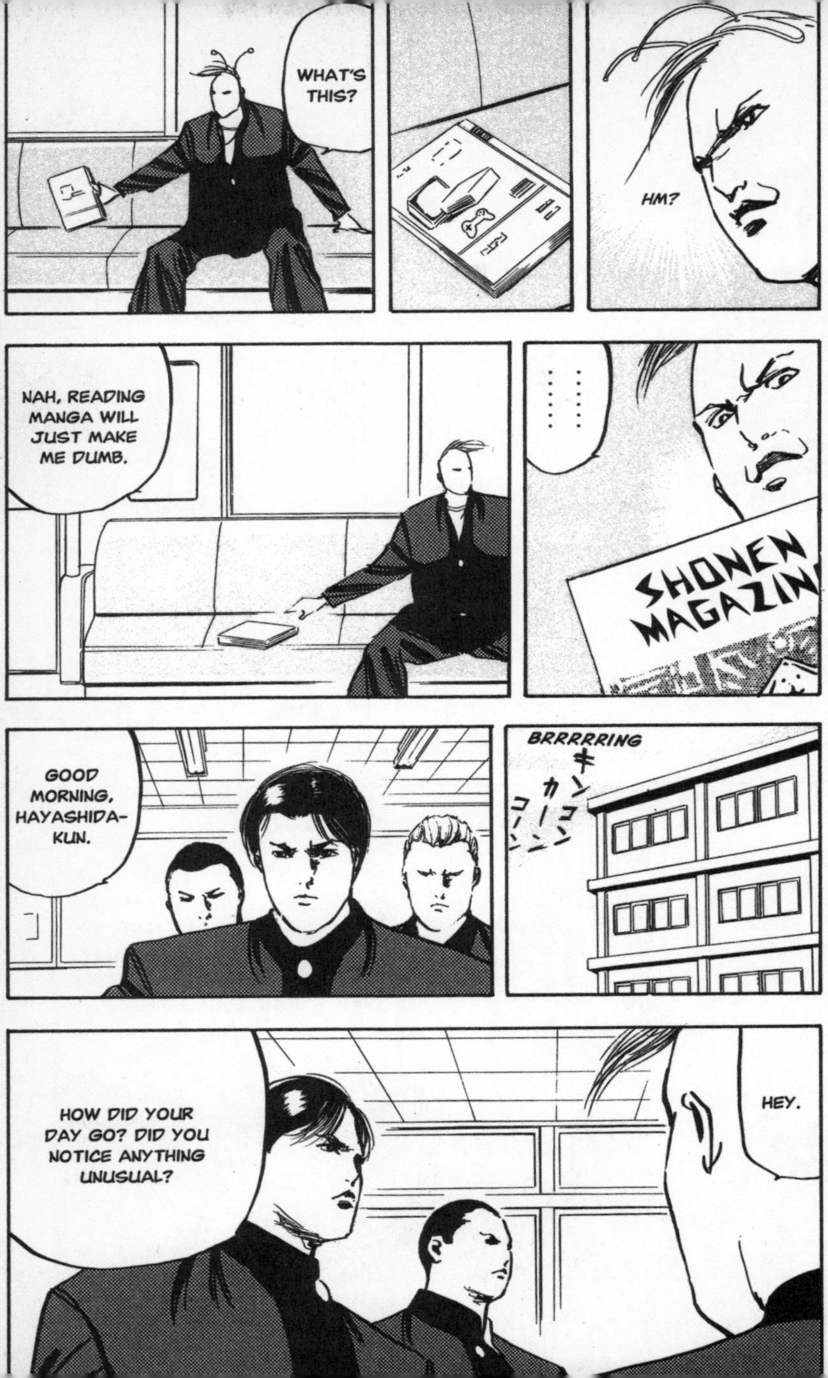
WHAT'S THIS?
HM?
NAH, READING MANGA WILL JUST MAKE ME DUMB.
......
SHONEN MAGAZINE
GOOD MORNING, HAYASHIDA-KUN.
BRRRRRING
HOW DID YOUR DAY GO? DID YOU NOTICE ANYTHING UNUSUAL?
HEY.

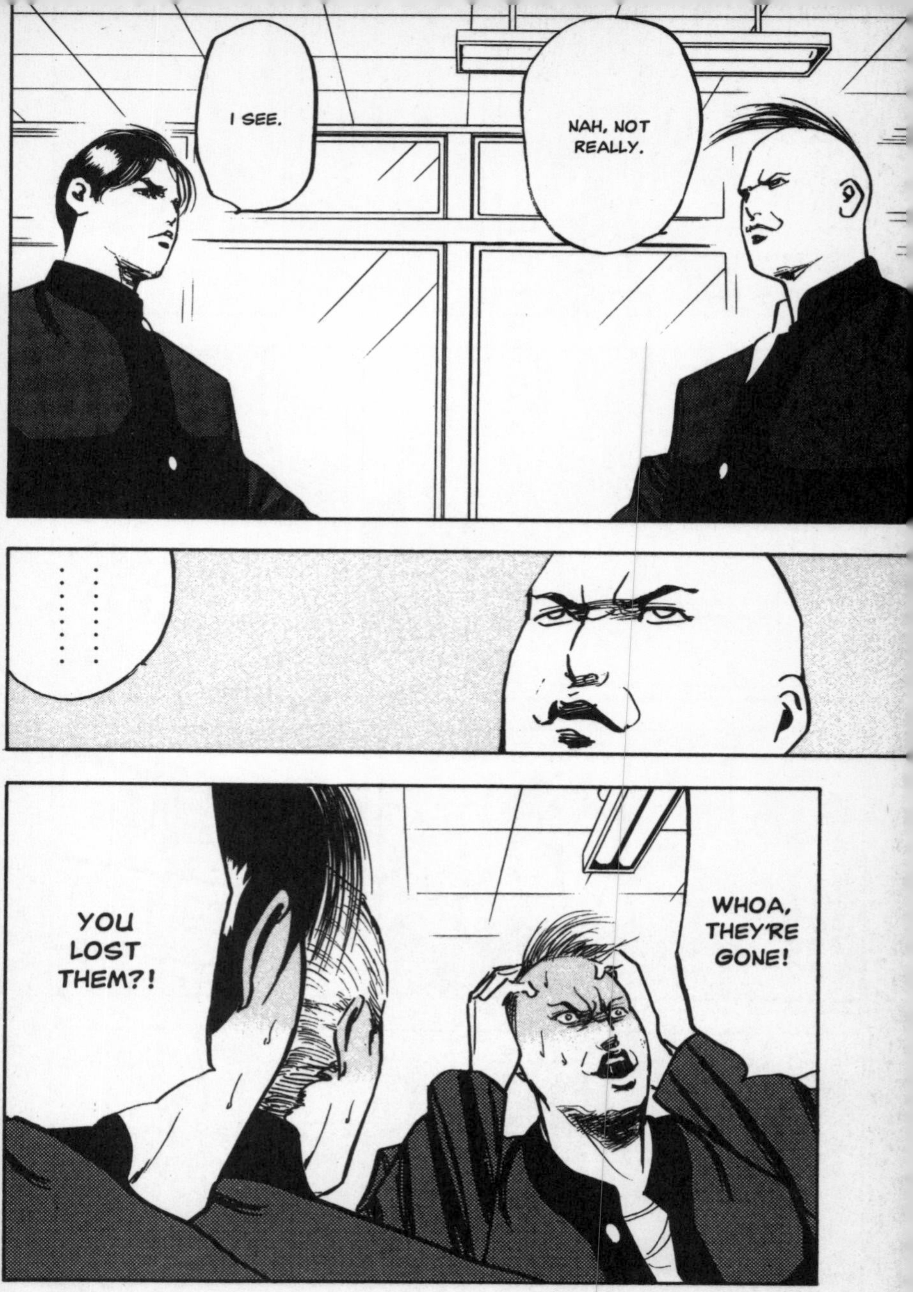
NAH, NOT REALLY.
I SEE.
......
WHOA, THEY'RE GONE!
YOU LOST THEM?!

THEY'RE ON THE TRAIN.

A HAPHAZARD INTRODUCTION TO THE CHARACTERS

SHINICHI MECHAZAWA

Known as "The Fighting Machine of Cromartie," Mechazawa has become the most popular character in this manga. He doesn't appear very often, but it's those unforgettable looks of his that captured the hearts of *Cromartie* readers. Maybe. Yes, hot blood runs through the steel body of this fellow, a manly man who's popular with men and women alike. In this volume, yours truly--in a fit of desperation--put Mechazawa into something of a pickle, but it goes without saying that none of the readers were particularly worried about this.

GORILLAS

These beasts are known as "the animals," 'cuz that's what they are! No need for further explanation. They're primates, and their catchphrase (if you can call it that) is "Ooga?" Even yours truly doesn't know if gorillas really vocalize that way or not--I've never heard one before. (LOL) At one point, there was a whole bunch of them, but they went away. I forget how many I had appear in the story.

MASKED TAKENOUCHI

Known as "the Masked Noble of the Heisei Era," Masked Takenouchi has become a familiar face in this manga, and readers seem unfazed by a mask-wearing high school student. That being said, having a student who wears a mask with his school uniform is enough to no longer qualify this as a joke-driven manga. Aah, what a headache.

A HAPHAZARD INTRODUCTION TO THE CHARACTERS

NOBORU YAMAGUCHI

Leader of Destrade High's 1st years, Yamaguchi is known as "the Greatest of the Joke Submitters." Actually, no one is aware that this gang boss so diligently submits jokes to late-night radio programs, so he is never called this. Yamaguchi previously thought *Pootan* was insipid and was enraged by its popularity, but he has since become a convert. Ishikawa no longer gets his ass kicked when he says that *Pootan* is "awesome" or that he's "a *Pootan* fan."

MECHAZAWA BETA

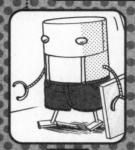

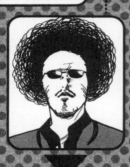

Known as "the lightest lightweight in the business," Beta is Mechazawa's little brother. He is quite small and tends to get broken (and repaired) quite often. Beta is a precocious child who looks oh-so-cute in his suspenders. As Mechazawa's younger brother, you'd think that he'd be a newer model with more and superior functionality...but unlike his big brother, he can't even carry on a conversation. In fact, the only word he can say is "Mekalatta," which he repeats over and over. I wonder if this even counts as joke-worthy material. (LOL)

CHAPTER 134: **LOVE BITES**

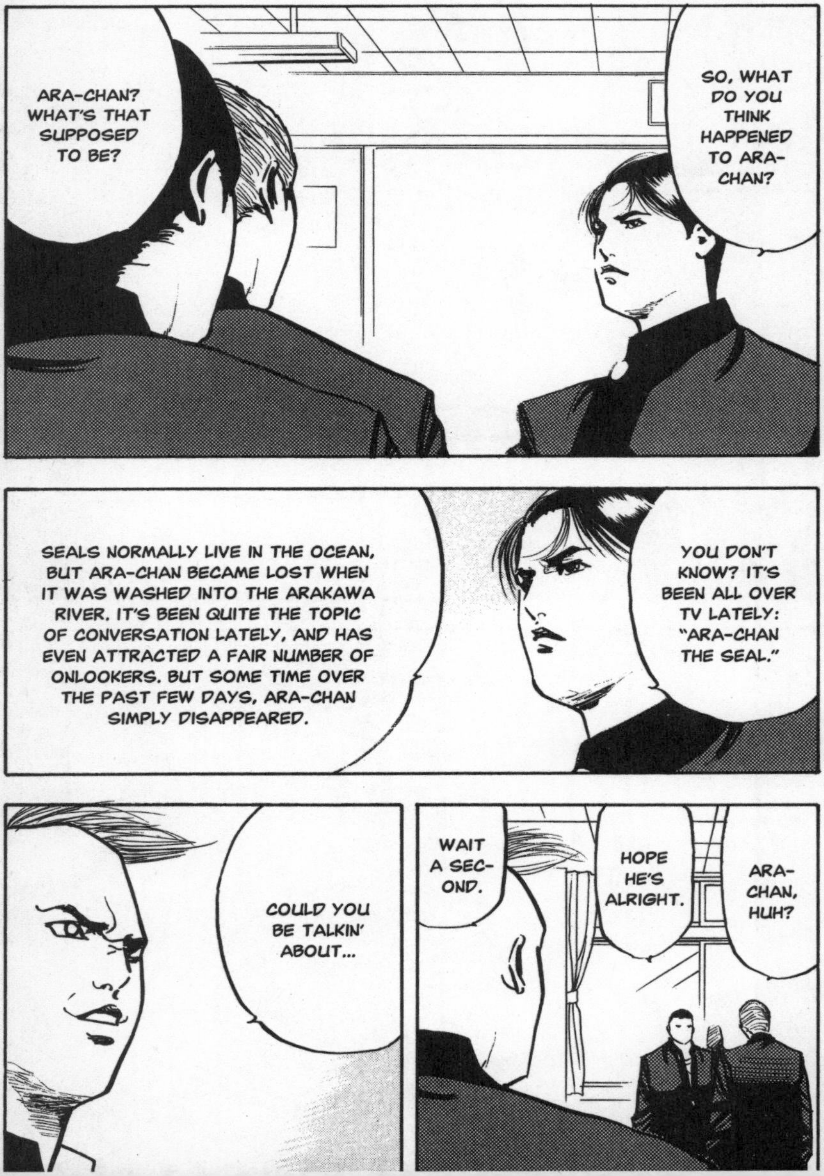
SO, WHAT DO YOU THINK HAPPENED TO ARA-CHAN?
ARA-CHAN? WHAT'S THAT SUPPOSED TO BE?
YOU DON'T KNOW? IT'S BEEN ALL OVER TV LATELY: "ARA-CHAN THE SEAL."
SEALS NORMALLY LIVE IN THE OCEAN, BUT ARA-CHAN BECAME LOST WHEN IT WAS WASHED INTO THE ARAKAWA RIVER. IT'S BEEN QUITE THE TOPIC OF CONVERSATION LATELY, AND HAS EVEN ATTRACTED A FAIR NUMBER OF ONLOOKERS. BUT SOME TIME OVER THE PAST FEW DAYS, ARA-CHAN SIMPLY DISAPPEARED.
ARA-CHAN, HUH?
HOPE HE'S ALRIGHT.
WAIT A SECOND.
COULD YOU BE TALKIN' ABOUT...

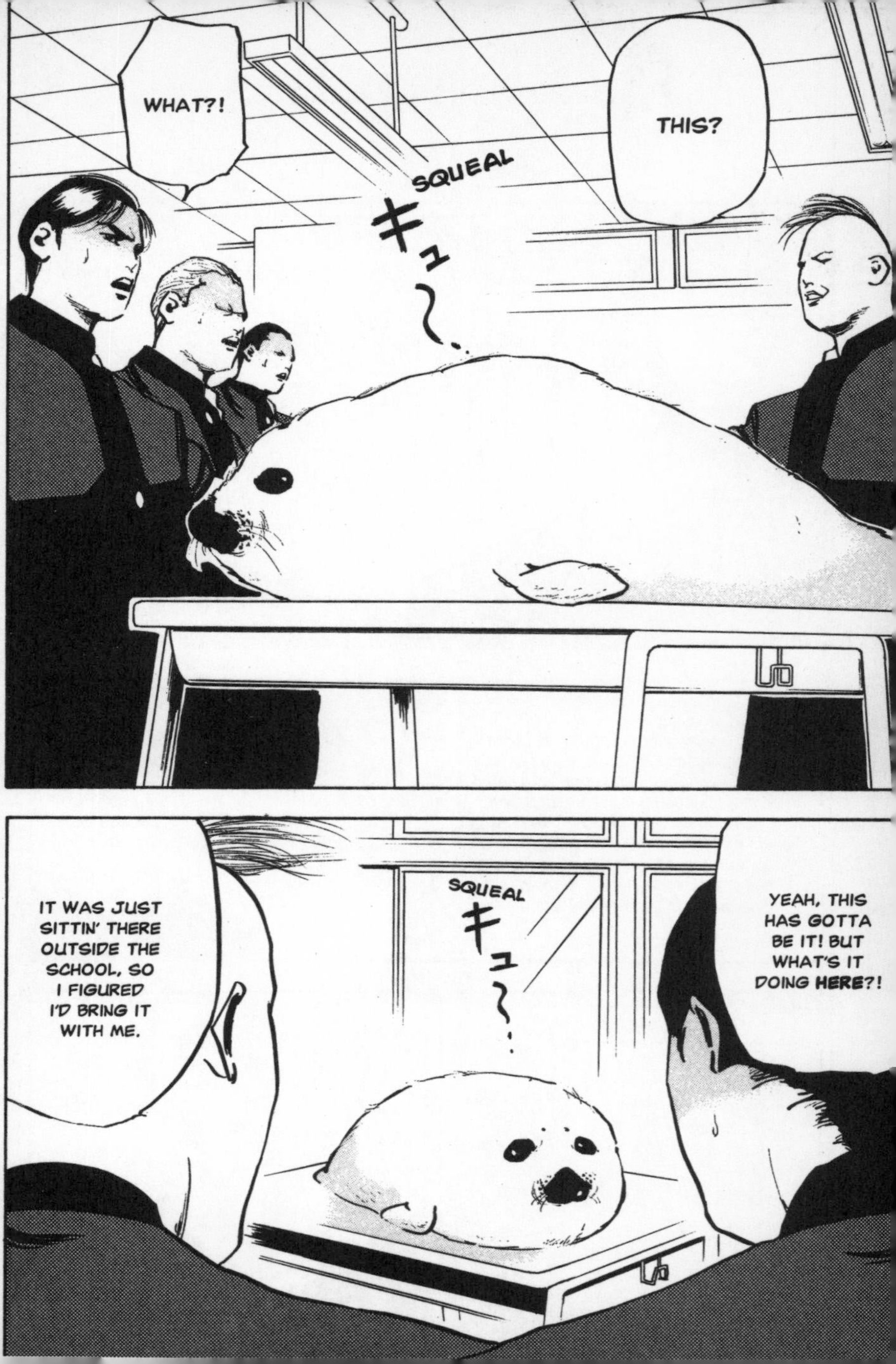
THIS?
WHAT?!
SQUEAL
キュ〜
YEAH, THIS HAS GOTTA BE IT! BUT WHAT'S IT DOING **HERE**?!
SQUEAL
キュ〜
IT WAS JUST SITTIN' THERE OUTSIDE THE SCHOOL, SO I FIGURED I'D BRING IT WITH ME.

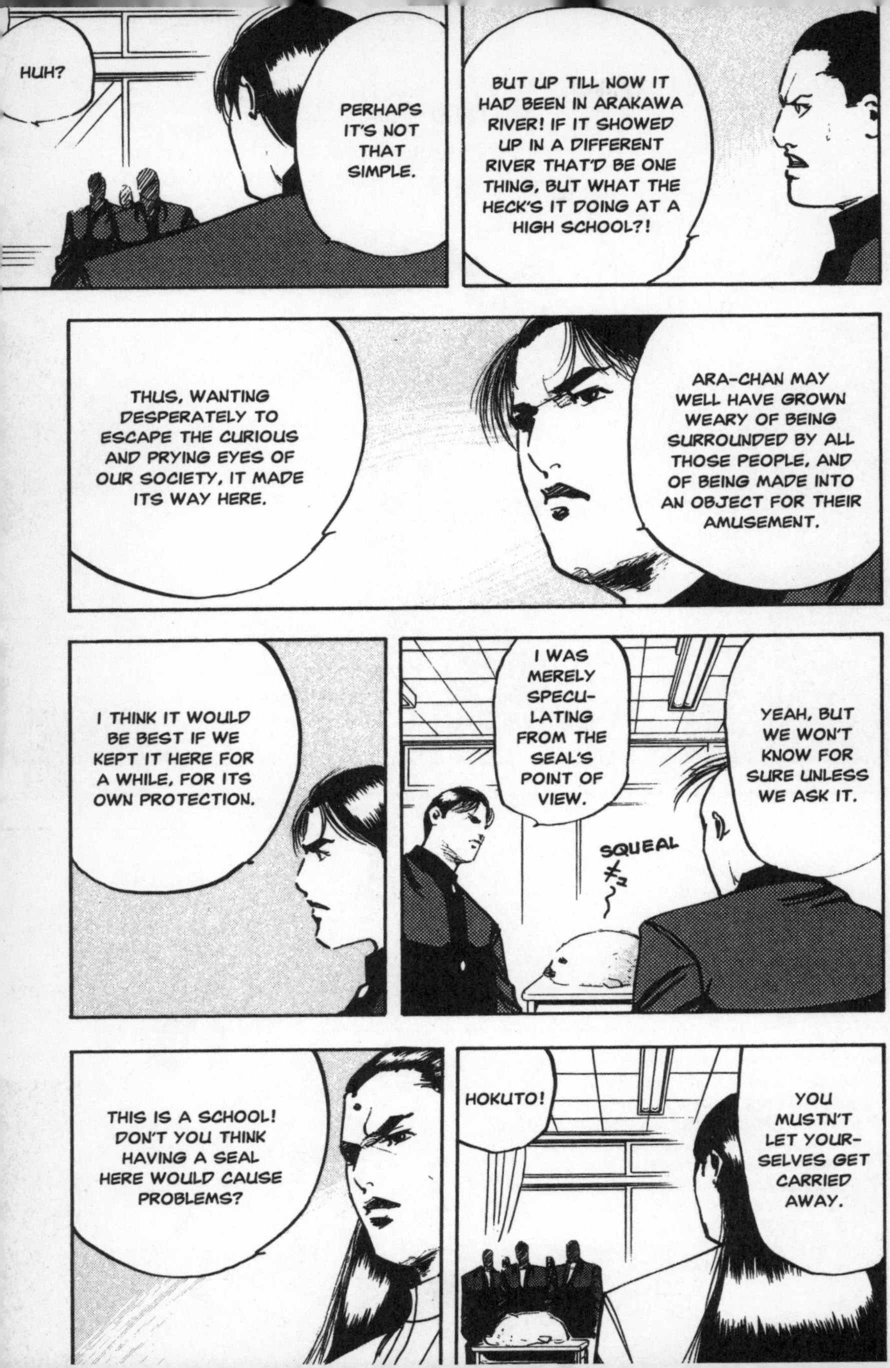
BUT UP TILL NOW IT HAD BEEN IN ARAKAWA RIVER! IF IT SHOWED UP IN A DIFFERENT RIVER THAT'D BE ONE THING, BUT WHAT THE HECK'S IT DOING AT A HIGH SCHOOL?!
PERHAPS IT'S NOT THAT SIMPLE.
HUH?
ARA-CHAN MAY WELL HAVE GROWN WEARY OF BEING SURROUNDED BY ALL THOSE PEOPLE, AND OF BEING MADE INTO AN OBJECT FOR THEIR AMUSEMENT.
THUS, WANTING DESPERATELY TO ESCAPE THE CURIOUS AND PRYING EYES OF OUR SOCIETY, IT MADE ITS WAY HERE.
YEAH, BUT WE WON'T KNOW FOR SURE UNLESS WE ASK IT.
I WAS MERELY SPECU-LATING FROM THE SEAL'S POINT OF VIEW.
SQUEAL
I THINK IT WOULD BE BEST IF WE KEPT IT HERE FOR A WHILE, FOR ITS OWN PROTECTION.
YOU MUSTN'T LET YOUR-SELVES GET CARRIED AWAY.
HOKUTO!
THIS IS A SCHOOL! DON'T YOU THINK HAVING A SEAL HERE WOULD CAUSE PROBLEMS?

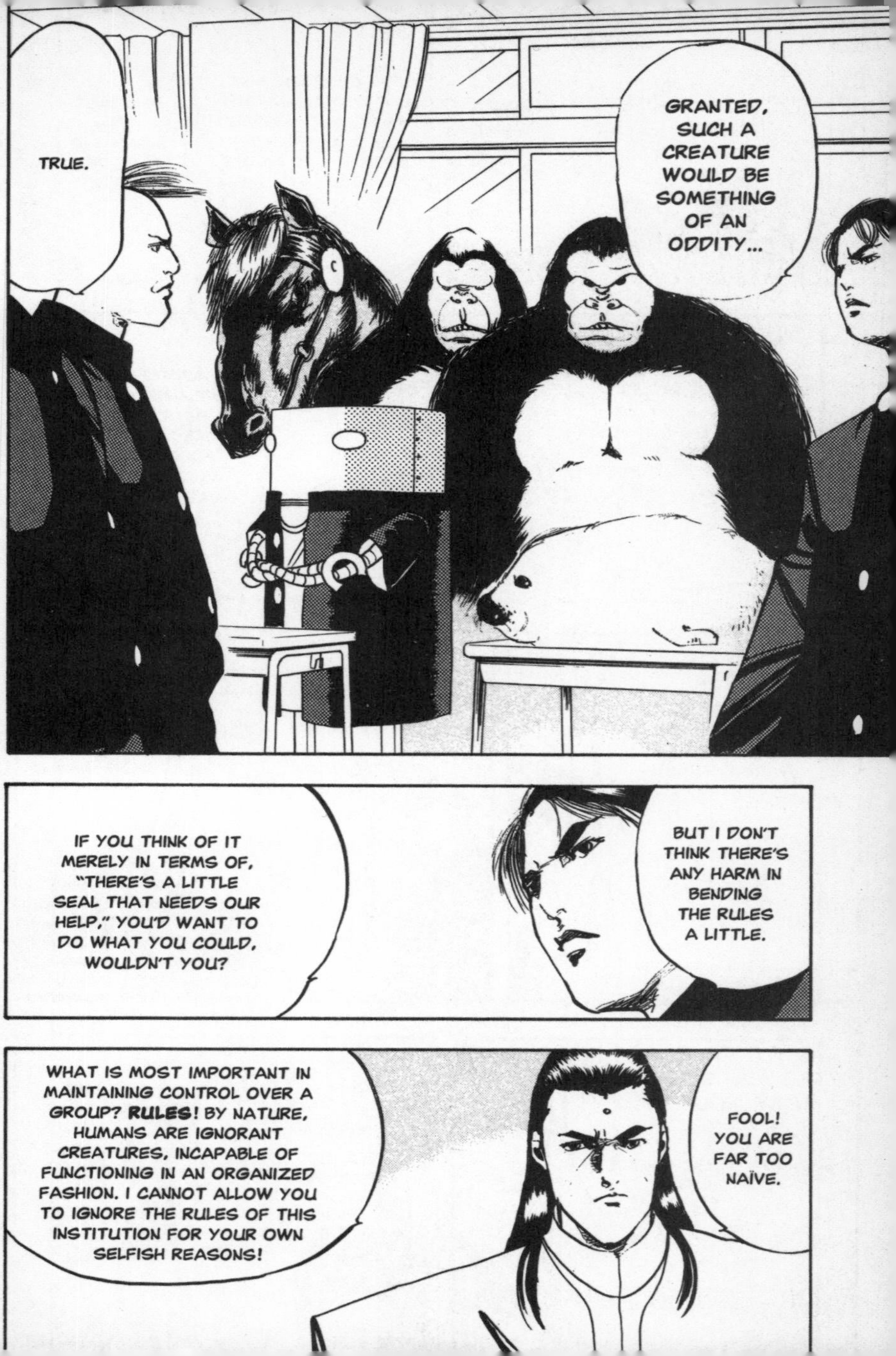

TRUE.
GRANTED, SUCH A CREATURE WOULD BE SOMETHING OF AN ODDITY...
BUT I DON'T THINK THERE'S ANY HARM IN BENDING THE RULES A LITTLE.
IF YOU THINK OF IT MERELY IN TERMS OF, "THERE'S A LITTLE SEAL THAT NEEDS OUR HELP," YOU'D WANT TO DO WHAT YOU COULD, WOULDN'T YOU?
FOOL! YOU ARE FAR TOO NAÏVE.
WHAT IS MOST IMPORTANT IN MAINTAINING CONTROL OVER A GROUP? **RULES**! BY NATURE, HUMANS ARE IGNORANT CREATURES, INCAPABLE OF FUNCTIONING IN AN ORGANIZED FASHION. I CANNOT ALLOW YOU TO IGNORE THE RULES OF THIS INSTITUTION FOR YOUR OWN SELFISH REASONS!

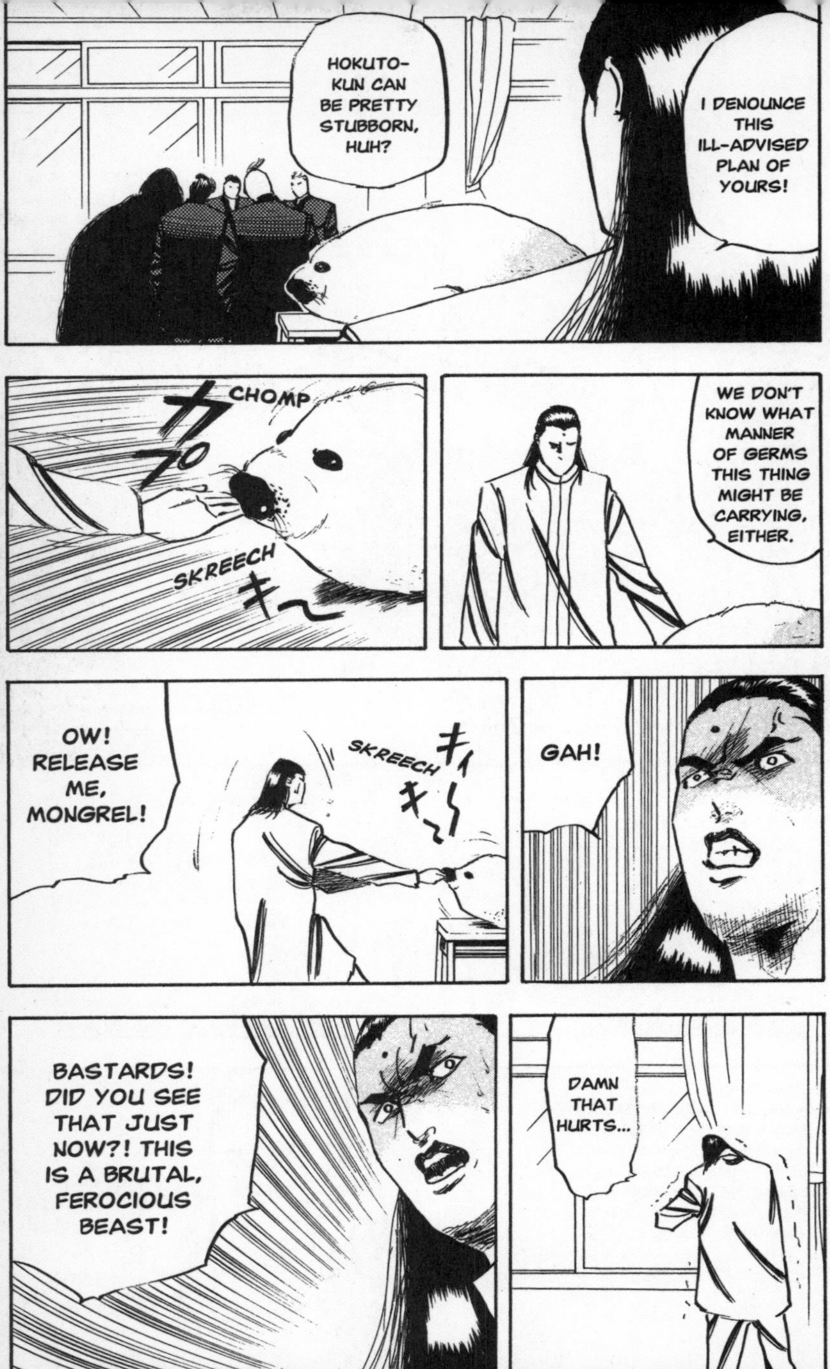

I DENOUNCE THIS ILL-ADVISED PLAN OF YOURS!
HOKUTO-KUN CAN BE PRETTY STUBBORN, HUH?
WE DON'T KNOW WHAT MANNER OF GERMS THIS THING MIGHT BE CARRYING, EITHER.
CHOMP
SKREECH
GAH!
SKREECH
OW! RELEASE ME, MONGREL!
DAMN THAT HURTS...
BASTARDS! DID YOU SEE THAT JUST NOW?! THIS IS A BRUTAL, FEROCIOUS BEAST!

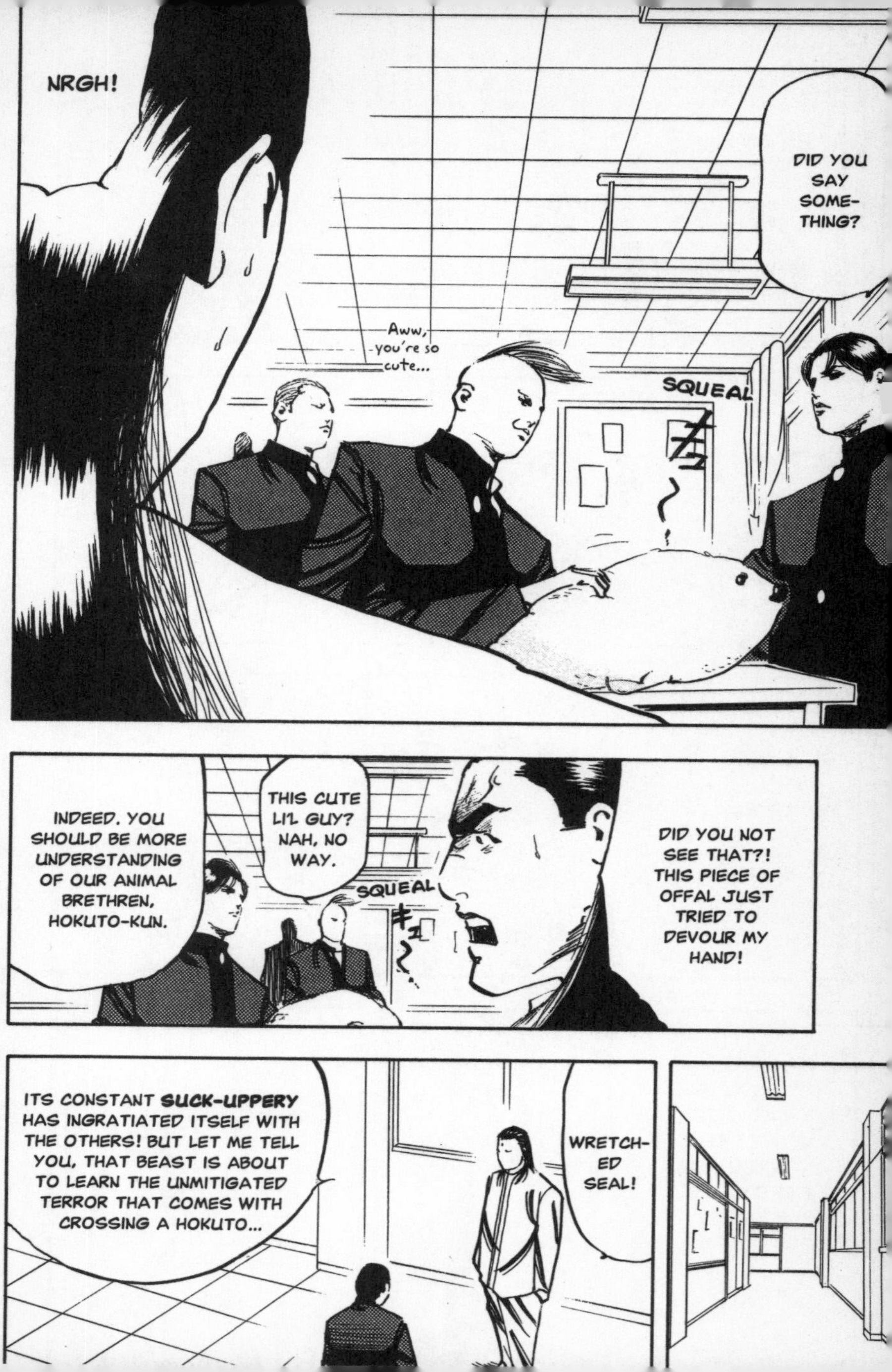
DID YOU SAY SOME-THING?
SQUEAL
Aww, you're so cute...
NRGH!
DID YOU NOT SEE THAT?! THIS PIECE OF OFFAL JUST TRIED TO DEVOUR MY HAND!
SQUEAL
THIS CUTE LI'L GUY? NAH, NO WAY.
INDEED. YOU SHOULD BE MORE UNDERSTANDING OF OUR ANIMAL BRETHREN, HOKUTO-KUN.
WRETCH-ED SEAL!
ITS CONSTANT **SUCK-UPPERY** HAS INGRATIATED ITSELF WITH THE OTHERS! BUT LET ME TELL YOU, THAT BEAST IS ABOUT TO LEARN THE UNMITIGATED TERROR THAT COMES WITH CROSSING A HOKUTO...

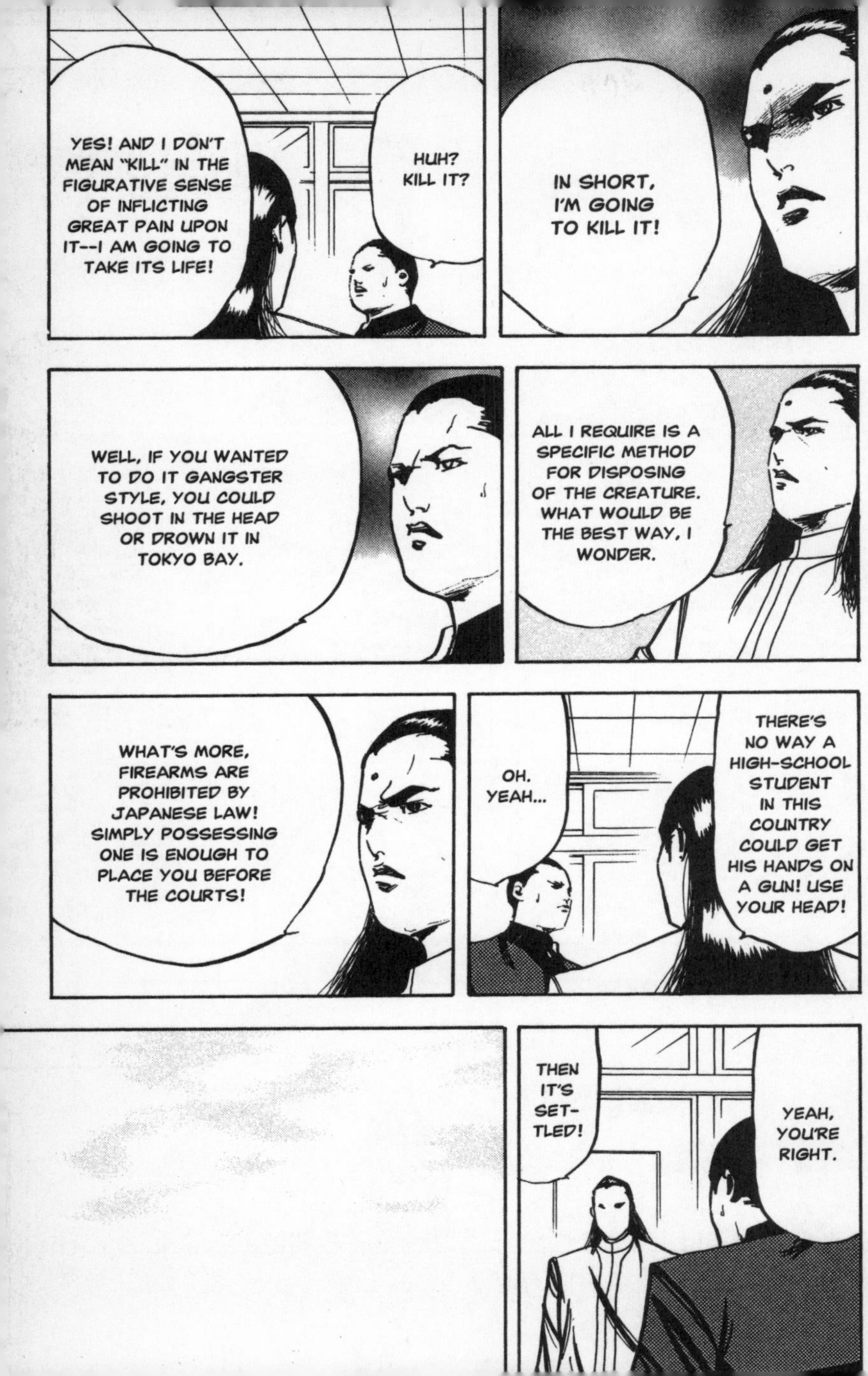
IN SHORT, I'M GOING TO KILL IT!
HUH? KILL IT?
YES! AND I DON'T MEAN "KILL" IN THE FIGURATIVE SENSE OF INFLICTING GREAT PAIN UPON IT--I AM GOING TO TAKE ITS LIFE!
ALL I REQUIRE IS A SPECIFIC METHOD FOR DISPOSING OF THE CREATURE. WHAT WOULD BE THE BEST WAY, I WONDER.
WELL, IF YOU WANTED TO DO IT GANGSTER STYLE, YOU COULD SHOOT IN THE HEAD OR DROWN IT IN TOKYO BAY.
THERE'S NO WAY A HIGH-SCHOOL STUDENT IN THIS COUNTRY COULD GET HIS HANDS ON A GUN! USE YOUR HEAD!
OH. YEAH...
WHAT'S MORE, FIREARMS ARE PROHIBITED BY JAPANESE LAW! SIMPLY POSSESSING ONE IS ENOUGH TO PLACE YOU BEFORE THE COURTS!
YEAH, YOU'RE RIGHT.
THEN IT'S SET-TLED!

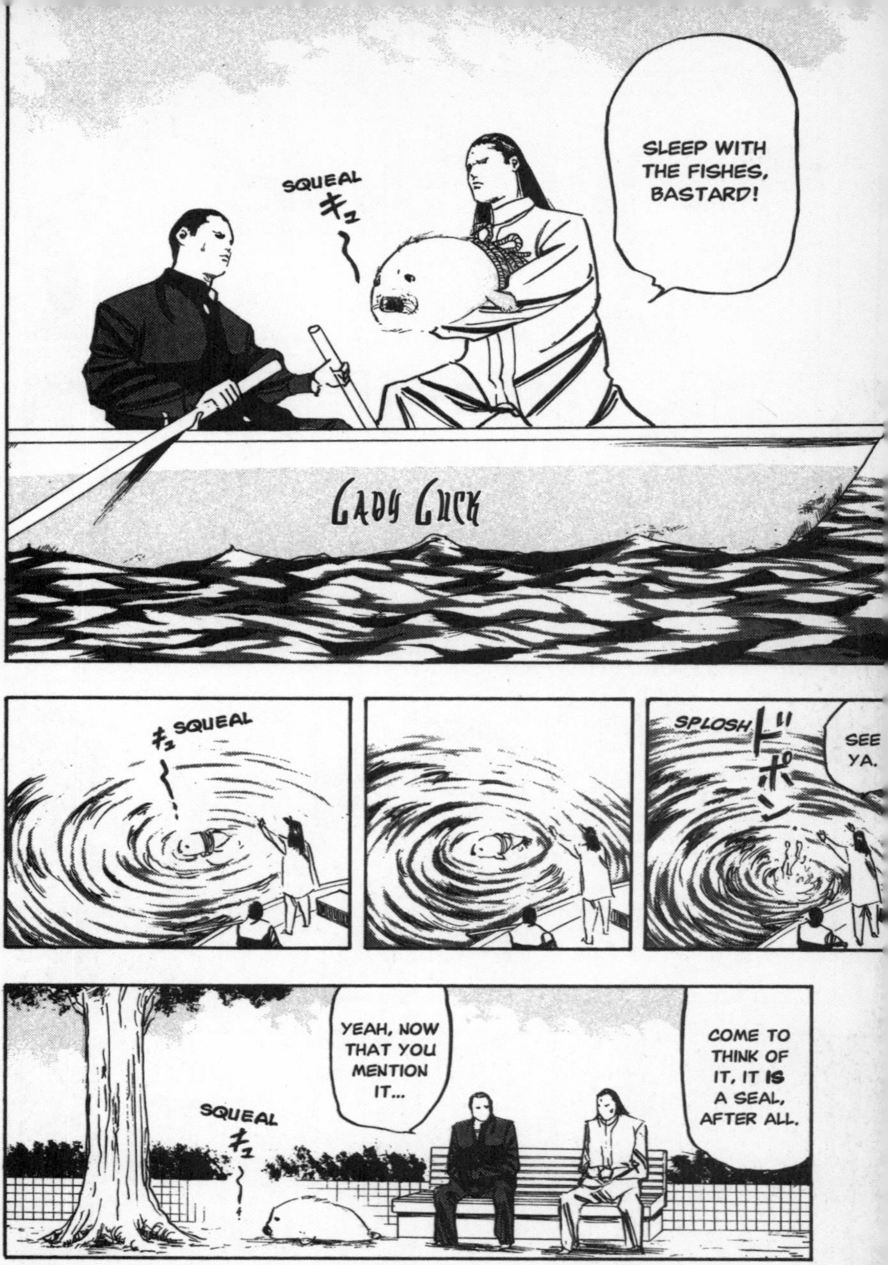
SLEEP WITH THE FISHES, BASTARD!
SQUEAL
キュ
LADY LUCK
SEE YA.
SPLOSH
ドボン
SQUEAL
キュ
COME TO THINK OF IT, IT **IS** A SEAL, AFTER ALL.
YEAH, NOW THAT YOU MENTION IT...
SQUEAL
キュ

IT CAN SWIM.

CHAPTER 135: **PAINT IT BLACK**

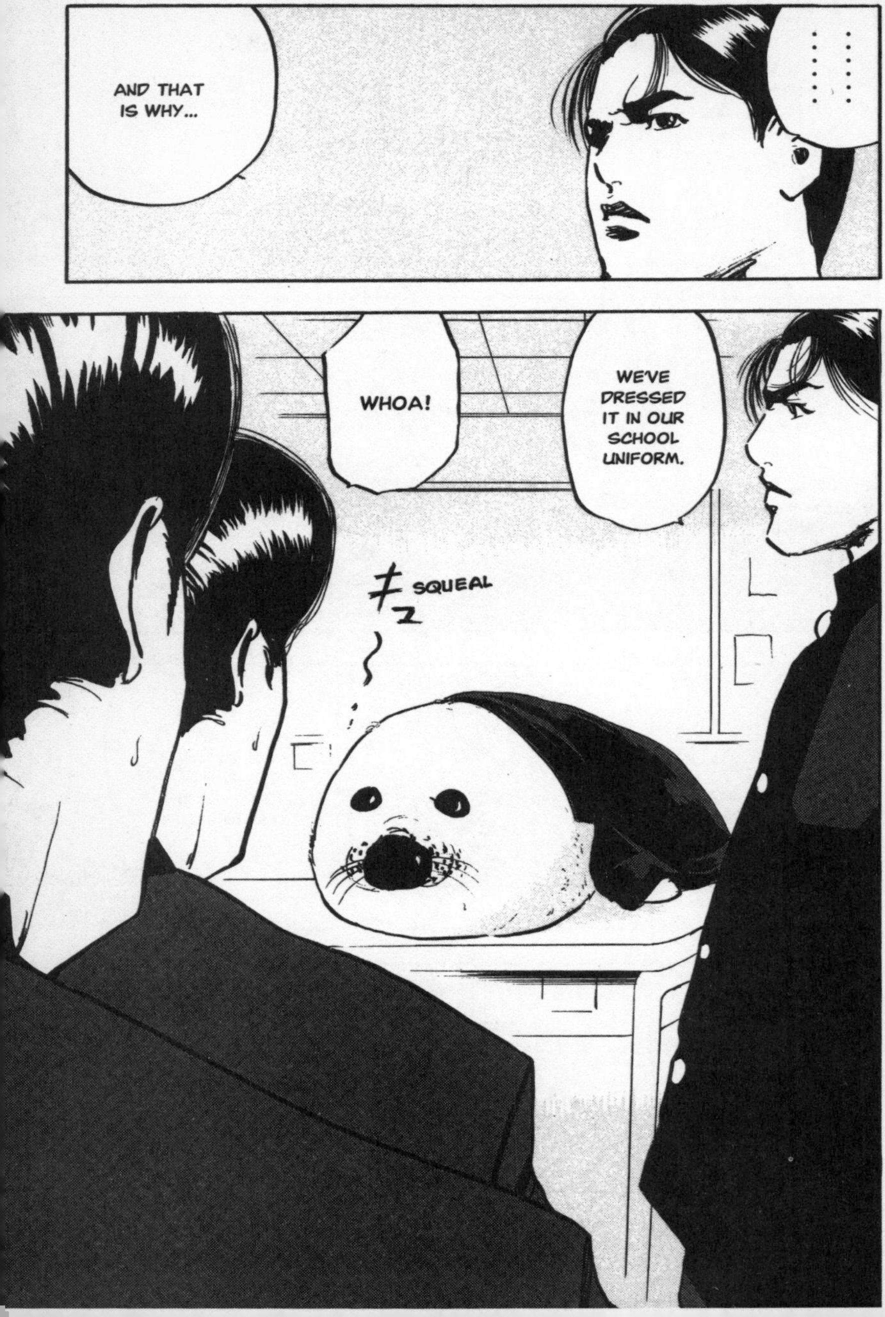
AND THAT IS WHY...
......
WE'VE DRESSED IT IN OUR SCHOOL UNIFORM.
WHOA!
SQUEAL

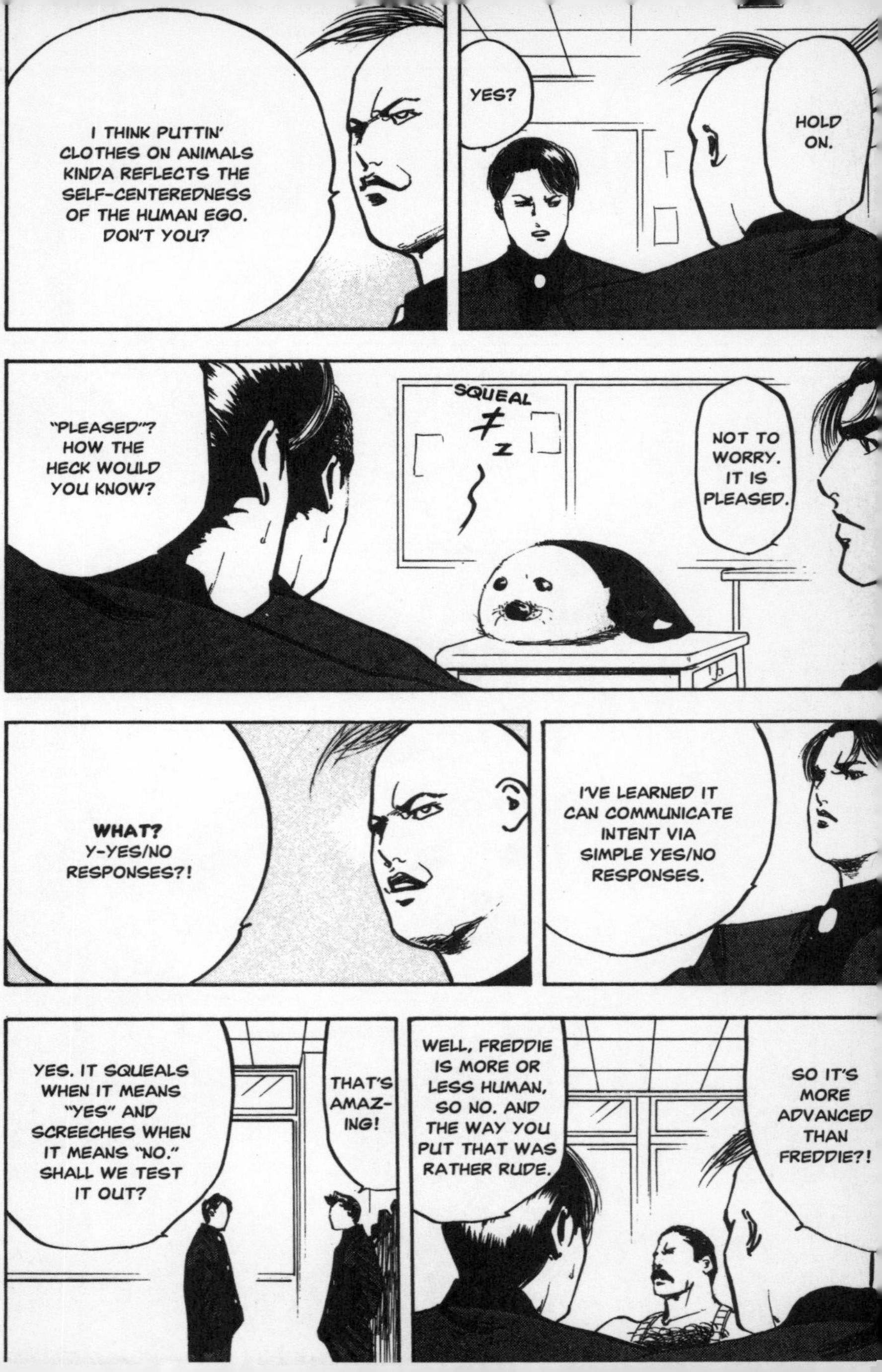
HOLD ON.
YES?
I THINK PUTTIN' CLOTHES ON ANIMALS KINDA REFLECTS THE SELF-CENTEREDNESS OF THE HUMAN EGO. DON'T YOU?
SQUEAL
NOT TO WORRY. IT IS PLEASED.
"PLEASED"? HOW THE HECK WOULD YOU KNOW?
I'VE LEARNED IT CAN COMMUNICATE INTENT VIA SIMPLE YES/NO RESPONSES.
WHAT? Y-YES/NO RESPONSES?!
SO IT'S MORE ADVANCED THAN FREDDIE?!
WELL, FREDDIE IS MORE OR LESS HUMAN, SO NO. AND THE WAY YOU PUT THAT WAS RATHER RUDE.
THAT'S AMAZ-ING!
YES. IT SQUEALS WHEN IT MEANS "YES" AND SCREECHES WHEN IT MEANS "NO." SHALL WE TEST IT OUT?

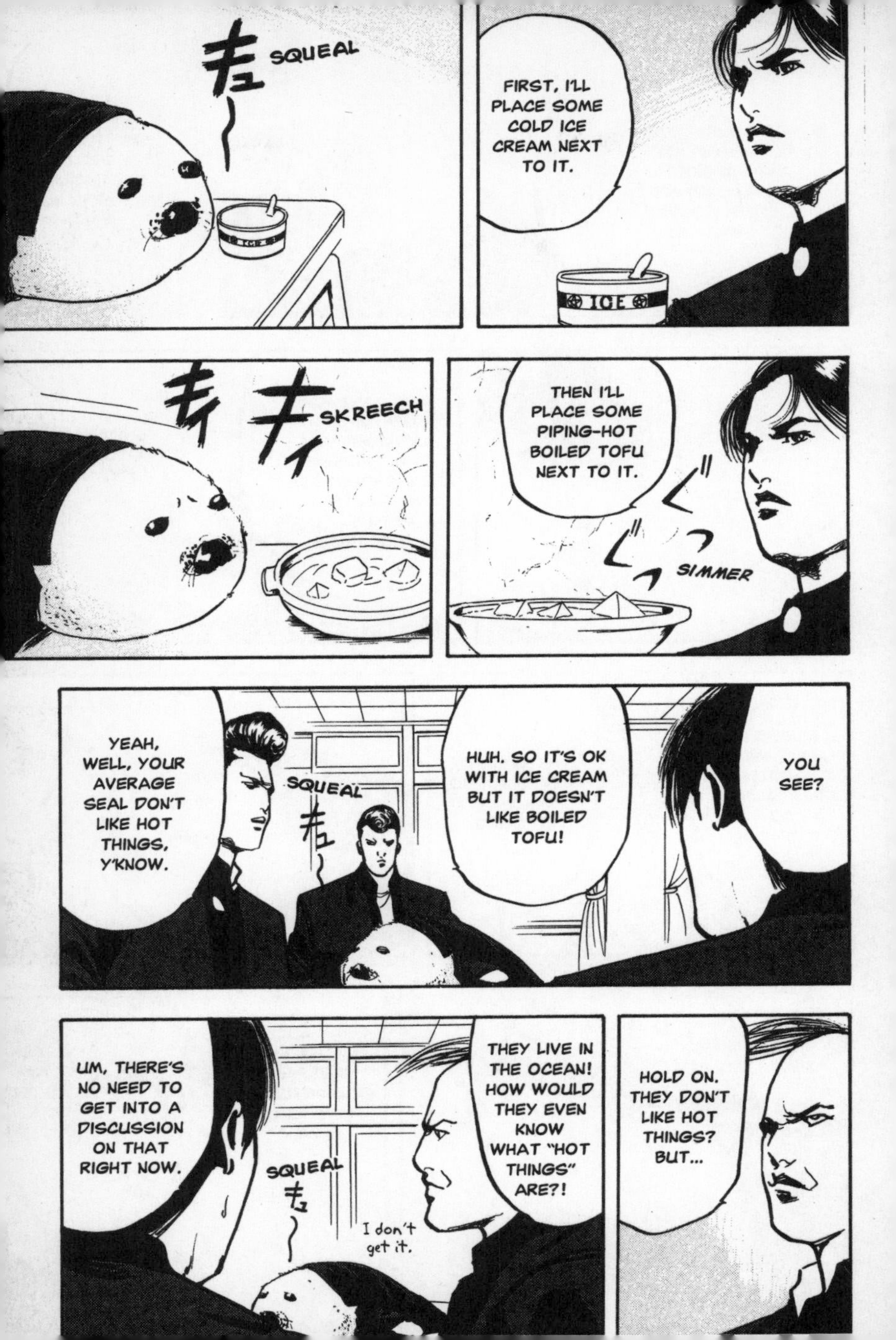
FIRST, I'LL PLACE SOME COLD ICE CREAM NEXT TO IT.
ICE
SQUEAL
THEN I'LL PLACE SOME PIPING-HOT BOILED TOFU NEXT TO IT.
SIMMER
SKREECH
YOU SEE?
HUH. SO IT'S OK WITH ICE CREAM BUT IT DOESN'T LIKE BOILED TOFU!
SQUEAL
YEAH, WELL, YOUR AVERAGE SEAL DON'T LIKE HOT THINGS, Y'KNOW.
HOLD ON. THEY DON'T LIKE HOT THINGS? BUT...
THEY LIVE IN THE OCEAN! HOW WOULD THEY EVEN KNOW WHAT "HOT THINGS" ARE?!
I don't get it.
SQUEAL
UM, THERE'S NO NEED TO GET INTO A DISCUSSION ON THAT RIGHT NOW.

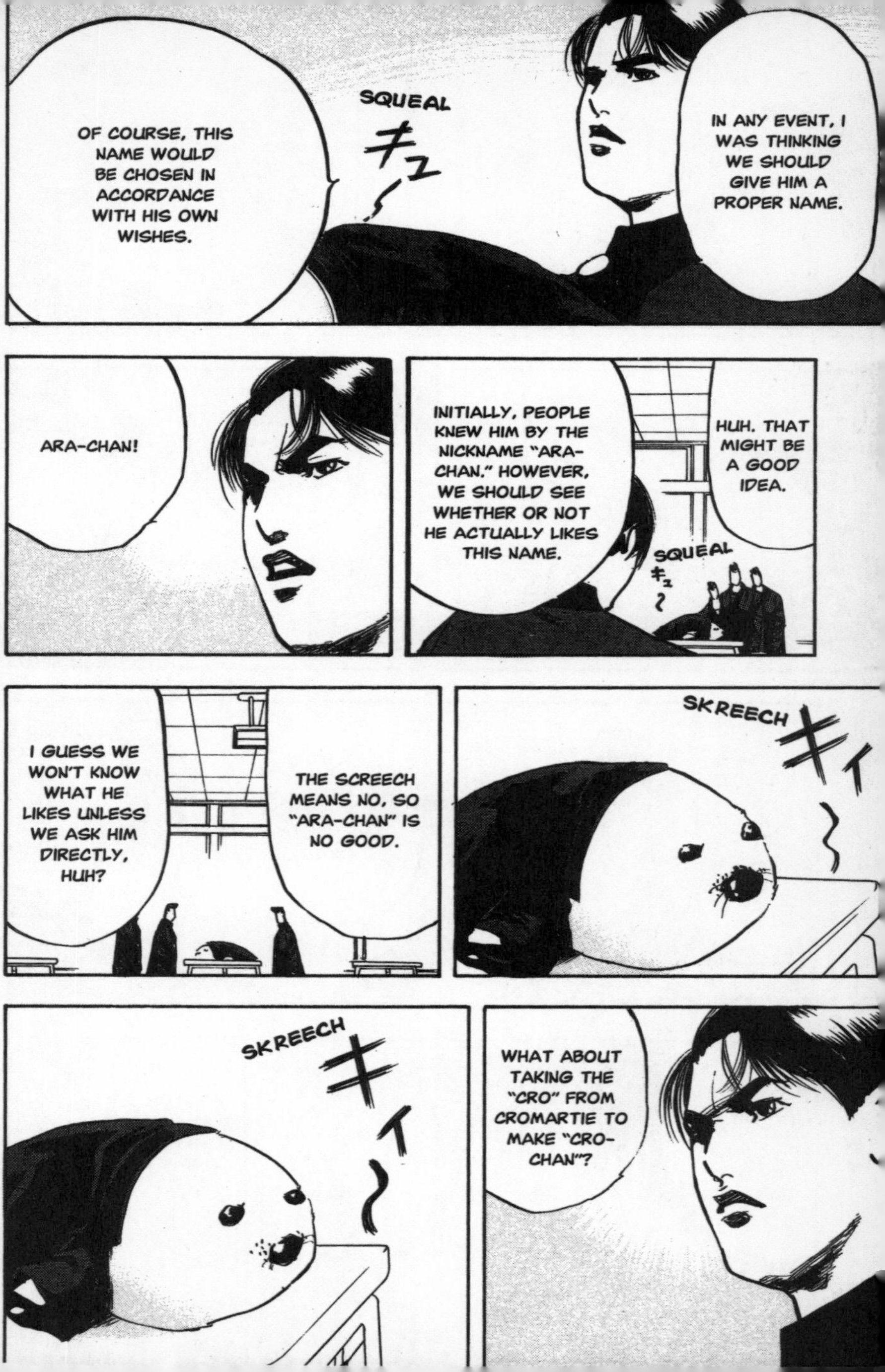
IN ANY EVENT, I WAS THINKING WE SHOULD GIVE HIM A PROPER NAME.
SQUEAL
キュ〜
OF COURSE, THIS NAME WOULD BE CHOSEN IN ACCORDANCE WITH HIS OWN WISHES.
HUH. THAT MIGHT BE A GOOD IDEA.
INITIALLY, PEOPLE KNEW HIM BY THE NICKNAME "ARA-CHAN." HOWEVER, WE SHOULD SEE WHETHER OR NOT HE ACTUALLY LIKES THIS NAME.
SQUEAL
キュ〜
ARA-CHAN!
SKREECH
キイ〜
THE SCREECH MEANS NO, SO "ARA-CHAN" IS NO GOOD.
I GUESS WE WON'T KNOW WHAT HE LIKES UNLESS WE ASK HIM DIRECTLY, HUH?
WHAT ABOUT TAKING THE "CRO" FROM CROMARTIE TO MAKE "CRO-CHAN"?
SKREECH
キイ〜

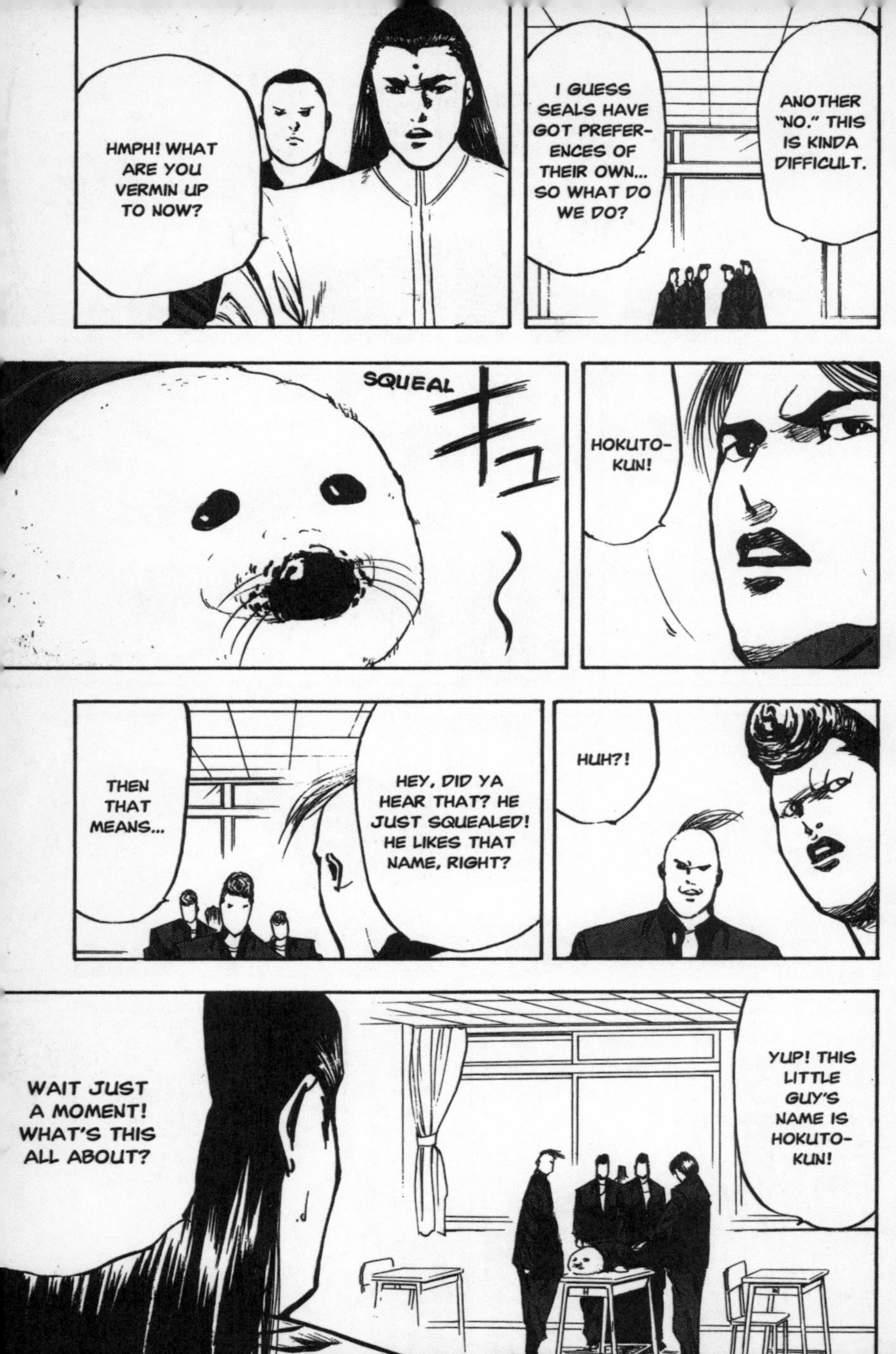
ANOTHER "NO." THIS IS KINDA DIFFICULT.
I GUESS SEALS HAVE GOT PREFERENCES OF THEIR OWN... SO WHAT DO WE DO?
HMPH! WHAT ARE YOU VERMIN UP TO NOW?
HOKUTO-KUN!
SQUEAL
キュ～
HUH?!
HEY, DID YA HEAR THAT? HE JUST SQUEALED! HE LIKES THAT NAME, RIGHT?
THEN THAT MEANS...
YUP! THIS LITTLE GUY'S NAME IS HOKUTO-KUN!
WAIT JUST A MOMENT! WHAT'S THIS ALL ABOUT?

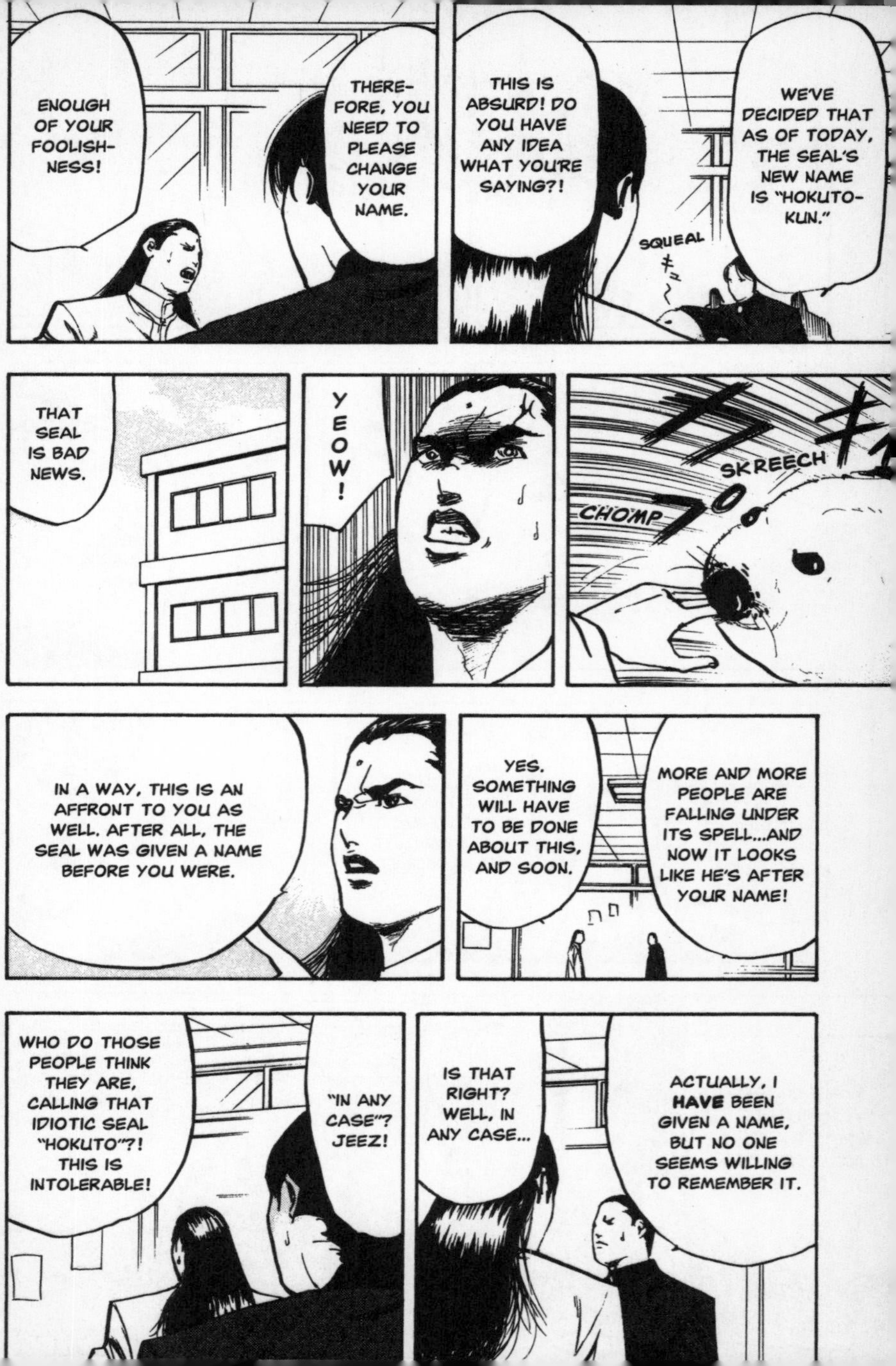

WE'VE DECIDED THAT AS OF TODAY, THE SEAL'S NEW NAME IS "HOKUTO-KUN."
SQUEAL
THIS IS ABSURD! DO YOU HAVE ANY IDEA WHAT YOU'RE SAYING?!
THERE-FORE, YOU NEED TO PLEASE CHANGE YOUR NAME.
ENOUGH OF YOUR FOOLISH-NESS!
SKREECH
CHOMP
YEOW!
THAT SEAL IS BAD NEWS.
MORE AND MORE PEOPLE ARE FALLING UNDER ITS SPELL...AND NOW IT LOOKS LIKE HE'S AFTER YOUR NAME!
YES. SOMETHING WILL HAVE TO BE DONE ABOUT THIS, AND SOON.
IN A WAY, THIS IS AN AFFRONT TO YOU AS WELL. AFTER ALL, THE SEAL WAS GIVEN A NAME BEFORE YOU WERE.
ACTUALLY, I **HAVE** BEEN GIVEN A NAME, BUT NO ONE SEEMS WILLING TO REMEMBER IT.
IS THAT RIGHT? WELL, IN ANY CASE...
"IN ANY CASE"? JEEZ!
WHO DO THOSE PEOPLE THINK THEY ARE, CALLING THAT IDIOTIC SEAL "HOKUTO"?! THIS IS INTOLERABLE!

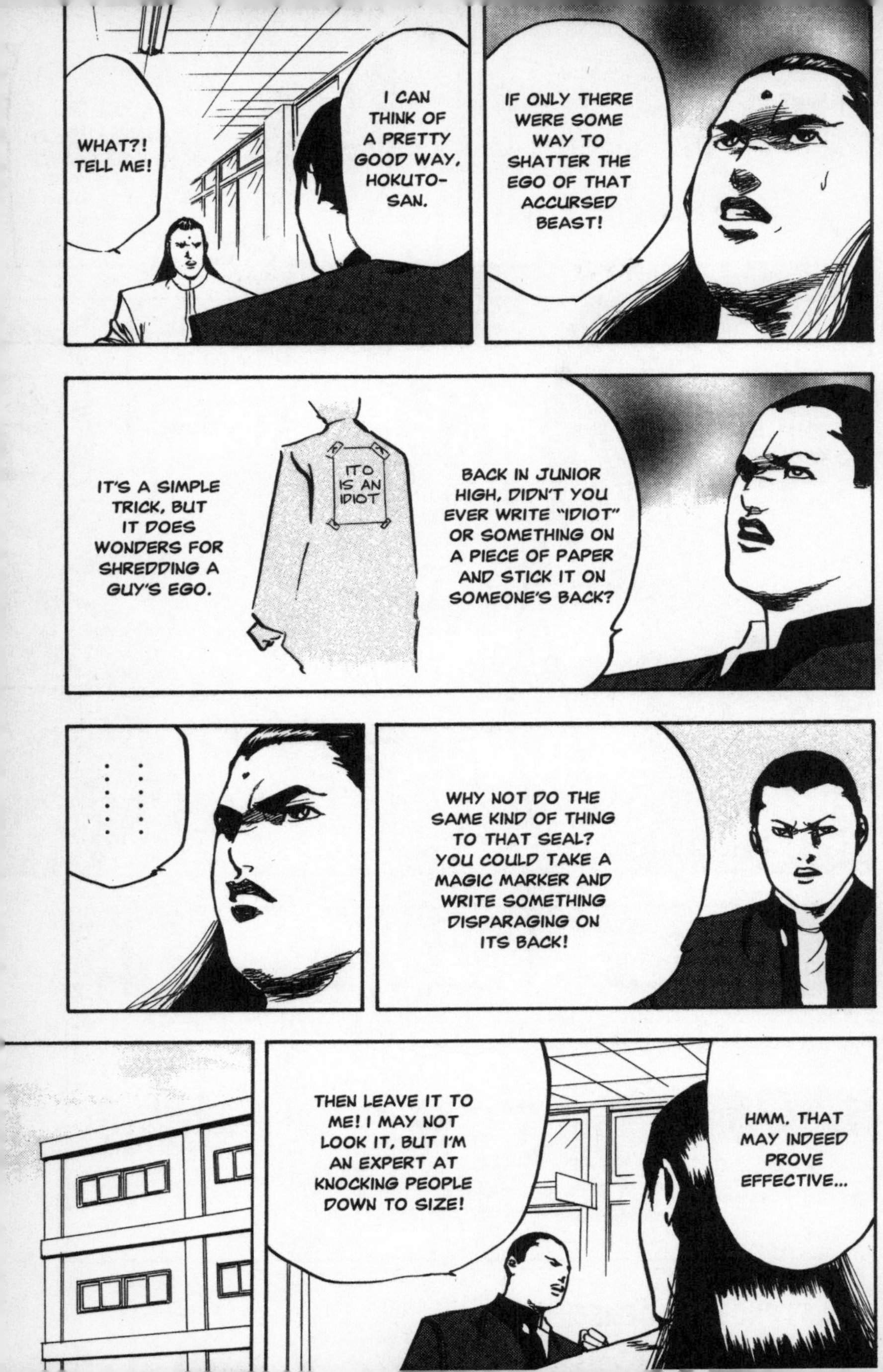
IF ONLY THERE WERE SOME WAY TO SHATTER THE EGO OF THAT ACCURSED BEAST!
I CAN THINK OF A PRETTY GOOD WAY, HOKUTO-SAN.
WHAT?! TELL ME!
BACK IN JUNIOR HIGH, DIDN'T YOU EVER WRITE "IDIOT" OR SOMETHING ON A PIECE OF PAPER AND STICK IT ON SOMEONE'S BACK?
ITO IS AN IDIOT
IT'S A SIMPLE TRICK, BUT IT DOES WONDERS FOR SHREDDING A GUY'S EGO.
WHY NOT DO THE SAME KIND OF THING TO THAT SEAL? YOU COULD TAKE A MAGIC MARKER AND WRITE SOMETHING DISPARAGING ON ITS BACK!
......
HMM. THAT MAY INDEED PROVE EFFECTIVE...
THEN LEAVE IT TO ME! I MAY NOT LOOK IT, BUT I'M AN EXPERT AT KNOCKING PEOPLE DOWN TO SIZE!

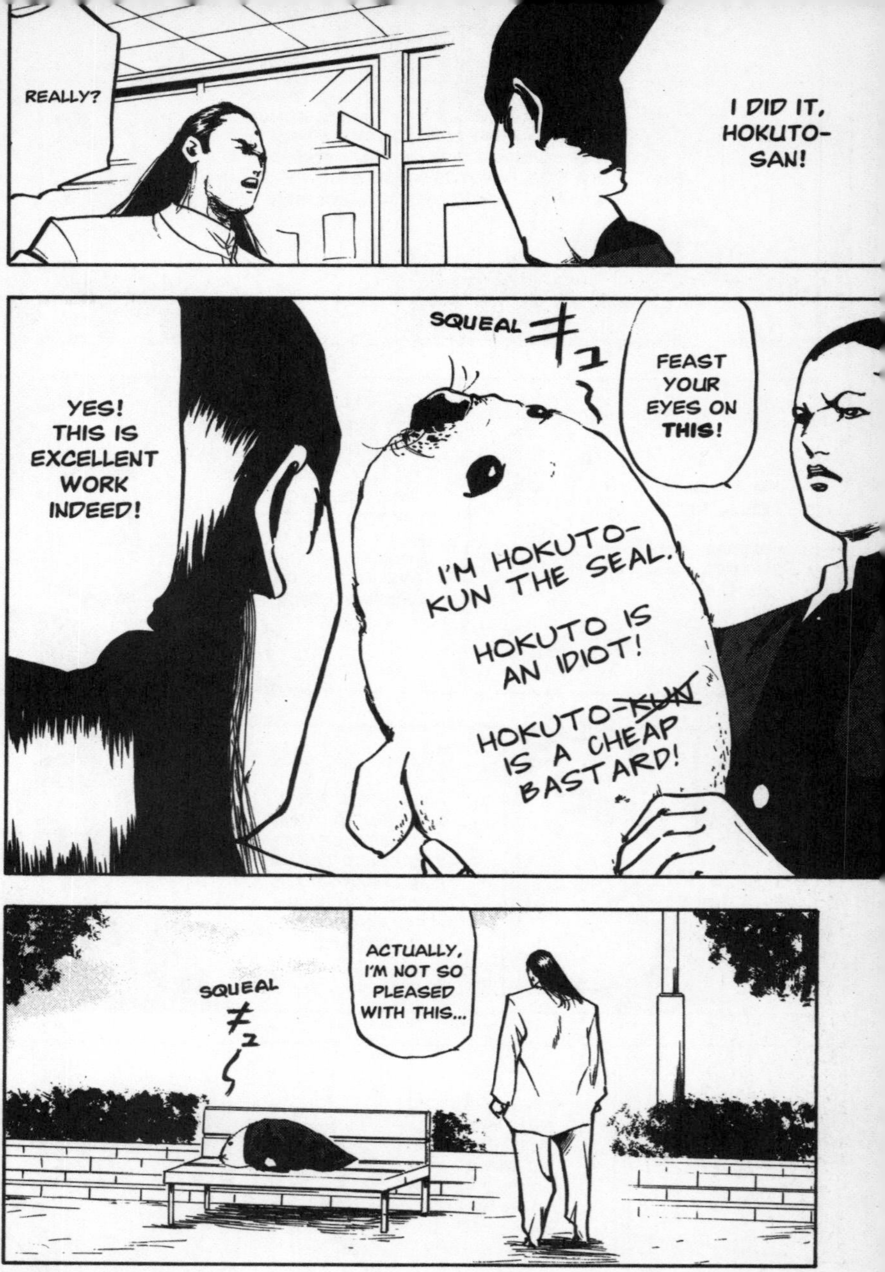
I DID IT, HOKUTO-SAN!
REALLY?
FEAST YOUR EYES ON THIS!
SQUEAL
I'M HOKUTO-KUN THE SEAL.
HOKUTO IS AN IDIOT!
HOKUTO-~~KUN~~ IS A CHEAP BASTARD!
YES! THIS IS EXCELLENT WORK INDEED!
ACTUALLY, I'M NOT SO PLEASED WITH THIS...
SQUEAL

IT WAS PROBABLY DELIBERATE.

CHAPTER 136: **CHANGE**

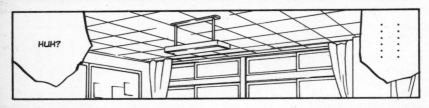

MY NAME IS TAKESHI HOKUTO. I AM HEIR TO MY FAMILY'S ZAIBATSU CONGLOMERATE AND NEXT IN LINE TO LEAD THE HOKUTO GROUP. I AM THE CHOSEN ONE, HE WHO WAS BORN TO RULE THE MASSES.

HUH?

I...I'VE BEEN TURNED INTO A SEAL!

WHAT?!

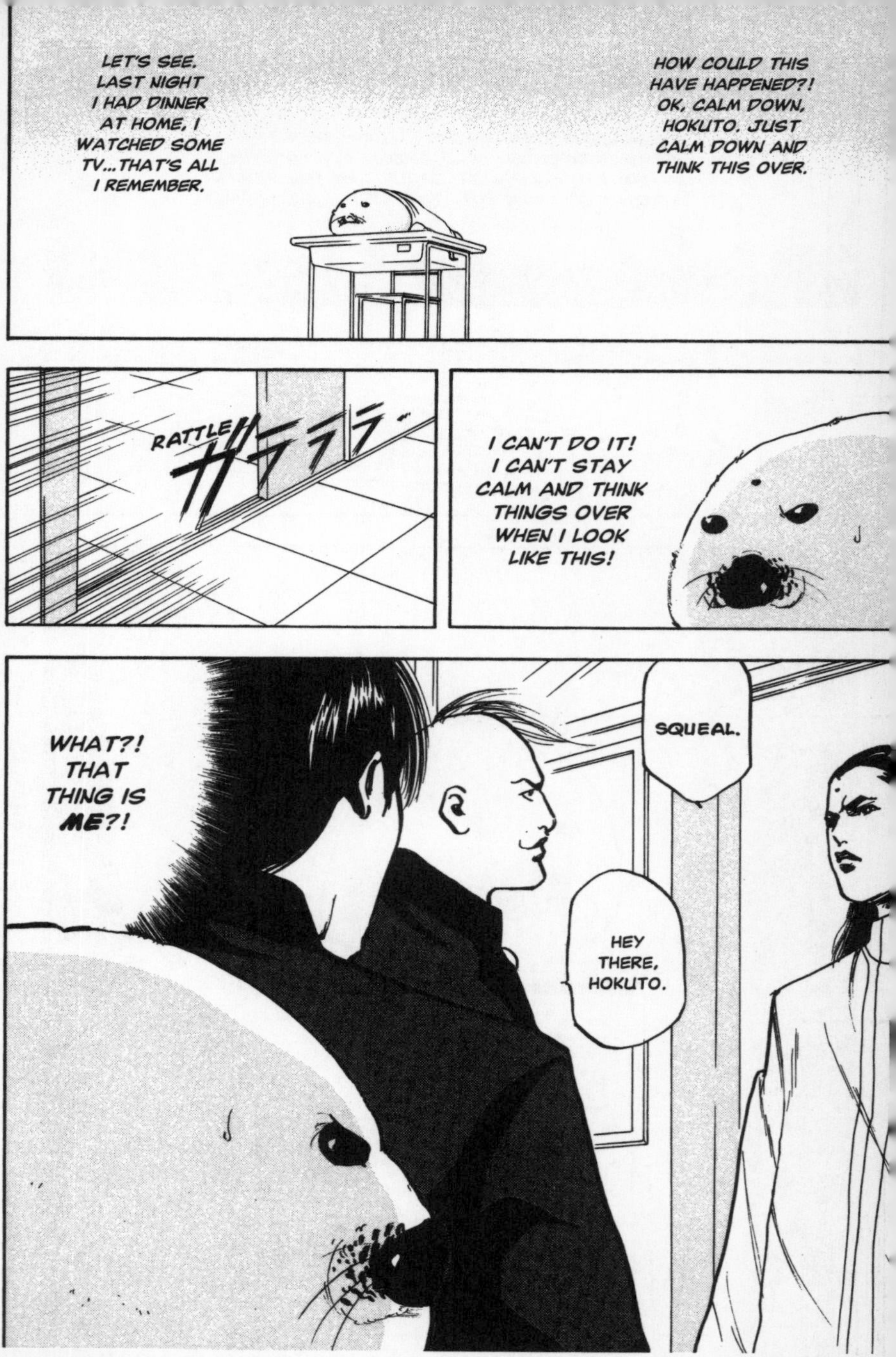
HOW COULD THIS HAVE HAPPENED?! OK, CALM DOWN, HOKUTO. JUST CALM DOWN AND THINK THIS OVER.
LET'S SEE. LAST NIGHT I HAD DINNER AT HOME, I WATCHED SOME TV...THAT'S ALL I REMEMBER.
I CAN'T DO IT! I CAN'T STAY CALM AND THINK THINGS OVER WHEN I LOOK LIKE THIS!
RATTLE
ガラララ
SQUEAL.
HEY THERE, HOKUTO.
WHAT?! THAT THING IS ME?!

THIS IS TRULY A SUPERNATURAL OCCURRENCE, SOMETHING FOR WHICH MODERN SCIENCE HAS NO EXPLANATION!

NOW I GET IT! SOMEHOW, THAT THRICE-DAMNED SEAL AND I HAVE SWITCHED BODIES!

WHACK
ボカ

SKREEK!

PUT A SOCK IN IT, YOU DUMB-ASS SEAL!

FLAP
FLAP

IN ANY CASE, I MUST TELL THE OTHERS WHAT HAS HAPPENED, AND FAST!

K-TNK

BASTARD! HE'S TREATED THE SEAL WELL ENOUGH UP TILL NOW, BUT THEN HE GOES AND DOES SOMETHING LIKE THIS?! THE WORTHLESS SON OF WHORE!

AGH!

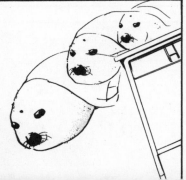

UH-OH.

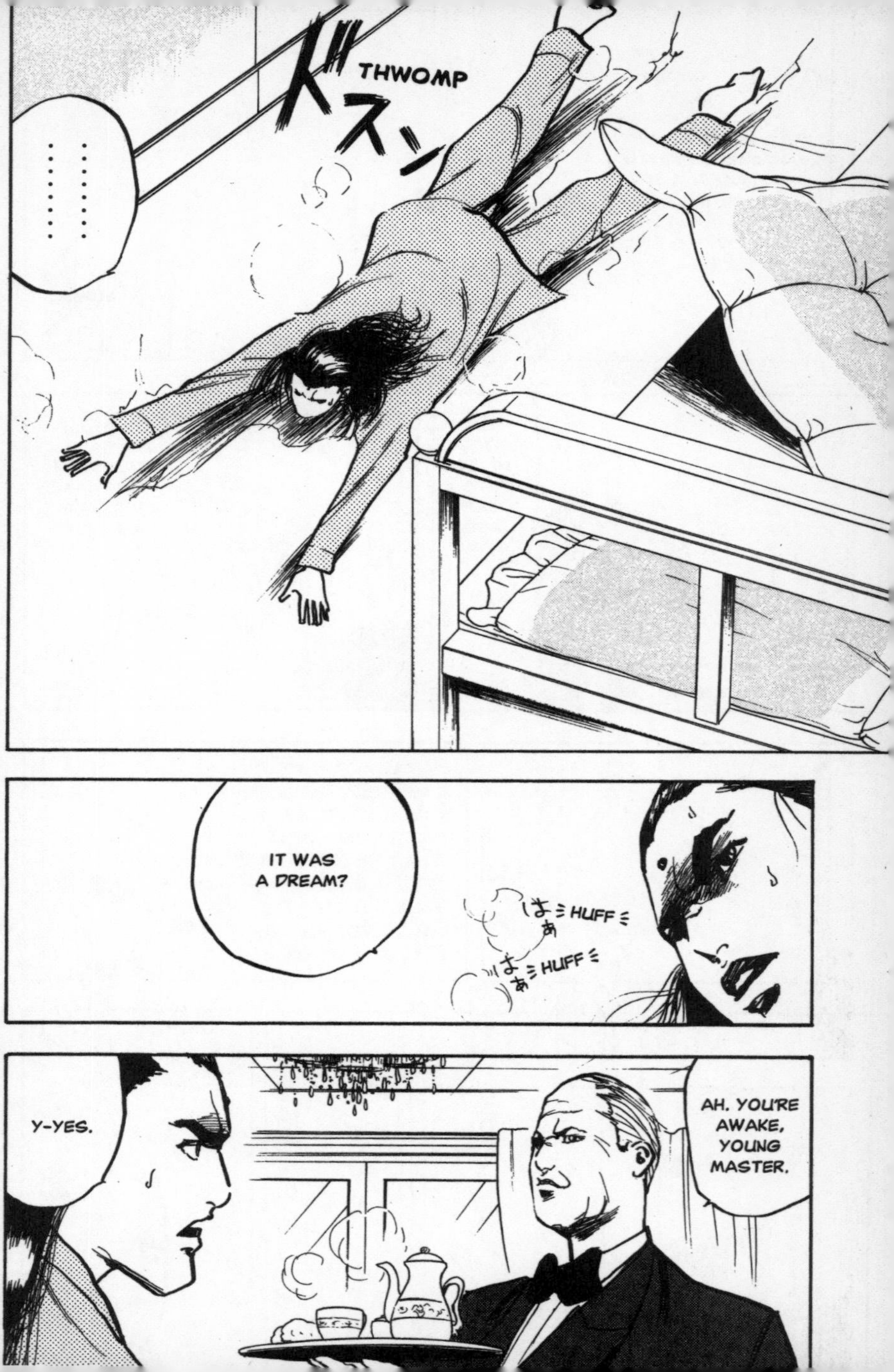

ドスン
THWOMP
......
IT WAS A DREAM?
はぁ HUFF
はぁ HUFF
AH. YOU'RE AWAKE, YOUNG MASTER.
Y-YES.

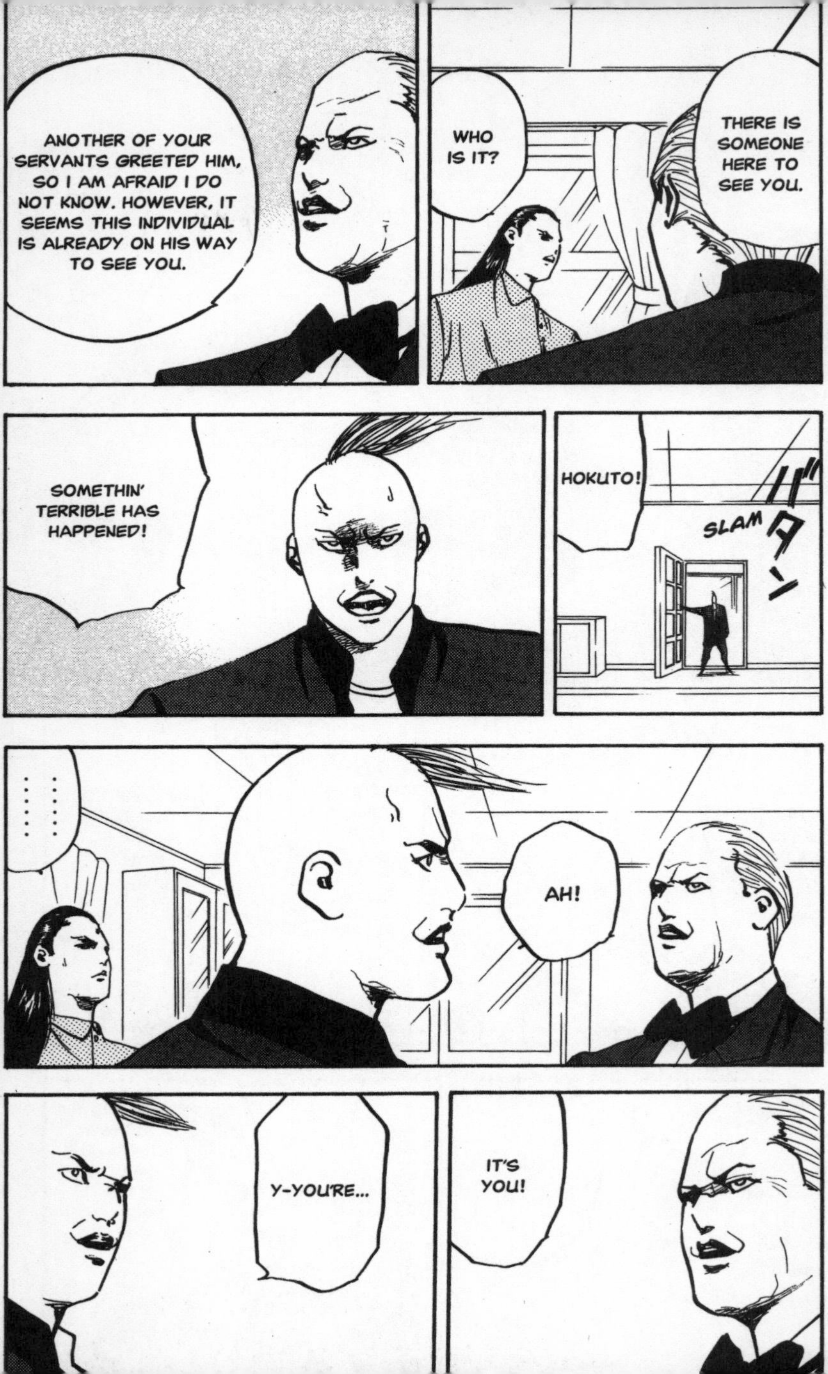
THERE IS SOMEONE HERE TO SEE YOU.
WHO IS IT?
ANOTHER OF YOUR SERVANTS GREETED HIM, SO I AM AFRAID I DO NOT KNOW. HOWEVER, IT SEEMS THIS INDIVIDUAL IS ALREADY ON HIS WAY TO SEE YOU.
バタン
SLAM
HOKUTO!
SOMETHIN' TERRIBLE HAS HAPPENED!
AH!
......
IT'S YOU!
Y-YOU'RE...

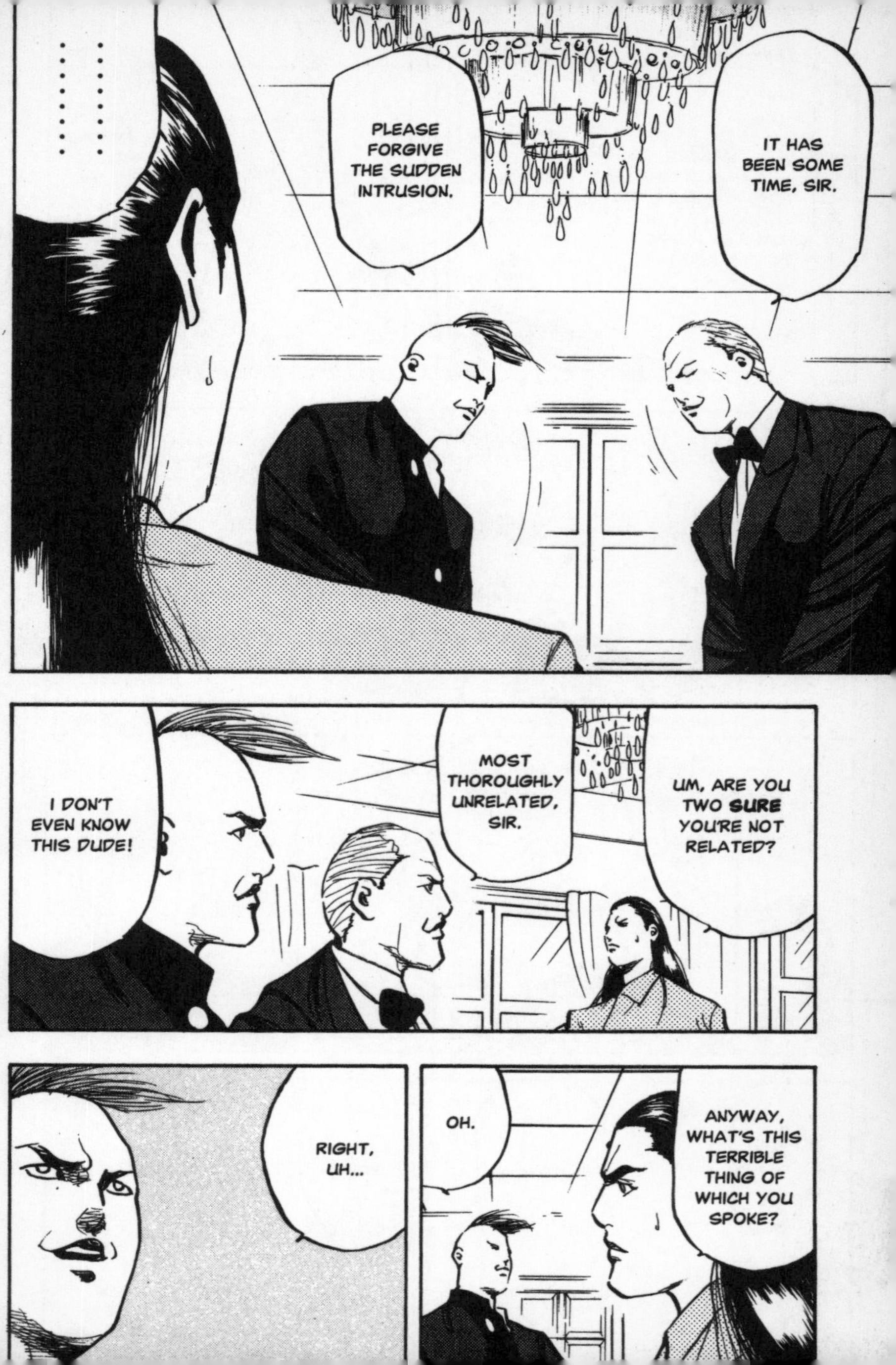
IT HAS BEEN SOME TIME, SIR.
PLEASE FORGIVE THE SUDDEN INTRUSION.
UM, ARE YOU TWO **SURE** YOU'RE NOT RELATED?
MOST THOROUGHLY UNRELATED, SIR.
I DON'T EVEN KNOW THIS DUDE!
ANYWAY, WHAT'S THIS TERRIBLE THING OF WHICH YOU SPOKE?
OH.
RIGHT, UH...

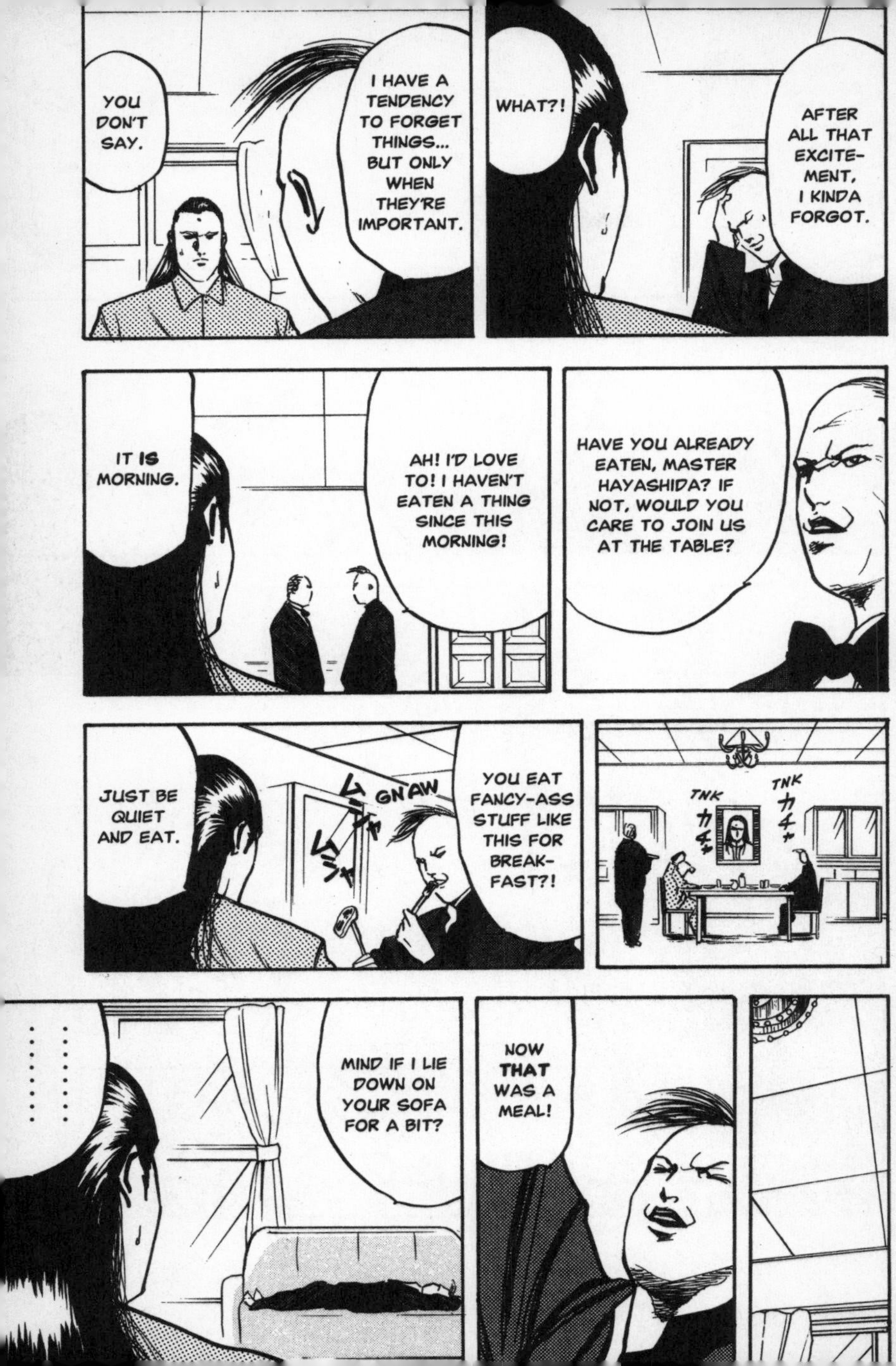
AFTER ALL THAT EXCITEMENT, I KINDA FORGOT.
WHAT?!
I HAVE A TENDENCY TO FORGET THINGS... BUT ONLY WHEN THEY'RE IMPORTANT.
YOU DON'T SAY.
HAVE YOU ALREADY EATEN, MASTER HAYASHIDA? IF NOT, WOULD YOU CARE TO JOIN US AT THE TABLE?
AH! I'D LOVE TO! I HAVEN'T EATEN A THING SINCE THIS MORNING!
IT IS MORNING.
TNK
TNK
YOU EAT FANCY-ASS STUFF LIKE THIS FOR BREAK-FAST?!
GNAW
JUST BE QUIET AND EAT.
NOW THAT WAS A MEAL!
MIND IF I LIE DOWN ON YOUR SOFA FOR A BIT?
......

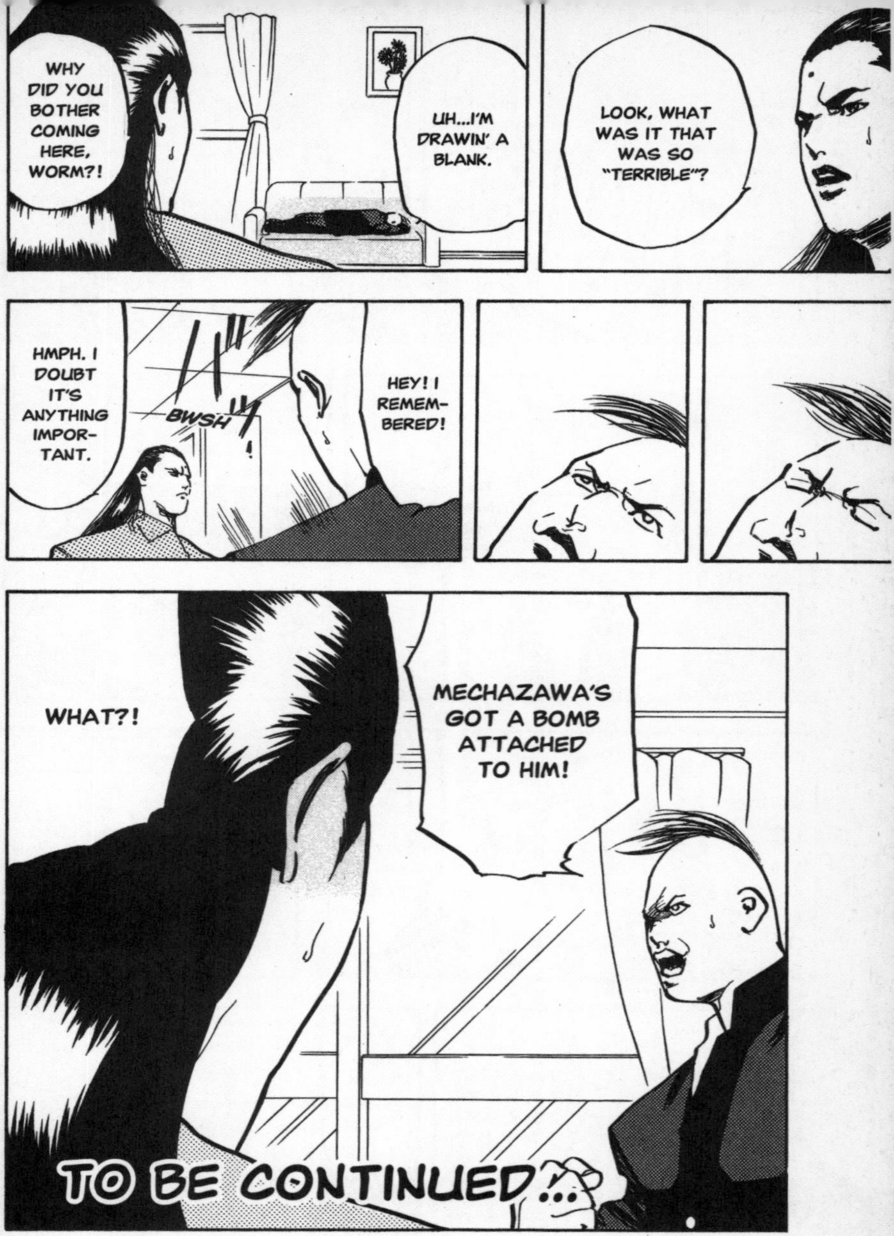
LOOK, WHAT WAS IT THAT WAS SO "TERRIBLE"?
UH...I'M DRAWIN' A BLANK.
WHY DID YOU BOTHER COMING HERE, WORM?!
HEY! I REMEMBERED!
BWSH
HMPH. I DOUBT IT'S ANYTHING IMPORTANT.
MECHAZAWA'S GOT A BOMB ATTACHED TO HIM!
WHAT?!
TO BE CONTINUED...

YEAH, THIS IS A PRETTY ORIGINAL MANGA.

A HAPHAZARD INTRODUCTION TO THE CHARACTERS

POOTAN

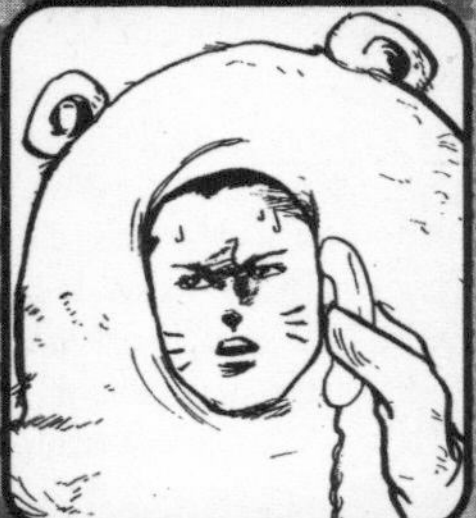

A comedian who performs in a plush animal outfit. When I first introduced this character, I never in a million years thought I'd get as much mileage out of him as I have. From the simplicity (and by simplicity, I mean "negligence") that typifies his design, you can probably guess that Pootan was intended to be a throwaway character. Every week on his TV show, you'll find him busily engaged in activities such as grinding sesame seeds and filing his income tax returns. Since Pootan has nothing whatsoever to do with Cromartie, it was a source of some consternation to see that the more Pootan showed up, the more the story strayed from its "high-school manga" scenario. This, of course, led to the surprise in noticing that I had *ever* intended for this to be a high-school manga. Huh. Anyway, Pootan's TV program is extremely popular, and Pootan himself is a successful comedian...Not that this ever happen in the real world, though.

POOTAN'S PARTNER

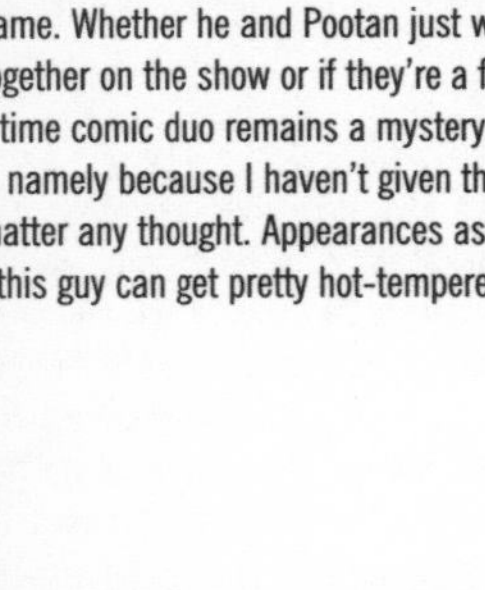

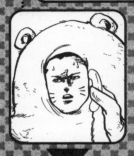

Character-wise, this guy is so insubstantial that after not drawing him for a while I flat-out forgot what he looked like. I have forgotten once again, so the next time he appears, there is a strong possibility that he'll be sporting a different face. This guy plays second fiddle to Pootan on the TV show, which is reason enough for him to not have a name. Whether he and Pootan just work together on the show or if they're a full-time comic duo remains a mystery... namely because I haven't given the matter any thought. Appearances aside, this guy can get pretty hot-tempered.

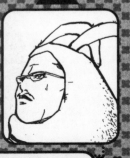

A HAPHAZARD INTRODUCTION TO THE CHARACTERS

Ara-chan was added almost as an afterthought, a kind of whim that came about while yours truly and his editor were watching TV. Something about all the fuss surrounding Tama-chan, a seal that showed up one day in the Tamagawa river, ticked us off so much that we wanted to pour a little cold water on the party. It makes me nostalgic to remember how the both of us were shouting things at the TV like, "If you wanna see a seal that badly, go to the frickin' zoo!" So anyway, I tried putting a seal into the manga...and it was an instant hit, which was of course the exact *opposite* of what we were after. Grarr, this always happens to us! Anyway, I've never once heard what kinds of sounds a seal makes, so having it go "squeal" was clearly the influence of some manga or other. (LOL) It's quite unusual for a "delinquent manga" to feature gorillas, seals and whatnot. Can Cromartie even be considered a delinquent manga?! I have a feeling this character will not be making another appearance.

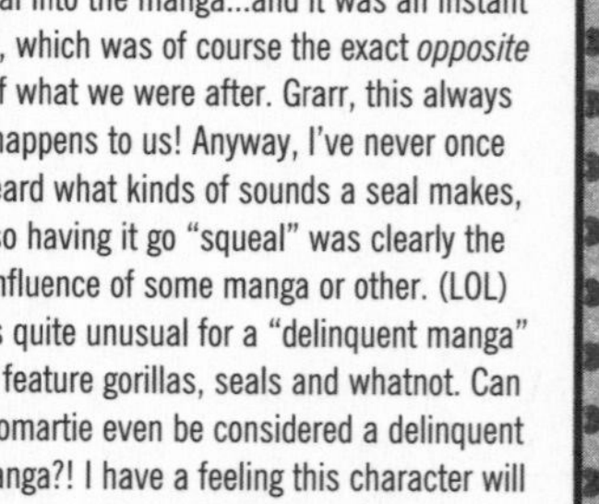

ARA-CHAN

ARA-CHAN

HIDEKI TAKAHASHI

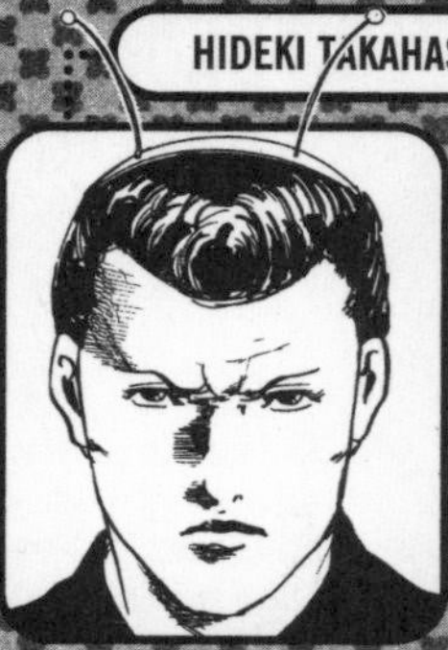

HIDEKI TAKAHASHI

At that den of thugs called Cromartie High, Hideki Takahashi commands the respect of all. Kamiyama, Hayashida and the other underclassmen look up to him with a kind of reverence. Takahashi is someone you can rely on, a man of limitless generosity. In addition to being a skilled fighter, this cool upperclassman is always looking out for his buddies. In other words, Takahashi is the ubiquitous "guy who walks the high road" found in most delinquent manga. It's amazing to see how schlocky he became after I added a little "spice" to the recipe. To stick with the food metaphors, I just wanted to add some subtle undertones to his overall flavor profile...still, there's nothing subtle about those things on his head! (LOL) Nobody knows what they're for, but eyewitness claim they help him locate people he's looking for. Takahashi is the first upperclassman we've seen who actually has his act together. It's just a shame that he has to wear those things everywhere--they end up getting noticed a lot more than the fact that he's a pretty decent guy.

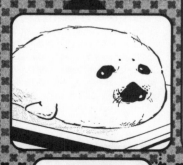

CHAPTER 137: **SPANISH BOMB**

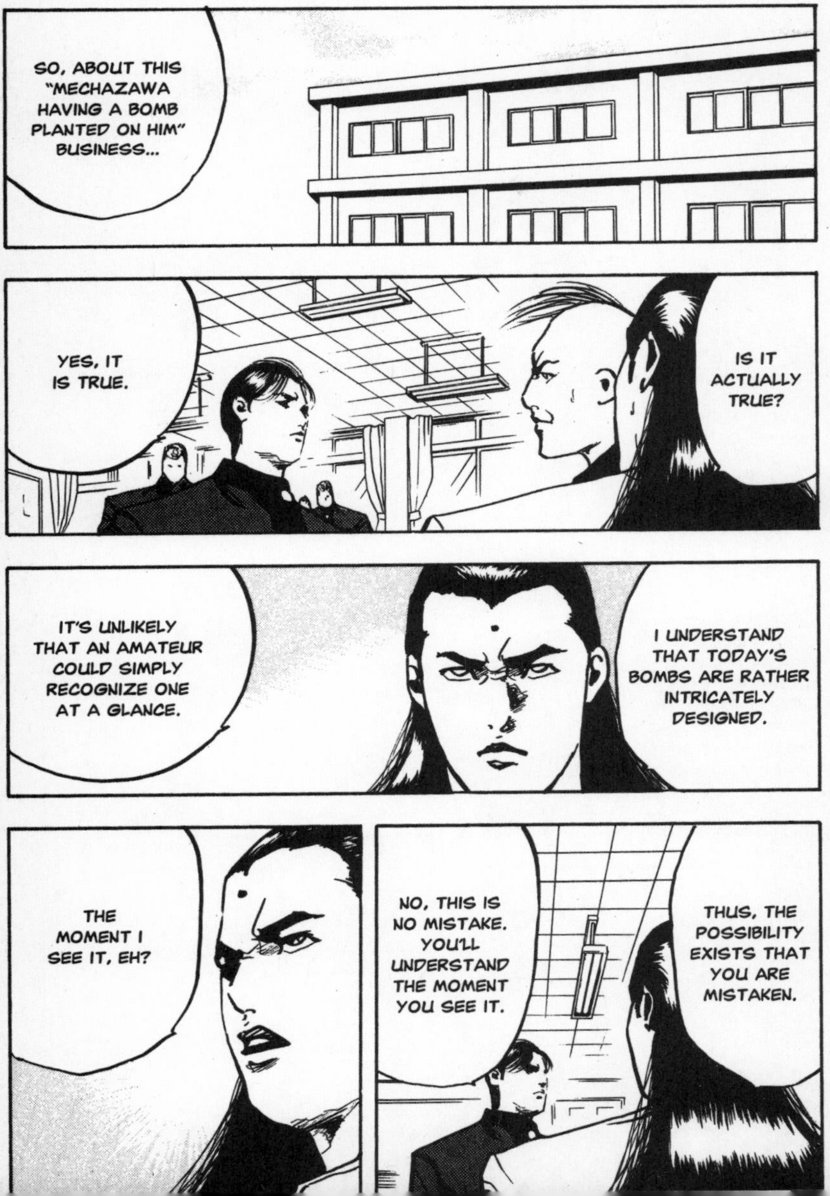
SO, ABOUT THIS "MECHAZAWA HAVING A BOMB PLANTED ON HIM" BUSINESS...
IS IT ACTUALLY TRUE?
YES, IT IS TRUE.
I UNDERSTAND THAT TODAY'S BOMBS ARE RATHER INTRICATELY DESIGNED.
IT'S UNLIKELY THAT AN AMATEUR COULD SIMPLY RECOGNIZE ONE AT A GLANCE.
THUS, THE POSSIBILITY EXISTS THAT YOU ARE MISTAKEN.
NO, THIS IS NO MISTAKE. YOU'LL UNDERSTAND THE MOMENT YOU SEE IT.
THE MOMENT I SEE IT, EH?

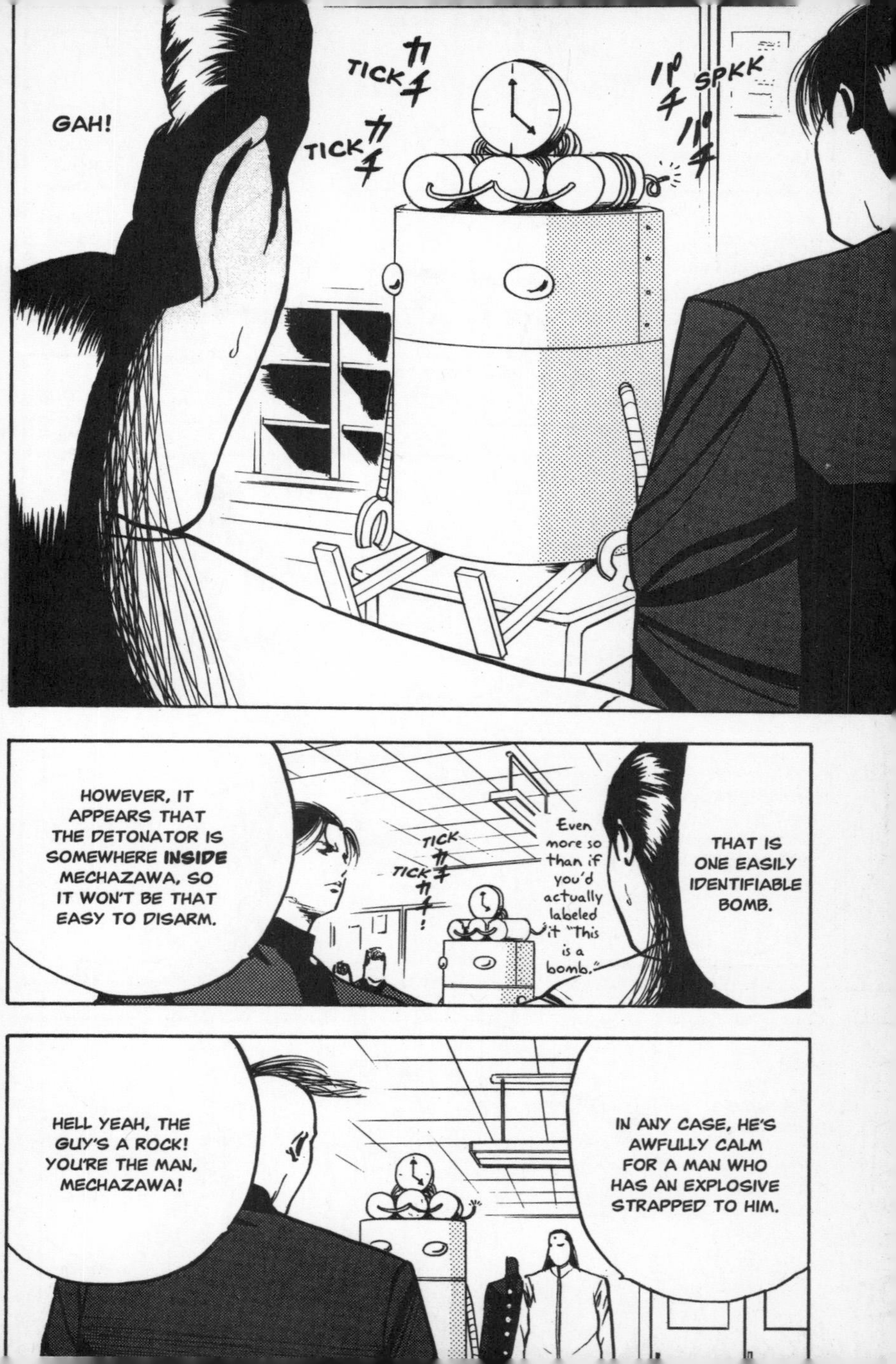
パチ
SPKK
パチ
TICK
カチ
TICK
カチ
GAH!
THAT IS ONE EASILY IDENTIFIABLE BOMB.
Even more so than if you'd actually labeled it "This is a bomb."
TICK
カチ
TICK
カチ!
HOWEVER, IT APPEARS THAT THE DETONATOR IS SOMEWHERE **INSIDE** MECHAZAWA, SO IT WON'T BE THAT EASY TO DISARM.
IN ANY CASE, HE'S AWFULLY CALM FOR A MAN WHO HAS AN EXPLOSIVE STRAPPED TO HIM.
HELL YEAH, THE GUY'S A ROCK! YOU'RE THE MAN, MECHAZAWA!

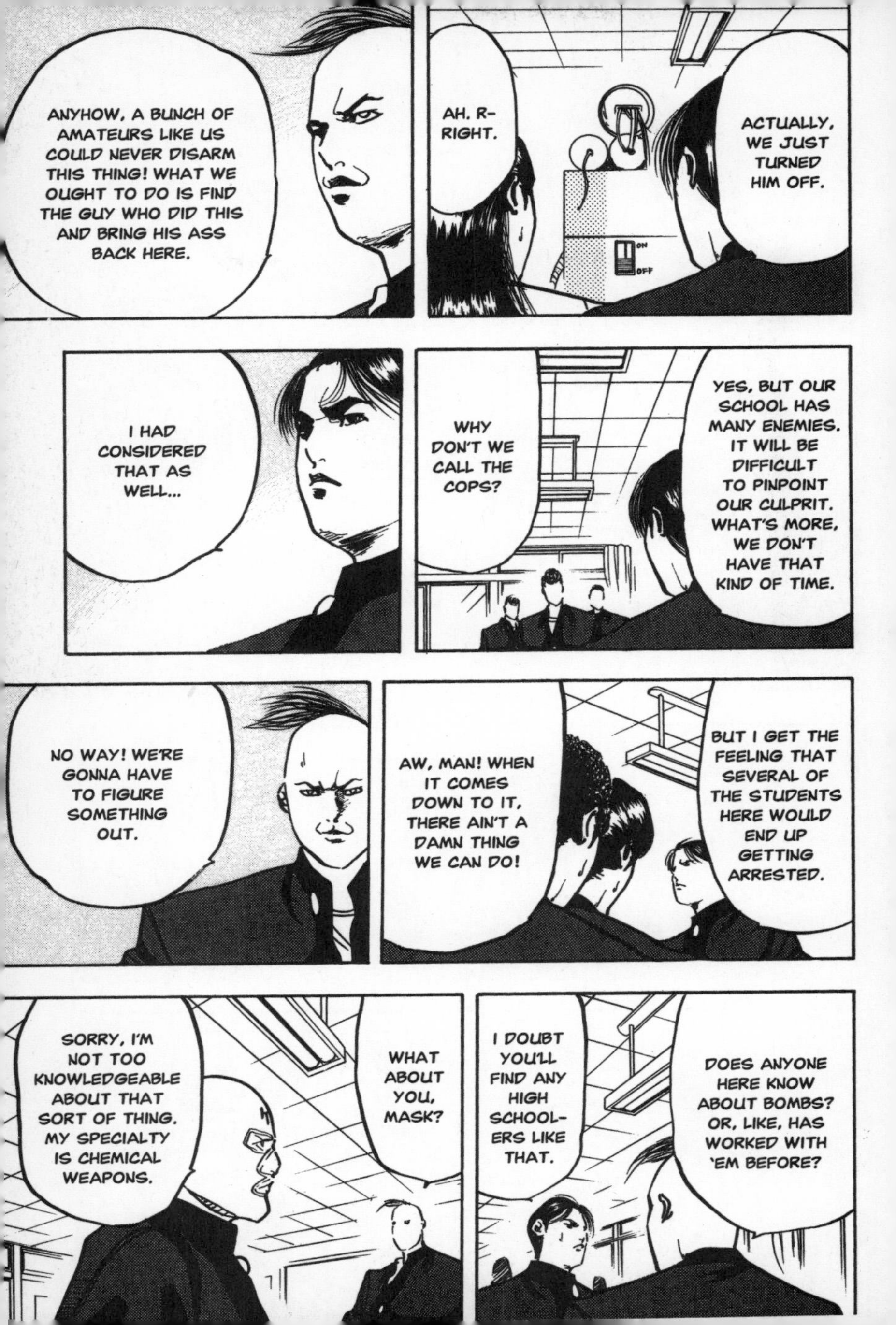
ACTUALLY, WE JUST TURNED HIM OFF.
AH. R-RIGHT.
ON
OFF
ANYHOW, A BUNCH OF AMATEURS LIKE US COULD NEVER DISARM THIS THING! WHAT WE OUGHT TO DO IS FIND THE GUY WHO DID THIS AND BRING HIS ASS BACK HERE.
WHY DON'T WE CALL THE COPS?
YES, BUT OUR SCHOOL HAS MANY ENEMIES. IT WILL BE DIFFICULT TO PINPOINT OUR CULPRIT. WHAT'S MORE, WE DON'T HAVE THAT KIND OF TIME.
I HAD CONSIDERED THAT AS WELL...
BUT I GET THE FEELING THAT SEVERAL OF THE STUDENTS HERE WOULD END UP GETTING ARRESTED.
AW, MAN! WHEN IT COMES DOWN TO IT, THERE AIN'T A DAMN THING WE CAN DO!
NO WAY! WE'RE GONNA HAVE TO FIGURE SOMETHING OUT.
DOES ANYONE HERE KNOW ABOUT BOMBS? OR, LIKE, HAS WORKED WITH 'EM BEFORE?
I DOUBT YOU'LL FIND ANY HIGH SCHOOLERS LIKE THAT.
WHAT ABOUT YOU, MASK?
SORRY, I'M NOT TOO KNOWLEDGEABLE ABOUT THAT SORT OF THING. MY SPECIALTY IS CHEMICAL WEAPONS.

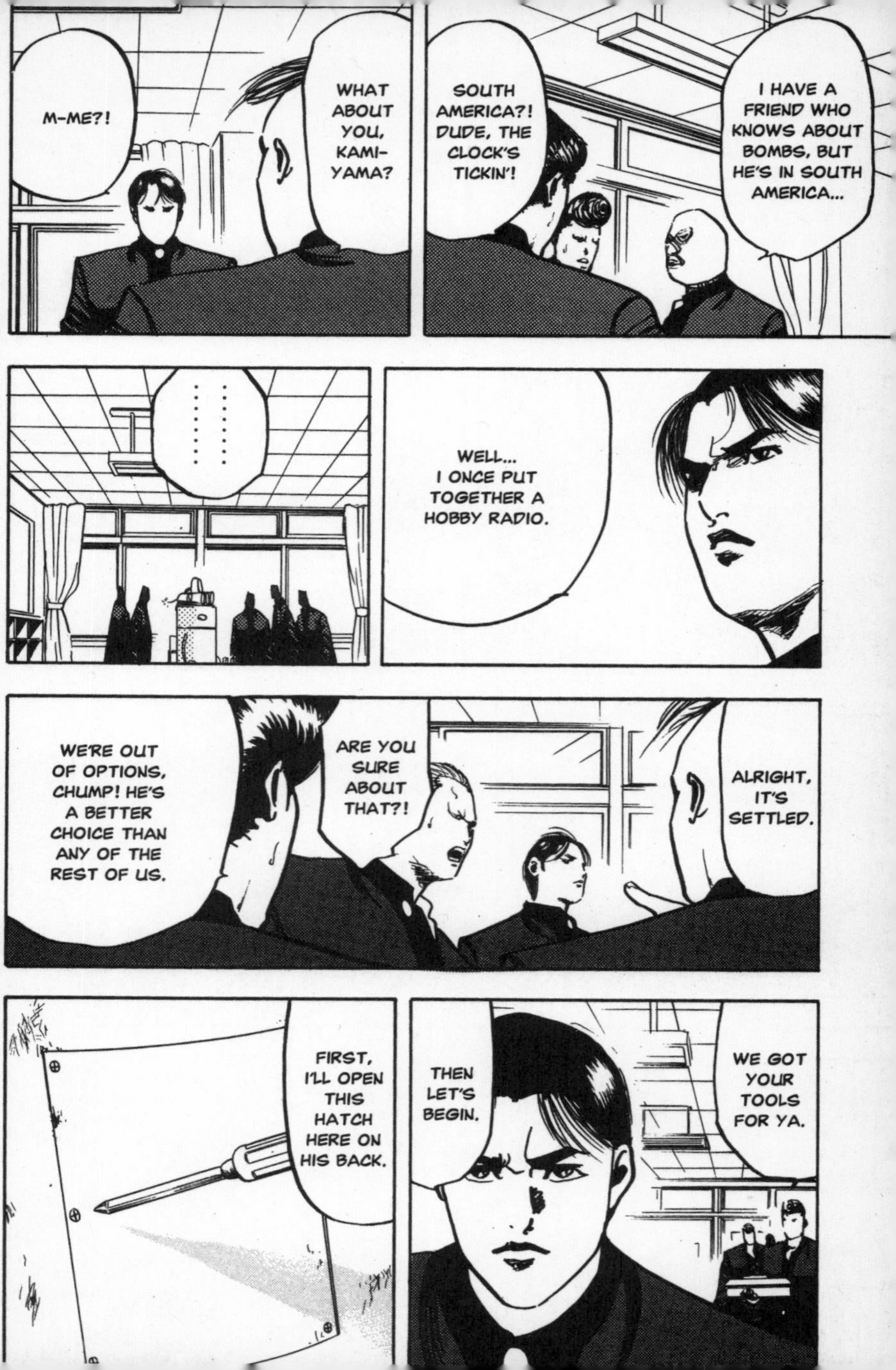
I HAVE A FRIEND WHO KNOWS ABOUT BOMBS, BUT HE'S IN SOUTH AMERICA...
SOUTH AMERICA?! DUDE, THE CLOCK'S TICKIN'!
WHAT ABOUT YOU, KAMI-YAMA?
M-ME?!
WELL... I ONCE PUT TOGETHER A HOBBY RADIO.
......
ALRIGHT, IT'S SETTLED.
ARE YOU SURE ABOUT THAT?!
WE'RE OUT OF OPTIONS, CHUMP! HE'S A BETTER CHOICE THAN ANY OF THE REST OF US.
WE GOT YOUR TOOLS FOR YA.
THEN LET'S BEGIN.
FIRST, I'LL OPEN THIS HATCH HERE ON HIS BACK.

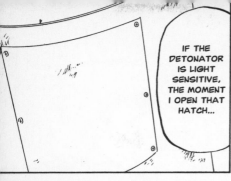

HMM, WAIT A MOMENT.
WHAT'S UP?
IF THE DETONATOR IS LIGHT SENSITIVE, THE MOMENT I OPEN THAT HATCH...
THERE COULD BE A VERY LOUD "BOOM."
HUH?!
WOULD YOU MIND EXTINGUISHING ALL LIGHT IN THIS ROOM?
GOTCHA!
カチン
CHK
K-CHAK
CREAK
WELL?
THERE DON'T SEEM TO BE ANY SENSORS... IT SHOULD BE SAFE TO TURN THE LIGHTS BACK ON.
カチン
CHK
......
HMM...

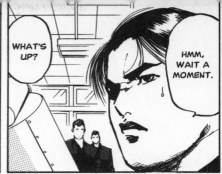

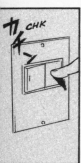

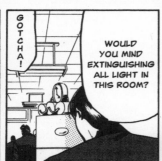

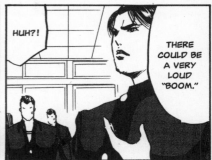

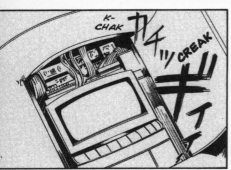

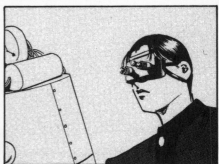

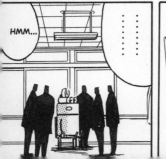

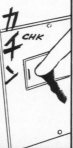

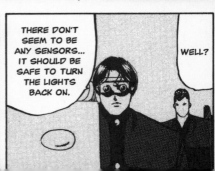

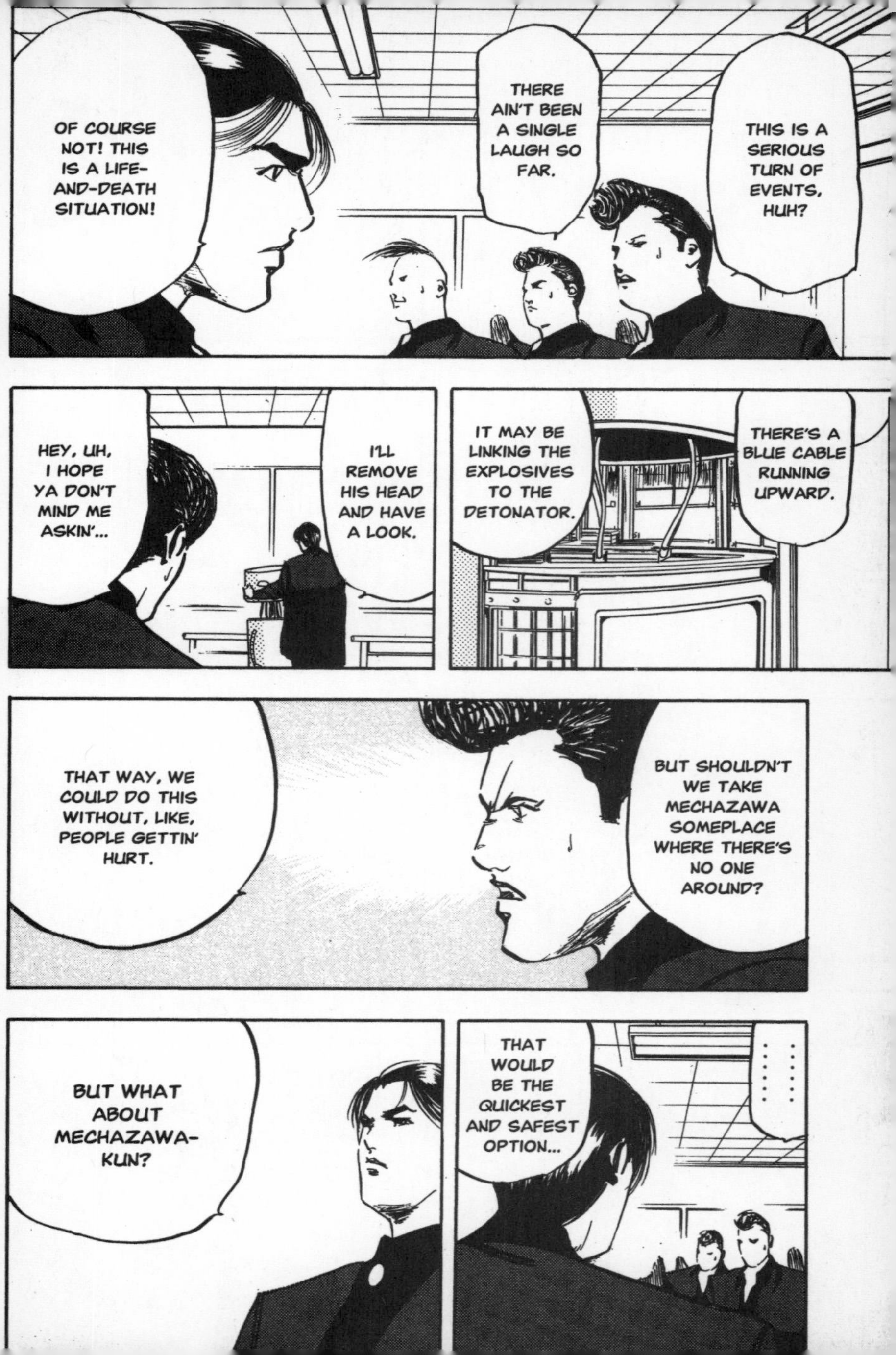
THIS IS A SERIOUS TURN OF EVENTS, HUH?
THERE AIN'T BEEN A SINGLE LAUGH SO FAR.
OF COURSE NOT! THIS IS A LIFE-AND-DEATH SITUATION!
THERE'S A BLUE CABLE RUNNING UPWARD.
IT MAY BE LINKING THE EXPLOSIVES TO THE DETONATOR.
I'LL REMOVE HIS HEAD AND HAVE A LOOK.
HEY, UH, I HOPE YA DON'T MIND ME ASKIN'...
BUT SHOULDN'T WE TAKE MECHAZAWA SOMEPLACE WHERE THERE'S NO ONE AROUND?
THAT WAY, WE COULD DO THIS WITHOUT, LIKE, PEOPLE GETTIN' HURT.
......
THAT WOULD BE THE QUICKEST AND SAFEST OPTION...
BUT WHAT ABOUT MECHAZAWA-KUN?

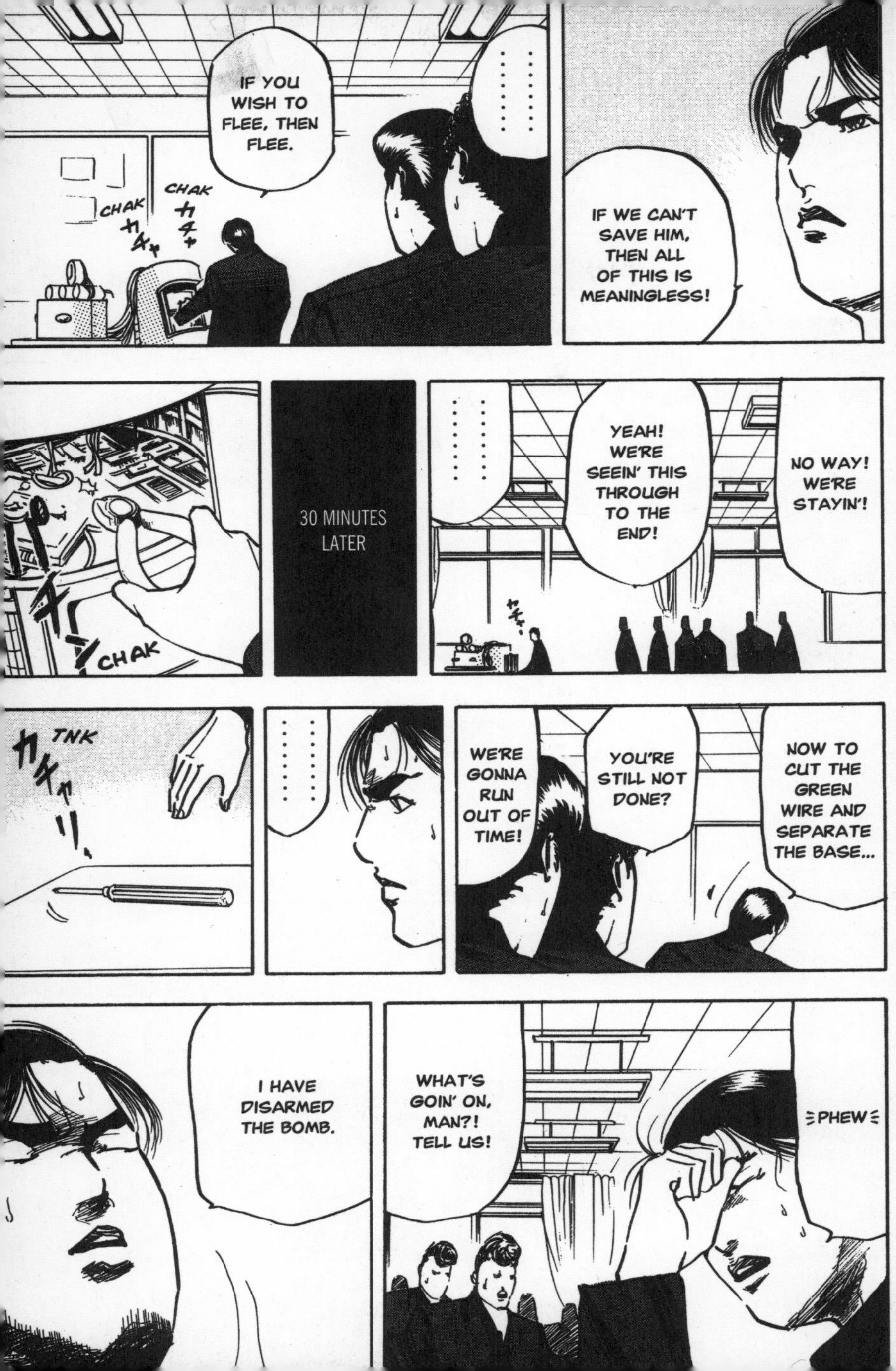
IF WE CAN'T SAVE HIM, THEN ALL OF THIS IS MEANINGLESS!
......
IF YOU WISH TO FLEE, THEN FLEE.
CHAK
CHAK
NO WAY! WE'RE STAYIN'!
YEAH! WE'RE SEEIN' THIS THROUGH TO THE END!
......
30 MINUTES LATER
CHAK
NOW TO CUT THE GREEN WIRE AND SEPARATE THE BASE...
YOU'RE STILL NOT DONE?
WE'RE GONNA RUN OUT OF TIME!
......
TNK
PHEW
WHAT'S GOIN' ON, MAN?! TELL US!
I HAVE DISARMED THE BOMB.

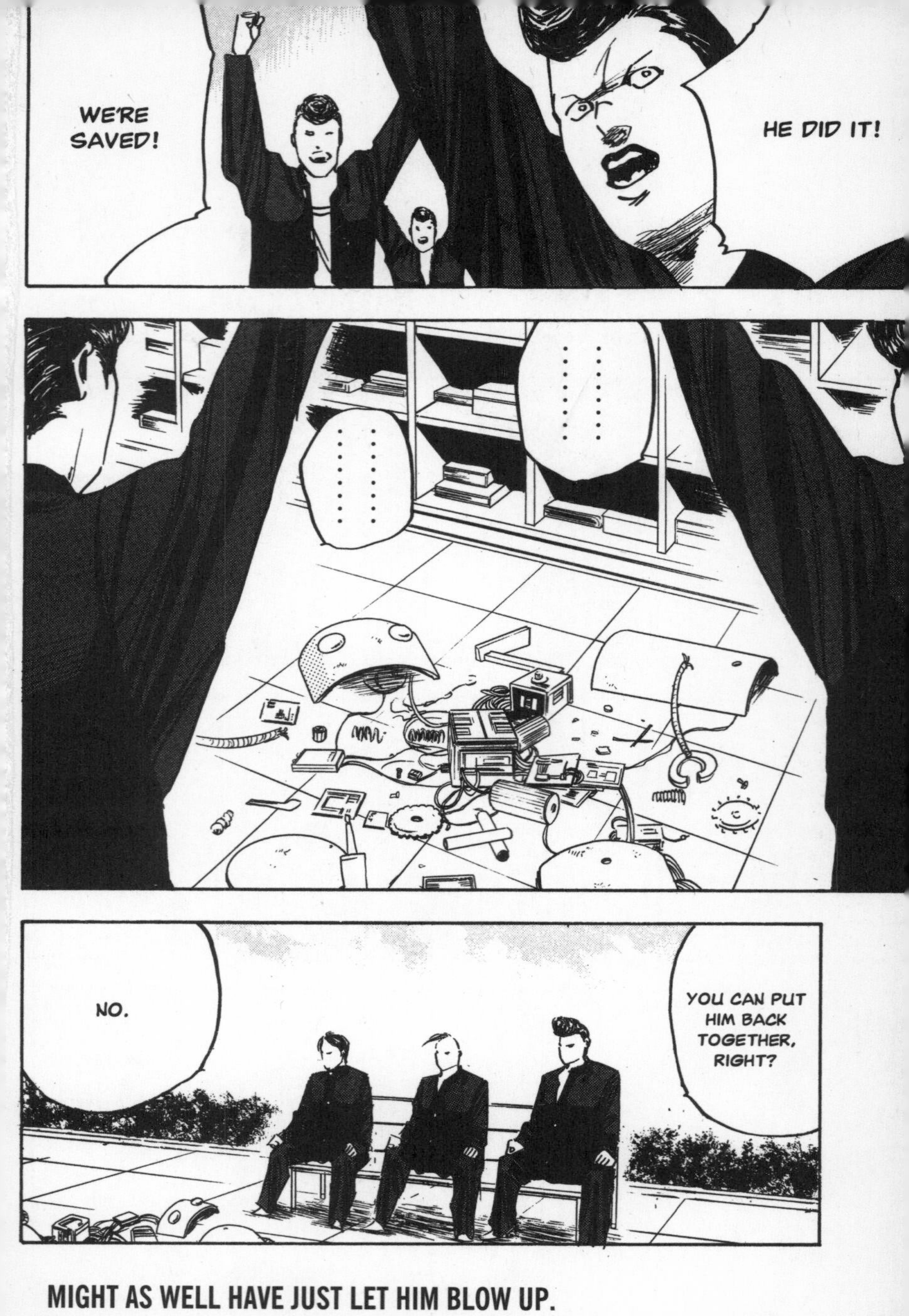
HE DID IT!
WE'RE SAVED!
......
......
YOU CAN PUT HIM BACK TOGETHER, RIGHT?
NO.

MIGHT AS WELL HAVE JUST LET HIM BLOW UP.

CHAPTER 138: **RADIO MAGIC**

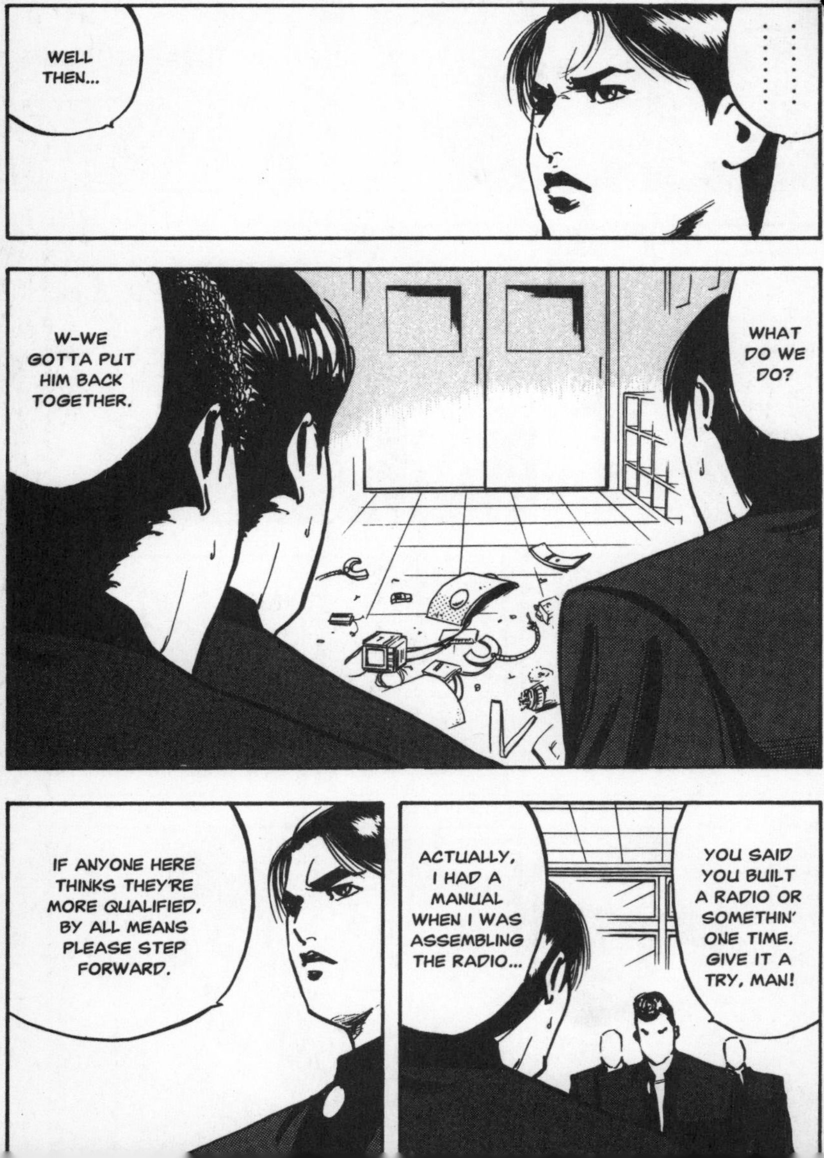
......
WELL THEN...
WHAT DO WE DO?
W-WE GOTTA PUT HIM BACK TOGETHER.
YOU SAID YOU BUILT A RADIO OR SOMETHIN' ONE TIME. GIVE IT A TRY, MAN!
ACTUALLY, I HAD A MANUAL WHEN I WAS ASSEMBLING THE RADIO...
IF ANYONE HERE THINKS THEY'RE MORE QUALIFIED, BY ALL MEANS PLEASE STEP FORWARD.

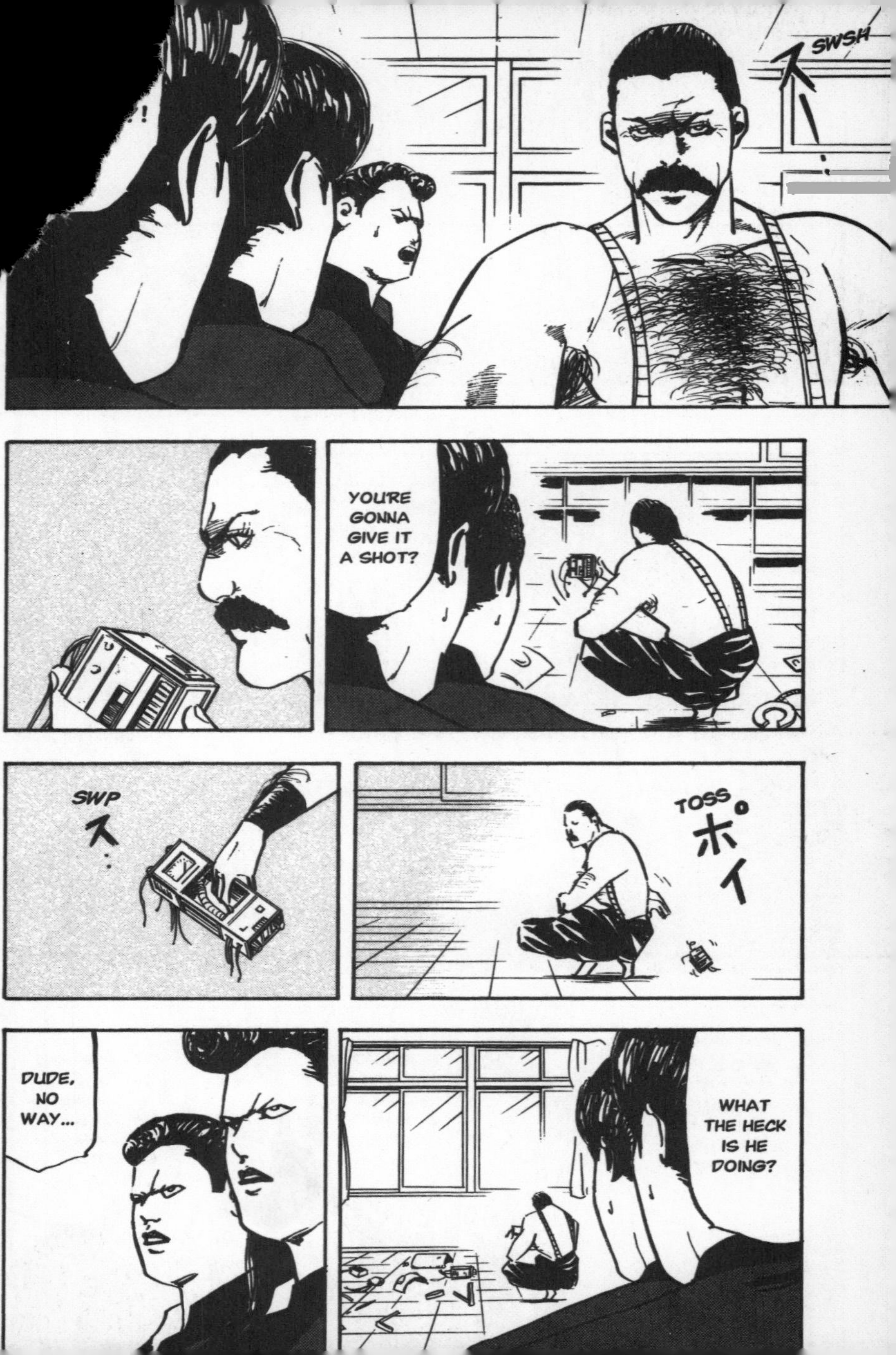
SWSH
ス
?!
YOU'RE GONNA GIVE IT A SHOT?
TOSS
ポイ
SWP
ス
WHAT THE HECK IS HE DOING?
DUDE, NO WAY...

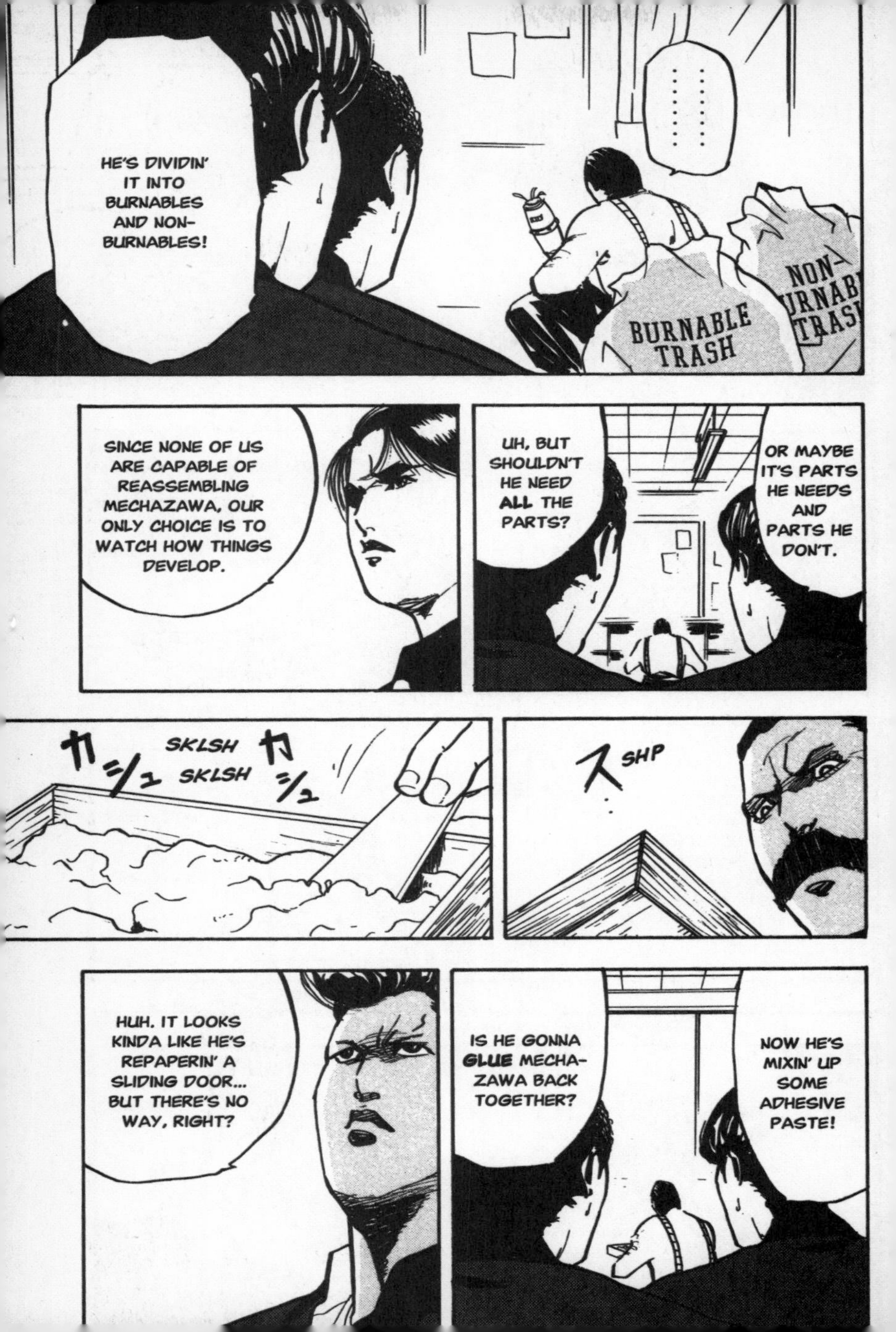
......
HE'S DIVIDIN' IT INTO BURNABLES AND NON-BURNABLES!
BURNABLE TRASH
UH, BUT SHOULDN'T HE NEED ALL THE PARTS?
OR MAYBE IT'S PARTS HE NEEDS AND PARTS HE DON'T.
SINCE NONE OF US ARE CAPABLE OF REASSEMBLING MECHAZAWA, OUR ONLY CHOICE IS TO WATCH HOW THINGS DEVELOP.
ス SHP
カシュ SKLSH
カシュ SKLSH
NOW HE'S MIXIN' UP SOME ADHESIVE PASTE!
IS HE GONNA GLUE MECHAZAWA BACK TOGETHER?
HUH. IT LOOKS KINDA LIKE HE'S REPAPERIN' A SLIDING DOOR... BUT THERE'S NO WAY, RIGHT?

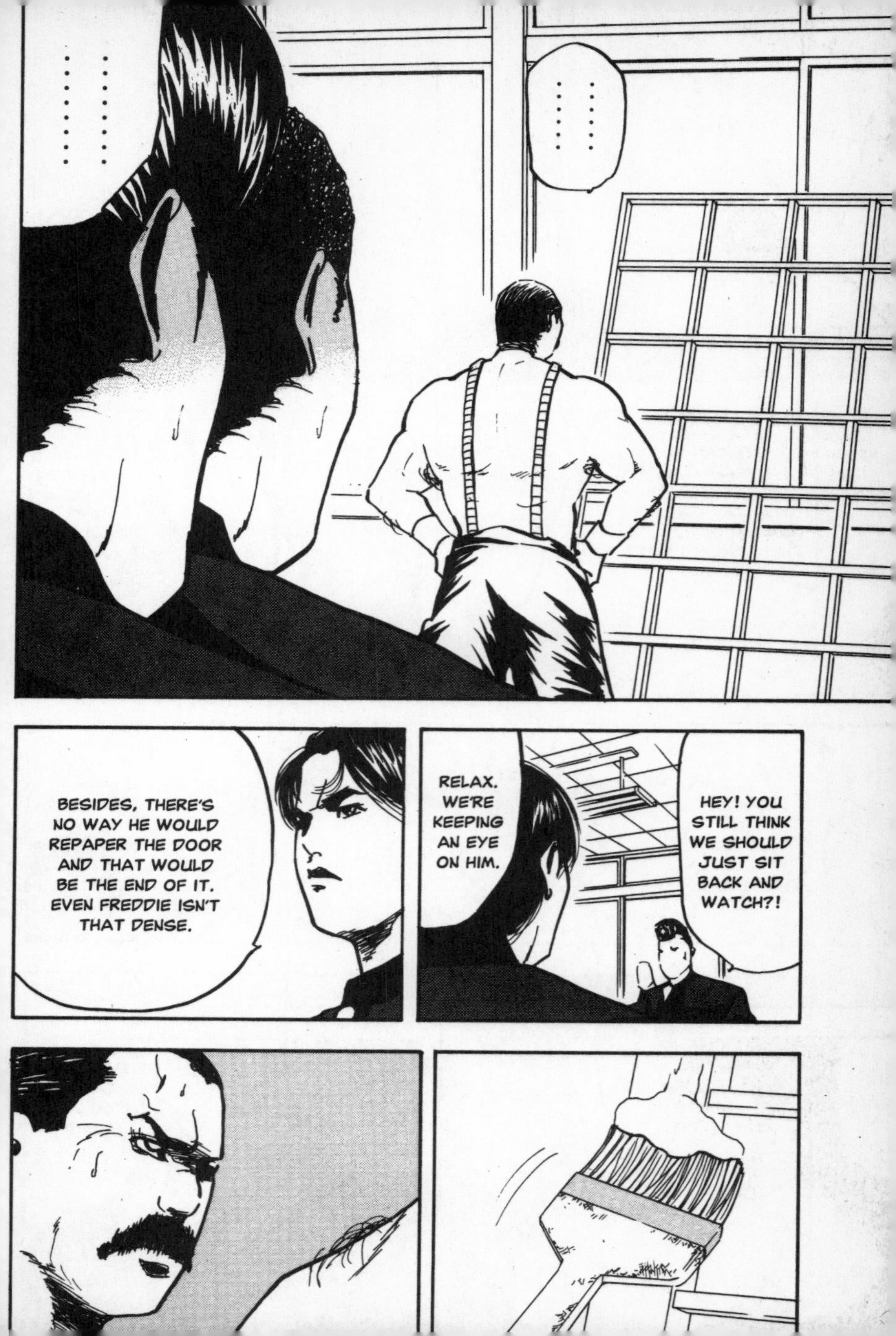
......
......
BESIDES, THERE'S NO WAY HE WOULD REPAPER THE DOOR AND THAT WOULD BE THE END OF IT. EVEN FREDDIE ISN'T THAT DENSE.
RELAX. WE'RE KEEPING AN EYE ON HIM.
HEY! YOU STILL THINK WE SHOULD JUST SIT BACK AND WATCH?!

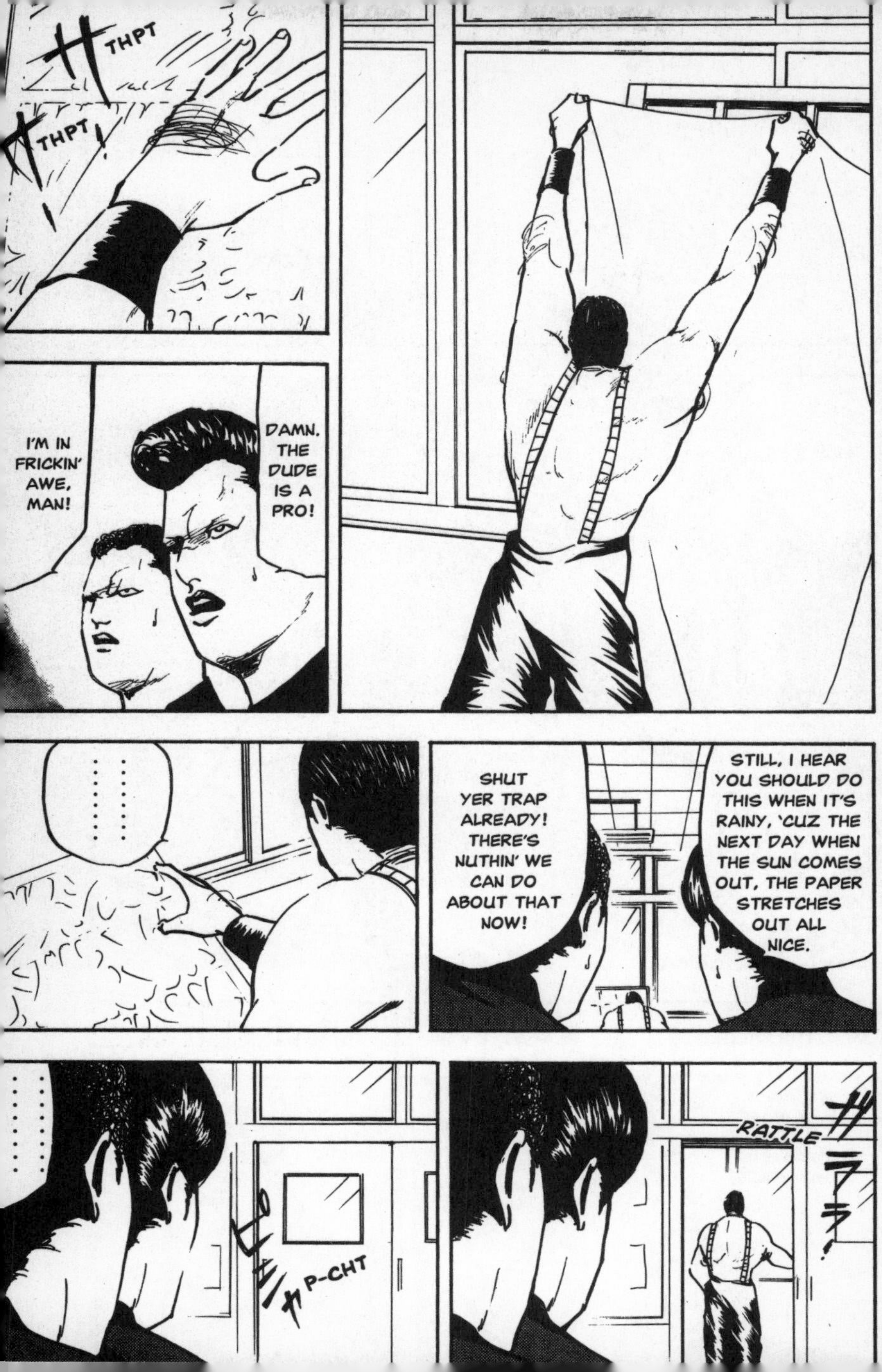
THPT
THPT
DAMN. THE DUDE IS A PRO!
I'M IN FRICKIN' AWE, MAN!
STILL, I HEAR YOU SHOULD DO THIS WHEN IT'S RAINY, 'CUZ THE NEXT DAY WHEN THE SUN COMES OUT, THE PAPER STRETCHES OUT ALL NICE.
SHUT YER TRAP ALREADY! THERE'S NUTHIN' WE CAN DO ABOUT THAT NOW!
......
RATTLE
P-CHT
......

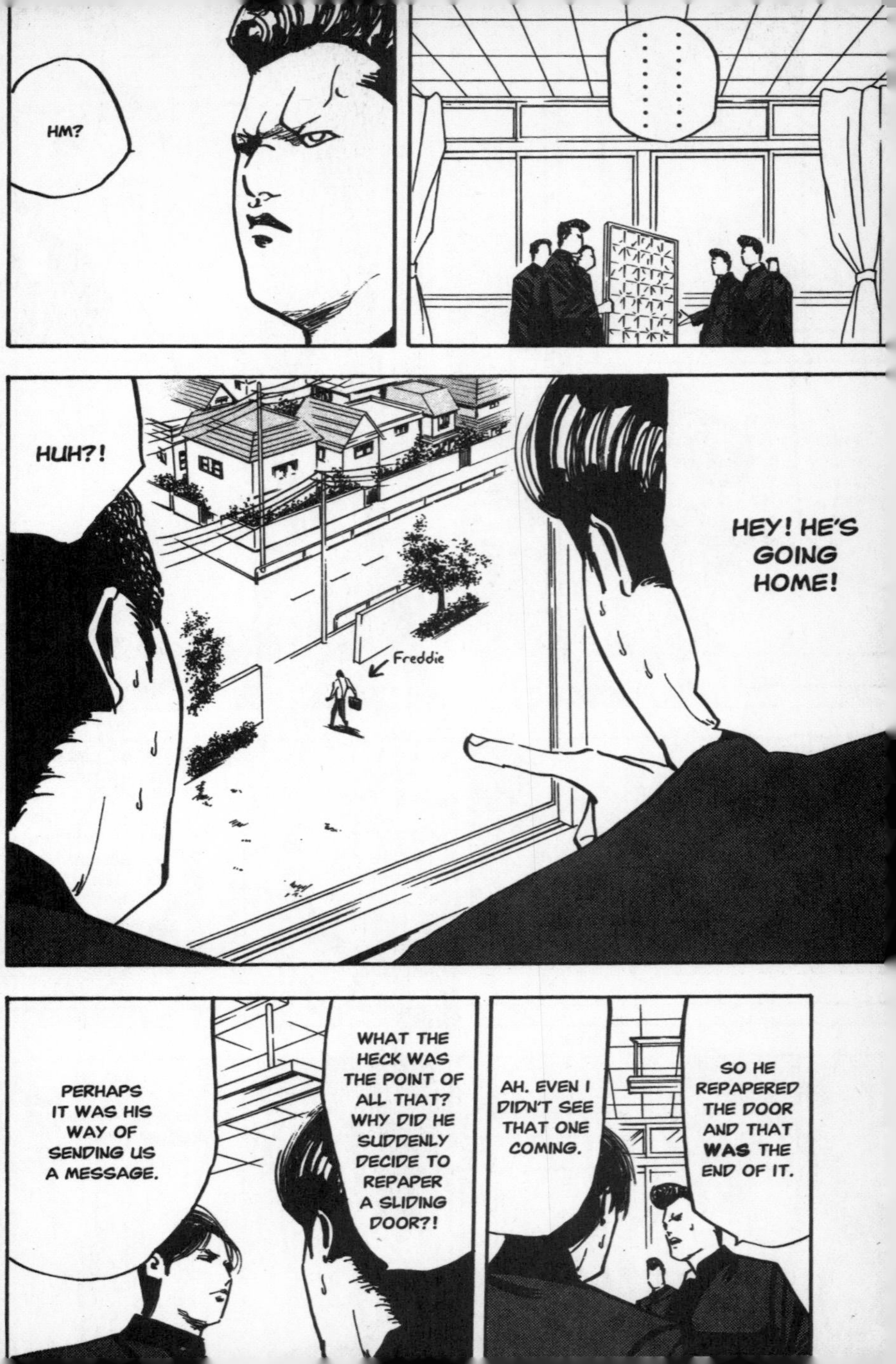
HM?
HUH?!
HEY! HE'S GOING HOME!
Freddie
WHAT THE HECK WAS THE POINT OF ALL THAT? WHY DID HE SUDDENLY DECIDE TO REPAPER A SLIDING DOOR?!
PERHAPS IT WAS HIS WAY OF SENDING US A MESSAGE.
SO HE REPAPERED THE DOOR AND THAT WAS THE END OF IT.
AH. EVEN I DIDN'T SEE THAT ONE COMING.

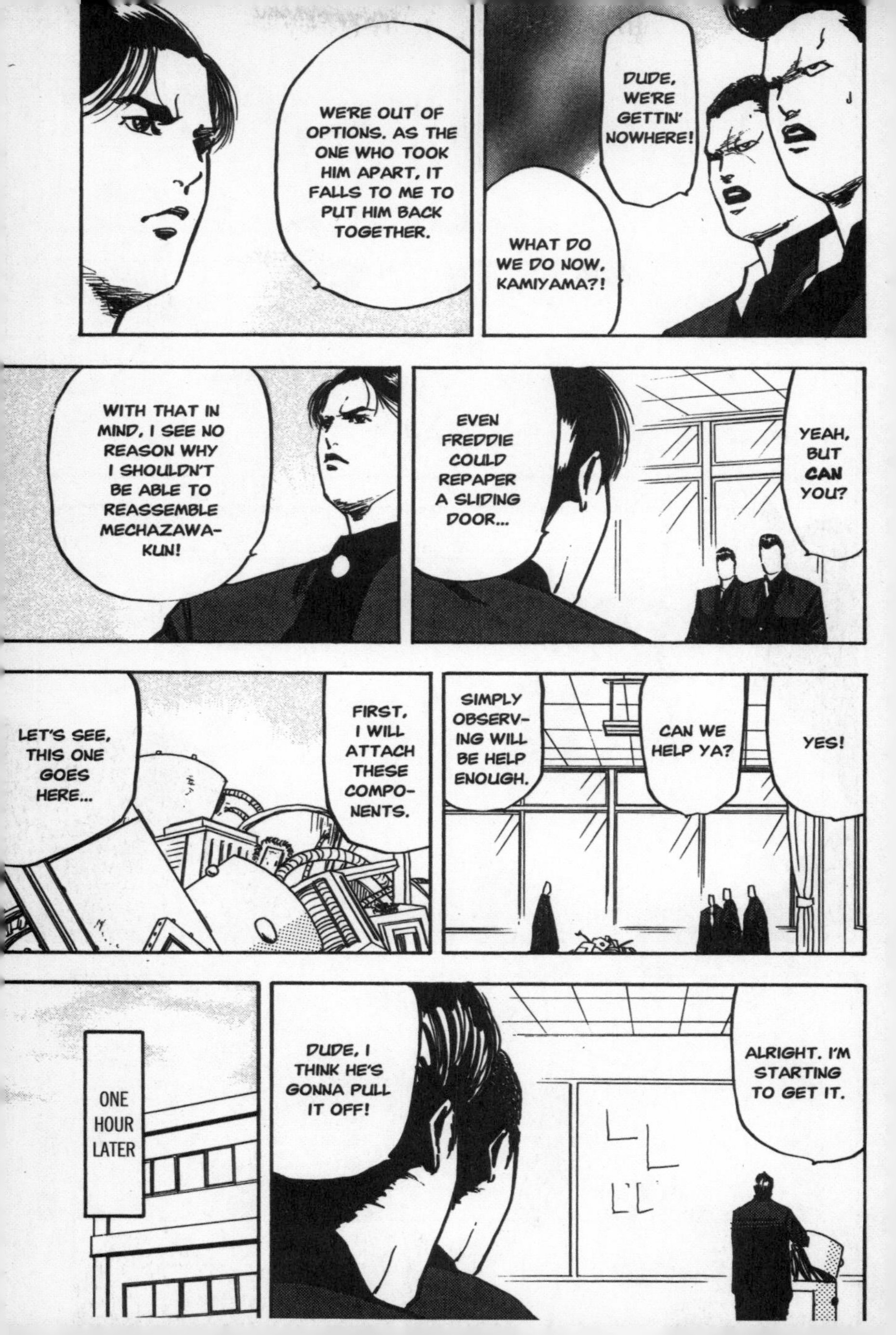
DUDE, WE'RE GETTIN' NOWHERE!
WHAT DO WE DO NOW, KAMIYAMA?!
WE'RE OUT OF OPTIONS. AS THE ONE WHO TOOK HIM APART, IT FALLS TO ME TO PUT HIM BACK TOGETHER.
YEAH, BUT CAN YOU?
EVEN FREDDIE COULD REPAPER A SLIDING DOOR...
WITH THAT IN MIND, I SEE NO REASON WHY I SHOULDN'T BE ABLE TO REASSEMBLE MECHAZAWA-KUN!
YES!
CAN WE HELP YA?
SIMPLY OBSERVING WILL BE HELP ENOUGH.
FIRST, I WILL ATTACH THESE COMPONENTS.
LET'S SEE, THIS ONE GOES HERE...
ALRIGHT. I'M STARTING TO GET IT.
DUDE, I THINK HE'S GONNA PULL IT OFF!
ONE HOUR LATER

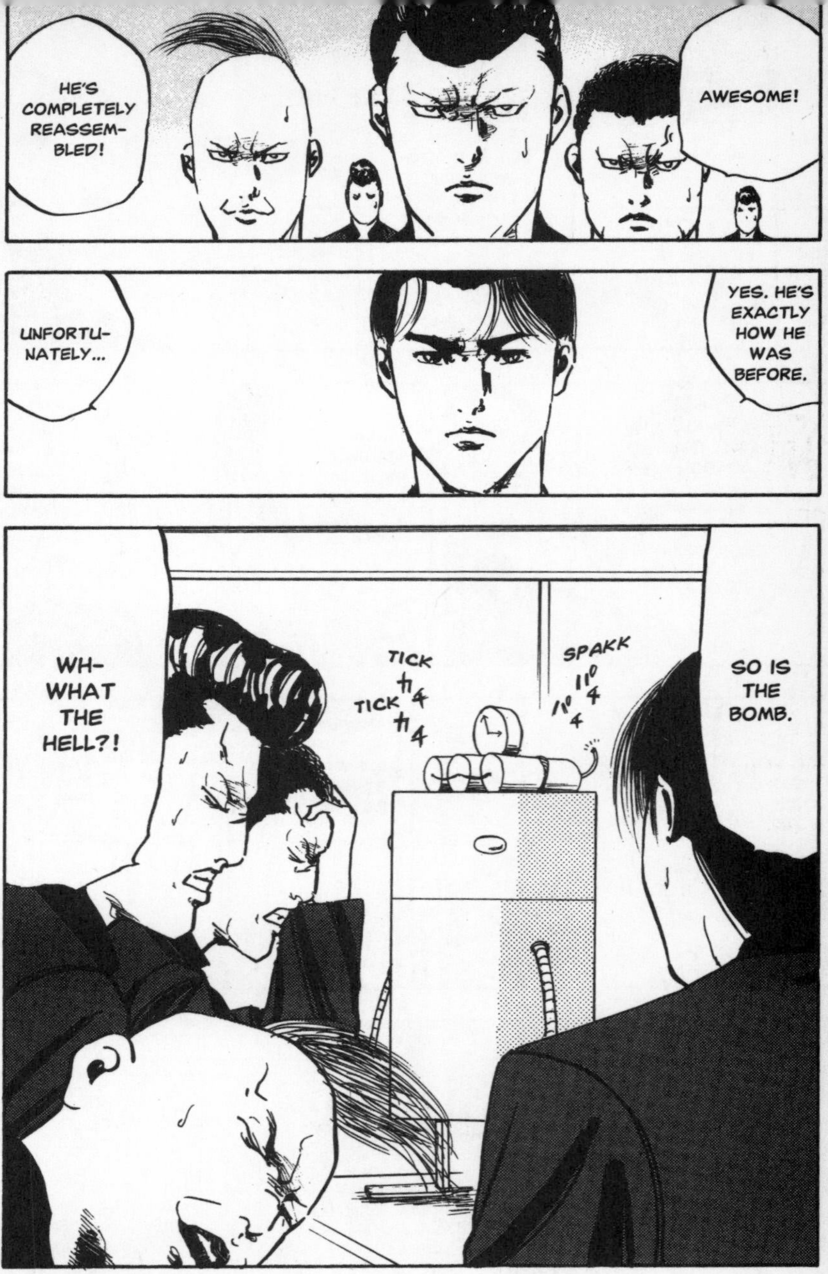

AWESOME!
HE'S COMPLETELY REASSEMBLED!
YES. HE'S EXACTLY HOW HE WAS BEFORE.
UNFORTUNATELY...
SO IS THE BOMB.
SPAKK
TICK
TICK
WH-WHAT THE HELL?!

SPEAK, MECHAZAWA!

CHAPTER 139: **WHO'S BAD?**

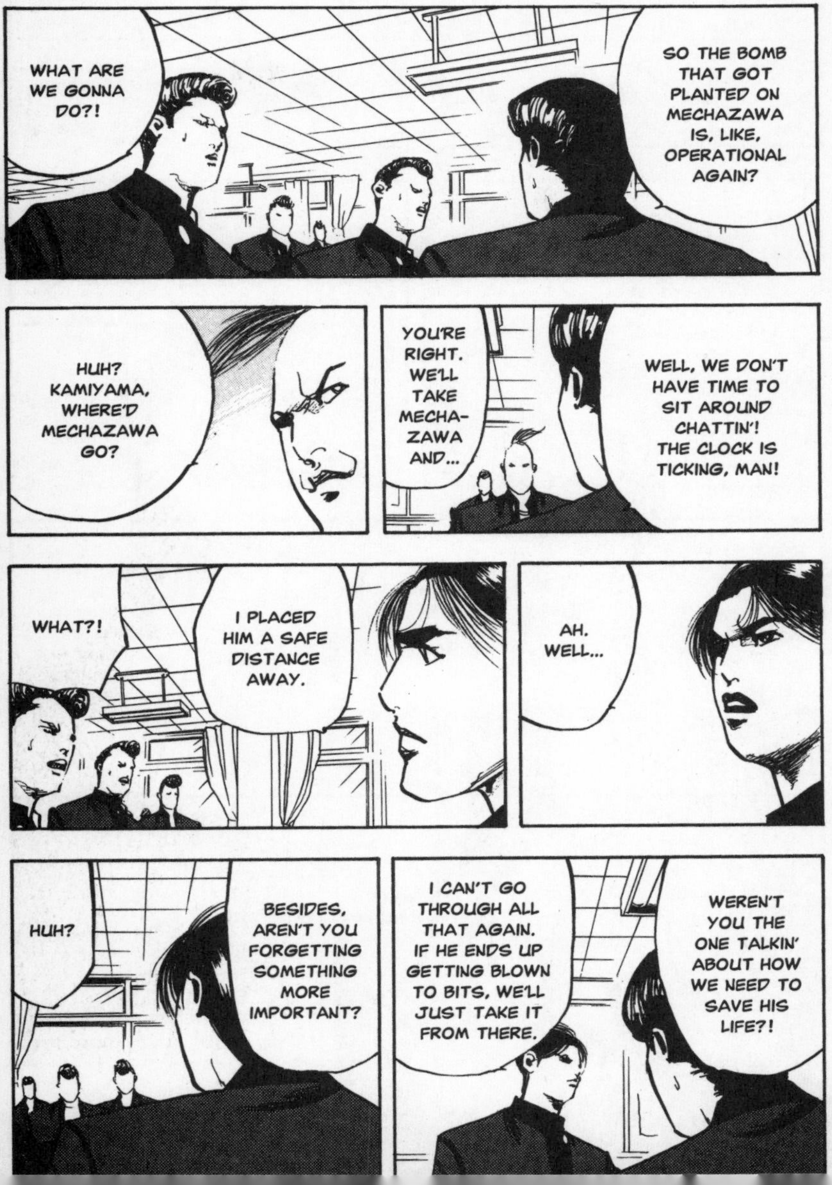

SO THE BOMB THAT GOT PLANTED ON MECHAZAWA IS, LIKE, OPERATIONAL AGAIN?
WHAT ARE WE GONNA DO?!
WELL, WE DON'T HAVE TIME TO SIT AROUND CHATTIN'! THE CLOCK IS TICKING, MAN!
YOU'RE RIGHT. WE'LL TAKE MECHA-ZAWA AND...
HUH? KAMIYAMA, WHERE'D MECHAZAWA GO?
AH. WELL...
I PLACED HIM A SAFE DISTANCE AWAY.
WHAT?!
WEREN'T YOU THE ONE TALKIN' ABOUT HOW WE NEED TO SAVE HIS LIFE?!
I CAN'T GO THROUGH ALL THAT AGAIN. IF HE ENDS UP GETTING BLOWN TO BITS, WE'LL JUST TAKE IT FROM THERE.
BESIDES, AREN'T YOU FORGETTING SOMETHING MORE IMPORTANT?
HUH?

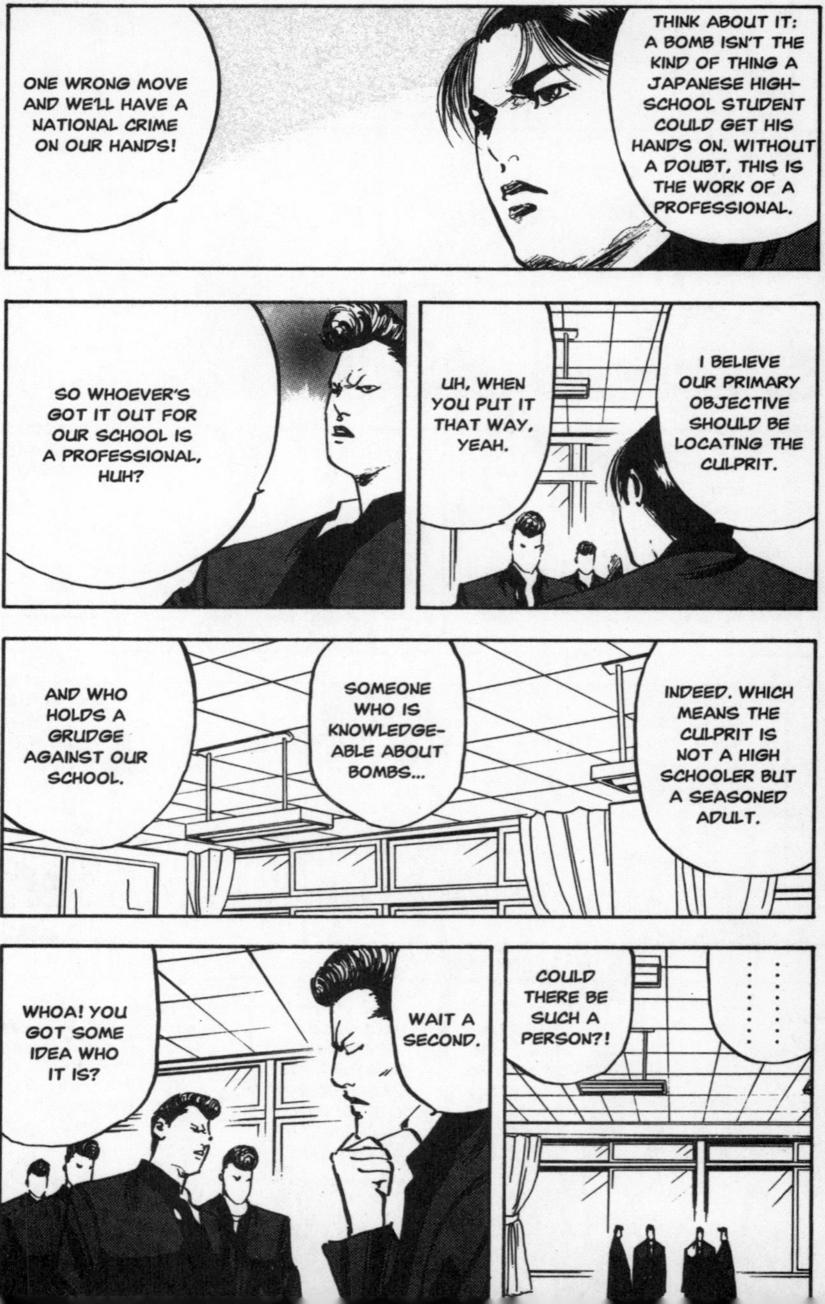
THINK ABOUT IT: A BOMB ISN'T THE KIND OF THING A JAPANESE HIGH-SCHOOL STUDENT COULD GET HIS HANDS ON. WITHOUT A DOUBT, THIS IS THE WORK OF A PROFESSIONAL.
ONE WRONG MOVE AND WE'LL HAVE A NATIONAL CRIME ON OUR HANDS!
I BELIEVE OUR PRIMARY OBJECTIVE SHOULD BE LOCATING THE CULPRIT.
UH, WHEN YOU PUT IT THAT WAY, YEAH.
SO WHOEVER'S GOT IT OUT FOR OUR SCHOOL IS A PROFESSIONAL, HUH?
INDEED. WHICH MEANS THE CULPRIT IS NOT A HIGH SCHOOLER BUT A SEASONED ADULT.
SOMEONE WHO IS KNOWLEDGE-ABLE ABOUT BOMBS...
AND WHO HOLDS A GRUDGE AGAINST OUR SCHOOL.
......
COULD THERE BE SUCH A PERSON?!
WAIT A SECOND.
WHOA! YOU GOT SOME IDEA WHO IT IS?

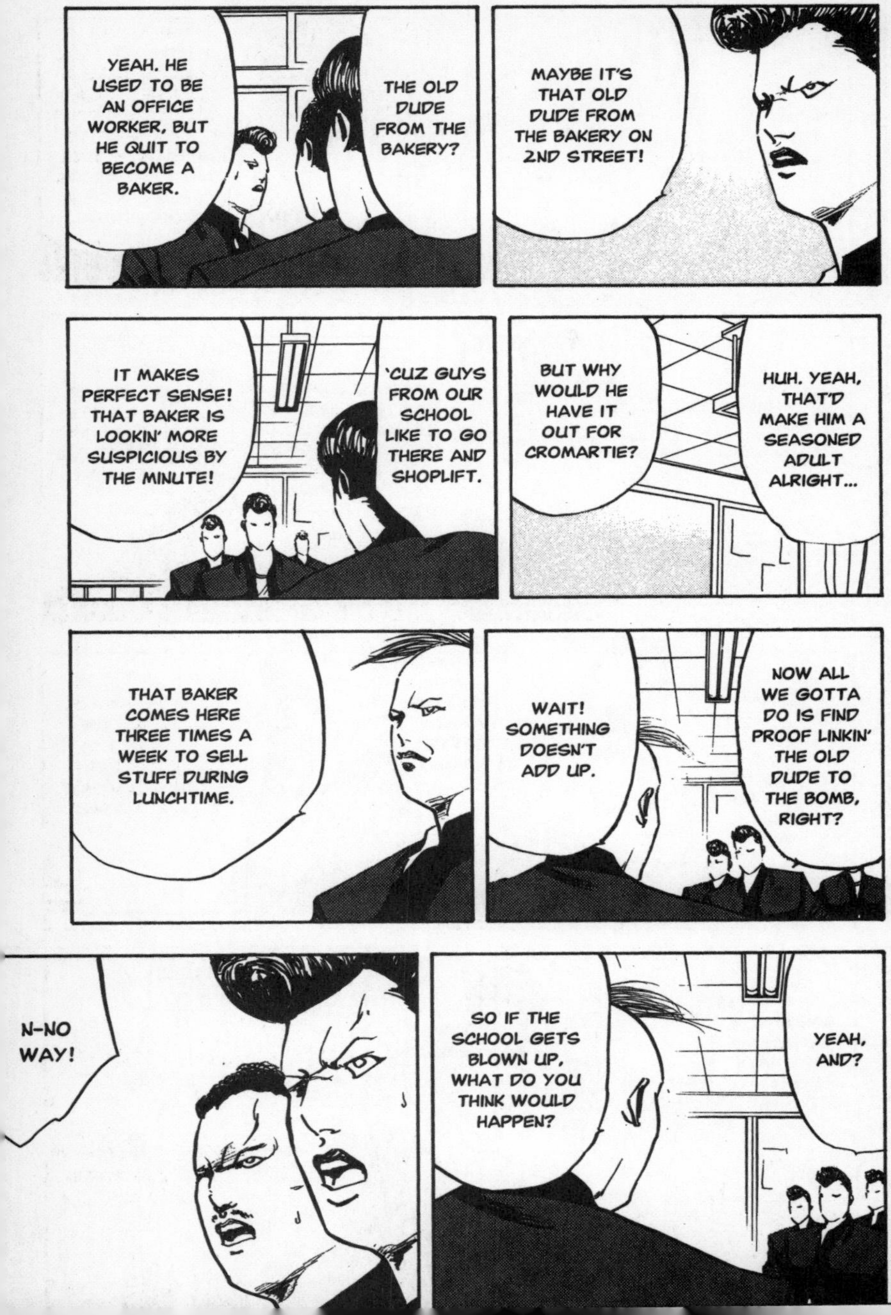
MAYBE IT'S THAT OLD DUDE FROM THE BAKERY ON 2ND STREET!
THE OLD DUDE FROM THE BAKERY?
YEAH. HE USED TO BE AN OFFICE WORKER, BUT HE QUIT TO BECOME A BAKER.
HUH. YEAH, THAT'D MAKE HIM A SEASONED ADULT ALRIGHT...
BUT WHY WOULD HE HAVE IT OUT FOR CROMARTIE?
'CUZ GUYS FROM OUR SCHOOL LIKE TO GO THERE AND SHOPLIFT.
IT MAKES PERFECT SENSE! THAT BAKER IS LOOKIN' MORE SUSPICIOUS BY THE MINUTE!
NOW ALL WE GOTTA DO IS FIND PROOF LINKIN' THE OLD DUDE TO THE BOMB, RIGHT?
WAIT! SOMETHING DOESN'T ADD UP.
THAT BAKER COMES HERE THREE TIMES A WEEK TO SELL STUFF DURING LUNCHTIME.
YEAH, AND?
SO IF THE SCHOOL GETS BLOWN UP, WHAT DO YOU THINK WOULD HAPPEN?
N-NO WAY!

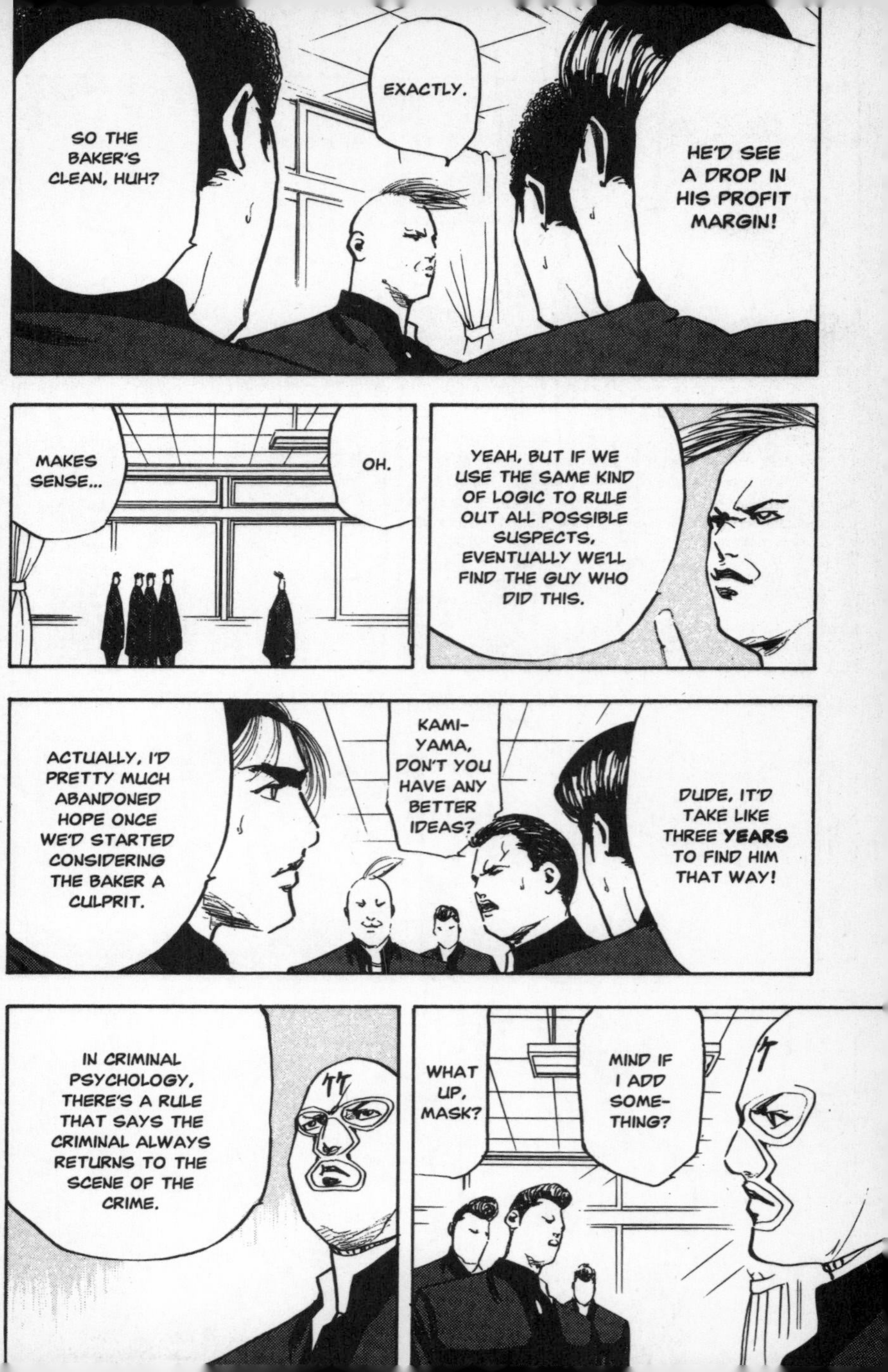
SO THE BAKER'S CLEAN, HUH?
EXACTLY.
HE'D SEE A DROP IN HIS PROFIT MARGIN!
MAKES SENSE...
OH.
YEAH, BUT IF WE USE THE SAME KIND OF LOGIC TO RULE OUT ALL POSSIBLE SUSPECTS, EVENTUALLY WE'LL FIND THE GUY WHO DID THIS.
ACTUALLY, I'D PRETTY MUCH ABANDONED HOPE ONCE WE'D STARTED CONSIDERING THE BAKER A CULPRIT.
KAMI-YAMA, DON'T YOU HAVE ANY BETTER IDEAS?
DUDE, IT'D TAKE LIKE THREE **YEARS** TO FIND HIM THAT WAY!
IN CRIMINAL PSYCHOLOGY, THERE'S A RULE THAT SAYS THE CRIMINAL ALWAYS RETURNS TO THE SCENE OF THE CRIME.
WHAT UP, MASK?
MIND IF I ADD SOME-THING?

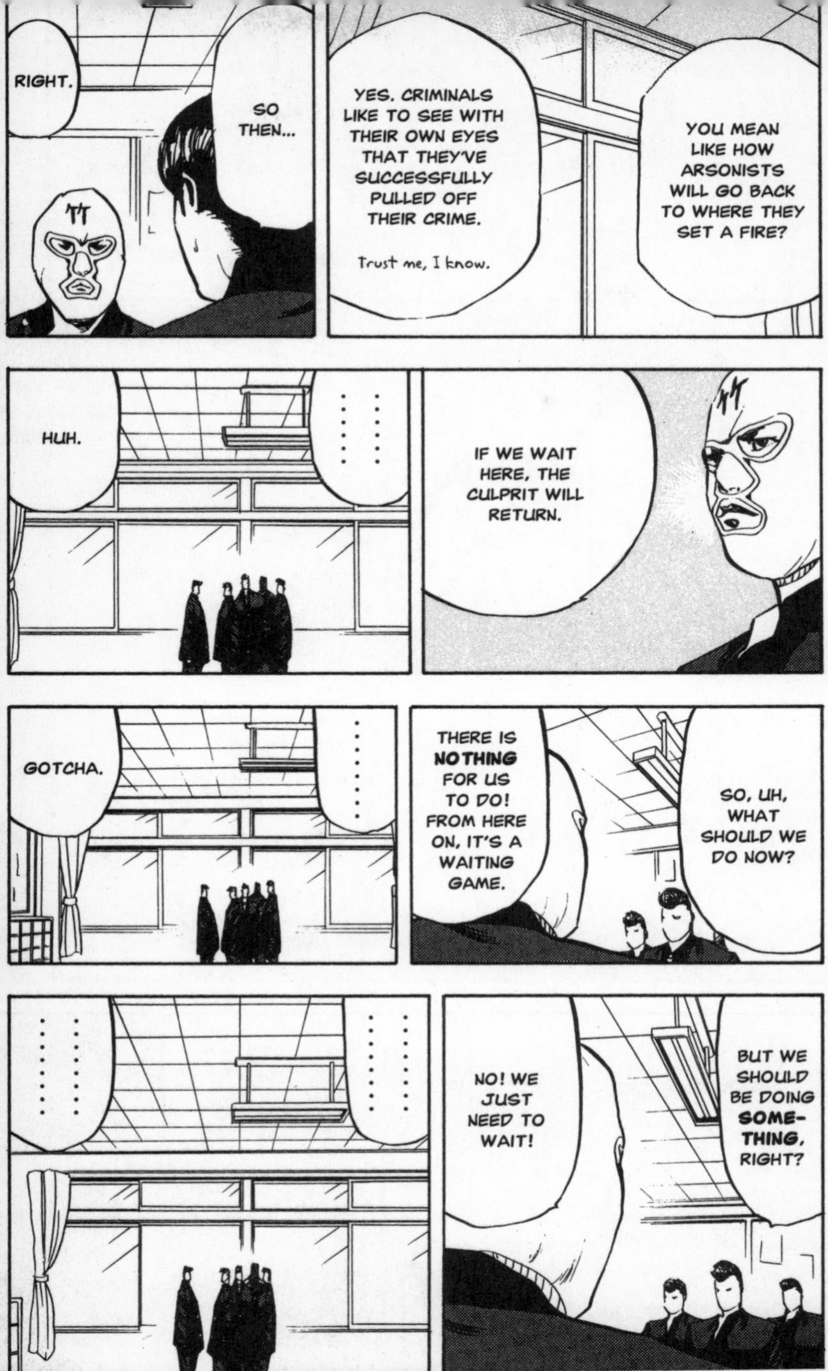
YOU MEAN LIKE HOW ARSONISTS WILL GO BACK TO WHERE THEY SET A FIRE?
YES. CRIMINALS LIKE TO SEE WITH THEIR OWN EYES THAT THEY'VE SUCCESSFULLY PULLED OFF THEIR CRIME.
Trust me, I know.
SO THEN...
RIGHT.
IF WE WAIT HERE, THE CULPRIT WILL RETURN.
......
HUH.
SO, UH, WHAT SHOULD WE DO NOW?
THERE IS **NOTHING** FOR US TO DO! FROM HERE ON, IT'S A WAITING GAME.
......
GOTCHA.
BUT WE SHOULD BE DOING **SOME-THING**, RIGHT?
NO! WE JUST NEED TO WAIT!
......
......

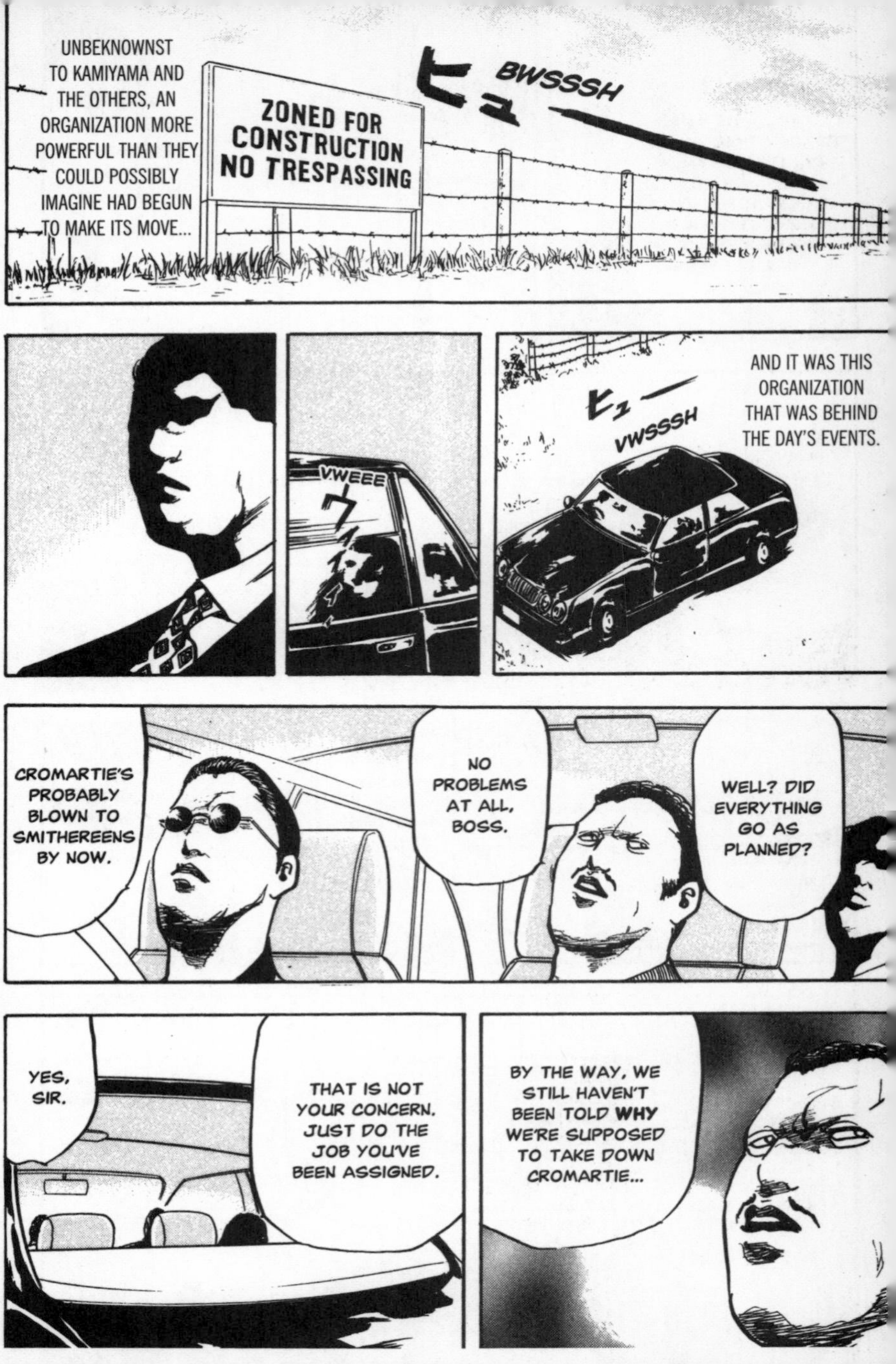
UNBEKNOWNST TO KAMIYAMA AND THE OTHERS, AN ORGANIZATION MORE POWERFUL THAN THEY COULD POSSIBLY IMAGINE HAD BEGUN TO MAKE ITS MOVE...
ZONED FOR CONSTRUCTION NO TRESPASSING
ヒュ
BWSSSH
AND IT WAS THIS ORGANIZATION THAT WAS BEHIND THE DAY'S EVENTS.
VWSSSH
VWEEE
WELL? DID EVERYTHING GO AS PLANNED?
NO PROBLEMS AT ALL, BOSS.
CROMARTIE'S PROBABLY BLOWN TO SMITHEREENS BY NOW.
BY THE WAY, WE STILL HAVEN'T BEEN TOLD **WHY** WE'RE SUPPOSED TO TAKE DOWN CROMARTIE...
THAT IS NOT YOUR CONCERN. JUST DO THE JOB YOU'VE BEEN ASSIGNED.
YES, SIR.

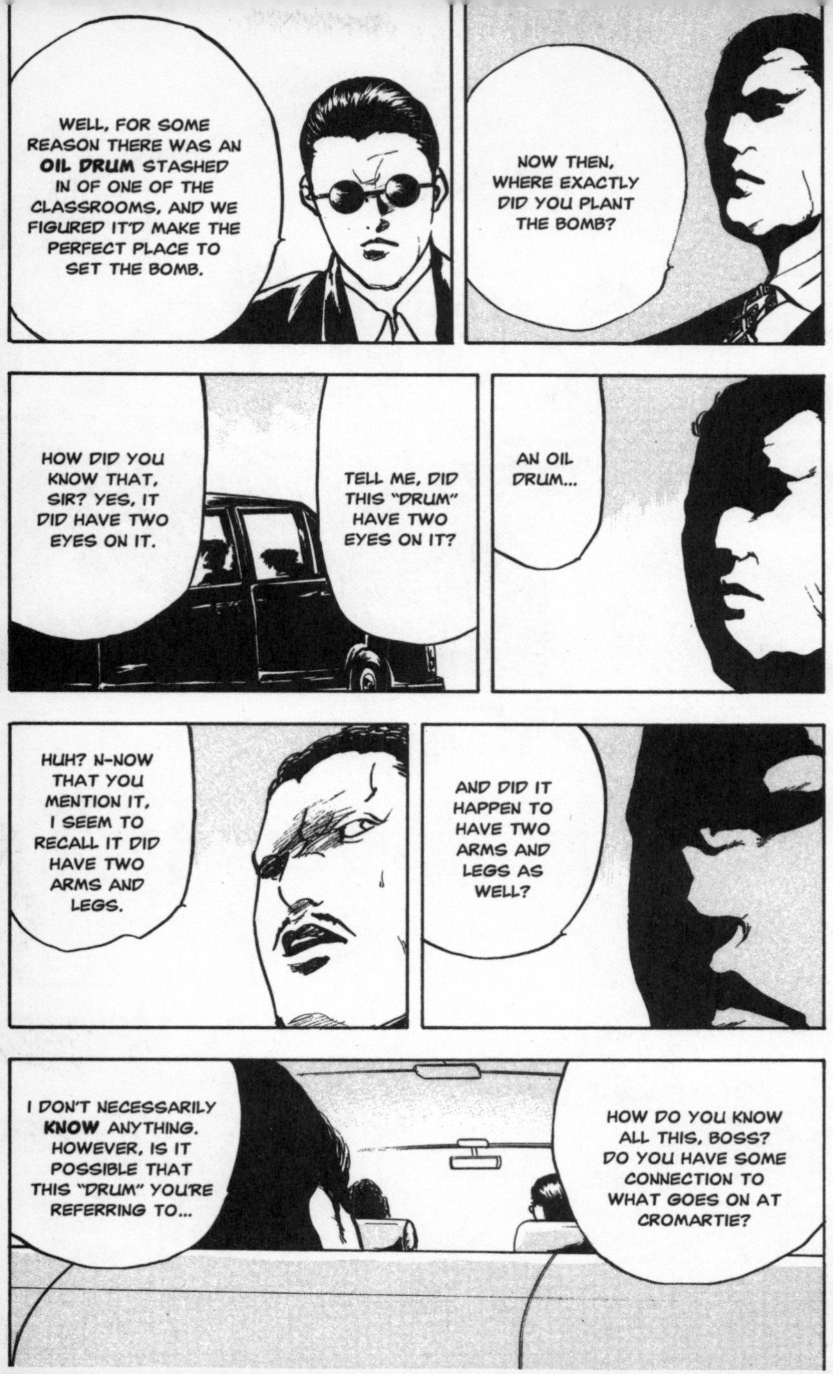
NOW THEN, WHERE EXACTLY DID YOU PLANT THE BOMB?
WELL, FOR SOME REASON THERE WAS AN **OIL DRUM** STASHED IN OF ONE OF THE CLASSROOMS, AND WE FIGURED IT'D MAKE THE PERFECT PLACE TO SET THE BOMB.
AN OIL DRUM...
TELL ME, DID THIS "DRUM" HAVE TWO EYES ON IT?
HOW DID YOU KNOW THAT, SIR? YES, IT DID HAVE TWO EYES ON IT.
AND DID IT HAPPEN TO HAVE TWO ARMS AND LEGS AS WELL?
HUH? N-NOW THAT YOU MENTION IT, I SEEM TO RECALL IT DID HAVE TWO ARMS AND LEGS.
HOW DO YOU KNOW ALL THIS, BOSS? DO YOU HAVE SOME CONNECTION TO WHAT GOES ON AT CROMARTIE?
I DON'T NECESSARILY **KNOW** ANYTHING. HOWEVER, IS IT POSSIBLE THAT THIS "DRUM" YOU'RE REFERRING TO...

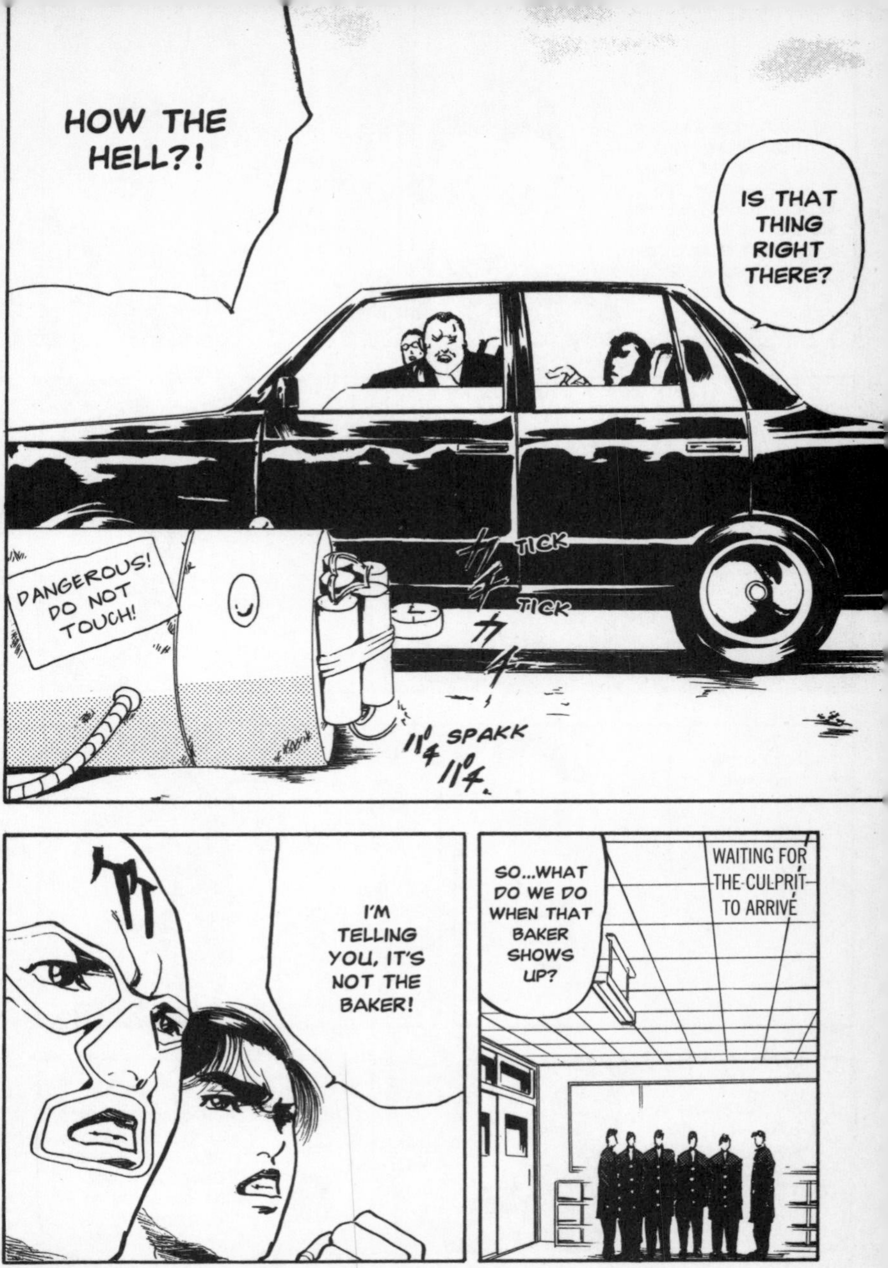
IS THAT THING RIGHT THERE?
HOW THE HELL?!
TICK
TICK
DANGEROUS! DO NOT TOUCH!
SPAKK
WAITING FOR THE CULPRIT TO ARRIVE
SO...WHAT DO WE DO WHEN THAT BAKER SHOWS UP?
I'M TELLING YOU, IT'S NOT THE BAKER!

NEXT CHAPTER: "BEHOLD! THE BAKER OF JUSTICE!" (JUST KIDDING)

CHAPTER 140: **GET BACK**

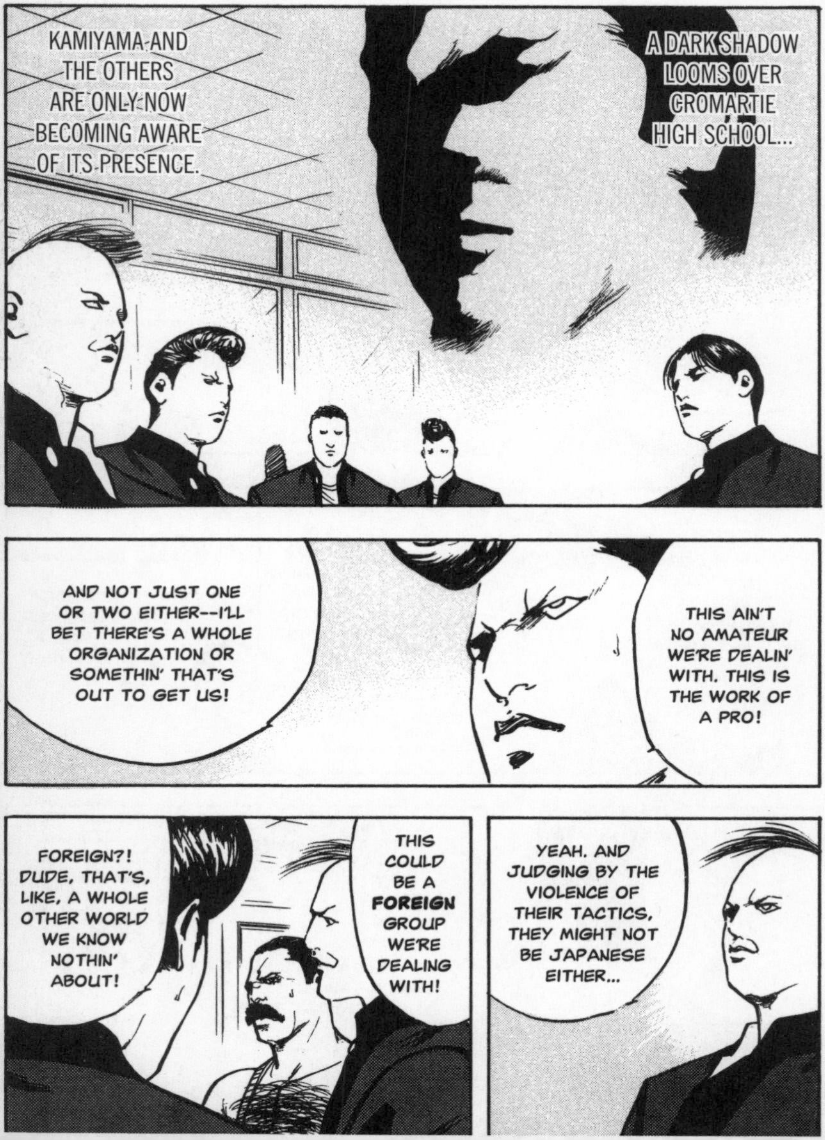

A DARK SHADOW LOOMS OVER CROMARTIE HIGH SCHOOL...
KAMIYAMA AND THE OTHERS ARE ONLY NOW BECOMING AWARE OF ITS PRESENCE.
THIS AIN'T NO AMATEUR WE'RE DEALIN' WITH. THIS IS THE WORK OF A PRO!
AND NOT JUST ONE OR TWO EITHER--I'LL BET THERE'S A WHOLE ORGANIZATION OR SOMETHIN' THAT'S OUT TO GET US!
YEAH. AND JUDGING BY THE VIOLENCE OF THEIR TACTICS, THEY MIGHT NOT BE JAPANESE EITHER...
THIS COULD BE A **FOREIGN** GROUP WE'RE DEALING WITH!
FOREIGN?! DUDE, THAT'S, LIKE, A WHOLE OTHER WORLD WE KNOW NOTHIN' ABOUT!

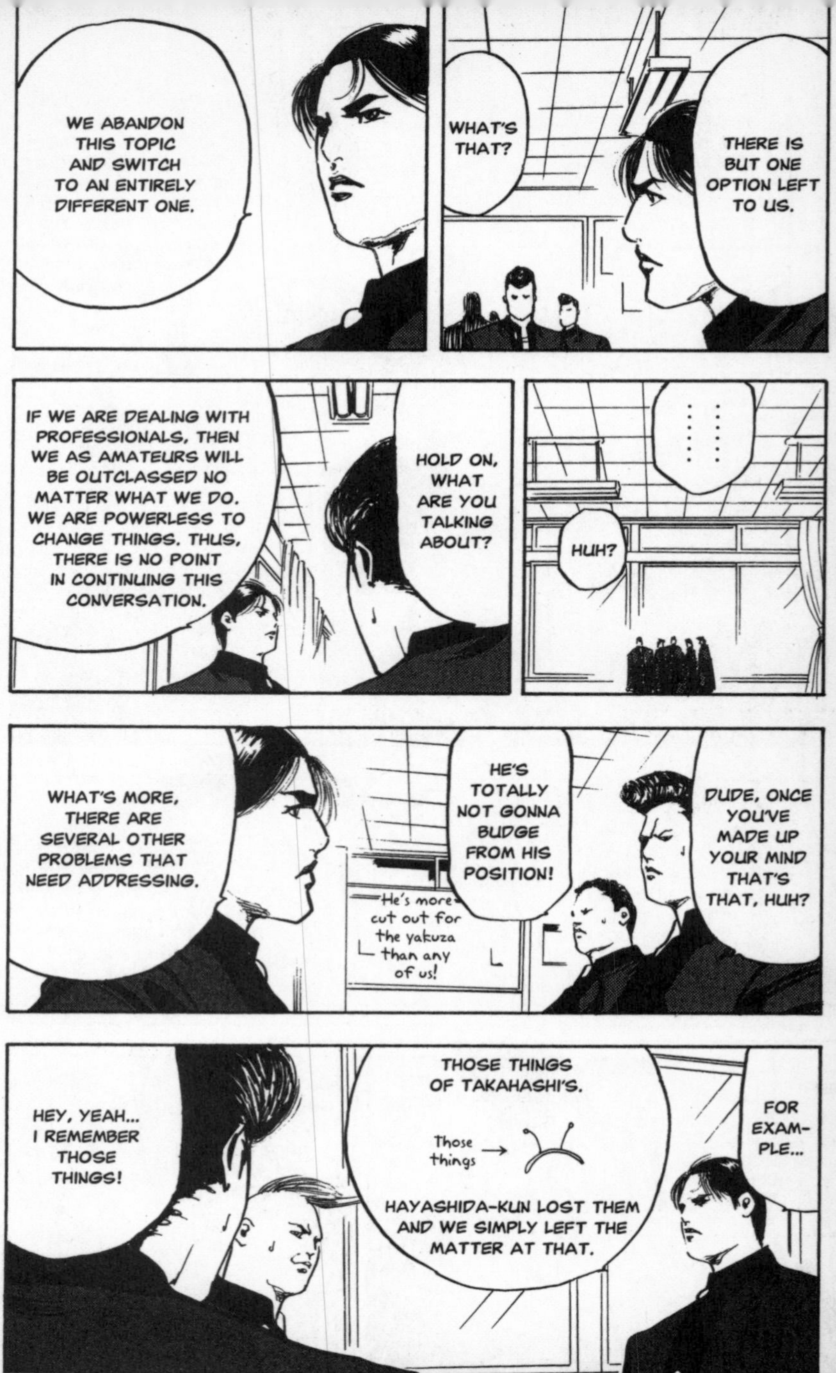
THERE IS BUT ONE OPTION LEFT TO US.
WHAT'S THAT?
WE ABANDON THIS TOPIC AND SWITCH TO AN ENTIRELY DIFFERENT ONE.
HUH?
......
HOLD ON, WHAT ARE YOU TALKING ABOUT?
IF WE ARE DEALING WITH PROFESSIONALS, THEN WE AS AMATEURS WILL BE OUTCLASSED NO MATTER WHAT WE DO. WE ARE POWERLESS TO CHANGE THINGS. THUS, THERE IS NO POINT IN CONTINUING THIS CONVERSATION.
DUDE, ONCE YOU'VE MADE UP YOUR MIND THAT'S THAT, HUH?
HE'S TOTALLY NOT GONNA BUDGE FROM HIS POSITION!
He's more cut out for the yakuza than any of us!
WHAT'S MORE, THERE ARE SEVERAL OTHER PROBLEMS THAT NEED ADDRESSING.
FOR EXAMPLE...
THOSE THINGS OF TAKAHASHI'S.
Those things
HAYASHIDA-KUN LOST THEM AND WE SIMPLY LEFT THE MATTER AT THAT.
HEY, YEAH... I REMEMBER THOSE THINGS!

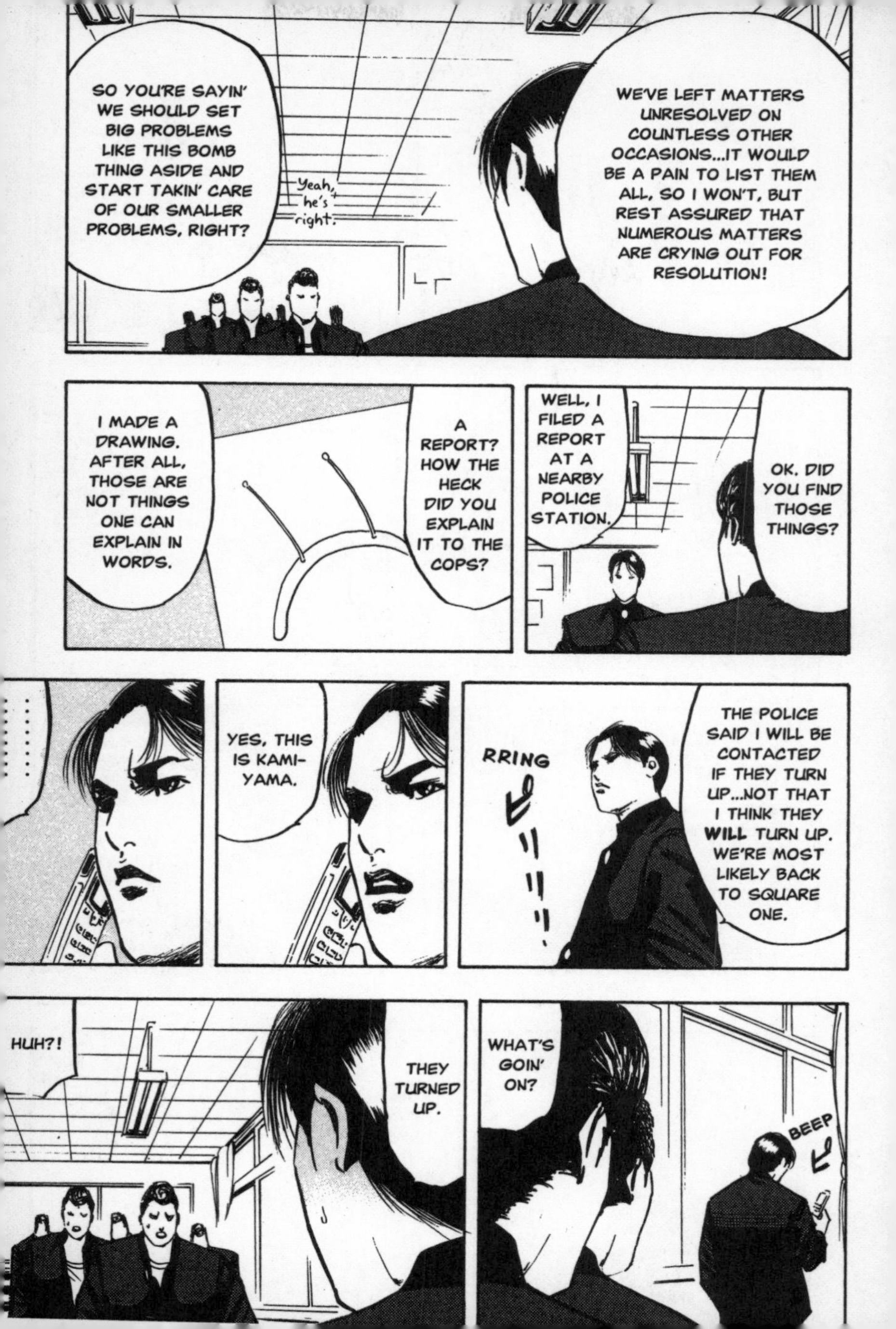

WE'VE LEFT MATTERS UNRESOLVED ON COUNTLESS OTHER OCCASIONS...IT WOULD BE A PAIN TO LIST THEM ALL, SO I WON'T, BUT REST ASSURED THAT NUMEROUS MATTERS ARE CRYING OUT FOR RESOLUTION!
SO YOU'RE SAYIN' WE SHOULD SET BIG PROBLEMS LIKE THIS BOMB THING ASIDE AND START TAKIN' CARE OF OUR SMALLER PROBLEMS, RIGHT?
Yeah, he's right.
OK. DID YOU FIND THOSE THINGS?
WELL, I FILED A REPORT AT A NEARBY POLICE STATION.
A REPORT? HOW THE HECK DID YOU EXPLAIN IT TO THE COPS?
I MADE A DRAWING. AFTER ALL, THOSE ARE NOT THINGS ONE CAN EXPLAIN IN WORDS.
THE POLICE SAID I WILL BE CONTACTED IF THEY TURN UP...NOT THAT I THINK THEY **WILL** TURN UP. WE'RE MOST LIKELY BACK TO SQUARE ONE.
RRING
YES, THIS IS KAMI-YAMA.
......
BEEP
WHAT'S GOIN' ON?
THEY TURNED UP.
HUH?!

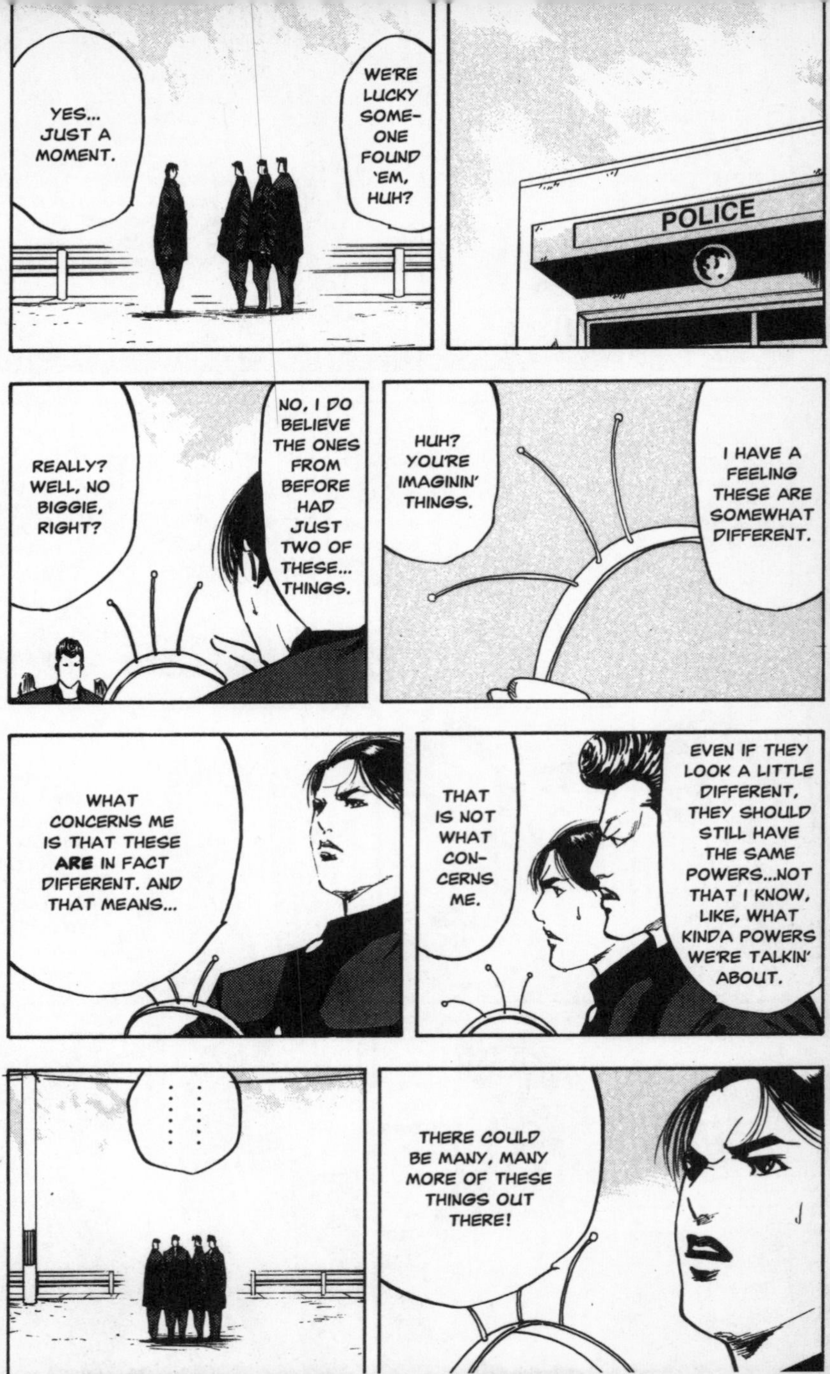
POLICE
WE'RE LUCKY SOME-ONE FOUND 'EM, HUH?
YES... JUST A MOMENT.
I HAVE A FEELING THESE ARE SOMEWHAT DIFFERENT.
HUH? YOU'RE IMAGININ' THINGS.
NO, I DO BELIEVE THE ONES FROM BEFORE HAD JUST TWO OF THESE... THINGS.
REALLY? WELL, NO BIGGIE, RIGHT?
EVEN IF THEY LOOK A LITTLE DIFFERENT, THEY SHOULD STILL HAVE THE SAME POWERS...NOT THAT I KNOW, LIKE, WHAT KINDA POWERS WE'RE TALKIN' ABOUT.
THAT IS NOT WHAT CON-CERNS ME.
WHAT CONCERNS ME IS THAT THESE **ARE** IN FACT DIFFERENT. AND THAT MEANS...
THERE COULD BE MANY, MANY MORE OF THESE THINGS OUT THERE!
....

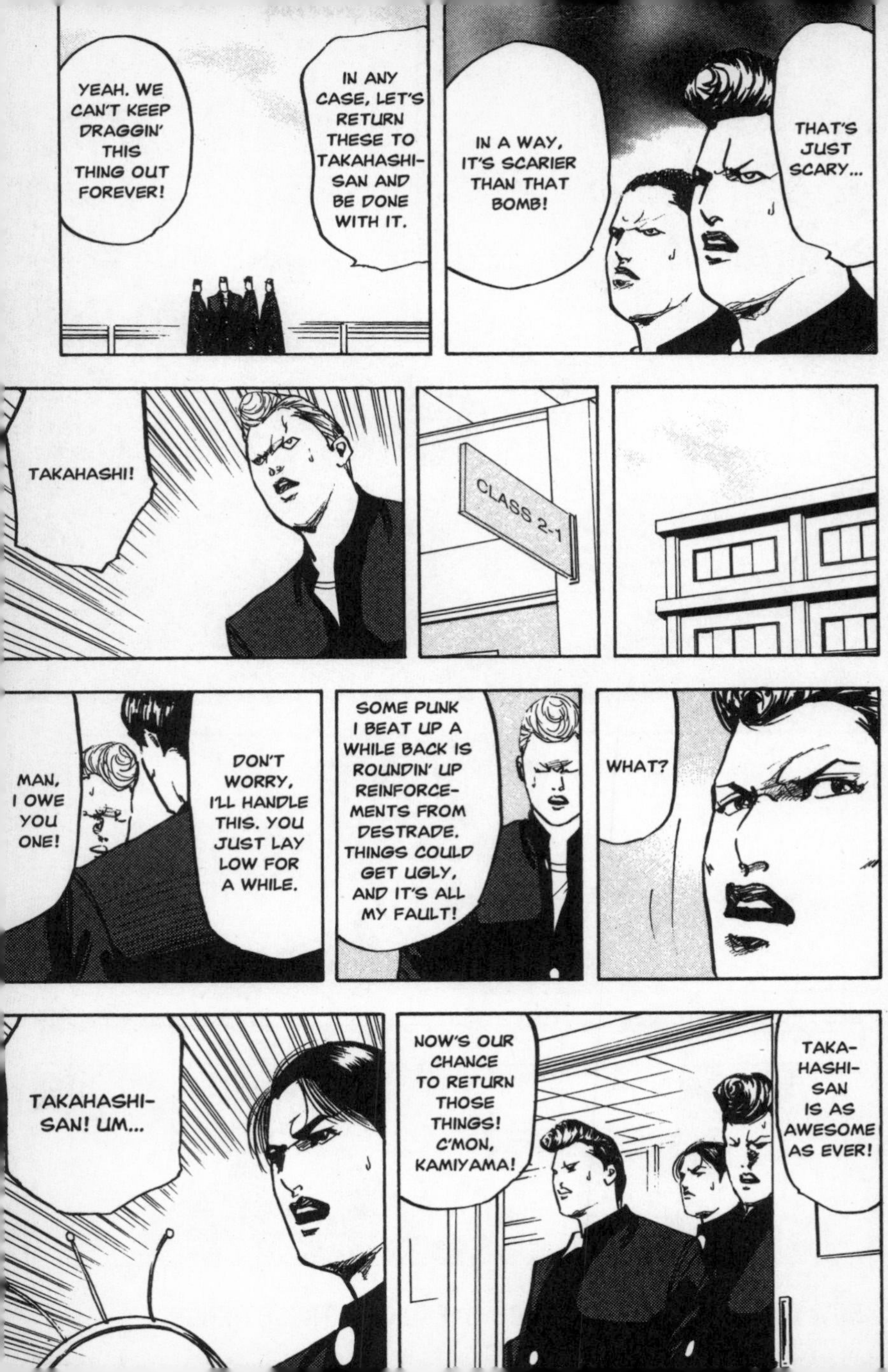
THAT'S JUST SCARY...
IN A WAY, IT'S SCARIER THAN THAT BOMB!
IN ANY CASE, LET'S RETURN THESE TO TAKAHASHI-SAN AND BE DONE WITH IT.
YEAH. WE CAN'T KEEP DRAGGIN' THIS THING OUT FOREVER!
CLASS 2-1
TAKAHASHI!
WHAT?
SOME PUNK I BEAT UP A WHILE BACK IS ROUNDIN' UP REINFORCE-MENTS FROM DESTRADE. THINGS COULD GET UGLY, AND IT'S ALL MY FAULT!
DON'T WORRY, I'LL HANDLE THIS. YOU JUST LAY LOW FOR A WHILE.
MAN, I OWE YOU ONE!
TAKA-HASHI-SAN IS AS AWESOME AS EVER!
NOW'S OUR CHANCE TO RETURN THOSE THINGS! C'MON, KAMIYAMA!
TAKAHASHI-SAN! UM...

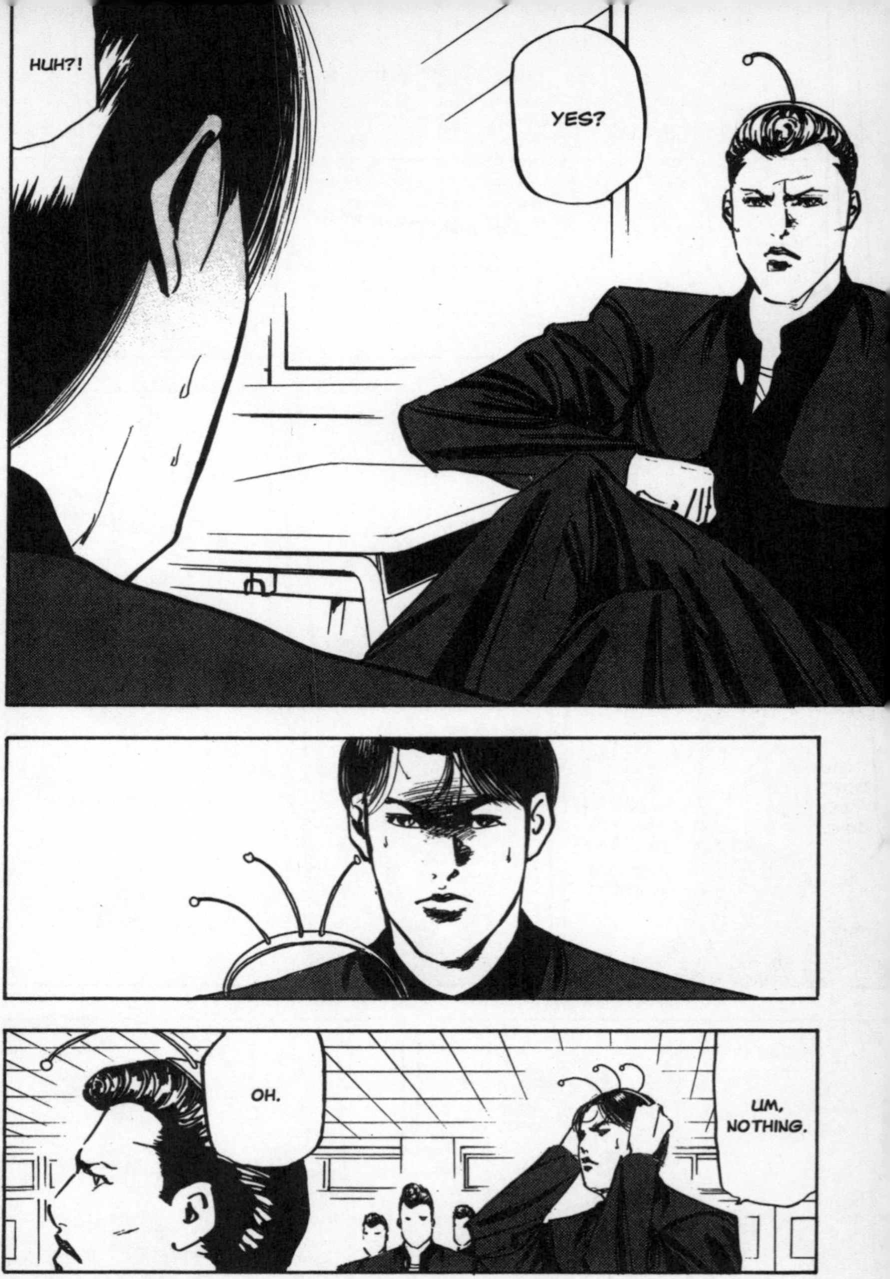
HUH?!
YES?
OH.
UM, NOTHING.

NOW TAKING SUGGESTIONS FOR WHAT TO CALL THOSE THINGS.

CHAPTER 141: **WHAT YOU'RE DOING**

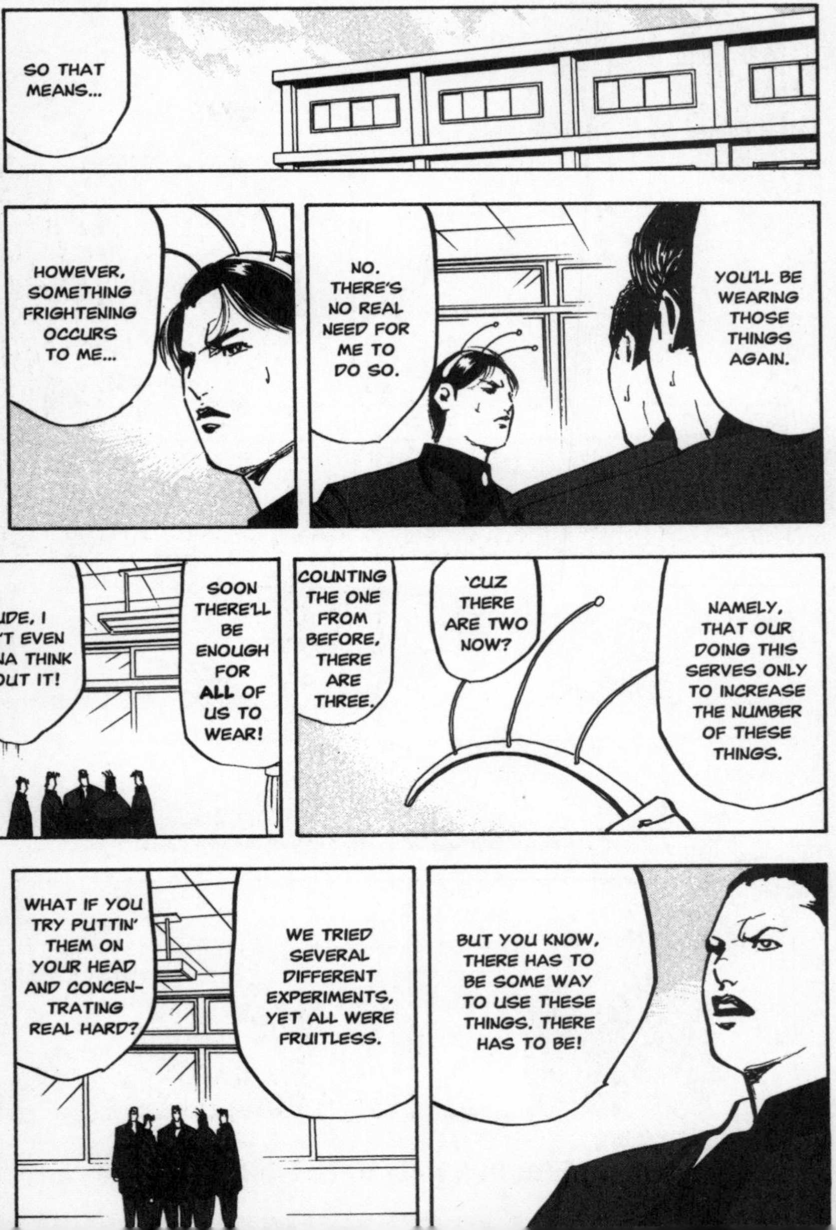
SO THAT MEANS...
YOU'LL BE WEARING THOSE THINGS AGAIN.
NO. THERE'S NO REAL NEED FOR ME TO DO SO.
HOWEVER, SOMETHING FRIGHTENING OCCURS TO ME...
NAMELY, THAT OUR DOING THIS SERVES ONLY TO INCREASE THE NUMBER OF THESE THINGS.
'CUZ THERE ARE TWO NOW?
COUNTING THE ONE FROM BEFORE, THERE ARE THREE.
SOON THERE'LL BE ENOUGH FOR ALL OF US TO WEAR!
DUDE, I DON'T EVEN WANNA THINK ABOUT IT!
BUT YOU KNOW, THERE HAS TO BE SOME WAY TO USE THESE THINGS. THERE HAS TO BE!
WE TRIED SEVERAL DIFFERENT EXPERIMENTS, YET ALL WERE FRUITLESS.
WHAT IF YOU TRY PUTTIN' THEM ON YOUR HEAD AND CONCEN-TRATING REAL HARD?

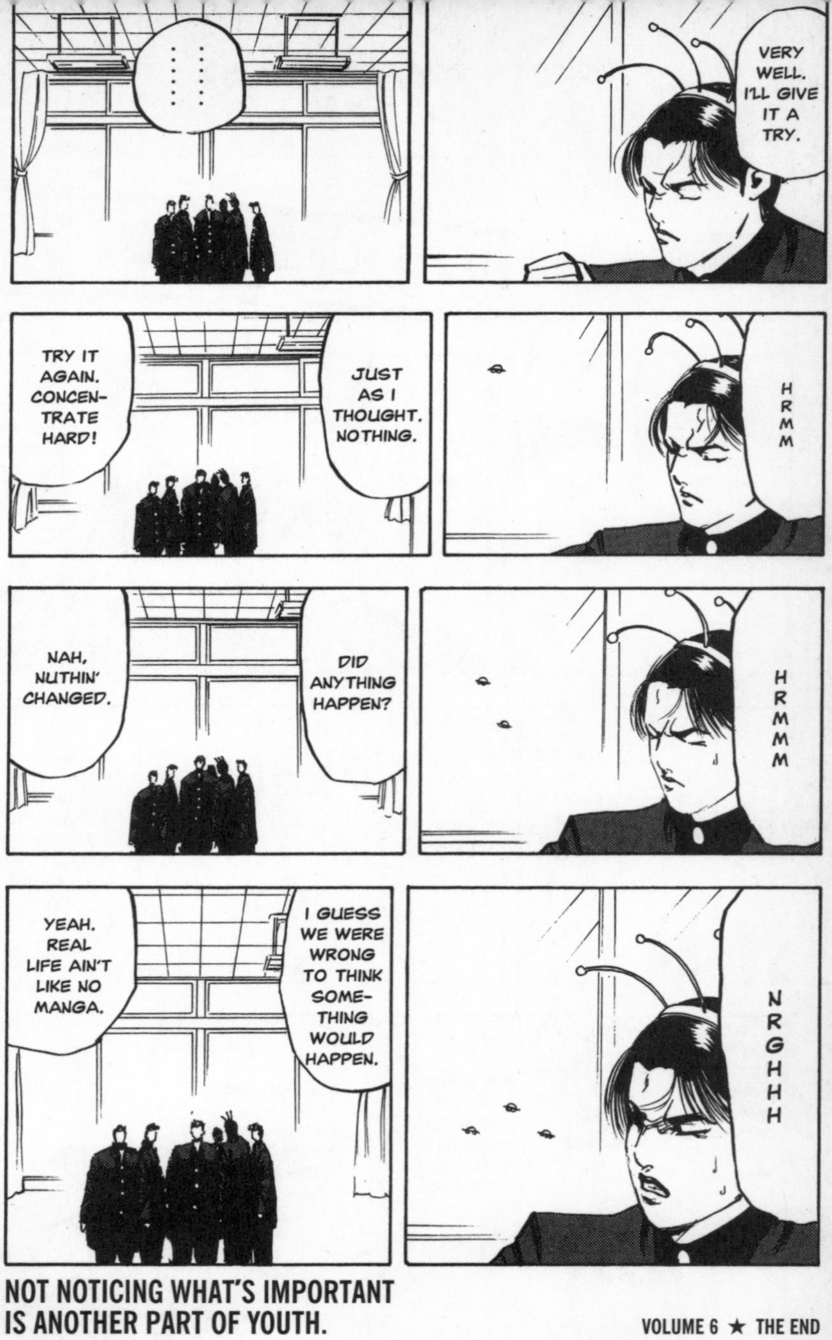
VERY WELL. I'LL GIVE IT A TRY.
HRMM
JUST AS I THOUGHT. NOTHING.
TRY IT AGAIN. CONCEN-TRATE HARD!
HRMMM
DID ANYTHING HAPPEN?
NAH, NUTHIN' CHANGED.
NRGHHH
I GUESS WE WERE WRONG TO THINK SOME-THING WOULD HAPPEN.
YEAH. REAL LIFE AIN'T LIKE NO MANGA.

NOT NOTICING WHAT'S IMPORTANT IS ANOTHER PART OF YOUTH.

VOLUME 6 ★ THE END

AN INTRODUCTION TO A NEW CHARACTER

Yet another man of mystery. If you're wondering just how much of a mystery he is, he's so mysterious that neither your humble author nor his editor know who he is...though, of course, it would be more accurate to say it's not so much a matter of mystery as it is a matter of us not having given him much thought. I haven't even come up with what his face looks like. It's an old rule of thumb in manga circles that when characters have their faces hidden in shadow it just means their design hasn't been finalized yet, so I wouldn't give such instances too much thought. I have no idea why such a fine adult would start showing up around the school (LOL), but since I've already made it out to be such a big deal, I'm sure it will end up being a very important reason. Who is this guy anyway?! If you have any good ideas, please let me know. Seriously.

MR. X

AND A ONE-TIME-ONLY INTRODUCTION TO AN ITEM

TAKAHASHI'S THINGS

A few people may wonder what these things are, while the vast majority couldn't care less. Even Hayashida found them to be a little odd. As usual, I wasn't thinking when I introduced them into the story, and my editor and I were hard pressed to think of a good way to handle them. When it came time for the serial run of this story, we tried putting in a request for readers to send in postcards to answer just what these things are. I'll take this opportunity to make it clear that no good ideas were forthcoming. (LOL) These things later came to be called "the two-antennae type," as it would seem there are in fact other kinds. I get the feeling I've seen these being sold before at street fairs...In any case, it's been established that they don't fire any kind of beam. Would these be considered gaudy? Subdued? Kinda lame? Truly, they are most difficult to pin down...

CROMARTIE HIGH SCHOOL VOLUME SIX

© 2003 Eiji Nonaka
All rights reserved.
First published in Japan in 2003 by Kodansha Ltd., Tokyo
English translation rights for this edition arranged through Kodansha Ltd.

Editor **JAVIER LOPEZ**
Translator **BRENDAN FRAYNE**
Graphic Artist **SCOTT HOWARD**

Editorial Director **GARY STEINMAN**
Creative Director **JASON BABLER**
Print Production Manager **BRIDGETT JANOTA**
Production Coordinator **MARISA KREITZ**

International Coordinators **TORU IWAKAMI AND MIYUKI KAMIYA**

President, CEO & Publisher **JOHN LEDFORD**

Email: editor@adv-manga.com
www.adv-manga.com
www.advfilms.com

For sales and distribution inquiries please call 1.800.282.7202

ADV MANGA™ is a division of A.D. Vision, Inc.
5750 Bintliff Drive, Suite 210, Houston, Texas 77036

ISBN: 1-4139-0262-6
First printing, May 2006
10 9 8 7 6 5 4 3 2 1
Printed in Canada

Coming up in

CROMARTIE HIGH SCHOOL VOL.7

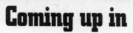

The winds of change blow through Cromartie's halls...

The school gorilla begins a career in banana-based sushi. Freddie makes the jump from the classroom to the boardroom. The Four Great Ones (all five of them) grapple with such burning questions as what makes a badass and how to get the ideal tan. But the biggest shock of all comes with the return of Takahashi and his...things!

Can the school weather this storm—or will it be razed to the ground (again)?! Find out in the stunningly obtuse seventh volume of **Cromartie High School!**

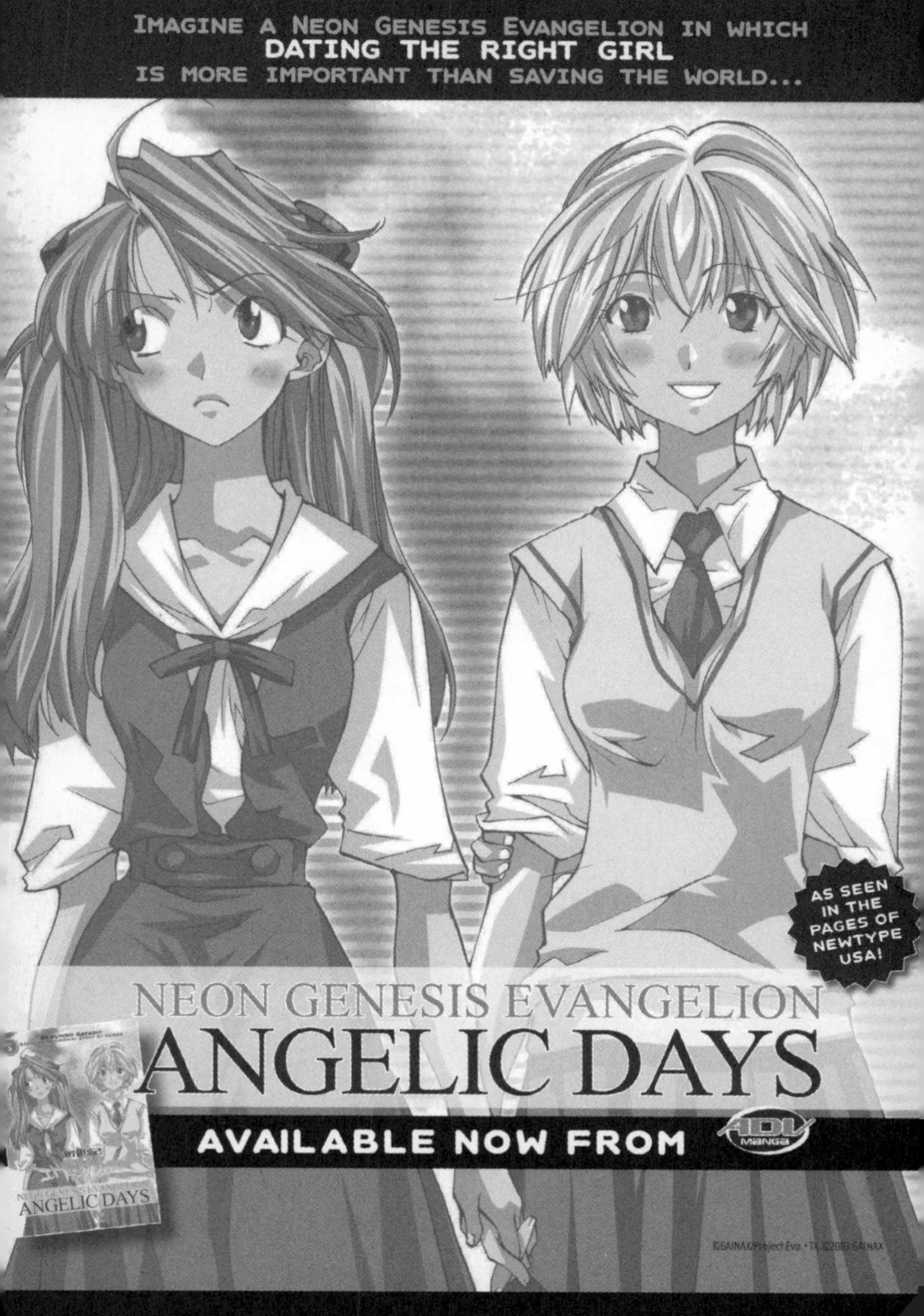
IMAGINE A NEON GENESIS EVANGELION IN WHICH
DATING THE RIGHT GIRL
IS MORE IMPORTANT THAN SAVING THE WORLD...
AS SEEN IN THE PAGES OF NEWTYPE USA!
NEON GENESIS EVANGELION
ANGELIC DAYS
AVAILABLE NOW FROM
ADV Manga
©GAINAX/Project Eva. • TX ©2003 GAINAX

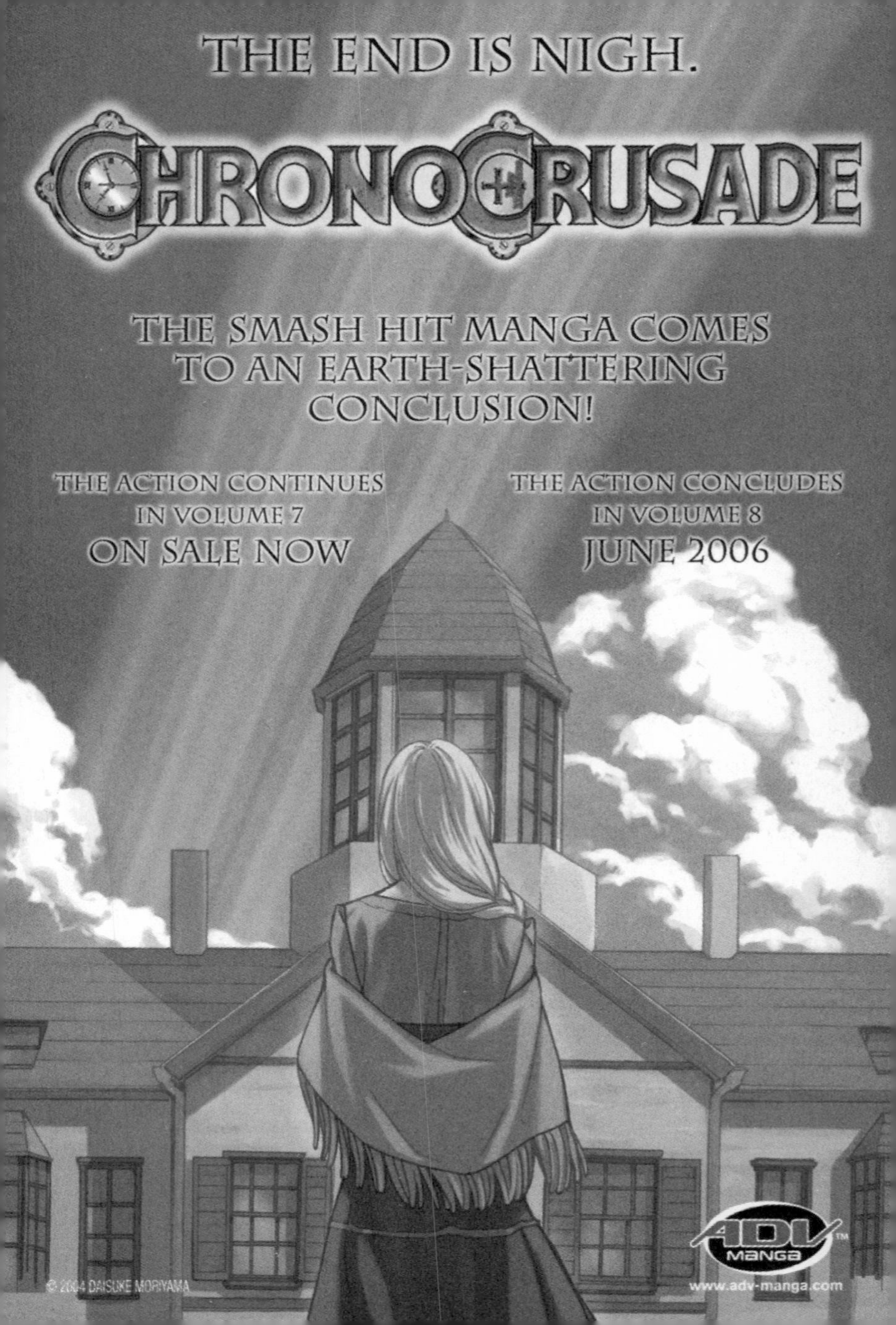

THE END IS NIGH.
CHRONO CRUSADE
THE SMASH HIT MANGA COMES TO AN EARTH-SHATTERING CONCLUSION!
THE ACTION CONTINUES IN VOLUME 7
ON SALE NOW
THE ACTION CONCLUDES IN VOLUME 8
JUNE 2006
ADV Manga
© 2004 DAISUKE MORIYAMA
www.adv-manga.com

Three people united by
a terrifying secret.

Yuri, a young man who
killed his own mother.

Mitsuba, who will gladly
murder to avenge the
sister that was taken
from him.

Anna, the mysterious
assassin with a
chilling beauty.

Together, they'll
stop at nothing
to bring down
a terrorist
organization...

And along the
way, they'll come
closer to the
truth that binds
them together.

Anne Freaks Vol. I
Thrilling new series
out now from
ADV Manga

© 2001 Yua Kotegawa

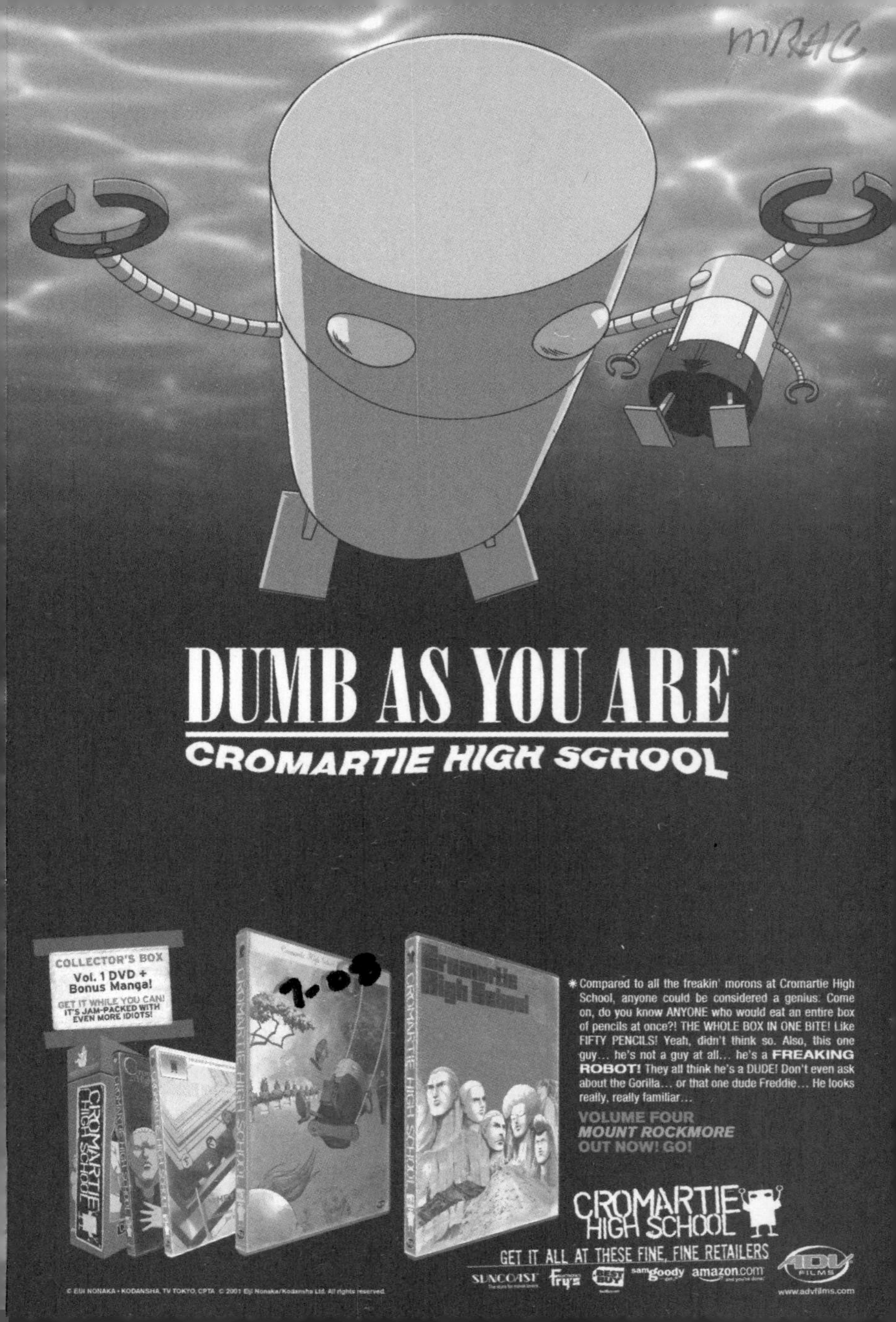

DUMB AS YOU ARE*
CROMARTIE HIGH SCHOOL
COLLECTOR'S BOX
Vol. 1 DVD + Bonus Manga!
GET IT WHILE YOU CAN! IT'S JAM-PACKED WITH EVEN MORE IDIOTS!
* Compared to all the freakin' morons at Cromartie High School, anyone could be considered a genius. Come on, do you know ANYONE who would eat an entire box of pencils at once?! THE WHOLE BOX IN ONE BITE! Like FIFTY PENCILS! Yeah, didn't think so. Also, this one guy… he's not a guy at all… he's a FREAKING ROBOT! They all think he's a DUDE! Don't even ask about the Gorilla… or that one dude Freddie… He looks really, really familiar…
VOLUME FOUR
MOUNT ROCKMORE
OUT NOW! GO!
CROMARTIE HIGH SCHOOL
GET IT ALL AT THESE FINE, FINE RETAILERS
SUNCOAST
Fry's
BEST BUY
samgoody
amazon.com
ADV FILMS
© Eiji NONAKA • KODANSHA, TV TOKYO, CPTA © 2001 Eiji Nonaka/Kodansha Ltd. All rights reserved.
www.advfilms.com